Named in remembrance of
the onetime *Antioch Review* editor
and longtime Bay Area resident,

the Lawrence Grauman, Jr. Fund

supports books that address
a wide range of human rights,
free speech, and social justice issues.

Better Judgment

The publisher and the University of California Press Foundation gratefully acknowledge the generous support of the Lawrence Grauman, Jr. Fund.

The publisher also gratefully acknowledges the generous support of the Chairman's Circle of the University of California Press Foundation, whose members are:

Elizabeth and David Birka-White
Patricia Klaus
Judith and Kim Maxwell
Robert Parker
The Richard and Lisa Kendall Fund
Meryl and Robert Selig

Better Judgment

HOW THREE JUDGES ARE BRINGING
JUSTICE BACK TO THE COURTS

Reynolds Holding

UNIVERSITY OF CALIFORNIA PRESS

University of California Press
Oakland, California

© 2025 by Reynolds Holding

All rights reserved.

Library of Congress Cataloging-in-Publication Data

Names: Holding, Reynolds, author.
Title: Better judgment : how three judges are bringing justice back to
   the courts / Reynolds Holding.
Description: Oakland, California : University of California Press, 2025. |
   Includes bibliographical references and index.
Identifiers: LCCN 2024058426 (print) | LCCN 2024058427 (ebook) |
   ISBN 9780520396616 (cloth) | ISBN 9780520396623 (ebook)
Subjects: LCSH: Judicial process—United States. | Judicial power—
   United States. | Judges—United States. | Justice, Administration
   of—United States. | Courts—United States.
Classification: LCC KF8700 .H53 2025 (print) | LCC KF8700 (ebook)
   | DDC 347.73/140922—dc23/eng/20241205
LC record available at https://lccn.loc.gov/2024058426
LC ebook record available at https://lccn.loc.gov/2024058427

Manufactured in the United States of America

GPSR Authorized Representative: Easy Access System Europe,
Mustamäe tee 50, 10621 Tallinn, Estonia, gpsr.requests
@easproject.com

34 33 32 31 30 29 28 27 26 25
10 9 8 7 6 5 4 3 2 1

For Joanna and Carolyn

Contents

Prologue 1

1. Heroes 15
2. Dear Top Banana 39
3. I Can Do This 64
4. Justice on Trial 84
5. What a Judge Does 109
6. Opening the Courthouse Doors 128
7. You Will Be Heard 150
8. Neither Admit nor Deny 177
9. No Life Wasted 206
10. Pure Gaslighting 225
11. The Troublemaker Prevails 234

Epilogue 246

Acknowledgments 257
Notes 259
Bibliography 281
Index 289

Prologue

Clarence Jamison was making his way to his home in South Carolina when the cop car came into view. It was on the right shoulder, a gray SUV tucked into the early evening shadows of the loblolly pines along a stretch of Interstate 20 in Pelahatchie, Mississippi, just east of Jackson. Jamison was driving within the speed limit, in no particular hurry to return from his vacation in Arizona. As he passed the SUV, he looked hard at the trooper inside, a white man with hair cropped to a stubble. Jamison was a Black man driving a silver Mercedes convertible.

The police car pulled out almost instantly. Seeing a flash of red and blue lights, Jamison slowed to a stop on the side of the road. He watched an officer, about thirty, stocky and thick around the shoulders, approach the passenger side of the convertible. Jamison lowered the window.

"You buy this automobile in Pennsylvania?" the officer asked. Jamison said he had, about two weeks before his trip to Arizona, from an online used car dealer who had attached a temporary license tag to the back. It read "Pennsylvania."

"Can I see the paperwork? You don't have a tag," the officer said. Jamison stared at the man for a moment, noting the name "Nicholas McLendon" on a tag above his shirt pocket. Jamison handed over his bill of sale, insurance card, and South Carolina driver's license.

McLendon walked back to his car to run a computer check on Jamison, and Jamison waited, his grip tightening around the steering wheel.[1]

It was July 29, 2013, and Jamison had cause to be tense. Interstate 20 ran on a line from West Texas to South Carolina and had gained a reputation among the officers who policed its path as a drug corridor—narcotics going east, cash moving west. The local cops tended to view almost any Black or Latino motorist as fair game for a close look and a quick arrest. Jamison did not know that at the time. But what he did know, what most of the nation could not ignore, was that sixteen days earlier a neighborhood watchman named George Zimmerman had been acquitted in Florida of murdering an unarmed African American high school student named Trayvon Martin.[2] On the day of the acquittal a Facebook post appeared, ending with "Black people. I love you. I love us. Our lives matter." It was written by Alicia Garza, a civil rights activist and an eventual cofounder of the Black Lives Matter movement.[3] In the following weeks, demonstrators across the country gathered to raise their fists in the streets and chant the dead teenager's name. Jamison shared their anger—and their fear.

The computer check came back clean, and McLendon returned to the Mercedes, handing back the documents through the open window. Relieved, Jamison reached for his keys.

"Hold on, hold on, hold on," drawled McLendon, resting his palm on the door. "Can I search the car?"

"For what?" Jamison asked.[4] McLendon changed the subject and inquired of Jamison what he did for a living. The forty-six-year-old divorced father was a welder who traveled the country for industrial jobs that typically lasted for months. The talk drifted to welding when McLendon asked again whether he could search the car.

"For what?" Jamison said.

This time McLendon explained that he had received a call about ten kilos of cocaine being in this very Mercedes.[5] "Can I search the car?" he asked again.

"There's nothing in my car," said Jamison, his voice perhaps a little too sharp as he let slip a comment about police officers "planting stuff" in cars.

McLendon leaned down so that his face, round and open with a five-o'clock shadow, filled the window. He reached inside the Mercedes. "C'mon, man," he said, slowly patting the door's interior. "Let me search your car. I got this call . . . ten kilos of cocaine . . . hey, if all I find is a roach, I'll let you go."

Jamison stared ahead. "There is nothing in my car," he repeated in slow and measured beats. He turned to meet McLendon's eyes and paused. Hours on the road had tired him, and resistance was surely foolish. "If I can see you in my plain sight," he said to the officer, you can search it.

McLendon walked around to the driver's side of the car and opened the door. "Get out," he said. He patted down Jamison, a taller man of slighter build than McLendon, and ordered him to stand in front of the police cruiser parked behind the Mercedes.

As Jamison obeyed, he asked why he had been stopped. "Your license plate," McLendon said. "It was folded up." Jamison leaned against the grill of the policeman's car and stared at the temporary plate, wondering what the officer was talking about. It was flat, secured by a screw in each corner.

McLendon commenced his search of the Mercedes. He climbed in the front and then the back, jammed his hands between and under the seats, twisted his finger through stitched seams in the leather upholstery. The sun was setting, and Jamison looked at his cellphone: 8:15 p.m., about forty-five minutes into the stop. McLendon poked around the trunk, the engine block, between the layers of the fabric roof, and underneath the car. All the while he talked: *This car's stolen. You sure you have insurance on this thing? I'm going to find the cocaine. Ninety percent of the time I think there's drugs in a car, I'm right.*

An eighteen-wheeler passed and Jamison heard a crack from the car. He approached to see what had happened. McLendon ordered him back. Jamison looked at his phone again: It was just before 9:00 p.m.

"You mind if I deploy my canine?" asked McLendon. Jamison nodded. A shepherd-like dog appeared and sniffed the car. McLendon emerged from the dark and faced Jamison, handing him a flashlight. "You look inside the car, and anything you find damaged, I'll pay for," he said. Jamison quickly passed the beam over the front and back seats, but eager to be on his way, he mumbled that things looked fine. As the police car pulled out, Jamison stooped to the pavement to pick up his possessions. It was about 9:30—almost two hours since he had pulled to the shoulder of Interstate 20.

Early the next morning, when Jamison arrived at his home in Neeses, South Carolina, he felt dead on his feet. And yet that night he could not sleep, playing over and over in his mind the encounter with Officer Nicholas McLendon. The following day Jamison placed a call to a lawyer he knew, Clyde Dean. The lawyer advised patience. Jamison was clearly upset, but the extent of his damages, the psychological and physical harm that led to medical expenses or loss of work, would only emerge with time. And suing the police was hard. It would require Jamison to prove not only that McLendon had committed a constitutional violation—an illegal stop and search of Jamison's car, for example—but also that the officer should have known that the search was illegal. The only way to do that was to scour the law books for cases so similar that the illegality was beyond dispute. Jamison would need a lawyer in Mississippi, someone who could pull off a time-consuming constitutional suit on behalf of a Black man against a white cop in a state of deep-bred racism.

Go slow, Dean counseled, the deadline for filing a lawsuit was three years away.

· · ·

Carlton Reeves strode to his chambers on the fifth floor of the Thad Cochran United States Courthouse in downtown Jackson, Mississippi, moving with impressive agility for a middle-aged man of powerful bulk. His broad grin and soft hellos brought smiles to the security officers he greeted along the way and often invited for a cup of coffee in his office. It was early, before 8:00 a.m., on a summer morning in 2016, and the building had yet to come to life. In his office, a spacious corner room of blond wood and wide windows looking southeast toward the Pearl River and the flatlands of poorer sections of town, scores of unhung plaques and photos were propped against the base of every wall and spread across the cushions of the big brown leather couch under a window. At the far end of the room, to the right as you enter, a tall bookshelf stood behind a desk that was buried beneath books and notepads and stacks of documents.

From somewhere in those stacks Reeves pulled a twelve-page document, captioned "Clarence Jamison Versus Nick McClendon [sic]," which claimed violations of Jamison's constitutional rights. The judge read of the stop that night three years before, of the humiliating accusations and interminable search, of the fear that at first kept Jamison from leaving his house for days at a time, of the anger and anxiety that often left him sleepless as he pondered the news about one Black man after another killed at the hands of the police. The document demanded an unspecified amount of compensation for the psychological pain Jamison had suffered, the wages he had lost, the doctors' bills he owed, and the damage to his car—torn upholstery, dented stereo speaker, broken air vent, the roof separated in spots from its frame.

Yet as Reeves could surmise, this suit, like similar civil rights cases, was about far more than compensating a single victim. It was about punishing and trying to end the persistent abuse of men and women whom cops and other authorities seemed prone to view as unworthy of treatment as human. Reeves's mind went back to a case that he had handled a decade earlier. He was still a defense lawyer then, and he was representing another Black man who had been stopped by police on a nearby road. Only that man had been handcuffed and hurled to the ground and stomped in the face. Like Jamison, this man had sued over the unconstitutional abuse inflicted upon him—and still he had lost.[6] The problem was what lawyers called "qualified immunity," a rule that the US Supreme Court had concocted decades earlier essentially to shield police officers and the towns they worked for from lawsuits.[7] There were exceptions, but they required obvious evidence that a "reasonable officer" would have known his behavior was illegal under the nation's founding document.[8] In legal terms that meant a case so on point that it involved almost precisely the same facts—a near impossibility.

Reeves couldn't find that case a decade earlier and believed he had let his client down. Now, as a judge, he was determined to see Clarence Jamison treated as fairly as the law would allow. This was about so much more than the law, though. Reeves had grown up Black in Yazoo City, Mississippi, a Delta town where his father had been arrested for raising his voice against a white grocer who had insulted his mother, where to see a movie he had to mount the balcony stairs because only white kids could sit in the cushioned seats below. Reeves had been blessed with the mind and optimism to overcome the condescension and scant opportunities, but he knew too many people who had not, and as a judge he often felt compelled to tell of what they had endured.

The case ground through the legal process over the next four years, prolonged by settlement negotiations, motions to drop charges, summary judgment hearings, and the ultimately successful efforts of the City of Pelahatchie, McLendon's employer, to wriggle out of liability. Meanwhile, the outside world intruded. Scores of unarmed Black people—Philando Castile in Minnesota, Breonna Taylor in Kentucky, George Floyd in Minnesota—died at the hands of police.⁹ And early in the summer of 2020, as Reeves and his three clerks talked, it became clear that they could not divorce the case from those events, the current context of discrimination.

Yet it was the weekly phone calls with Reeves's family, the group conversations among his sisters and brothers and their children during the COVID-19 lockdown, that most moved him. His relatives had fresh stories of being harassed by police. Reeves's nephew in Dallas, Texas, spoke of being pulled over on the interstate in January, his wife and kids with mouths agape as he had been searched. "Unc, you don't know how degrading it is to be stripped of your manhood before your family," Reeves recalled his nephew saying. "You get sick of it. One false move, one raised voice, could get you killed." By the end of that conversation Reeves had decided what he needed to say in the Jamison case. On August 4, 2020, he issued his opinion.¹⁰

"Clarence Jamison wasn't jaywalking," it began, followed by a footnote: "That was Michael Brown," the twenty-eight-year-old Black man shot dead by police in Ferguson, Missouri. "He wasn't outside playing with a toy gun," it continued, followed by another footnote: "That was twelve-year-old Tamir Rice," killed in a Cleveland, Ohio, park. "He wasn't suspected of 'selling loose, untaxed cigarettes.'" Footnote: "That was Eric Garner," the Staten Island man who died in a police chokehold. And on it went through nineteen footnoted examples of unarmed Black people killed by the police over the past several years. "No, Clarence Jamison was a Black man driving a Mercedes convertible." And though he left a police encounter "with his life, too many others have not."

The opinion then told the story of that terrifying evening in 2013 on Interstate 20, but it didn't stop there. It recounted the troubling history of the law that Jamison was suing under, a statute known as Section 1983 that flatly barred state officials from violating people's constitutional rights and that had its origins in Reconstruction after the Civil War. Over dozens of pages of stark and rhythmic prose, the opinion detailed how the statute was one of several laws—most notably the Thirteenth, Fourteenth, and Fifteenth Amendments—that offered "a glimpse of a different America," only to be crushed under a backlash of white supremacy, terror, and violence that had lasted for almost a century. When in 1961 the Supreme Court revived Section 1983, allowing a Black family to sue thirteen Chicago police officers for ransacking their home, the promise of the federal courts as guardians against officials' abuse seemed realized, Reeves wrote, only to be trampled again in 1967 by a Supreme Court worried that the fear of being sued could stop police from doing their jobs. The court fabricated the doctrine of "qualified immunity," a concept nowhere in the statute, its legislative history, or the Constitution.

The argument for overcoming that immunity in Jamison's case was powerful, Reeves wrote in his opinion. A Black man had been pulled over in a state with a deep history of racial violence, in a year when more than six hundred people had been killed by the police, at a time when Black Lives Matter was shining a light on "police brutality writ large." The tensions between the police and Black people had grown more visible since, but even in that earlier context, he wrote, there was no way to conclude that Jamison had freely given the permission required for the police to search his car. "In an America where Black people 'are considered dangerous even when they are in their living rooms eating ice cream, asleep in their beds, playing in the park, standing in the pulpit of their church, birdwatching, exercising in public, or walking home from a trip to the store to purchase a bag of Skittles,'" Reeves wrote, "who can say that Jamison felt free that night on the side of Interstate 20? Who can say that he felt free to say no to an armed Officer McClendon [sic]?" There seemed no doubt that McLendon had violated Jamison's constitutional rights.

As Reeves reached the end of the opinion, he wrote something extraordinary. He addressed the US Supreme Court directly, calling on the justices to abolish qualified immunity, to cease perpetuating, in the justices' own words, "something we all know to be wrong only because we fear the consequences of being right." And then, being a judge and having sworn to comply with the law, Reeves did the only thing that he believed the law—as wrong as it was—would allow him to do. He dismissed Clarence Jamison's lawsuit.

. . .

That Carlton Reeves could not deliver the justice he believed was Clarence Jamison's due was a disturbing symptom of what has become of our federal courts. At their best they can act as a kind of whistleblower in our democracy, sending an early signal that a serious problem needs repair. They can also bring us together with persuasive rulings that broaden support for shifts in what society views as good or appropriate or desirable. They can offer a direct and effective way for us to voice our concerns and have them addressed.[11] And the courts are one of the few places where facts—tested, proven facts—can emerge to shed light on disasters so that lawmakers can sensibly gauge what happened and enact reforms. Yet over the past six decades federal courts and, even more important, people's access to them have been constrained or blocked—by Congress, by the Executive, and especially by the Supreme Court itself—to the point where they can no longer do what we count on them to do.

In too many cases, federal courts cannot make police officers or other officials pay for the abuse that they inflict on their victims. And it's not just police. A virtually impenetrable legal shield has protected the likes of prosecutors and judges from answering for even the most horrific misconduct. Courts cannot allow employees harassed or worse at work to reveal in public their bosses' misconduct. Judges cannot force banks to come clean about frauds that force the economy to its knees. In case after case, criminals cannot get just sentences, immigrants fair hearings, or Americans generally the day in court that they once imagined was their right.

So how did this happen? The current effort to kick shut the courthouse doors started about seventy years ago, initially fueled by racism. In 1956 a group of Southern senators aghast at what *Brown v. Board of Education*—the Supreme Court case that ruled racially segregated schools unconstitutional—would do to their home states' way of life issued the Southern Manifesto, a declaration of war on the federal courts.[12] In the following decades, the effort gained momentum from a politics of retribution, errant attempts at reform, and a fear that courts fully capable of delivering justice would be too costly and slow. Today the federal bench is full of men and women inclined to view their role narrowly, to duck cases and defer to state lawmakers and governors and let pass rather than scrutinize and perhaps challenge the toughest issues of our day.

It is not the first time that the federal courts have suffered diminished stature. They have periodically risen and fallen in the eyes of Americans—liberals and conservatives and libertarians, Democrats and Republicans and Progressives—throughout our nation's history. The federal courts and especially the Supreme Court have been on the side of some of the most regressive forces in society. But just as often, they have given Americans hope and relief on everything from racial equality to economic progress to criminal justice. This history has long provoked intense debate among politicians and scholars and judges themselves over how powerful and accessible to the public the courts should be.

Former Harvard Law School professor and Supreme Court justice Felix Frankfurter famously vexed liberal allies with the notion that courts should generally restrain themselves in favor of the democratic process: the judgment of voters and the laws that elected officials enact.[13] One of Frankfurter's law clerks, the influential Yale law professor Alexander Bickel, startled liberal admirers by arguing that judges and justices should exercise "passive virtues"—find ways to return thorny, unsettled questions to the political branches so courts could avoid unnecessary entanglements with controversial problems and gain room to determine what constitutional principle best applied to particular issues. Though initially supportive of *Brown*, Bickel turned fierce critic of the Supreme Court's activism under Chief Justice Earl Warren.[14] Legal scholar John Hart Ely staked a sort of middle ground, arguing that judges' constitutional duty was largely procedural—"policing the process of representation" by making sure that democracy worked fairly and allowed as many people as possible, especially minorities, to participate in it.[15] Even before they became judges and then Supreme Court justices, Thurgood Marshall and Ruth Bader Ginsburg as civil rights lawyers pushed the federal courts to act boldly in securing the rights of Americans when the political system would not.[16]

In recent years, though, it seems a swath of America has about given up on the federal courts. On the right, the work of making it harder for people to seek redress and vindicate their rights still thrives, and to the extent conservative judges and justices are considered activist, it is a starkly negative activism, an effort to get the federal courts out of the business of, say, upholding erstwhile principles like the right to abortion or the notion that no Americans—not even presidents—are above the law. On the left the talk is of imposing term limits on judges and justices and limiting their ability to hear certain types of cases and relying instead on elected officials to make law and interpret the Constitution.

Giving up on the courts, though, would be a mistake. The best argument for why is revealed throughout this book, in the stories of three remarkable judges. They are of different races and genders, from different backgrounds and parts of the country, and with different views of their roles on the bench, and they have strengthened our democracy in a host of extraordinary ways. One judge is Carlton

Reeves. Another is Jed Rakoff, a white, well-educated child of a prosperous Philadelphia neighborhood, who after nearly three decades as a US district court judge in New York routinely challenges power and legal precedent as one of the nation's leading advocates for judicial independence. The third judge is Martha Vázquez, a Mexican American and daughter of an undocumented immigrant, who grew up in a scruffy neighborhood in 1960s Southern California working alongside her parents in the gardens of the well-to-do and became a US district court judge in Santa Fe, New Mexico.

Each of these judges came of age as people's access to the courts and the power of judges were declining, and each was personally and profoundly affected by the experience. What's more, on the bench, each has resisted growing and harmful constraints on a judge's power to discover the truth and right wrongs: Rakoff by confronting those constraints directly through the force of logic, Vázquez by digging deep into the lives of the people who come before her, and Reeves by making his case to the ultimate authority—the people. Their diversity demonstrates both the breadth of the opposition to limiting court access and power and the range of people who practice audacious and consequence-focused judging. Their story is very much the story of widespread resistance to a war on the courts.

There is another reason for telling their stories together. Thinkers on the left argue for largely sidelining the courts in favor of the elected branches of the federal government, which, they believe, can better confront a growing crisis: political and economic inequality in the United States. This crisis threatens American democracy by putting too much power in the hands of too few, creating an oligarchy. Elected officials can confront the crisis with legislation to, say, invest in downtrodden regions and create jobs, offer health-care insurance and childcare support, and limit political contributions and tax excessive wealth—that is, to broaden the distribution of wealth and power. Yet conservative courts block much of this legislation based on a view that the Constitution essentially protects property and rugged individualism. But this view, this theory of political economy—basically how economic power affects politics and vice versa—is, say these thinkers on the left, at odds with democracy and the republic that the Constitution is meant to preserve.

Among the most compelling of these thinkers are two law professors, Joseph Fishkin at UCLA Law School and William Forbath at the University of Texas at Austin. They argue that essentially three things are required to ease the crisis of inequality. One is stricter constraints on the excessive money and power that creates oligarchy. Another is a broader middle class, meaning more people with a basic American standard of material comfort and security and the opportunity to live a life of value. The third thing is the inclusion of more people across all races and genders in American society, its politics, and the economy. The basic idea is that democracy works better—*only* works, really—when as many people as possible have a voice and the power to be heard. Fishkin and Forbath call it, as President Franklin Roosevelt called it, the "democracy of opportunity."[17]

They see a lesser role for the federal courts in all this, believing judges should generally step aside and let the other branches of government get on with the work. Yet that sells judges short, as Reeves, Rakoff, and Vázquez tell us. Each judge has powerfully promoted one or more of the three principles that Fishkin and Forbath describe as necessary for a democracy of opportunity. Rakoff has taken on the denizens of Wall Street and other oligarchs throughout his career, most famously calling banks to account after the 2008 financial crisis. Vázquez has worked to ensure that the troubled people who come before her get help, get educations, and get jobs so that they are not discarded but have a shot at living lives of value and becoming members of the middle class. Reeves has consistently upheld the rights of women, gay people, Black people, Latinos, and other minorities in his opinions and on the bench but also in the dozens of eloquent speeches he gives every year. He has worked to include them more deeply in American society.

Far from undemocratic, these three judges advance democracy as effectively as any elected official, and their story is also the story of what engaged judges can do toward that end. Our story begins near the first blossoming of resistance to the federal courts, in a town on the edge of the flat, dark land of the Mississippi Delta.

1   *Heroes*

The photo is faded now, its colors no longer vivid. The white line of a crease runs from its left edge toward its center, and a smudge, maybe from a thumbprint, clouds a corner above the crease. Faint, spidery scratches scatter about. It is a photo that has been handled often, looked at, smiled at, shared and loved and passed from friend to friend. At its center, a blonde girl, maybe six years old, her hair pulled tightly back, her sleeveless T-shirt striped across with bright lines of color, leans toward the camera with mouth agape in a joyous shout. Behind her, his hands on his hips in a confident pose, stands a tall African American boy wearing a short-sleeved red plaid shirt and a grin so friendly you feel like saying hello. Beside and behind them and seated in front are twenty-two other boys and girls gathered in a haphazard mix of faces—white, white, Black, white, Black—all smiling, all delivering a holler as cheerful as the late-spring light.

It is a photo of Miss Thornton's first-grade class at the Annie Ellis Elementary School on Grand Avenue in Yazoo City, Mississippi. It was taken near the end of the school year in 1971. There was a time when such a portrayal of school kids together in Mississippi would have been unthinkable, and in certain parts of the state it was unthinkable still.[1] Yet moments of token desegregation aside, for essentially the first time in history, these children and others in thirty school districts across the state had attended a full year of racially integrated classes. They had attended because in 1969, in a case originally filed up Route 49E from Yazoo City in Holmes County, the US Supreme Court had ordered recalcitrant educators and complicit judges to stop procrastinating and comply with *Brown v. Board of Education*.[2] Unlike those in DeKalb and Tunica and other Mississippi towns, these children went without controversy, without a mass exodus of white boys and girls to private schools created to skirt the demands of integration. And they are smiling. They are, after all, just six-year-olds, and you can easily believe that over the course of first grade they have not learned anything about prejudice. They have not learned anything but how to read and do a little math and engage in fun and childish things. They have not learned how to view each other with suspicion because of their race or their families' status in town but merely how to play together. You can believe that is why, in the photo of their last day in first grade, they are smiling at the camera with unreserved glee.

For one child in particular, the Black child wearing a pressed white shirt directly to the right of the blonde girl in the striped T-shirt, the feeling of joy in those smiles mattered deeply. It stayed with him, shaped him, made him into a compassionate man who saw goodness and hope in a society and especially a state that had long inflicted brutal racism on its Black inhabitants. He would mention the photo often, to members of Congress, to prosecutors at the US Department of Justice, to acquaintances who were curious about what made him tick. That child was Carlton Reeves.

Reeves was born two states to the west, in Fort Hood, Texas, in 1964. He and his three older siblings soon moved with their father, First Sergeant Jesse W. Reeves, and mother, Wilhelmina Reeves, to Germany before settling four years later back in Yazoo City, his parents' hometown. Yazoo sits on hills at the edge of the Mississippi Delta, about forty miles north of Jackson, the state capital, and forty-five miles east of the Mississippi River itself. The delta land that spreads to the horizon west is flat, its alluvial soil black and loamy, its swamps and small rivers and creeks remnants of a prior existence under the sea. In 1969 just over eleven thousand people, a little more than half of them Black, lived in Yazoo. The ones with jobs worked at the Mississippi Chemical Corporation or much smaller businesses like the lumberyard or tire store in town. Yet poverty persisted. Almost a quarter of Yazoo residents were on food stamps in 1970, and more than a third of families earned less than $3000 a year.[3]

Growing up, Reeves might have had reason to be bitter; like most Black people in town, he was admonished to "know his place." On his first day of school in the first grade, he walked from home along the loose gravel of Ninth Street before turning left and heading up Prentiss Avenue's paved surface toward the Annie Ellis school. On his side of Prentiss, the west side, with bungalows like his family's of wood boards and brick and cement-slab patios in small yards close together, lived the teachers and shopkeepers and families of the Black middle class. On the east side, not a stone's toss away, were the notables of white society: the Barbours and the Stevenses and their homes of wraparound verandas and weighty columns and manicured lawns thick with shade. As Reeves grew, more Black families moved in, prompting the whites to move out until, eventually, even the east side was largely Black.

At school, the teachers and textbooks too often reminded him of where he stood. In fifth grade he went on a field trip with his fellow honor-roll students to Jackson, and standing in the rotunda of the state capitol was a statue of former governor and senator Theodore G. Bilbo, among the most infamous of the state's infamous race-baiters.[4] The bus driver, a father of a classmate and the guide on the children's tour, hugged the statue and, according to Reeves, told the students: "Y'all should be very proud of this man, the greatest Mississippian ever." In seventh grade, when Reeves reached out to a classmate offering him candy, his white teacher falsely accused Reeves of throwing some sort of obscene gesture with his hand and ordered him to the principal's office. Ignoring Reeves's protestations of innocence, the principal delivered twenty-five licks with a paddle to his backside. The memory of the injustice and humiliation can still bring Reeves to tears. In ninth grade, during a class on civics and Mississippi history, the teacher—the white football coach—said that slaves didn't know how to handle freedom and were better off enslaved.

Outside of school, it was no easier. Best buddies like Henry Barbour—the nephew of future Mississippi governor Haley Barbour—often vanished into a white world that Reeves could only imagine. To see a movie on Saturday mornings at the Yazoo Theater, Reeves and his friends trudged up three flights of steps to the balcony for want of the extra fifty cents required to sit with the white boys and girls eating popcorn and holding hands in the padded seats downstairs. It was the theater owner's way of separating the races despite the 1964 Civil Rights Act's ban on segregation in public accommodations.[5] In the summers Reeves played baseball in the all-Black Campanella League, which at first lacked the wherewithal to supply its players with uniforms. When the kids in the all-white Dixie Youth League and Babe Ruth League received new uniforms of lightweight cotton, though, their old ones of hot and itchy wool were handed down to the players in the Campanella League, along with whatever used bats and balls could be spared. After the public pool was forced to admit Black swimmers, the town filled it and replaced it with a tennis court.

Reeves cringed at how his parents were sometimes treated. In 1972, when he was about eight, his sister came home close to tears and told him that she had just been at the grocery store with her parents. The white manager had insulted their mother with a racial slur, and his father had yelled at the man, prompting a call to the police. A year later, when her now-seven children were old enough to mind themselves or each other, Reeves's mother took a job as a housekeeper washing sheets and towels at the Yazoo Motel. She was paid a dollar an hour. Reeves's father was home periodically but more often away, continuing the army tours in places like Pennsylvania and Georgia that eventually provided an excuse for him to be gone for good.

Yet Reeves was far from bitter about all this, no doubt because it was just the world as he knew it but also because of who he was. At the Annie Ellis school he would join the "A section." It consisted almost entirely of white students, and they would in later years learn algebra and biology rather than the general science and shop that students in the bottom, almost entirely Black, section C would be taught. "The way you knew if you were in the smart class," Reeves recalled, "was when you looked around and you were the only black person in there."[6] He would thrive in the public schools not just because of his smarts but also because of an ebullience that made people smile. They called Reeves—still call him—Baba (pronounced "Bay-bay"), his eldest brother's name for him as an infant.

Reeves would grow close to many of his classmates, white and Black. In high school they would elect him president of his junior-year class and by secret ballot MVP of the tennis team even though he was far from the best player. And though many had come or gone over the past twelve years, they would largely retain the joy in each other's company that they had displayed in that photo back on the last day of first grade. It meant a lot to Reeves that their high school graduation song was Stevie Wonder and Paul McCartney's "Ebony and Ivory."

Reeves had a strong sense of optimism, in part by nature but also as the result of a precocious appreciation for the law and what it had done and could do for people who looked like him. That appreciation first came in a childish way, while he was watching an episode of the sitcom *Sanford and Son*, and its star, the Black comedian and actor

Redd Foxx, got sued by his wife for divorce. It seemed to Reeves that a lawyer's job must be to help people in tough situations. During the US Senate's Watergate hearings, in 1973, when Reeves was just nine years old, he devoured the unfolding drama of testimony and examinations and startling revelations about a corrupt White House. In spare moments he would attend trials at the Yazoo County Courthouse, enthralled to see what lawyers did. His first chance to watch the wheels of justice turn up close came one summer when, as a favor for a friend on vacation, he cleaned the office of Judge William Barbour downtown in Yazoo City. It had a copying machine, and having never seen such a contraption, Reeves clicked the "on" button and flinched in near panic as it hummed and whirred. He didn't know how to stop it, so he pushed the emergency shut-off button, cutting all power, and felt compelled to confess to the judge that he believed he had broken the machine.

With interest in the law came a fascination with politics. Reeves would watch the presidential nominating conventions deep into the night over several days. His mother would make sure that he and his siblings understood the power of the vote, and come every election day, she would take them to watch her cast her ballot. They would return home and listen on the local radio station for the results. Throughout his childhood, for most of the 1970s, those electoral results were inevitably disappointing. The contests were often close, but Black candidates for mayor or the board of aldermen or county supervisors lost time and again until, in 1979, Wardell Leach won his race for supervisor.[7] Reeves was ecstatic. In 1982 politics and law met for Reeves in a federal courtroom, where Judge Barbour denied a Black mayoral candidate's challenge to his latest election loss. The defeat stung, but what mattered most for Reeves was that the candidate could go into court and try to ensure that the election had been fair and the system had worked.

That same year, Reeves started college at Jackson State University, a historically Black institution of close to ten thousand students and the scene of a deadly police shooting of fourteen students in 1970.[8] Future students like Reeves "relived that shooting a lot in their minds," said Patricia Bennett, who taught Reeves at the university and recently stepped down as dean of the Mississippi College of the Law, "and it became part of their stories." For better or worse, the deadly shooting also put the school on the nation's map as a locus of Black resistance to racism. Reeves might have gone to almost any college in the country and, given his preference to stay in Mississippi, certainly the University of Mississippi—Ole Miss—but he refused. One reason, he said, was "simply because I knew that these white kids in my [high school] class loved Ole Miss so much. If they loved it that much, I didn't want it."[9] But he also saw in Jackson State an opportunity to gain "an understanding of who I am." He continued: "You learn so much more about yourself because you see your own people."

While at Jackson State, Reeves took a series of American history courses, many with teacher Dennis Mitchell, who became his favorite, a thoughtful scholar of Mississippi's past and its writers and artists. From Mitchell, Reeves learned that a certain group of people—individuals who worked mostly out of the public eye and, aside from an occasional encounter with Judge Barbour, had never much drawn Reeves's attention—had played an enormously consequential role in his life. Those people were federal judges, and Reeves learned that over the past thirty years they had withstood sometimes violent resistance to breathe life into his rights and into the rights of every American. He came to learn that, in his eyes, "judges are heroes."

Some of the greatest heroes among them, Reeves believed, were the justices of the US Supreme Court under Chief Justice Earl Warren. Reeves had been allowed to go to the good schools once reserved for white students largely because those justices had decided that racially segregated schools were unconstitutional and that desegregation with "all deliberate speed" was required.[10] Reeves's mother, still working for paltry wages at the Yazoo Motel, could vote in federal elections without paying a poll tax because in 1966 the court declared the levy unconstitutional in *Harper v. Virginia Board of Elections*.[11] Reeves had the right to rent or buy a house regardless of his race because of the court's decisions in cases like *Jones v. Mayer* in 1968.[12] He could eat at most any restaurant, stay at most any motel, and generally function in society as freely as he did in part because the court upheld the provisions of the 1964 Civil Rights Act.[13]

He saw heroes among lower court judges too, individuals like Frank M. Johnson, a federal trial judge in Alabama, whose courageous decisions included joining a 1956 opinion striking down the Montgomery law that Rosa Parks had challenged and required Black patrons to sit in the back of city buses.[14] A cross was burned on Johnson's lawn after the decision came down, his mother's house was bombed a few years later, and a series of death threats led the government to assign federal marshals to protect him over almost twenty years.[15] Four judges on the Fifth Circuit—the federal court of appeals that before 1981 had jurisdiction over Mississippi, five other states of the old Confederacy, and the Panama Canal Zone—came to be known as "the Four" when they took on the task of ensuring that desegregation went forward despite harsh resistance. All four judges—John Minor Wisdom, Elbert Tuttle, John Robert Brown, and Richard Rives—put their lives at risk for their efforts.[16]

A Rough Lesson

What Reeves could not fully appreciate at the time, though, was how fragile the progress that these judges and justices had made possible could be. He would come to realize that the Warren Court was largely an aberration, that for much of the nation's history, the judiciary, and especially the Supreme Court, had often given strength to the most regressive and even terrifying forces in society. It was a rough lesson to learn.

Consider slavery. In 1842 the Supreme Court reversed the conviction of Edward Prigg, a professional slave catcher found guilty under a Pennsylvania law that barred spiriting Black people out of the state and back into enslavement. The justices decided that the law violated the requirement of the federal Fugitive Slave Act of 1793—and the Constitution's fugitive slave clause—that slaves gone to free states be returned to their owners.[17] Then there was, of course, the Dred Scott decision in 1857.[18] The Supreme Court held that even free Blacks weren't US citizens, and Congress's efforts to abolish slavery in the nation's territories were unconstitutional. In the court's majority opinion Chief Justice Roger Taney wrote that African Americans are "beings of an inferior order" with "no rights which the white man was bound to respect." This was too much for Abraham Lincoln, who delivered an early and high-profile challenge to the Supreme Court's undemocratic ways. "If the policy of the Government upon vital questions affecting the whole people is to be irrevocably fixed by decisions of the Supreme Court, the instant they are made . . . ," he said, "the people will have ceased to be their own rulers, having to that extent practically resigned their Government into the hand of that eminent tribunal."[19] Sure enough, as president, Lincoln suspended habeas corpus without Congress's say-so and ignored Taney's ruling, in 1861, that the suspension was unconstitutional.[20]

Then there was the Supreme Court's endorsement of the system of apartheid that white leaders had established after stymieing Reconstruction efforts toward racial equality. In 1896, in *Plessy v. Ferguson*, the justices ruled that a Louisiana law requiring the segregation of Black people from white people on railway cars did not violate the Fourteenth Amendment's guarantee of equality between the races.[21] The guarantee applied to political rather than social equality, the court reasoned, and besides, the Louisiana law did not impose second-class status on Black people, even though "the colored race chooses to put that construction upon it." And thus the Supreme Court blessed the notion of "separate but equal."

Consider the back of the hand that the Supreme Court delivered to ordinary Americans, Black and white, trying to make a go of life in an emerging industrial society. At about the time of the *Plessy* decision, Populists and then Progressives were rising as potent political forces on their behalf and, in response, states enacted a host of economic regulations. They included laws setting minimum wages and maximum hours for workers, prohibitions on so-called "yellow dog contracts" barring workers from creating labor unions, and regulations establishing health and safety standards for living and working conditions.[22] Yet this reform movement made leaders of the Republican Party—the party of Lincoln—nervous, especially lawyers. The most successful among them, people like reformer David Dudley Field, the brother of future Supreme Court Justice Stephen Field, had powerful corporations as clients, and this lawyer-client relationship may have skewed their view of what it meant to support worker freedom. Rather than risk more legislation dictating how they treated employees, companies should steal the thunder of radical reformers, Field and others advised, and put workers on a similar footing as stockholders by allowing them to share profits and exercise voting rights in corporate matters.[23]

The idea was essentially to create a sort of big happy family where everyone—workers and their employers alike—had an interest in protecting the freedom of labor and contract as well as making the business and private property secure.[24] The idea took hold in the federal courts, in part because the Supreme Court bench was filling with Wall Street lawyers and other attorneys sympathetic to this view—and especially to the idea that corporations could have constitutional rights alongside workers.[25] Their sympathies were soon apparent in their reactions to states' economic reforms, most famously in the

1905 case of *Lochner v. New York*.[26] New York state had prohibited employers from requiring bakers to work more than ten hours a day or sixty hours a week because hot ovens were ruinous to people's health. The court, though, concluded that baking was no riskier than a lot of jobs and ruled that the prohibition violated the freedom of contract protected by the Fourteenth Amendment. The majority opinion in the 5–4 decision was written by Justice Rufus Peckham, a "confidant of tycoons" like "Morgan, Rockefeller, and Vanderbilt."[27]

Lochner's antipathy to economic limits was no aberration. Over the next several decades the Supreme Court would overturn laws that banned the firing of employees for joining unions, that weakened constraints on strikes and boycotts, or that otherwise strengthened workers' bargaining power or redistributed wealth from employers to laborers. The backlash to the Supreme Court's embrace of tycoons and big business was emphatic, swift—and from the left. In an opinion dissenting from the majority in *Lochner*, Justice Oliver Wendell Holmes wrote: "This case is decided upon an economic theory which a large part of the country does not entertain.... The Fourteenth Amendment does not enact Mr. Herbert Spencer's Social Statics," which famously advocated limited government, but rather is "made for people of fundamentally differing views."[28] The court, in other words, had overreached by imposing its policy preferences on the people and their elected representatives. It's simplistic but fair to say that Holmes was often on the left, given his many opinions advancing progressive causes. A more obvious liberal was Louis Brandeis, a sharp defender of social justice and an enemy of the "Money Trust" who joined Holmes on the court in 1916. Brandeis typically favored deferring to legislatures and restraining the courts, often in dissenting opinions.[29]

Holmes, Brandeis, and the many other critics of the Supreme Court's power were engaged in a rearguard action, though, until 1937, the first year of President Franklin Roosevelt's second term.

FDR had tried mightily to goose the US economy out of the Depression with his New Deal works projects and financial reforms, but the court, led by four conservative justices derided as the "Four Horsemen of the Apocalypse," blocked him at almost every turn. So after his landslide victory in 1936, Roosevelt floated the idea of packing the court—adding a justice for each geezer over the age of seventy, up to five justices. The plan went nowhere but relief came basically in the form of one Owen Roberts, a genial and easily swayed justice who had often supplied a fifth vote for the Four Horsemen.[30]

It came in *West Coast Hotel Co v. Parrish*, a case involving Elsie Parrish, a hotel maid who sued for back pay under Washington State's minimum wage law.[31] The Supreme Court had struck down these sorts of laws before, saying they violated the freedom of contract, but this time it upheld Washington State's. "What is this freedom?" asked Chief Justice Charles Evans Hughes in the majority opinion. "The Constitution does not speak of freedom of contract. It speaks of liberty," and liberty requires protecting "against the evils which menace the health, safety, morals, and welfare" of essentially powerless people like Elsie Parrish.[32] Roberts liked this logic, and he voted with the majority in a shift that earned the catchy description "the switch in time that saved nine."[33]

The New Deal was on a roll—and the so-called Lochner Era on the outs. The court upheld railway labor regulations, limits on banks' ability to seize farms, and, after the retirement in 1937 of Justice Willis Van Devanter, one of the Four Horsemen, a slew of other ambitious laws governing economic life.[34] For a while at least, the justices generally deferred to Congress and the president on matters of economic policy. In a 1938 case called *United States v. Carolene Products Co.*, in an opinion upholding a ban on adulterated milk, Justice Harlan Fiske Stone added a footnote—the famous footnote 4—that suggested the court would instead scrutinize more closely laws involving minority or political rights. Advocates for African Americans took the hint and began to turn to the courts for racial justice.[35]

By the early 1950s, with Jim Crow and rock-ribbed Southerners having Congress and Democrats in a hammerlock, federal jurists were about the only option left. The likes of Thurgood Marshall at the NAACP Legal Defense and Education Fund made their case to the Supreme Court, and the justices often found in their favor, sometimes unanimously, reviving the power of the federal courts to a level rarely higher in the nation's history. This was the judiciary Reeves revered, its judges in his mind heroes, stalwarts who would stand up for him and his friends and family and their ambitions. He felt lucky that just in time for his first day at Annie Ellis Elementary School, the federal courts had prevailed. Yet as he came of age and spent long hours in Dennis Mitchell's class at Jackson State almost thirty years later, Reeves learned of a furious backlash against that judiciary. The shame of it was that the backlash had emerged so close to home, helped along by his neighbors and the parents of his neighbors and his own state's senator, James Eastland, who grew up in a Delta town just north of Yazoo City. Reeves took it hard.

A Declaration of War

It began on a Monday morning in March 1956. Vice President Richard M. Nixon, the presiding officer of the US Senate, strode to his honored spot at the top of the dark-marble dais that faced the ornate chamber and glanced at the scene before him. Reporters, legislative aids, and a few plaid-shirted tourists gathered in the gallery above. Below them senators in scattered clumps hobnobbed and murmured. Nixon called the chamber to order, but his words fell unheeded, and not until Democratic Majority Leader Lyndon Johnson bellowed for a quorum did most senators jostle back to their mahogany desks tiered in semicircles facing the front of the room. In the center of the first row, Georgia's Walter George, the lanky seventy-eight-year-old president pro tempore—the Senate's number two—eased to his feet and prepared to speak.[36]

"Mr. President," George began in a sonorous drawl, "the increasing gravity of the situation following the decision of the Supreme Court in the so-called segregation cases, and the peculiar stress in sections of the country where this decision has created many difficulties . . . have led some senators and some members of the House of Representatives to prepare a statement of the position which they have felt and now feel to be imperative."[37] The "decision" to which he referred was *Brown v. Board of Education*. The "peculiar stress" he mentioned was the fury and horror in Mississippi and other Southern states over the legal evisceration of a principle at the heart of their way of life: the separation of Black people and white people. And the "statement" he named was the Declaration of Constitutional Principles or, as it came to be known, the Southern Manifesto. All but three of the twenty-two senators from former Confederate states signed it, along with seventy-seven members of the House of Representatives.[38]

The manifesto had been years in the making, its genesis the furious denunciations of *Brown* by several Southern senators—including Eastland, Richard Russell of Georgia, and Olin Johnston of South Carolina—on the Senate floor the day after the decision came down. Eastland had declared: "The South will not abide by nor obey this legislative decision by a political court."[39] Those senators agreed that an even more powerful rebuttal to *Brown* was essential. What emerged was a savvy and legally meticulous document arguing that *Brown* violated six decades of court precedent, misread the Fourteenth Amendment's right to equal treatment, undermined the Constitution's protections for states' rights, and endangered Black people while creating chaos. As George neared a close, Johnston nodded in quiet approval from his desk in the second row—a desk that had belonged to South Carolina's John C. Calhoun, the strident defender of slavery, more than a century before.[40]

Unlike Calhoun, Johnston had no talent for oratory and theatrics. His Southern accent, thick as butterscotch, earned him the nickname "mush-mouth Olin" from the *Washington Post*, and his contributions to the manifesto were strictly behind the scenes.[41] Yet he considered the document a personal victory. It set the stage for taking the bite out of *Brown* with an interpretation of *Brown II*'s "all deliberate speed" language as an invitation to move carefully—to flat-out delay. And no one could read its opening line—especially the bit about "naked power"—and mistake the Southern Manifesto for anything but what it was: a declaration of war against the federal courts. It was that war, a campaign to intimidate the nation's tribunals and force the selection of judges who would toe the Southern line, that Johnston was determined to lead. While many of his colleagues treated the manifesto as a kind of rebel yell that would keep them united for the fall elections, Johnston was playing the long game—and had little patience for provocative but empty gestures.[42]

For Johnston, the war against the courts had already begun. The year before, President Dwight Eisenhower had nominated Solicitor General Simon Sobeloff, who had argued for the implementation of *Brown*, to the US Court of Appeals covering the region that included South Carolina, and Johnston had attacked.[43] It was just a lower court appointment, but he knew lower court judges did the real work of the judiciary, having the final say in nearly all federal cases and leaving a comparative handful to the headline-grabbing grandees of the Supreme Court.[44] Controlling the lower courts was the key to limiting *Brown* and the judiciary generally, and in 1955 Johnston introduced a bill that, had it passed, would have given the US district courts—the federal trial courts—final say over all school desegregation cases. As a member of the Senate Judiciary Committee, Johnston initially blocked the Sobeloff appointment and launched an investigation into the nominee's supposed conflicts of interest. "It's an insult," he told the full Senate in July 1956, agreeing with Eastland that "we are in an era of judicial tyranny."[45] Johnston ultimately lost that battle, but in delaying the confirmation for more than a year, he set a template for generations of rancorous hearings over judicial nominations.

Johnston's next target was Thurgood Marshall, the civil rights hero and storied architect of *Brown* whom President John F. Kennedy nominated in 1961 to the US Court of Appeals in New York. Johnston upped his game, stalling the nomination with hearings so interminable that even supporters in the Senate and among his constituents turned against him.[46] It took Eastland, Johnston's colleague on the Judiciary Committee, to end the stalemate. Eastland wanted his friend from law school at the University of Mississippi, Harold Cox, appointed to the bench, and so he cut a deal with the president's brother, Attorney General Robert Kennedy, allegedly saying, "Tell your brother that if he will give me Harold Cox, I will give him the nigger."[47] Although Johnston lost these battles, he was winning the war, with Presidents Eisenhower, Kennedy, and Johnson rejecting advisers' recommendations of court nominees in part because they might rub Johnston the wrong way. After Johnston died in 1965, Strom Thurmond and other Southern senators wielded their power over nominations with even harsher and sometimes personal attacks against the nominees.[48] The upshot was an increasingly deferential federal judiciary prone to do conservative senators' bidding—with no better example than the lower courts' delay in implementing school desegregation.

At the Supreme Court, though, Chief Justice Earl Warren and his liberal majority were, for the time being, firmly in control, and they continued to uphold civil rights relating to everything from voting to prisons. On October 29, 1969, they finally lost patience over integrating schools and issued their decision in the *Holmes County Board of Education* case. Yet as much as that and other rulings compelled Reeves to view them as heroes, the justices of the Warren Court could sometimes disappoint—and in fundamental ways that Reeves would famously speak out against many years later.

The Perfect Choice

In September 1961, fifteen Episcopal priests—three Black, twelve white—in clerical attire took a cab from Tougaloo, Mississippi, down to the Continental Trailways bus terminal in nearby Jackson, planning to continue in Chattanooga, Tennessee, their "prayer pilgrimage" for racial justice. They walked through the waiting room, disobeying a whites-only sign, and turned toward the terminal restaurant for lunch. Two police officers were ready. They ordered the priests to move on, the priests refused, and, though by all accounts polite and peaceful, they were arrested, convicted, and each sentenced to four months in jail and a $200 fine for breaching the peace.

The charges were eventually dropped, but the priests sued the trial judge and the cops for violating their civil rights. The case made its way to the Supreme Court, and in 1967 the justices decided in *Pierson v. Ray* that judges were immune from suit and that police officers had, in the infamous phrase that would provoke Reeves, "qualified immunity"—that is, essentially they were protected so long as they acted in good faith. The new rule made some sense: How else could a good cop do his job? "A policeman's lot is not so unhappy," wrote Chief Justice Warren for the court, "that he must choose between being charged with dereliction of duty if he does not arrest when he has probable cause and being mulcted in damages if he does."[49]

Yet the rule began a weakening of Americans' ability to vindicate their rights in court, a weakening that a new president, a new chief justice, and a new lineup on the Supreme Court would extend in all sorts of ways to various areas of the law. The new president was Richard Nixon, elected in 1968 in part on a law-and-order platform that featured swipes at the Warren Court for boosting the rights of criminals.[50] An accomplished lawyer, Nixon had argued before the Supreme Court and came into office with clear notions of what made a good judge or justice. When it came to nominating people to the federal bench, he got plenty of advice, and some of the most passionate came from an unlikely source: an obscure and very young political operative named Tom Charles Huston. A conservative hard-liner with a sharp, narrow face and receding hairline, Huston was only twenty-five when he first met Nixon, in 1966. He had already gained prominence in right-wing politics as chairman of the Young Americans for Freedom, and the former vice president hired him to help with the youth vote and, after the election, to work in the White House.[51]

The sign on Huston's door said "staff assistant," but that failed to capture his role. He compiled the presidential news summary and wrote proclamations and minor speeches, but most of all he was the one who answered to the president's demand to "get Huston on this," with "this" typically a dodgy task like finding out who financed antiwar protesters. It was, Huston assumed, a sign of trust.[52] Behind that plain white door, in the small hours of March 25, 1969, under a portrait of John C. Calhoun, Huston was about to test that trust with an audacious document titled "Memorandum for the President."[53] It began: "Perhaps the least considered aspect of Presidential power is the authority to make appointments to the federal bench—not merely to the Supreme Court, but to the Circuit and District benches as well." It is the opportunity, the memo continued, "to influence the course of national affairs for a quarter century after he leaves office." This, Huston figured, was the key to a durable domestic policy for Nixon.

Huston made his case. A recent Gallup survey showed that three-quarters of Americans were dissatisfied with the courts, likely because of rulings on crime and segregation that showed judges were "soft on criminals and blacks."[54] The real problem, though, was that judges had strayed into politics and "forfeited their claim to impartiality." That meant Nixon should pick "the type of men" who would reach decisions that he liked—and to create a system for doing that—

so that "the appointments will be his, in fact, as in theory." More than just policy advice, the memo was a strident call for undermining the independence of the courts. When Huston finished, he gave the memo to chief of staff H. R. Haldeman, who handed it to domestic policy chief John Ehrlichman, who turned it over to the staff secretary. Two days later, Nixon scrawled across the cover page "RN agrees— Have this analysis in mind in making judicial nominations."[55]

Huston probably confirmed what Nixon was already thinking, and it would be a stretch to say the memo influenced the president's choice of particular judges. Yet no one else seemed to articulate the strategy so clearly, giving it weight with the president. In any event, two months later Nixon announced the appointment of the kind of person Huston had in mind, and it was the most consequential judicial appointment in decades—Warren Burger, who would replace the retiring Earl Warren, chief justice of the United States for the previous sixteen years.[56] Burger had been a federal appeals court judge for more than a decade, and as an outspoken critic of the Warren Court, won Nixon's admiration.[57] The year before, *U.S. News & World Report* had reprinted a speech in which Burger compared the US judicial system unfavorably with those of Norway, Sweden, and Denmark. In those countries, Burger said, courts "go swiftly, efficiently and directly to the question of whether the accused is guilty. No nation on earth goes to such lengths or takes such pains to provide safeguards as we do, once an accused person is called before the bar of justice and until his case is completed."[58] For a president eager to crack down on crime, the rights of criminals, and the ability of Americans generally to go to court, Burger seemed the perfect choice.

To be sure, Burger joined, sometimes even wrote, opinions progressives would celebrate, most notably siding in 1973 with the majority in *Roe v. Wade* establishing the right to abortion.[59] On Americans' access to court, though, there was plenty about Burger and his allies to criticize. At first, the new chief justice often found himself in the minority, left to dissent in landmarks like the 1971 decision *Bivens v. Six Unknown Named Agents of Federal Bureau of Narcotics*, which gave people the right to sue federal officials for violating their constitutional protections.[60] Nixon's second appointment to the court, Harry Blackmun, also dissented in *Bivens*. By the end of the year, however, the president had named two more justices to the court—Lewis Powell and William Rehnquist—who, along with Blackmun and Byron White, gave Burger enough conservative allies to change the law dramatically. The approach was not so much to reverse decisions that strengthened equality and other constitutional rights as to put so many conditions on those rights that they withered. Take the ability to sue federal officers. Starting in 1983, the Supreme Court began limiting the *Bivens* decision, ruling eventually that no one could sue if there was an alternative, like a remedy under civil service regulations, or the suit involved military service, or it just didn't seem desirable to allow a lawsuit—mostly for fear of a "flood of litigation."[61]

Then there were the various sorts of immunity for state officials. The Warren Court touched on them in 1967, but the Burger Court gave them breadth and power. In 1976 it ruled that absolute immunity protected a prosecutor from being sued by a man wrongly convicted and imprisoned for nine years because the prosecutor knowingly used perjured testimony.[62] In 1983 it gave cops who lie on the stand absolute immunity from lawsuits.[63] As for qualified immunity, the kind that shielded the police officers who arrested the priests in Jackson, the court granted it to the Ohio governor who sent the national guardsmen who shot four Kent State University students dead in 1970, ten days before the shootings at Jackson State University. The dead students' representatives claimed the guardsmen were unnecessary and had been instructed to "act illegally," and the court set the test of liability as whether the governor had acted reasonably, and whether he thought he had acted reasonably.[64] Over the following years the court tightened the test into its present form: clear evidence that a reasonable state official would know his behavior was illegal under the Constitution, with the proof of illegality shown by a case so on point that it involved almost precisely the same facts.

The court found still other ways to close the courthouse doors. In 1974 it blocked Americans from using their status as taxpayers to challenge government conduct such as keeping the CIA's budget secret.[65] In 1973 and in several later cases it barred prisoners from claiming they should be released because their conviction was unconstitutionally flawed if they had never mentioned that flaw at trial.[66] And the privacy right granted in 1965 to engage in intimate practices did not, according to the court, apply to gay couples.[67] In fact, the Burger Court refused even to acknowledge that gay marriage might be a federal issue or that state laws criminalizing sodomy could be unconstitutional.[68] This cramped view of rights and judicial power to address them was reflected in the lower courts and in the selection of judges to them. Nixon delegated most picks to John Ehrlichman, whose main selection criterion seemed to be strict political loyalty to the president.[69] Burger himself imposed on the federal courts a sweeping administrative regime that rewarded speed, efficiency, and the resolution of cases without trials. It was the template for a judiciary whose job it was to administer, rather than actually do, justice.

A Sense of Purpose

Reeves began to notice this retreat from his notion of justice when he learned the significance of the speech that Ronald Reagan gave in 1980 to open his presidential campaign.[70] The candidate delivered it at the Nashoba County Fair, just east of Yazoo City, near the site of the murders of three civil rights workers in 1964, and in the speech Reagan embraced "states' rights," to many critics a wink of approval to Southern segregationists who had long rallied around the phrase.[71] That same year, in *Mobile v. Bolden*, the Supreme Court rejected claims that at-large voting in Mobile, Alabama—a system of allowing all voters in a district to vote for all candidates, with the top vote-getters winning—was unconstitutional because it had resulted in a largely all-white city commission since 1911.[72] The court ruled that a discriminatory intent, not just this sort of discriminatory result, was necessary to make a case for racial discrimination.

These signals put a fear in Reeves that the progress he believed had taken hold in Mississippi—especially on broadening the vote—would not last without a furious defense. He spoke out in class at Jackson State and among his friends and as a member of the student government in favor of the Voting Rights Act of 1982, one of whose provisions overrode the Supreme Court's *Bolden* decision and established discriminatory results as essentially enough to support a claim of voting discrimination.[73] He did much the same in support of a law that in 1983 created a national holiday to honor Martin Luther King—a law that passed despite a filibuster by Senator Jesse Helms of North Carolina and that Mississippi only begrudgingly complied with by observing it together with Robert E. Lee's birthday.[74]

The politics bug and long-standing admiration for lawyers led Reeves to dream of attending law school near the nation's capital, and in 1986 he gained admission to the University of Virginia Law School, becoming one of only a handful of students from Mississippi to attend at that point. UVA was a shock. Reeves may not have thought it possible, but the school seemed light years behind Mississippi in dealing with issues of race. "They were still studying 'the negro,'" he recalled. "There was a task force on Afro-American affairs. Just the nomenclature was false." There were other problems too. One of the first things Reeves saw near campus was a statue of the confederate general Stonewall Jackson. A Black student had never been named to the *Virginia Law Review*, a position of high prestige granted to the very best students. That changed shortly after Reeves's arrival when a Black woman, Dayna Matthew, joined, an obviously well-deserved honor for the future dean of George Washington University Law School that nonetheless drew criticism as ostensible evidence of preferential treatment for Black students.

In classes, many discussing landmark civil rights cases, students and professors often seemed incapable of talking about race without setting off bulletin-board screeds, spats between professors, or discussion groups convened by the dean. Reeves understood the anger and "the need to fight for all Black folk," as he put it, but this talking past each other, this ignorance of each other's experiences, it all seemed such a broken way to be. What Reeves might try to do about it was becoming clear to him. He would not join a corporate law firm, viewing it as "working with the system, with the man." He would spend summers during law school with the ACLU in Mississippi and then with the firm of renowned civil rights attorney Julius Chambers in Charlotte, North Carolina. "I was just mesmerized by the good that the lawyers at the firm were doing in their community," he said. But Reeves wanted to return home, to Mississippi, and clerk for a judge because he knew from his time at Jackson State how important judges were to his state and its people and his ambitions for his own community. His C+ average in law school wouldn't cut it with the prestigious judges on the federal bench, but he impressed Reuben Anderson, the first African American justice of the Mississippi Supreme Court, and in 1989 he joined Anderson in Jackson as a clerk.

It was not an easy time for Reeves. His girlfriend, Lora, had been diagnosed with cancer and was about to undergo surgery. "I saw the burden in his face," recalls Shirley Byers, Reeves's co-clerk and a friend of Lora. "He cared about her, and I could see from his face that he wanted to be there with her and stand by her, but he carried it very well. It didn't upset his job performance at all." His work with Justice Anderson was hard, though, and it often kept him in the office until two or three in the morning. Yet Reeves was eager, the cases that came before the court covered every interesting issue imaginable, and Lora's surgery went well. A year later, she would become his wife. By then his time at the state supreme court had led to friends and connections and lunches with the movers and shakers of Jackson and the beginnings of a sense of purpose: to bring his experience, a Black experience that included optimism and opportunity along with the scars of discrimination, to the legal system.

Reeves would bring it first through the practice of law and then, he hoped, as a judge, with the aim of doing justice as he understood it—revealing the truth so it could be determined what is fair, what is reasonable, what is owed. He remembered from Jackson State that Abraham Lincoln had said *Dred Scott* was wrong for a simple reason: It was "based on assumed historical facts which were not really true."[75] Blacks had been excluded from society based on those "facts" that were really falsehoods, and they and other minorities were to a great degree still excluded. Without them, American democracy—a republican form of government—could not truly work. He did not put it this way, but Reeves's view was squarely in the tradition of the democracy of opportunity's third element—the principle that everyone, no matter their gender or race, deserved a voice in the nation's economy and political system. He had seen judges go far in ensuring that people had that voice, although he was beginning to discover how fragile their progress could be.

· · ·

Meanwhile, more than a thousand miles away, in a city as different from Mississippi as any place in America could be, another lawyer was confronting a force at the heart of the democracy of opportunity's first element—the moneyed interests and corporate power that could lead to oligarchy.

2   *Dear Top Banana*

In the morning half-light, Eli Black stirred from a fitful sleep and set about his day. Six feet tall and balding, with a round face, soft voice, and delicate hands, he moved quickly, quietly, so as not to disturb his wife still sleeping. He showered, shaved carefully, combed what was left of the hair on his head, and padded to the closet for a navy-blue suit and patterned tie to match. He dressed with the haste of habit, pausing at a mirror to adjust his knotted tie and the stiff collar of his white shirt.

Black snatched a brown satchel-style briefcase from a chair by the door and entered the living room, barely registering the arresting view east from his apartment at 900 Park Avenue. From a wall of shelves, he grabbed as many books—big, heavy books—as would fit inside the briefcase. The sound of soft knocking caused him to stop and snap the satchel shut. It was the doorman, come to deliver the *Wall Street Journal* and announce that Black's chauffeur was waiting on the street below. Black glanced at the newspaper's front page—Monday, February 3, 1975—running his eyes down the "What's News" column before grabbing a scarf, fedora, and wool overcoat against the chill. Once outside, he delivered a good-morning nod to Jim Thomas, his chauffeur, and slid into the back seat of the Cadillac Fleetwood limousine.

"Will you be needing me, Mr. Black?"

"No, Jim, this will be an in day," Black answered, gazing out the window as the car glided down Park Avenue toward his office in the Pan Am Building.[1]

Black was the chairman, chief executive officer, and, some still hoped, savior of United Brands, a conglomerate of sprawling clout that started in 1899 as United Fruit Company and, in 1969, sold most of its stock to Black's company, AMK Corporation. United Fruit had been infamous as a practitioner of brutal corporate power, a company that came to dominate the economies and governments of Costa Rica, Honduras, and Guatemala in service of the banana trade. United Fruit had earned notoriety as "The Octopus," doling out bribes, evading taxes, engineering coups, exploiting impoverished workers, and by the 1930s owning some 3.5 million acres of land in Central American and Caribbean nations that became known as "banana republics." In 1954, the company helped the CIA topple the government of Guatemala, supplying the agency with money, intelligence, and ships for smuggling guns and men.[2]

The coup brought United Fruit intense scrutiny and an antitrust case, and the price for settling it, in 1958, was the sale of a third of its Guatemalan fields and facilities to a competitor, Del Monte, which bumped United Fruit from the top banana seller to number three. Its profits soon plummeted, and its reputation followed: In the minds of many Americans, or at least those on the political left, the company was an avatar of a corrupt system, and its New York offices on Pier Three were bombed by Weather Underground radicals in 1969.[3] Black saw promise in United Fruit, however, and wanted it enough to overpay by an astronomical amount: $630 million for 80 percent of a $286 million enterprise, by one accounting.[4] He merged it into AMK in 1970, changing the combined company's name to United Brands, and immediately set about trying to improve the sullied image and deplorable finances United Fruit had left behind.

The task was tougher than Black had imagined, however. The company lost money for several years, but he told shareholders that he expected 1974 to be a banner year.[5] It was anything but. Early in the year, seven South and Central American nations formed the Union of Banana Exporting Countries to raise fruit prices, and in August, Panama, Costa Rica, and Honduras enacted a tax on banana exports, with the Honduras tax weighing in at a hefty fifty cents per forty-pound box.[6] United Brands executives feared passing the tax to consumers might dissuade them from buying Chiquita bananas—the company's best-known brand. But by January 1975, with a banana crop coming in at quantities much greater than predicted, it looked as if things might be looking up.

Black may have been musing on these matters as his limousine passed the elegant apartment houses on Park Avenue toward the Pan Am building looming over Grand Central Terminal. Jim Thomas, who had served as chauffeur for six of the company's CEOs, pulled the car to the curb and jumped out to hold open the door. Before he could grab Black's briefcase, the CEO said, "Careful Jim, it's a ton of bricks." The chauffeur smiled as he grabbed the case, surprised by its weight, and handed it to his boss.

Black took the elevator to the forty-fourth floor, unlocked the outer double doors, then locked and bolted them behind him. He was, as usual, the first to arrive. He walked down the long hall to his corner office, went through the door, and locked that one too. He set his hat, scarf, and coat on a chair, picked up the briefcase, and moved toward the floor-to-ceiling windows facing north up Park Avenue. He opened the venetian blinds and paused, taking in the view. With a wide swing of his right arm, he heaved the heavy case toward the quarter-inch-thick plate-glass window, putting a halo crack in it. He swung again, punching a three-by-four-foot hole in the glass and sending shards to the street below. He hurled the case through the opening and watched it hit the pavement, scattering books and papers. Black stepped on the sill, pivoted on his right foot, and with a final shove pushed away from the building.

Drivers headed north on a ramp to Park Avenue watched in horror as Black's body landed before them. Police arrived in minutes, traffic backing up, and searched his pockets: cash, keys, a wallet, a black notebook—no suicide note. Later, as the police began to gather and sift through the papers scattered near his briefcase, they found a note he had written in pencil. "Early retirement—55," it said.[7] The following days brought words of praise and sadness from the worlds of business, politics, and beyond. The financial press portrayed Black's reign at United Brands as initially difficult but the company as on the verge of success and strong profits. Within the confines of United Brands, however, a darker story was emerging.

One version had it that the year before, just after Honduras announced its banana tax, Black met with the nation's ex-president, General Oswaldo Lopez, to offer a payment in return for a cut in the tax, and Lopez refused. Black's friends disputed that version. In any event, in July 1974 the Honduran economic minister approached United Brands's banana-operations vice president, Harvey Johnson, about a possible deal: $5 million could buy the company some relief from the tax. Johnson conveyed the proposition to Black, who told him to take it to Johnson's immediate boss, who in turn handled the details. At the end of August 1974 the company announced that it and Honduras had hammered out an "understanding" to cut the tax from fifty cents a box to twenty-five cents.[8]

The bribe did little to slow the company's financial slide, however, and rumblings began among top executives in the Boston office that Black seemed "disoriented," maybe even on drugs (a possibility his family and doctors denied), and that his ouster was in the offing. In late January, while reviewing the company's books, an auditor came across a cryptic entry, an expense of $1.25 million for "cost of European sales." He poked around and discovered that this was code for the payment to Honduras. "The entry stuck out like a sore thumb," one company official, unsurprised by the discovery, would say later.[9] On the advice of its auditor, United Brands hired a law firm, Covington & Burling, that eventually disclosed the bribes to the US Securities and Exchange Commission (SEC). The company issued a statement that it was all Black's fault.[10]

Getting past the scandal would not be so easy. The SEC is the top financial-markets watchdog in America, and its enforcement chief at the time—an ice-chewing, Falstaffian figure named Stanley Sporkin—had earned a reputation for moving against suspected miscreants quickly and aggressively. The United Brands case presented the kind of juicy corporate wrongdoing that could make an impressive splash for Sporkin and a recently revitalized SEC. On April 9, 1975, the agency sued the company, accusing it of not only bribing Honduran officials but also paying $750,000 to European government officials. In a court filing a month later, the SEC added an allegation that United Brands was trying to cover up details of the schemes.[11]

Yet the potential for punishment was limited. The SEC could not seek criminal penalties or, until the 1980s, even the payment of money as a civil penalty.[12] Almost all it could get was an injunction, a court order requiring a company or person to do, or not do, certain things. In this case the agency sought an order that would block United Brands from paying any more bribes or hiding bribes with false entries in its books. There was another reason the SEC's options were limited. Sporkin managed to move record-high numbers of cases through the enforcement division—an accomplishment that would earn him the sobriquet "the Father of Enforcement"—by adhering to a policy of settling them with a sweetener that would ensure a quick resolution: Targets were generally not required to admit wrongdoing, but they could not deny it either. This neither-admit-nor-deny bargain would cause its own problems years later, but after a series of tough negotiations the company agreed to it and the other conditions that the SEC demanded.[13]

There was little doubt though that United Brands had gotten off easy. So as the SEC was investigating and before it filed its lawsuit, Sporkin referred the case to a federal agency that might inflict the pain of criminal prosecution on the company and its executives.

Our Colt 45

The scandal surely looked bad. But was it illegal? That Eli Black had authorized United Brands' bribe was undisputed. That the company had paid the bribe was beyond question. Yet, crazy as it sounded, nothing in the US criminal code quite covered this nefarious conduct, with one possible exception—and it was at best a stretch.

John "Rusty" Wing, the prosecutor running the case, and his younger colleague, Jed Rakoff, had a notion that the provision against wire fraud might work. Like its older but otherwise similar sibling mail fraud, wire fraud is essentially the use of an interstate communication—a phone call, say—to engage in trickery like trying to sell counterfeit goods.[14] The victim can be in Honduras or any other foreign country, and still the wire fraud statute applies. The problem in the United Brands case was, what was the fraud? Bribing a public official might qualify—you're inducing the official to deny his constituents his honest services—but bribing a *foreign* official was not considered illegal at the time. Besides, what possible interest did the US government have in protecting Hondurans from their no-good, lying economic minister?

The other problem had to do with where Wing and Rakoff worked. They were assistant US attorneys in the US attorney's office for the Southern District of New York, the Manhattan-based outpost of the US Department of Justice, which prosecuted federal crimes across Manhattan, the Bronx, and five New York counties to the north. It was a unique place, fiercely independent (it was nicknamed the Sovereign District), self-important (lawyers who worked there invariably call it The Office), prestigious (it generally hired on merit, not political connections), and an undeniably plum perch for lawyers aspiring to the highest echelons of American law. Since its earliest days, it had also prosecuted, almost exclusively, actual people rather than corporations because corporations acted only through their employees and, besides, corporations could not be put in jail, so what would be the point of pursuing them? As best anyone could figure, Eli Black was behind the bribery scheme, and he was dead, so who was worth prosecuting?

Yet Wing and Rakoff were on to something—and Rakoff could not be more delighted. The mail fraud statute fascinated him. Its breadth and flexibility allowed a creative prosecutor to stretch its words to cover surprisingly varied misconduct. He would, a few years later, write a law review article celebrating the statute as prosecutors' "Stradivarius, our Colt 45, our Louisville Slugger, our Cuisinart—and our true love."[15] With this case, though, Rakoff was just beginning to appreciate what wire fraud could legally be, and over the next few years he and Wing would engage in dozens of conversations over what to do with United Brands. They were well matched: whip smart, smitten with the law, Rakoff slight and wry and quick with a corny joke, Wing tall and quiet and keen to offer a smile. Rakoff was especially adamant about finding a way to punish the company. It had been perhaps the most infamous corporate giant of the two lawyers' time, using chicanery, subversion, extortion, bribery, and strong-arm tactics to control markets and whole nations and enrich its owners and executives. At some point someone had to stand up and inflict real punishment for what it had done wrong.

Few in the US attorney's office were willing to take on that task. Some argued that there was no case without Black. Others conceded that at least the company might be prosecuted—under a 1909

Supreme Court decision[16] a company could be held liable for the actions of a single employee—but believed the absence of any antiforeign bribery law was an insurmountable problem. The top boss, US Attorney Robert Fiske, was torn, and being extraordinarily thorough and careful, he could not come around to the view that this was a winnable case. But Rakoff and Wing would not let up. The two were by now close friends, and in 1977, on vacation in the Bahamas with their wives, Rakoff purchased a postcard depicting an idyllic beach with lush palm trees. On the back he wrote: "Dear Top Banana, Thinking of you, Rusty and Jed." He mailed it to Fiske. The humor was typical Rakoff, and so was its implicit message: It was time for Fiske to vote yea or nay on their novel approach to the United Brands case. The approach essentially expanded the wire fraud statute to reach a Honduran foreign minister who had deprived his people of his honest services with the help of a US company. It would require indicting United Brands itself, but Rakoff argued that the bribery was too blatant, and the value of exposing corporate wrongdoing too great, to allow the policy of prosecuting only individuals to get in the way.

On July 3, 1978, an indictment was filed in the US District Court in the Southern District of New York charging United Brands with one count of conspiring to commit bribery and five counts of wire fraud.[17] The company agreed to plead guilty. Thus concluded the latest, but far from the first, display of the creativity and audacity and delight at challenging corporate power that Rakoff brought to pretty much everything he did.

What a Judge Could Do

It was easy to see where Rakoff's best qualities came from. He learned gentle confidence and persistence from his father, Dr. Abraham Rakoff, a renowned fertility specialist in Philadelphia and a teddy bear of a man whose early research on hormones helped lead to the contraceptive pill. Abe Rakoff's success did not come easily, though. Despite excelling in college at the University of Pennsylvania, he was denied admission to its medical school because he was Jewish. He instead graduated from Jefferson Medical College, where he would later teach and Jed would work in the lab one summer during college.

But it was Jed's mother, Doris Rakoff, a striking, garrulous English teacher with lively opinions and a genius-level IQ, who taught him that originality and independence separated merely admirable people from the truly extraordinary. She started her career at Overbrook, a school in a poor neighborhood where one of her students was a gangly kid named Wilt Chamberlain, but she soon moved on, becoming the first woman to teach at Philadelphia's elite Central High School. Like her husband, she had to deal with discrimination—first at the hands of her own mother. In 1921, when Doris was seven, her school selected her for its science program, the favored course of study for the brightest students. Doris's mother vetoed the idea, arguing that it would hurt her daughter's chances of finding a husband. Later, near the end of her teaching career and wanting to continue working despite the school's mandatory retirement age, Doris sought to become an attorney. She applied to her alma mater, the University of Pennsylvania, for law school and, like her husband, was rejected—but not because of her religion. She was too old, the admissions officer told her, and the school refused to waste its resources educating someone who might practice for only ten or fifteen years. Doris never became a lawyer.

Jed was born in 1943, the middle of three brothers, Jan being the oldest and Todd the youngest. Life at the Rakoff home in the white middle-class Germantown neighborhood of 1950s Philadelphia felt warm and fun and serious. Dinner conversation covered theater, books, music, politics, and social issues. The Rakoffs and their frequent guests talked of Gilbert & Sullivan and the Marcel Proust novels Jed and his two brothers should read. They talked critically of neighbors posting for-sale signs as African Americans, many professors and ministers and lawyers, moved in nearby. They laughed a lot, thanks to Doris and her wonderful guffaw but also her brother, a raucously funny ladies' man who lived with the family for a while and, much to the delight of Jed and his two brothers, would have sex on the living room couch as they secretly watched from the stairs. The Rakoffs weren't especially religious—Jed attended synagogue on Saturdays with his friend Mike Kean just so they could go to the Phillies baseball game after—but their Jewish sense of social justice was strong, stirred by ire over McCarthyism and the racism that emerged at startling moments. Jed would never forget being jeered upon exiting a men's room marked "colored" that he had accidentally used during a camping trip to Natural Bridge State Park in Virginia.

Jed and Todd excelled at Central High School, but Jan was a nearly impossible act to follow. He was at or close to the top of his class. His genius on stage and resonant bass voice put an opera career within reach. Yet Jan struggled with something about himself that was, at that time and place, too difficult to share: He was gay. All his family knew for sure was that he often seemed unhappy. He would awaken at night, screaming from terrible nightmares. He would snap unexpectedly at people and speak with brutal honesty. It was as if he were consumed with a simmering anger at his failure to fit in. Yet it was the quality of being different that many people, and especially his brother Jed, so admired. In fact, Jed was different—and bold and creative—in his own right. When he arrived in 1960 at Swarthmore College, a school infused with the liberal tradition of its Quaker founders, Jed sensed a strong spirit of "cock-eyed optimism," as he put it, there and in the nation generally. *Father Knows Best*, *Leave It to Beaver*, and the other cozy sitcoms he had grown up with in the 1950s recounted the quotidian hijinks of middle-class families overcoming difficulties. John Kennedy, newly elected president, would soon beseech Americans to ask what they could do for their country. Poverty and racial discrimination were emerging as issues that many of Jed's generation were thoroughly convinced they could resolve. Anything, it seemed, was possible.

Yet for most of Jed Rakoff's friends, it was typically a matter of reach exceeding grasp; they had no clue how to get things done. Near the top of their list was convincing Swarthmore to create a sociology department, a course of study that would go beyond history and political science and economics to address what was happening in the world at that moment: the Cold War and segregation and the aftermath of the previous fall's brush with nuclear annihilation from Soviet missiles headed for Cuba. Almost a decade of pleading had failed to persuade the administration and faculty, whose members insisted that sociology was intellectually squishy, inappropriate at the academically rigorous institution.

In February 1963, telling no one, Rakoff took the half-hour train ride to the University of Pennsylvania and told the associate chairman of the school's sociology department that he would pay Penn professors seventy-five dollars a class to teach sociology at Swarthmore one or two nights a week, figuring he could get the money from the student council budget. A few days later, the educator agreed to the deal, and Rakoff's fellow student council members voted to supply the money. Rakoff then wangled permission to speak at the next all-school meeting under the guise of offering an update on student council activities. In front of some eight hundred students and Swarthmore's president, Courtney Smith, he rambled on a while before getting to the point. "Students have long agitated in favor of bringing sociology and cultural anthropology to Swarthmore," Rakoff said. "The administration has hesitated, made long-range promises, then hesitated some more." He laid out his plan. The place erupted in cheers, laughter, and applause. At first, President Smith said nothing. After the meeting ended, he pulled Rakoff aside. "You should not have sprung this on me" is all he said, his voice tight with anger. Rakoff could not help enjoying the moment, admitting he "got a kick out of it." Within a year Swarthmore had created a sociology department.

Clever accomplishments would continue for Rakoff. He would go from Swarthmore to Oxford University on scholarship for two years and, in writing his master's thesis, find a way around British secrecy laws by traveling to India to review reports of the British secret police that he needed to explain the success of Mahatma Gandhi's independence movement. He would attend Harvard Law School, doing well enough to earn membership in the school's legal aid bureau, which gave him his first chance to perform in court and experience the sometimes wrenching but often satisfying feeling of representing people who truly needed his help. The optimism—the sense that progress was inevitable—would be harder to sustain.

In 1969, when Rakoff graduated from law school, the horror and apparent futility of war in Vietnam and the regression in civil rights and plain decency that the election of President Richard Nixon seemed to portend rattled him and his friends. These graduates of Swarthmore and Harvard Law School were largely smart and liberal and obviously privileged but still deeply proud that being middle class and having a life of value was possible for so many Americans. Now, though, they wondered whether the certainty that they and most others would be better off than their parents was certain at all, whether democracy, in the political but especially the economic sense, could still work in a land of persistent inequality and wealth and power for the few. Rakoff had already decided that he could best help it work—to have the most impact—by practicing law. Exactly how he would do that was still a bit hazy.

After law school Rakoff became a judicial clerk, a sort of judge's apprentice who drafts memos, fields calls, and absorbs the judge's teachings for a year. Rakoff clerked for Abraham Freedman, a native of Philadelphia who began his career as legal counsel to Democratic politicians there, served as the city's chief lawyer, became a US district judge, and finally a judge on the US Court of Appeals in Philadelphia. Freedman was smart—so smart that his brilliance prompted Rakoff at one point to think, if that was the standard for being a lawyer, maybe he was not cut out for a legal career. This crisis of confidence aside, Rakoff soon learned how his own inclination to use creativity in solving problems could, in the hands of a master like Freedman, lead to a just result in a high-stakes legal case. It was his first lesson in what a judge could do.

The case was called *Shultz v. Wheaton Glass*, one of the first and most important tests of women's right to equal pay.[18] The US Department of Labor had sued a New Jersey manufacturer of glass containers for violating the Equal Pay Act of 1963 by paying men and women different amounts—$2.35 and hour for the men, $2.16 an hour for the women—for inspecting the containers and packing them in boxes on a conveyor belt. The judge in the trial court, the district court, heard the case and decided that the difference in pay was justified because the jobs were different: Men sometimes—though only sometimes—had to lift the boxes off the conveyor belt. The Labor Department appealed.

Three-judge panels typically hear appeals court cases, with one judge writing the opinion and otherwise taking the lead. This case was Freedman's, and he assigned Rakoff to research the law that would apply to it. Being fresh from law school and filled with the spirit of stick-it-to-the-man, Rakoff believed the Labor Department—and so the women workers—should prevail over the company and its discriminatory ways. The details of the arguments he plucked from the law books lining the judge's sumptuous library are hazy to him now, but Rakoff recalled his legal memo to Freedman mentioning in passing that the pay difference might be illegal under the Civil Rights Act of 1964, which said people should be judged as individuals, not with blanket assumptions like, say, women are weaker than men. The trouble was that the Labor Department had sued under the Equal Pay Act, in part because it provided successful plaintiffs with back pay, and the Civil Rights Act did not.

Rakoff took the memo to Freedman's hushed office and watched the judge, a formal and somewhat icy man, cast his eyes across the memo without expression. Suddenly Freedman called for his secretary and, off the top of his head, dictated a legal opinion. He had picked up on the mention of the Civil Rights Act and in the course of dictation used the phrase *in pari materia*—a Latin expression that means essentially that when two statutes cover the same matter, the more recent one is assumed to have amended the other and so governs the case. After Freedman persuaded his two colleagues of his view, the court ruled that the manufacturer had in fact violated the Equal Pay Act, as amended by the Civil Rights Act, and the women on the assembly line would get their back pay after all. Rakoff was in awe. Not so much because Freedman had in his view reached the just result, but because he had done it with creative logic that was nonetheless squarely within the bounds of the law.

In 1970, Rakoff left Freedman's chambers and joined Debevoise & Plimpton, a prestigious law firm in New York whose practice centered on representing insurance companies and other corporations. His heart was not in the work, which rarely required going to court. But others at the firm had served in the US attorney's office in Manhattan, describing it as "the best job in New York." Despite his skepticism about becoming a federal prosecutor, Rakoff applied and was accepted as an assistant US attorney. It was there that he learned his second lesson about what a federal judge could do. On Rakoff's first day, in January 1973, an older prosecutor rapped on his door and invited him to watch a colleague perform in court. The two took the elevator from their drab offices on the fourth floor of the federal courthouse in Foley Square to the nineteenth floor, walked across the ornate hallway, and heaved open the doors of Judge Morris Lasker's courtroom. The judge had not yet taken the bench, and almost immediately someone caught Rakoff's eye, a long-haired man about his age slouching near the front of the courtroom. The man gave Rakoff a wave and came over. It was Cohen, *somebody* Cohen—Rakoff blanked on his first name—a classmate from Central High School in Philadelphia.

"Jed!" Rakoff recalls Cohen saying. "What brings you to court?"

"Well, I'm a brand-new assistant US attorney," Rakoff responded with pride. "What brings you to court?"

"I'm about to be sentenced," Cohen said. The charge was selling LSD, and Cohen had pleaded guilty. Rakoff was not prepared for this. Here he was, on the side that was about to send his former classmate to prison. Poor what's-his-name Cohen. Prison. There but for the grace of God. The judge took the bench, and the prosecutor made his pitch. Here's an upper-middle-class white man, the prosecutor said, with all the advantages of a good family and education, who had nonetheless flouted the law with no excuse and therefore deserved a long sentence. Next, the defense lawyer rose, ran through a list of his client's good qualities, and sat down. That was it. Case closed, Rakoff figured.

But Judge Lasker, brows arched over kindly eyes, began to speak. It was as if the prosecutor and the defense lawyer were no longer there. "Mr. Cohen," Lasker said in measured tones, "tell me about your background." A half-hour interrogation ensued. *Where did you grow up, how did you do in school, why did you start selling drugs*, that sort of thing. A very different story unfolded, one about a troubled soul with mental health problems that neither side had bothered to mention. In the end the judge sentenced him to probation and psychiatric treatment. As Rakoff rode the elevator with his colleagues down to their offices, he thought he had witnessed something extraordinary, a thought that he would have again in other courtrooms with other judges who asked pointed questions and spoke their minds and took on dissemblers with the force of logic and independence and who, to his mind, did justice. And then he had another, more thrilling thought: Maybe, someday, he could be one of them.

A third lesson for what a judge could do—but also shouldn't do—came from Milton Pollack. Judge Pollack had two flaws. One was that he seemed to decide on day one which side—usually the government—should win a criminal trial, and he wasn't shy about steering a jury to his way of thinking with subtle but devastating questions. Pollack's other flaw was that he had a habit of speaking with the lawyers on one side of a case without the other side's lawyers present. These so-called ex parte conversations were unethical, but no attorneys complained for fear of putting themselves at a disadvantage before the judge. One of the first cases Rakoff tried as a prosecutor was before Pollack, and after a particularly grueling day, at about 6:00 p.m., the phone rang in Rakoff's office. "This is Milton Pollack," Rakoff recalls the voice on the line saying. "How come you haven't made such-and-such procedural motion?" Taken aback, the young lawyer said something to the effect of not having thought of it and assured the judge that he would make the motion the next day. Believing the call had been improper, he asked his boss what to do. "Oh, that's just Pollack doing his thing," came the answer, along with the admonition that Rakoff should tell the opposing lawyer about the conversation. Rakoff took his boss's advice, made the motion—and the other attorney never objected.

As best Rakoff could tell, Pollack's excesses aside, being bold and brave and determined to get to the facts and the right result within the law was what all judges did. To Rakoff, it meant being like Freedman and finding the legal logic to do justice for, say, working women and stand up to their corporate employer. It meant being like Lasker and going beyond lawyers' arguments to figure out why the person before you committed a crime and what he deserved as punishment. It even meant being, to an extent, like Pollack and controlling a case and the courtroom to ensure that the truth came out. "There they were," Rakoff recalls, "administering justice, and it was real justice, and you felt you were getting justice, and you felt these were smart, dedicated, balanced, fully informed people who were dedicated to getting the right result. And it was just very impressive."

It was what Rakoff had seen through most of his life from the Supreme Court, with its groundbreaking efforts to strengthen equality and economic opportunity and the political voices of the powerless, and from lower court judges like Richard Rives, the Alabama native who defied his Confederate roots to enforce desegregation at great risk to his own safety. There might be judges who believed their role was to get out of the way of Congress and the president, but they were exceptions, he thought. Rakoff was wrong of course, as history showed, and he would soon learn—especially when it came to challenging the power of corporate America.

Disquieting Voices

On August 23, 1971, the lawyer Lewis Powell mailed a memorandum to the US Chamber of Commerce at the request of his close friend Eugene B. Sydnor Jr., the head of the Southern Department Stores chain and chairman of the chamber's education committee. Powell was a partner at a prominent Richmond, Virginia, law firm, a former president of the American Bar Association, and a director of more than a dozen major American corporations that included the cigarette maker Philip Morris—in Sydnor's view the perfect person to write the memo, a kind of call to arms and battle plan for defending against what the two men perceived as a growing threat to American life: a lack of reverence for big business.[19]

In words more typical of a wild-eyed polemicist than a cautious lawyer of gentle Southern voice, Powell laid blame for the threat on the usual lefty suspects—defense lawyer William Kunstler, Yale professor Charles Reich, and especially consumer advocate Ralph Nader—but also on something "quite new in the history of America," he wrote. "The most disquieting voices joining the chorus of criticism, come from perfectly reputable elements of society: from the college campus, the pulpit, the media, the intellectual and literary journals, the arts and sciences, and from politicians." Yet it was the courts, Powell wrote, that might be "the most important instrument for social, economic and political change." He pointed out that "labor unions, civil rights groups and now the public interest law firms are extremely active" litigating in the courts. "This is a vast area of opportunity for the Chamber," Powell continued, "if it is willing to undertake the role of spokesman for American business and if, in turn, business is willing to provide the funds."[20]

Less than two months later, President Richard Nixon nominated Lewis Powell to the US Supreme Court. The memo was marked "confidential," but months after Powell took his seat on the court, in January 1972, it leaked, and its impact as a business cri de coeur after at least a decade of setbacks was undeniable. A host of moves—enactment of consumer and environmental laws, creation of the Environmental Protection Agency, the backlash against big tobacco and the companies that profited from the Vietnam War—had scared the bejeesus out of corporate America, and it fought back. Right-wing magnates financed think tanks, litigation firms, media organizations, university research, and political movements dedicated to advancing the causes of business. In 1977 the US Chamber of Commerce established its litigation center and, true to Powell's advice, now regularly files friend-of-the-court briefs and rivals the US Solicitor General's office in its ability to influence the US Supreme Court.[21] As with the Southern Manifesto almost two decades before, the memo's greatest significance might have been as a turning point: in this case the moment when American business made the Supreme Court an ally again.

Evidence of the turn permeates the decisions of the court under then chief justice Warren Burger. Its hundreds of opinions dealing with business issues included landmark rulings that ranged from protecting Major League Baseball's antitrust exemption to expanding corporations' free speech rights to curtailing the power of labor unions.[22] For Rakoff, however, the court's most troubling decisions may have been in the area where he was developing a deep expertise—combating corporate fraud. Over the next decade the court would weaken the rights of investors to sue companies for financial wrongdoing. In 1961 the SEC decided for the first time that trading on a company's confidential and significant information (so-called insider trading) was improper under federal rules, a kind of fraud on other investors, and anyone with such information had to either disclose it or abstain from trading on it.[23] Three years later, the Supreme Court expanded the concept by allowing investors themselves, not just the SEC, to sue for securities fraud.[24] And four years after that, the US Court of Appeals in New York, known for its sophistication in matters of Wall Street and finance, became the first court to rule that insider trading violated federal securities laws.[25]

By the end of the 1960s these and similar decisions had given the victims of corporate cheats fresh hope that they could hold their malefactors accountable in court. That hope began to fade with the new decade. Powell took his seat on the nation's highest court in 1972 and, to the surprise of probably no one, soon made good on his Chamber of Commerce screed, leading an effort to deny the critics of corporate America one of their most potent weapons: lawsuits.[26] He and his colleagues started with class actions, the kind of lawsuits that allowed multiple victims to band together in suing an alleged wrongdoer. Class actions were a godsend for individuals who could not afford to pursue a case on their own but often hellish for companies faced with the prospect of shelling out damages to dozens, if not thousands, of people. One way to limit class actions was to make banding together harder. In a 1974 case involving excessive stock-trading commissions, Powell wrote for the court majority that the lawsuit could not continue until the small investor who had filed it had officially notified each and every person on whose behalf he was suing—more than two and a quarter million individuals—at his own expense.[27] The investor had neither the money nor the means to do that, so he dropped the suit. Consumer groups were outraged. A lawyer for Ralph Nader's advocacy organization Public Citizen put the absurdity of the court's lesson succinctly: "It's better for business to cheat a million people out of a dollar each than to cheat one person out of $1 million."[28]

The court was just getting started. In 1975 it further hamstrung investors, ruling that the securities laws protecting them applied only to buyers and sellers of stock rather than to, say, someone persuaded by lies *not* to buy shares that might end up worth a fortune. From the majority opinion in *Blue Chip Stamps v. Manor Drug Stores*, the court's motivation was clear: protect corporations by cracking down on cases from investors done wrong.[29] This type of litigation "presents a danger of vexatiousness different in degree and in kind from that which accompanies litigation in general," wrote Justice William Rehnquist, adding a frightening reference to companies being forced into "in terrorem" settlements.[30]

The court's effort to keep business safe from litigation continued. In 1976 the justices ruled that a company could not be sued for stock fraud unless it had *intended* to cheat shareholders—being sloppy or even reckless was not enough.[31] The same year, they stressed that the fraud had to be about something that was more than just significant; it had to be, in legal terms, "material," and the court stiffened the definition of material from "might be" important to a reasonable investor to "a significant likelihood" it will be important.[32] The change was a subtle but effective way to keep investors far from court. A year later, the justices made it clear that shareholders had to show that they had been victims of a lie or a failure to disclose information; companies had no duty to be fair or straight with them.[33] Finally, at about the same time, the court narrowed the definition of "security"—the very thing people had to buy or sell to be protected from fraud; it would not include, say, shares in a government-subsidized housing co-op or an interest in a pension plan.[34]

That big business needed protection from lawsuits or prosecutors or zealous enforcement of the law in general was news to Rakoff. Time and again during his first three years as a federal prosecutor he had seen corporations and the men, always men, who ran them have their way with shareholders and politicians and the consumers who fed their coffers—profits faked, risks undisclosed, unfriendly leaders ousted—invariably steered from trouble by the best lawyers and accountants and publicity agents that money could buy. Even when caught in blatant misconduct, companies could often expect little more in the way of punishment than a small contribution to Uncle Sam and a smug mea culpa.

In the case of United Brands the company did agree to plead guilty to serious crimes. Yet on a Wednesday in late July 1978, with much of New York's millions away at the beach, United Brands's lawyer, Robert Morvillo, walked into the federal courthouse in lower Manhattan to enter the plea to all six counts for the maximum fine that the law would allow. It was a whopping $15,000. Later, on the courthouse steps, Morvillo downplayed the conduct of his client, and the company issued a statement stressing that "management had concluded that it was far better to settle with the government for this modest amount than to engage in prolonged litigation."[35] Even so, Rakoff and his colleagues had made their point—their efforts had been Exhibit A in the case for enacting the Foreign Corrupt Practices

Act the year before, a law that essentially prohibited bribing a foreign person—but few people may have noticed.[36] A story about the plea deal ran the next day, buried on page D3 of the *New York Times*. Despite Lewis Powell's fears, and thanks to the Supreme Court's efforts, corporate America seemed safer than ever.

A Judge-Picking Machine

Like most young federal prosecutors in Manhattan, Rakoff left the US attorney's office after seven years to join a private law firm, propelled by the need "to put some bread on the table," he said. Partners at large law firms could expect hundreds of thousands of dollars a year, while assistant US attorneys earned a small fraction of that amount. In 1980, Rakoff became a partner at Mudge, Rose, Guthrie, Alexander & Ferdon, a large firm best known for representing issuers of municipal bonds—and having among its former partners Richard Nixon and his attorney general, John Mitchell.

Rakoff thrived at Mudge, Rose, representing executives at the firm's existing clients and also working his network of former federal prosecutors to bring in lucrative white-collar crime cases that involved top bankers and other financial bigwigs. He became, in the parlance of Wall Street, a rainmaker. The nature of the firm's largely corporate practice led him to court far less often than his tasks as a prosecutor had, but he still encountered from time to time judges who inspired and surprised him with their extraordinary skill and creativity at using the law to do what they believed was right. Yet as the decade of the 1980s played out, other, very different considerations for evaluating judges grew more important. Ronald Reagan had staked his successful presidential run in part on appointing judges who held a modest view of their roles—"judicial restraint" was the buzzword—and politically conservative principles like being tough on crime.[37] Though Reagan's first attorney general, William French

Smith, established the administration's judge-picking process, the opinion of one of the president's top aides carried tremendous weight.[38]

He was Edwin Meese, a strident proponent of law and order who had overseen the cracking of student heads at Berkeley as then California governor Reagan's chief of staff in the 1960s. Meese was a Yale University and University of California–Berkeley law graduate who had prosecuted felonies in the Oakland, California, district attorney's office before joining Reagan's gubernatorial staff. Though a sometimes-clumsy sidekick nicknamed "Poppin" for resembling the Pillsbury Doughboy, Meese could simplify confusing ideas in a way that made him indispensable to Reagan, who hired him to run his 1980 presidential campaign and transition team and serve as one of his closest confidants.[39] Meese succeeded Smith as attorney general in 1985 and created a system of selecting judges that dramatically transformed the judiciary. He had long despised the Warren Court's expansion of the rights of individuals to an extent that he believed violated the Constitution's original meaning. In a speech at Tulane University in 1986, Meese argued that Supreme Court decisions inconsistent with that "meaning"—as presumably determined by him and his adherents—were not "binding on all persons and parts of government."[40]

This theory of "originalism" rankled the legal establishment but had for some time been gaining favor among conservative law professors, and Meese aimed to make it the touchstone of American jurisprudence. All he needed was the right sort of judges on the bench. Meese took Tom Huston's model of judicial selection and turned it into a judge-picking machine. First, he used the Justice Department's Office of Legal Policy as not only a clearinghouse for potential nominees but a "think tank" to "shape the terms of national debate."[41] Second, he sought a network of lawyers to ferret out candidates for the bench and promote originalism in the administration. He wanted experienced advisers and asked his counselor, Kenneth Cribb, to "bring me people with gray hair."[42] But few seasoned attorneys believed in originalism, and so Meese was forced to recruit young lawyers from an upstart network of conservative and libertarian lawyers quickly gaining prominence around Washington, DC—the Federalist Society.[43]

The move propelled the society to dizzying heights. In large part through Meese's patronage, it rose from little more than a debating club created in 1982 to one of the most influential legal organizations in America.[44] On the current Supreme Court alone, six of nine justices are affiliated with the Federalist Society. There may in fact be no single force more responsible for transforming the modern federal judiciary into an institution at war with itself—willing, even eager, to weaken its power to help the people before it and to undermine its own credibility by seeming to serve a political agenda.[45]

· · ·

Rakoff's desire to become a federal judge was nonetheless as keen as ever, and after a decade as a partner in major New York law firms, he figured that he was finally prominent enough, financially comfortable enough, to make an appointment to the bench realistic. Maybe more important, he had gained enough experience to know exactly the kind of judge he hoped to be—principled and fair, creative and sufficiently courageous to get to the truth and hold the powerful accountable—but also able to laugh at himself, as evidenced later in his lyrics for the annual Courthouse Follies: "You can't become a doctor, you would wind up a quack / You can't become a porn star, you're no good in the sack / But you can be a judge because you're such a big hack." Early in 1995, Rakoff applied to Daniel Patrick Moynihan, the senior US senator from New York, for an appointment as a federal district judge.

As with Carlton Reeves, the judge that Rakoff aspired to be also fit within the tradition of the democracy of opportunity, although he did not put it this way—someone who would stand up to the corporate power that could lead to an oligarchy. It would be a third lawyer, though, one of a very different background and far across the country from either Reeves or Rakoff, who would seek to broaden the middle class by refusing to give up on anyone capable of living a life of value.

3   *I Can Do This*

They called her Chacha. He was Chacho. When Martha Vázquez and her older brother, Ricardo, were teenagers in the 1960s, they would arrive every summer in Guadalajara, Mexico, on the afternoon bus from their home in Santa Barbara, California, and haul their suitcases across the street to the third-class bus, the one that would return to the villages with the people who had come in the morning to sell flowers and buy chickens and cheese. Martha and Ricardo's cousins owned this bus, and as they were taking tickets, they would see the two siblings and cry out, "The chachas are here!"

The warmth of the welcome was nothing compared with the greeting that awaited Martha and Ricardo after the jostling half-hour drive south to Atotonilquillo, the tiny village where their father was born and their grandparents lived and near everyone's last name was Vázquez. After alighting from the bus in the main square, the brother and sister would walk along the cobblestones to their grandfather's house, and gradually people would leave their homes to shake hands and hug and pat them on the back. Both siblings were loved, but Ricardo was special. His gentle laugh and glow of a smile with two deep dimples drew people to him, and after five or six blocks he would be surrounded by close friends and shy girls and boys bouncing on the balls of their feet.

It was like that everywhere for Ricardo. In the fall, back home at Bishop Garcia Diego High School on Santa Barbara's north side, he would bring soccer fans to their feet on an afternoon as he juked and jittered his way to another goal. With his family he was, in his mother's words, "noble"—meaning, in Spanish, generous and forgiving—"a child with a heart of gold." Ricardo protected his siblings and especially Martha, grabbing her hand when older boys would taunt her and taking the blame when she swiped apricots from a neighbor's tree. School, though, was difficult. When Ricardo first went, he knew little English, and his teachers judged him so quiet and slow at learning that he was shifted from mainstream classes to special education a few hours each day. If there was a stigma to his shortcomings, though, it did not stick, because he was too well liked and hardworking.

Ricardo and Martha would take gardening jobs with their parents at nights and on weekends. At age fourteen he worked after school as a bag boy at the Safeway in town. His earnings would help pay for the groceries, his clothes, his siblings' clothes, and the phone and electric bills. He paid most of his tuition when he went to Santa Barbara City College and when he transferred to Sacramento State College. Ricardo did not graduate from college, falling a few credits short, but by other measures he did well. He took a job at yet another grocery store, Jumbo Markets in Sacramento, earning raises and promotions and marrying his college sweetheart and having two children with her, boys who spent hours with their dad shooting baskets and gazing at his baseball card collection. Ricardo rose to assistant manager of the Jumbo Markets, but he developed high blood pressure and other ailments, and one afternoon he collapsed to the floor at work. He recovered but then Jumbo Markets went bankrupt and closed. His marriage faltered, and he and his wife divorced, and the need to help care for his children made out-of-state jobs, the only ones available, impractical. For a while, Ricardo helped at the catering business of a friend, a guy named Lenny Lizalde, but the pay was lousy and the business too far from home.

Temptation can be hard to resist for a desperate man with three kids to feed and an ex-wife to support, and it came for Ricardo on March 26, 1990, at a Black Angus Steakhouse in Burbank, California.[1] Lenny Lizalde had invited him there with a business proposition: *Let's you and me and some friends set up a drug deal—nothing crazy, just some pot, enough to get you out of the hole.* Ricardo would have been far down anyone's list of likely drug pushers, but he went along with the idea, and as they sat at a booth in the restaurant, a stranger plopped down beside Lizalde. He said his name was Adam Cobb. He said he was a pilot and understood from a contact in Guadalajara that the two men and a few of their buddies were looking to import some contraband. *That's right*, said Lizalde, *marijuana*. Cobb scoffed. He explained that the big money was in cocaine, and it was much easier to handle than pot. Ricardo was adamant. He said it would be marijuana or nothing.

Maybe Cobb sensed Ricardo's simple nature, a trusting personality eager to please and open to persuasion. In any event he locked on to Ricardo like an eagle to its prey. Over the next month, Cobb phoned Ricardo eight times, offering to arrange a cocaine shipment of 650 kilos from Guatemala and telling Ricardo that he could even supply the drugs. *Seven times* Ricardo said no. On the eighth call, completely broke, Ricardo accepted Cobb's offer of a $10,000 loan. On the ninth call, after a discussion with his compatriots, Ricardo said they would agree to the cocaine deal. Ten people, not including Cobb, were now in on the scheme, and while Ricardo was by no means its leader, he could speak Spanish better than his collaborators and so played an active role, mostly by talking with the people in Mexico. It was a shit show.

At first the plan was for a pilot to fly the drugs from Colombia to a landing strip near Guadalajara, where Cobb would pick them up and fly them to Los Angeles. Then the pilot from Colombia got arrested and the plan was off. Then it was on again. This time the drugs would be delivered to Guatemala for pickup. Ricardo and his buddies agreed that they would pay $2,000 for each kilogram of cocaine delivered, and Cobb would get 30 percent of the total. The drugs didn't show up on the appointed date, though, and a third plan came together. A month later Cobb returned to Guatemala, and on June 30, 1990, twenty-two duffel bags containing 650 kilograms of cocaine were unloaded from a twin-engine Cessna and onto a plane bound for Los Angeles. Ricardo and his friends would pay $200,000 for half the cocaine—325 kilograms—and would meet Cobb's associates at a designated spot to close the transaction.

Early in the afternoon on August 1, 1990, two Chevy Blazers, one white, one black, pulled into the parking lot of a Denny's restaurant in San Dimas, California. Ricardo and a friend got out of the white Blazer and approached the men they had been told to meet. After Ricardo showed them the cash, the men said the cocaine was in a van parked a mile away at an industrial park and that a white BMW parked nearby would take them there. Ricardo signaled his friends in the black Blazer to follow the BMW and watched the cars turn a corner and disappear. Within seconds he lay face-down over the hood of the white Blazer in handcuffs. Cobb was an informant for the US Drug Enforcement Administration (DEA). The other men Ricardo had met in the parking lot that day were agents with the DEA, Los Angeles County deputy sheriffs, and a local police officer, all operating undercover. The cocaine deal was an elaborate sting operation. For the first time in his life, Ricardo was under arrest. As his friends in the black Blazer were meeting a similar fate, Ricardo and an agent were on their way to the DEA office in Los Angeles. The agent seemed the silent type, and Ricardo could not resist making small talk, asking about the agent's background and family and this and that, and then the remorse of his arrest overwhelmed him.

"I'm guilty," Ricardo said, according to government documents. "I know that."

Oranges and Avocados

Martha Vázquez was in Guadalajara when she got the phone call. She was with her grandmother, whose early-stage Alzheimer's disease made it hard for her to believe that her younger sister had died, and so Martha figured a visit to the sister's grave in Mexico might persuade her. They had barely left the airport when the phone rang, and Martha's sister gave her the news: Ricardo was in jail in Los Angeles.

Early the next morning, Martha was on a plane to LA and after arriving went straight to the Metropolitan Detention Center downtown to see her brother. He seemed in shock; she felt numb. He turned his smile and dimpled cheeks toward her and said, "Don't worry, sis. It will all be okay." Martha was a lawyer now, a thirty-seven-year-old partner at a Santa Fe, New Mexico, firm, and she wanted of course to believe him, could readily believe him because he had never been in trouble before, and at that point neither he nor she had any idea how severe the charges would be. She would take care of it. She would make sure that he had the best lawyer that she could find. She would do everything possible to help him because he was her Chacho, just about her favorite person on Earth, the sibling she most admired but also could not stop worrying about.

Martha worried because that was her way in a family whose success through the generations, such as it was, had often felt precarious. Her father, Remigio Vázquez, had grown up in modest circumstances in Atotonilquillo, going to school and playing soccer every day on dusty lots to fill the idle hours. As luck would have it, he was good at soccer, great even, and through word of mouth he attracted the attention of a scout from the professional football club in Guadalajara. The team soon put him on its roster and turned him into a local hero and a minor national celebrity. After several years dazzling fans, he caught another break. A wealthy uncle—a banker in Guadalajara—cottoned to him and agreed to pay for his education as an accountant in Guadalajara. When he graduated from a local university, Remigio joined his uncle's bank and his future seemed secure. Then Consuelo Mendez caught his eye.

Even at fifteen, Consuelo was poised and elegant, with thick hair the color of midnight and almond eyes. Remigio first saw her on a visit home to Atotonilquillo. Consuelo and her mother and brother had moved there from Guadalajara several years before. She had been born in Dallas, Texas, the daughter of an engineer on the Union Pacific railroad who traveled the tracks to Port Arthur and back until he slipped from a train and hit his head so hard that he was forced to quit working. He died soon after, and when Consuelo was nine, the family moved to Guadalajara and then to Atotonilquillo. When she met Remigio, Consuelo was starstruck. But he was in love. He took it hard when she told him that she and her mother and brother needed money and were leaving town to work at a lemon-packing company in Carpinteria, California. Remigio arranged to follow them, finding work digging dirt in an Arizona copper mine and then plucking oranges and avocados from endless rows of trees near Santa Barbara, able to stay close to Consuelo. In 1951, Remigio, finally bold enough, and Consuelo, finally old enough, agreed to marry, eventually enabling him to become a US citizen.

With $300 to their name, the two settled in East Santa Barbara, where most of the residents were Mexican. Ricardo was born in 1951 and Martha two years later, with two more sisters and a brother to follow. The family moved briefly back to Guadalajara then, when Martha was six, returned to Santa Barbara so that she and her brother could attend US schools. Martha, like the rest of her family at the time, spoke no English, and it was the policy at the Catholic school she attended to teach Spanish-speaking students separately, making it easier for them to learn math and other subjects but harder to learn English. A classmate (soon to become an exceptionally good friend) recognized this and insisted that Martha hide under her desk when the time came to divide the class so she could remain with the English-speaking students. The trick worked, and the friend agreed to interpret, when necessary, but it was tough. Other classmates would laugh at Martha when she could not understand a question or comment delivered in English. Mostly, though, Martha succeeded in finding her way and working hard and getting good grades.

In the afternoons after school Martha would join her parents to work in the gardens of rich people in nearby Montecito. Far from resenting the tasks that deprived her of time with friends, she found nobility in the labor—and a deep admiration for her parents' willingness to hold three or four jobs just to make a tolerable living. It was an ethic common to many of the immigrants Martha knew, especially those who had risked their lives and the lives of their children to come to the United States illegally. They were her neighbors, her coworkers, the people with whom she joked and shared secrets and whom she even came to love. As early as third grade, Martha sensed that they and those like them deserved better, and it was then that she determined to become an immigration lawyer, having only the haziest notion of what that might mean.

What struck her most, though, was that by and large these people, and especially her father, had an almost irrational faith in the United States and its capacity to treat them fairly. Her father would contrast the corruption he believed was rampant in Mexico with a basic honesty he saw in Americans and particularly their politicians, who to his mind actually meant what they said. He would walk around the apartment reciting the preamble to the Constitution, and his faith in the nation's goodness seemed unshakable, even in the face of humiliating discrimination. Martha would see people, kids her age, make fun of his heavy Mexican accent and giggle when he tried to make small talk. She would watch him recoil, stunned at the mocking, confused that his love for America and Americans would be so cruelly received. And yet he persevered. At night he worked as a dishwasher at the Hotel Marisol and during the day managing a laundromat. He then got a job as a bus driver for the city and later as the early-morning host of a Spanish-language radio show. He continued to juggle jobs—as a radio host and an accountant for a local company and a tax preparer during tax season—until, with his savings and a $20,000 loan from his uncle, the banker in Guadalajara, he bought a small Spanish-language radio station in Santa Barbara. It was successful enough that he eventually opened a profitable restaurant and moved the family from the apartment in East Santa Barbara to a four-bedroom house in an upscale neighborhood near the Santa Barbara mission.

As for Martha, she lived in a kind of cocoon, forbidden from going on dates, required to attend Catholic school and church regularly, largely shielded from popular culture—rock music, sitcoms, McDonald's. She spent most summers back in Atotonilquillo, missing out on the casual encounters and experiences that typically help American kids decide who they want to be. Martha had no notion, for example, of college. Her father had attended university in Guadalajara, but even a high school education was rare for the women in her family, and the possibility of college just never came up. Yet Martha had been a star at school—a top student, a leader of the homecoming committee, and the secretary of her class. She was particularly close with the class president, and when she told him of her bewilderment when other kids talked of college, he persuaded her to come to his house for dinner. There she met his father, a devout Catholic who had graduated from Notre Dame. Along with the university's beauty and academic quality, his father stressed to Martha how safe and proper it was, a place where she could feel comfortable and thrive. Martha applied, was accepted, and received a scholarship, and in the fall of 1972 she was on a flight to South Bend, Indiana.

Martha took to Notre Dame quickly. The campus was beautiful, her classmates kind and helpful, the prospect of a top education exciting. But even then she was not fully prepared for university life in 1972.[2] Her high school friend's father had stressed that Notre Dame was safe, but not that until that year the student body had been all male. Martha discovered that she would often be the only woman in classes, some as large as sixty students. She was shy to begin with and sticking out like a sore female thumb made her uncomfortable. When a teacher taking attendance would call her name, she would respond in a low-pitched voice, hoping that it would somehow make her less conspicuous. When she would gather with male students outside of class, they would fidget and shift their eyes away, as if they did not know what to do with her. One boy took a liking to her, but when they were both on a plane home to Los Angeles for a holiday break, she rejected his advances, and he called her a "spic." She had never heard the slur before, and only later did she realize that, like her father, she had been ridiculed because of her ethnicity.

Usually Martha would drive home for breaks, steering her aging Ford southwest through Saint Louis, Tulsa, Amarillo, first alone and later with her boyfriend. They would linger in Santa Fe, among the thick-walled adobe buildings and Spanish voices that brought strong and happy memories of her father's village. The trips continued after she graduated from college and during the following three years at Notre Dame law school. There was little doubt in her mind that she wanted to practice law in Santa Fe, although she had no idea how she would get a job there. With the help of a priest who was good friends with the governor of New Mexico, Jerry Apodaca, Martha and her boyfriend, whom she had recently married, got jobs as summer associates at a Santa Fe law firm. As she fell more in love with the place, she sensed even in Santa Fe, where so many Mexican Americans lived, that she was a second-class citizen. They seemed to want to be Spanish, not Mexican; Mexican food was called Spanish food. It stunned her that people did not give more respect to the country that her parents were so proud to be from.[3]

After graduation in 1978, Martha landed a job in Santa Fe with the New Mexico Law Office of the Public Defender, a state agency that represented poor people accused of crimes. It was demanding, sometimes heartbreaking work: street addicts accused of theft, teenagers charged with assaulting abusive parents, prisoners beaten by guards for mouthing off. Early in her second year there, Vázquez represented Modesto Martinez, a Mexican American in his early sixties who was small and weak and walked with a limp—he faced the death penalty for shooting dead a police officer who had approached his car window. Vázquez and her co-counsel's investigation in the desert area where Martinez lived led them to Reies López Tijerina, a renowned activist and hero of the Chicano rights movement to reclaim land grants for the descendants of Hispanic and Mexican settlers.[4]

Tijerina greeted the two lawyers at his mobile home, weapons drawn, a nearby sign saying "Land or Death." He made clear that the cop had been a bully and that he expected Martinez to be convicted of nothing more serious than voluntary manslaughter, as he had unintentionally killed the officer. Vázquez hardly needed the added pressure—she was pregnant at the time and often nauseous and losing weight—but after a two-week trial she persuaded the jury to find Martinez guilty of voluntary manslaughter, an extraordinary feat for a lawyer so young. Given Martinez's age and failing health, the judge sentenced him to only a few years in prison. That approach—tailoring the punishment to fit the individual—was typical among judges at the time and what Vázquez would learn to expect. It was, however, already losing favor. In 1979, one year after Vázquez became a public defender, the so-called sentencing reforms that New Mexico had enacted two years earlier took effect.[5] Gone were "indeterminate" sentences whose length could depend on factors like the prisoner's age, record, and behavior, and in their place were sentences of a fixed number of years chosen from a range: ten to twenty-five years for kidnapping, say, or one to five years for stealing a TV, with in all cases at least a year tacked on for the use of a pistol or other "deadly weapon."

The point of the law was, of course, to "get tough on criminals" with harsher sentences because, as one New Mexico state senator put it, the current system did not adequately protect society.[6] It soon became horrifically evident that putting people away for fixed and longer terms in already overcrowded prisons was not a great idea. The trouble began at 1:40 a.m. on February 2, 1980, in a dormitory at the Penitentiary of New Mexico, just south of Santa Fe. Two guards were counting prisoners as they squeezed between the two rows of single cots that stretched the length of the sixty-foot room. A third guard was at the locked door. When the shift commander arrived unexpectedly to help with the count, the third guard unlocked the door and two inmates—drunk with a homemade brew that many of the prisoners had earlier imbibed—tackled him. The other prisoners soon overpowered the three remaining guards and flooded out of the room.

Over the next thirty-six hours raged the most violent prison riot in the nation's history. When it was done, when the wardens and subwardens had appeased inmate negotiators with vague promises about meeting their demands and state troopers had stormed the prison's charred remains, at least thirty-three prisoners were dead and more than two hundred injured. Seven guards had been beaten and raped but survived. An investigation commenced, but the causes of the riot were not much in dispute. Leading the list was overcrowding. On the night of the riot there were 1,157 prisoners in a penitentiary designed for about 900. Other problems followed from there: rotten food, cockroach and mice infestations, disbanded education and recreation programs, and violent and nonviolent people housed together.[7]

The breadth and severity of the mistreatment prisoners endured was one reason few of them were prosecuted successfully. They also had savvy lawyers: Santa Fe chief public defender Mark Donatelli and his staff, which included Martha Vázquez. Vázquez would visit the prison and witness the filth and repulsive conditions in which some of her clients were forced to live, and she would develop an indelible sense that this was no way to treat people, even criminals—to "throw them away like garbage," as she would later say so often. Yet the tough-on-crime impetus for fixed or mandatory sentences that limited judges' discretion and led to longer prison terms had spread far beyond New Mexico, with forty-nine of fifty states having adopted the measures in some form by 1983.[8] And since all politics is local, as former Speaker of the House Tip O'Neill would put it, national policy soon reflected the states' approach.

The Politics of Fear

In a sense it started in the spring of 1981, about when Joseph Persico, the prominent author and former speechwriter for New York governor Nelson Rockefeller, was sifting through a mass of notes and data, kneading his craggy brow in puzzlement. He was a hired pen, recruited to write a report for President Reagan's advisory committee on crime, a motley nineteen-member group of political up-and-comers and has-beens charged with polishing the administration's tough-on-crime bona fides. The new president had vowed to make the nation safe from murder and mayhem, "to strengthen the hand of the law against the lawless," as his attorney general William French Smith put it, and this report would show how.[9]

But the data wouldn't cooperate. The committee's months of interviews and reams of research hadn't come close to identifying what truly caused crime. Potential solutions remained elusive. Harsher penalties might be popular, but Persico knew from working on Rockefeller's draconian 1970s drug laws that such punishments packed prisons more than cut crime. The kicker: US rates of serious and violent offenses were dropping—making it seem absurd to spend even more money on expanding a US prison population that had already doubled in the past decade.[10] Suspecting that Reagan would not welcome these facts, the committee's members came up with a plan. They would emphasize in the report that the real problem—more damaging than crime itself—was the fear of crime, which the committee argued could devastate neighborhoods by driving out people and businesses.

Fear: The concept caught the imagination of top Reagan adviser Ed Meese. Meese ended up dumping the advisory committee's report and its provocative blood-red cover as too cautious on solutions and too wedded to the facts. He seized on the fear of crime as an opportunity for voters to view Reagan as their great protector, and he played an integral role in shaping the federal sentencing guidelines—an effort to make punishments for the same federal crime uniform across the nation.[11] Many on the political left backed sentencing uniformity as fair: a way to stop judges from discriminating against certain, often minority offenders. The right embraced it as an antidote to leniency on the bench. The result was the Sentencing Reform Act of 1984, sponsored in the Senate by the rock-ribbed Strom Thurmond and the liberal Ted Kennedy.[12] Based on states' experience, the legislation established a commission of seven members—three federal judges and four nonjudges—that many supporters expected would fit punishments to crimes based on scientific research and the characteristics of each offender.[13] But after the seven Reagan-appointed and Senate-approved commission members went to work, what emerged in 1987 was quite different. The commission basically just calculated the average length of past US sentences—and increased them for most violent crimes and drug crimes because they were considered simply "inadequate."[14]

The new system burnished Reagan's and his conservative allies' anticrime image but at the cost of denying federal judges almost any discretion in sentencing. Punishment would now depend essentially on what offense prosecutors chose to charge—one of the most significant transfers of power from the judiciary to the executive branch, of which prosecutors were a part, in American history. Meese's machinations and the transformation of the federal justice system seemed at the time far away and of small consequence for Martha Vázquez. As a New Mexico public defender, she practiced in state court, where stricter sentencing laws were still loose enough for her empathy and persistence and exhaustive preparation to turn a judge her client's way. Yet the money was tight (her salary was $15,000 a year) and the job all-consuming (she was married, with four kids), and she left the position in 1982 for private practice at a Santa Fe law firm. She handled mostly civil cases—business disputes, personal injury suits, employment matters—and just a smattering of criminal cases. Her main clients were teachers, members of the National Education Association of New Mexico, which her firm had represented since the early 1970s. She successfully represented members of the governor's cabinet in a federal corruption investigation and was keenly aware of the sentencing guidelines, but she had no idea of how profoundly they would soon affect her life.

Treated Like Garbage

After visiting Ricardo in jail on August 3, 1990, Vázquez arranged with the DEA to get his stuff from his car at the agency's impoundment lot. As she opened the car door, a jumble of sandy beach toys spilled out, and the reminder of Ricardo's children made her cry. The DEA agent who had met her at the lot seemed sympathetic, telling her how shocked he had been to find that her brother's record was spotless—no arrests, no run-ins with the law—and offered to support his release on bail if Ricardo would speak with him. Vázquez was in no mood to chat, but she would remember the offer.

Her most pressing task was to get her brother the best lawyer she could find. The federal defender who had been appointed to represent Ricardo was telling her that it looked like an open-and-shut case, that the government had him on tape, and when she heard how much time he could face in prison—a minimum of twenty-five years—Vázquez said she "completely lost it." Ricardo had been swept up in a drug sting after all, and he was far from the scheme's mastermind, so how could the case be open and shut? Her colleagues told Vázquez that the guy to hire was Barry Tarlow, one of the best-known criminal defense lawyers in LA. He was expensive but worth it, they said, so to scrape together the money, Vázquez's mother pledged her home in Santa Barbara to secure a loan, and Martha's sister, Rosanna, agreed to save money by deferring her plan to attend law school in the fall. Yet they didn't get much of Tarlow. Instead, another lawyer in his firm, a former prosecutor named Mark Heaney, handled the case. Heaney remembered Ricardo as "a totally, totally decent guy. It was heartbreaking to see him in jail." As for Martha, she was clear and insistent on how things should go. "I thought the world of her," Heaney said. But Vázquez wasn't happy. "He was a very nice man," was all she would say about Heaney's legal acumen. "He didn't want to investigate, and he wanted Ricardo to plead guilty."

That was not going to happen. The next move, Heaney and Vázquez agreed, was to get Ricardo out of jail. On September 20, 1990, more than a month after Ricardo's arrest, a hearing was held on whether he could be released while awaiting trial. It was Martha's first encounter with the federal judge who would preside over the case, Manuel Real. Real, to put it kindly, was a character. Appointed by President Lyndon Johnson in 1966, Real may have been best known for ordering the Pasadena Unified School District to desegregate its schools and approving a busing plan to accomplish the task. He was infamous for capricious decisions, harsh treatment of criminal defendants, and rude and domineering behavior in court.

He was often reversed on appeal, and in 2006 he faced a potential impeachment hearing in Congress for allegedly interfering in a bankruptcy case.[15]

At Ricardo's hearing, Martha testified about her brother's clean record, stable life, and strong family support, saying she would agree to take care of him, even moving to California if necessary. She testified about the DEA agent's offer to support Ricardo's release. The government lawyers and the agent himself denied that he had said any such a thing, however. "That was a good lesson for me," Vázquez said later. "It taught me not to believe the police." She held her tongue, hoping the judge would believe her and see the goodness in Ricardo and the righteous nature of his request. It was not to be. At the end of the hearing, Real sided with the government. "Well, I think that there are no conditions that can be met" to justify Ricardo's release, Real declared from the bench. "I think the bond, if anything, that would guarantee his return [to court] would have to be probably in the million-dollar range, and that just cannot be met."[16]

And yet Martha and her family would not give up. They took the judge at his word—the bit about the million-dollar range—and proceeded to scrounge together more assets to secure Ricardo's release. In addition to Martha's house and the houses of her parents, they would pledge Martha's second home and the house of her aunt and uncle. In total, the equity value of the property was well over $1 million. The family requested that the judge reconsider, and at a hearing on October 10, he dismissed them out of hand. "He treated us like garbage," Vázquez recalled. "It was if I was considered a criminal and must have known about the drug dealing, that all of us in the family must have known." Six days later, Ricardo would go to trial on four counts involving cocaine and one for carrying guns.

The trial was short, not much more than a few days of testimony. Real behaved as advertised. "He jumped down our throats at every turn," recalled Heaney. There had been no motions to suppress evidence, no evaluation of Ricardo's limited mental capacity, no effort to undermine the credibility of Cobb, the government informant. Heaney did argue that Ricardo had been entrapped: that Cobb had pressured him to convert a pot deal into a cocaine deal that Ricardo did not want to do. It seemed a promising defense. The trick was to show that Ricardo was not in legal terms "predisposed" to carry out the cocaine deal, and demonstrating that depended on five factors. The first was essentially whether Ricardo had a clean record. He did, so that weighed heavily in his favor. The second turned on whether the government agent had first suggested the crime. How that one played for Ricardo was less clear because he *did* want to do the pot transaction—though not the cocaine deal. The third factor was whether Ricardo had committed the offense for money, and the answer was clearly yes. The fourth was whether Ricardo did not want to commit the particular crime, but the government persuaded him to do it, and on this one he had a pretty good argument. The final factor was how strong the government's effort had been to persuade Ricardo, and the answer here was very strong—multiple phone calls, a $10,000 loan to a flat-broke man, and an offer to supply the drugs.[17]

Yet the defense of entrapment rarely succeeds. Even when it seems persuasive from a commonsense point of view, the law skews heavily in the government's favor. Still, it takes only the slightest evidence of entrapment for the defense to be put before the jury for consideration, and once it's before the jury, anything can happen. The insurmountable obstacle for Ricardo, however, was again Judge Real: He refused to instruct the jury that it could even *consider* entrapment.

As Bad as It Could Get

Early in the afternoon of November 1, 1990, just after Heaney and the government had finished their closing arguments, Vázquez and her mother, Consuelo, walked from the Edward R. Roybal Federal Courthouse in the Little Tokyo section of Los Angeles to a small park nearby. On the edge of the park there was a church whose doors were open in a gesture of welcome. The two walked inside and knelt to pray in the silence. Ricardo had been praying the rosary bead by bead throughout the trial, and it had broken Vázquez's heart to watch him; she and her mother were compelled to believe that he still had a chance, that God would grant him that chance of acquittal, and so in the church they prayed.

After they finished and walked back through the chilly air to the courthouse, they sat in the hallway outside Judge Real's courtroom and waited. Before day's end came word that the jury had reached a verdict. As Vázquez and her mother stood in the first row of benches at the back of the courtroom, as they watched the judge sit down at his bench and call in the jury, they waited some more. Finally the judge spoke. *Have you reached a verdict? We have your honor. On all five counts. Guilty.* Ricardo turned and looked back at his mother and sister. His role had always been to comfort them, and now he could not, and it was if he did not know what to do. Vázquez's mother turned to her in confusion, and Vázquez had to explain what had happened. "It just didn't seem real," she recalled. The best hope now for Martha Vázquez and her family was to convince the judge—and it would be up to the judge alone—to go easy on Ricardo when the time came to sentence him. Yet even if Real wanted to show leniency, the sentencing guidelines strictly limited his options. In 1990 the guidelines had been in force for only three years, and few if any judges had yet displayed the confidence to interpret them other than strictly. In Ricardo's case here's how they worked: For a defendant with no criminal history the range of sentences was 292 to 365 months (about twenty-four to thirty years) in prison for each offense involving 500 to 1,500 kilos of powder cocaine. In addition, a drug offense involving a gun carried a mandatory minimum of sixty months (five years).[18]

On the morning of January 14, 1991, Ricardo, wearing an orange jumpsuit with his hands cuffed in front of him, stood before a wooden lectern with Heaney and faced Judge Real. Vázquez and her mother were again there, sitting stiffly on the benches behind him. The judge listed the charges of which Ricardo had been convicted, ran through the boilerplate about the range of months each charge carried, added and subtracted the points pertaining to the details of the crime and Ricardo's role and behavior, and came up with a number. It was 352 months, or almost thirty years. Considering the guidelines, it could have been worse. Judge Real had chosen the low end of the range—292 months—for each of the four cocaine counts and, as is typical, said they should be served concurrently. He then added the mandatory five-year gun sentence.

Considering everything else, though, it was about as bad as it could get. Consuelo, the woman who had borne Ricardo and worried him through school and a career and repeated as a kind of mantra that "Ricardo tiene un corazón de oro," *Ricardo has a heart of gold*, collapsed in tears in Vázquez's arms. It was at about that moment, as her anger at a callous judge and the senseless ordeal that they had all been through over the past five months rushed through her, that an idea Vázquez had only toyed with before took sharp form. *I can do this*, she thought. She could seek to understand people who, like Ricardo, had made a bad mistake, to treat them as humans whose lives still had value, to offer them compassion—or at least a daily "good morning"—as they made their way through a terrifying system of criminal justice. She could get them true justice, even if it required her to send them to prison. She decided that she would try to become a federal judge.

. . .

Over the next three years Martha Vázquez would continue to practice law in Santa Fe. She would spend spare moments working with

Ricardo's lawyers on his appeal, and in 1992 the US Court of Appeals in San Francisco affirmed his conviction. The decision was not unanimous, though. One of the three judges on the court's panel dissented, ruling that Ricardo deserved a new trial because Judge Real should have allowed the jury to consider his defense of entrapment.[19] At the time, Ricardo was being held at Terminal Island, a low-security prison near Los Angeles, but he would soon be moved, and Martha was trying to ensure that he would end up in a decent place. She refused to give up on his case, working with Heaney to file a petition for clemency with President Bill Clinton.

As for Martha's dream of joining the bench, her chance came late in 1992, when Judge Santiago Campos in Santa Fe took senior status—a sort of semiretirement that allows a judge to cut back on his caseload but also opens a spot for a replacement. A founder of her law firm, Jerry Wertheim, knew one of the US senators for New Mexico, Jeff Bingaman, and told him that Vázquez would be a compelling choice: smart, experienced, a Mexican American woman. She had something else going for her. Like Carlton Reeves and Jed Rakoff, she had a strong sense of purpose. It had formed as she watched her parents rise from impoverished immigrants to citizens of respect and relative wealth in Santa Barbara, as she herself discovered that education and focused toil could bring an honorable career and, painfully, as she saw the promising life of her brother effectively thrown away. She believed that everyone deserved the chance at a middle-class life of value and, when they stumbled, the help to get right again. It was an obligation of the judicial system—and of our democracy—to give them that help. She just wasn't counting on how hard it would be.

4 *Justice on Trial*

The August heat of a Deep South dawn creeps into the cabin of the Cessna four-seater, and Carlton Reeves begins to sweat. He is squeezed tight in his seat away from the door. To his left sits Lance Stevens, a prominent Mississippi trial lawyer. Across are Kathy Nester, an attorney and lobbyist of imposing physique, and David Baria, president-elect of the state's trial lawyers' association. As the plane awaits departure on the tarmac of Hawkins Field in Jackson, Mississippi, the temperature rises beyond any notion of bearable, and the pilot offers a suggestion for cooling the cabin. Leave the door open as we taxi down the runway, he says, and slam it shut just before takeoff. The four passengers, their desire for relief overwhelming their comprehension of risk, comply.

The Cessna gathers speed, and as it nears the runway's edge, the pilot gives the signal to close the door. Stevens delivers a push. The door does not budge. Baria pulls from the other direction. Still the door is stuck. Together they push and pull to no effect. Panic sets in. *We are going to die.* Then Stevens hears a low voice of soothing calm.

"We will be fine," says Carlton Reeves, and he reaches across to help give the door a decisive shove.

"Carlton's pulse never increased," marvels Stevens. "That is just how he is. Deliberative. Absolutely steady." And that is one reason Reeves was along for the ride. It was 2002. He was an attorney with the Jackson firm of Pigott Reeves Johnson & Minor, and with his trial-lawyer colleagues was embarking on a one-day barnstorming tour across the state: north to Greenville, east to Tupelo, south to Meridian and Hattiesburg and Gulfport, then back to Jackson. They were going, it is fair to say, largely because of what George W. Bush had done the week before.

On August 8 the president had touched down in Madison, Mississippi, just north of Jackson, to deliver a speech in the gym of Madison Central High School. A crowd of twenty-three hundred had greeted him with homemade placards, American flags, and cries of adoration. "We love you!" came a shout across the bleachers. Bush spoke a bit about homeland security, low taxes, and the evils of corporate fraudsters. But his reason for being there, the point of his speech, was to rake trial lawyers over the coals. "Litigation," he declared, "is no way to prosperity."[1]

Animosity toward trial lawyers—the people who argue in court on behalf of the injured, the cheated, the workaday person ripped off—was a fever running high across the nation but nowhere hotter than in Mississippi. The president's speech helped stoke it to a frenzy. At this point some six thousand lawsuits in the state had accused Gulf Coast shipbuilders of killing employees with asbestos, and the cases had enriched the attorneys who filed them with tens of millions of dollars in fees.[2] The litigation launched with the state's attorney general against the nation's tobacco companies had bestowed on courtroom conjurers like Dickie Scruggs the image of scallywags exploiting tragedy for astronomical payoffs. Doctors were scaring the bejeesus out of Mississippians with threats of fleeing the state because jury verdicts had put the price of malpractice insurance beyond their reach. The message implicit in Bush's speech was that Mississippi's very survival came down to dissuading people from going to court.

The lawyers jammed into the Cessna ascending that morning toward Greenville believed they could not let the message stand. It put their livelihoods at risk, of course, but in their eyes it was also wrong. They figured bad investments, rising interest rates, and collusion among insurers had more to do with higher insurance premiums than big jury verdicts did, and besides, seeking legal justice was a right whose erosion would harm society more than the occasional excessive damage award. The lawyers believed, in other words, that the facts and common sense were on their side, and there were few better at articulating facts and common sense to the people of Mississippi than steady, deliberative Carlton Reeves.

The impending showdown in Mississippi and across the United States over lawsuits was the culmination of an almost three-decade struggle over how legislators and judges and Americans at large viewed the purpose of civil justice. While giving people a fair hearing and getting to the truth in court were once considered paramount, many folks now viewed lawyers and lawsuits as impediments to prosperity, necessary but irritating elements of a system whose message to judges was to "do everything you can to end cases as quickly and summarily as possible," as one former federal judge observed.[3] It was a national effort, already under way at the time of the Powell memo and the Burger Court crackdown on securities lawsuits and class actions and other forms of litigation in the 1970s. Its harshest impacts, though, would fall on the poorest and most vulnerable regions of the nation, states like Mississippi, where Reeves would come of age as a lawyer and grapple with this shift in attitude toward civil justice, first as a counselor to corporations, then as a lawyer for the United States, and later as a trial attorney on behalf of clients seeking redress.

Working for the Man

On June 30, 1986, a couple of months before Reeves began his first year at law school, readers flipping through *Newsweek* magazine might have come across a startling image on page 27. It was a photograph of a newborn baby, superimposed over a block of text under the bold, black headline "The Lawsuit Crisis Is Bad for Babies." The text accused "the civil justice system" of putting obstetricians out of business and risking the lives of mothers-to-be and ultimately their babies. Readers might have seen the same image in *Time*, *Reader's Digest*, or the Sunday magazines of newspapers around the country. They might have seen or heard, at various times and in various publications or on various radio or television stations, similarly arresting ads with similar messages. The messages were paid for largely by the Insurance Information Institute, an industry association that in 1986 rolled out a $6.5 million campaign to convince Americans that, as the campaign slogan put it, "We All Pay the Price" for lawsuits.[4] The institute had plenty of company in its efforts to persuade through fear, including the *Wall Street Journal* editorial page and the Department of Justice, which called lawsuits "a major issue in the insurance crisis."[5]

The catalyst for all this was a precipitous rise in insurance rates. Total premiums for general liability insurance increased more than 70 percent in each of 1985 and 1986, and corporate America, led by insurance companies, was determined to find a culprit.[6] Lawyers seemed a ripe target, and rather than investigate and report admittedly complex facts, insurers and their allies commissioned public-opinion polls with questions (*Do people bring more lawsuits than they should? Are the size of awards and settlements too large?*) designed to suggest that lawsuits were excessive, frivolous, and unfair.[7] Predictably, a lot of people agreed that they were, helping the industry tailor a public relations campaign that blamed lawyers and lawsuits for propelling insurance premiums through the roof. The evidence for that argument was inconclusive at best, but the success of the campaign was resounding. In 1986 more than thirty states enacted substantial limits on when, how, and for how much people could bring lawsuits.[8] Yet one person's frivolous case is another's vindication of a constitutional right, and the campaign's smearing of the civil justice system did real damage to it by diminishing the stature of lawyers and judges and the courts—and the right of Americans to seek their help. So unimportant had the most basic functions of courts become in the eyes of some politicians that, when Congress turned to cutting the budget in 1986, the thirty-dollars-a-day fee paid to federal jurors was among the items sacrificed, prompting the nation's first suspension of civil jury trials.[9]

In 1989, when Reeves clerked for Justice Reuben Anderson, the campaign's impact was evident in the numerous appeals to the Mississippi Supreme Court claiming someone had won excessive damages that needed to be cut or thrown out completely. The appeals were filed by defense firms—advocates most often for companies and the like—whose practices interested Reeves much less than that of the Charlotte, North Carolina, civil rights firm where he had worked in the summer during law school. Yet at the end of his first year with Anderson, when he had to decide what to do next, reality intervened. Reeves wanted to stay in Mississippi. Lora, his girlfriend and future wife, had just undergone surgery, and the prognosis was not yet clear. And a large corporate firm in Jackson called Phelps Dunbar had asked Justice Anderson to join. Corporate practice was unfamiliar and vaguely suspect territory for Anderson as well as Reeves—"Black people did not work for these big law firms," Reeves said—and the two discussed the possibility, with the older man asking Reeves whether he would go with him.

As it happened, Anderson went while Reeves stayed at the Supreme Court as a staff attorney, only to join the justice at Phelps Dunbar a year later. When he arrived there in 1991, consensus continued to build in Washington, DC, that the federal courts had become overburdened, slow, and expensive. Conservatives and their corporate backers again blamed a "litigation explosion"—too many frivolous lawsuits that raised the cost of doing business. Those on the left also worried that even meritorious litigation failed to deliver swift and affordable justice. Rhetoric about budget deficits blocked one reasonable response: more judges and resources to handle the load. Instead, in 1990, then senator Joseph Biden sponsored the bipartisan Civil Justice Reform Act, which required courts to make plans for cutting delays and expenses.[10] The plans' details were mostly up to the courts, but the act offended plenty of judges, who accused Congress of trying to micromanage their profession. Maybe worse in their view was that they received no additional money to cover the tens of millions of dollars the plans would cost. This was part of a pattern: Congress would pass pricey laws like the Americans with Disabilities Act or the Civil Rights Act of 1991 or, most notably, federal antidrug statutes but refuse to pay for the soaring caseloads that resulted. In fact, shortfalls in the federal courts' annual budget neared $400 million in the early 1990s, and rather than meet the financial obligations of civil justice, lawmakers like Senator Chuck Grassley of Iowa held hearings on cutting the number of judges.[11] Getting a case heard in federal court became tougher than ever.

This was the world Reeves encountered as a young lawyer. Most cases against clients of Phelps Dunbar's Jackson office were probably filed in Mississippi state court, either because they had to be there or because the plaintiffs—the people who filed them—wanted them there. It gets complicated, but in broad strokes they had to be there if a federal court did not have jurisdiction because, say, the plaintiffs and at least one of the defendants were based in the state and the case did not involve a federal law.[12] The plaintiffs might want the cases in state court for a bunch of reasons, but a big one was that the juries and judges—often from plaintiffs' hometowns or counties and suspicious of big companies—were generally sympathetic, tending to find in their neighbors' favor and award them more money. For essentially the same reasons, corporate defendants preferred federal court. Being in state court was "what you wanted to avoid at all costs," said Chuck Barlow, who joined Phelps Dunbar two years before Reeves did and often worked with him on cases. "It really didn't matter what the facts were, a [state] judge was never going to dismiss a case; it was going to go to trial." So Reeves and his colleagues spent much of their time trying to get their clients' cases moved to federal court through a process called "removal."

In theory, removal was easy if the jurisdictional requirements were met. In practice, though, it was completely up to federal judges to decide whether to accept cases from state court, and given their already onerous caseloads and dwindling resources, many were happy to find any reason to say no. The federal courthouse doors were closing fast for everyone—including corporate defendants. In at least one area of the law, however, there was still room to maneuver. It was qualified immunity, the troubling judge-made concept of shielding most government bodies and public officials from liability for their misbehavior. In the early 1990s the standard for finding immunity was not yet so strict that any lawsuit against, say, a cop was all but laughed out of court. For Phelps Dunbar this meant plenty of work in defense of clients like the Mississippi Municipal League, the organization whose various affiliates represented and insured and lobbied for the state's towns and counties and their employees. If a city got sued, the call typically went out to Phelps Dunbar, often putting Reeves in the awkward position of helping to defend against a claim of, for example, racial discrimination.

Reeves was not so bound by ideology that he would deny the benefits of toiling at a corporate firm, "working . . . with the man," as he had viewed it in law school. "I was still on the partnership track, I was doing good work" after three years, he said, and he liked his colleagues. "These people grew up in a different Mississippi. These guys who were young partners, they experienced a different Mississippi," one that no longer saw Black lawyers as any less talented or intelligent or deserving than their white colleagues. "And I was treated that way. It was also the most money I ever made." As luck would have it, a turn in Reeves's career would keep him from having to further test his tolerance for the life of corporate law.

Doing the Right Thing

On the occasional weekday at noon, eight or so local alumni of the University of Virginia Law School would gather for lunch in Jackson. Reeves was often among them, as was a lawyer who had graduated from the school nine years before him. That lawyer had gained a modicum of renown for the law firm he had built with John L. Maxey, a civil rights advocate in his early days and a close friend of Reeves's mentor, Justice Anderson, and for his unsuccessful bid for Congress in 1988. He was a McComb, Mississippi, native, son of a state court judge, and a summa cum laude graduate of Duke University, skilled at spinning a story and cultivating connections and charming the waitresses at the place-to-be-seen Mayflower coffee shop downtown. That lawyer's name was Brad Pigott, and he and Reeves hit it off.

It was later, in early 1993, as the two walked together toward the door of a fundraiser for the soon-to-be congressman Bennie Thompson, that they got to know each other better. Reeves had interned for Thompson during college, when the older man served on the Hinds County Board of Supervisors, and had kept in touch with him through law school. Thompson had urged Reeves to return to Mississippi, and Reeves said he revered Thompson as a "rabble-rouser around here; he was the man." Pigott, a vice chairman of the Mississippi State Board of Education and already politically connected, was on the short list to become the next US attorney—the chief federal prosecutor—for the Southern District of Mississippi. Whether Pigott would be selected depended on the outcome of a delicate political dance. Word had come down from the new president, Bill Clinton, that a Black person had to fill at least one of the two open US attorney positions in the state. Pigott, being white, would have to wait but eventually received the appointment after a Black nominee agreed to serve in the Northern District. When it came time to select his lieutenants, Pigott believed his choice to head the office's civil division was clear—Carlton Reeves.

It was a big job, and Reeves was young, just thirty years old. Yet he had proven himself a careful and thorough lawyer who worked with thoughtful poise, and that gave Pigott confidence in his choice. What's more, Pigott had big plans. With a Democrat in the White House and a Justice Department that for the first time seemed eager to bring its Mississippi outpost into its cases, the new US attorney began aggressively pursuing actions at the core of his party's concerns—health-care fraud, civil rights violations, and degradation of the environment. Although many of those actions were criminal prosecutions, plenty were civil lawsuits, putting them squarely in Reeves's remit. He would sue doctors and defense contractors and others for submitting false claims to the government, landlords for violating housing laws, employers for discriminating against their workers, and local governments for undermining Americans' right to vote. He would also defend the government against lawsuits, but by and large the cases Reeves handled were in line with his compassionate view of the world. "I was pretty much satisfied that we were doing the right thing," he said.

His experiences in the US attorney's office also removed him from the fractious developments roiling the world of private practice. It had been troubling enough for Reeves to work against people trying to vindicate their rights in court or to witness federal judges pushing away cases for a lack of resources and congressional respect. But in 1994, with the Republican Party just months away from taking control of Congress, what had been shaping up as a war against lawsuits and victims and the courts themselves was about to explode into a self-righteous cause.

Hot Fudge Sundae of Politics

On February 27, 1992, Stella Liebeck, a delicate seventy-nine-year-old with a yen for morning coffee, sat in the passenger seat of her grandson's 1989 Ford Probe as he eased the car to the McDonald's drive-through window in Albuquerque, New Mexico. He reached for his breakfast, passed her a cup of coffee, and pulled forward to park so that she could add cream and sugar. As Liebeck struggled to lift the lid of the Styrofoam cup, though, the near-boiling beverage washed over her thighs, soaking the thick cotton of her sweatpants. At the emergency room the doctors said her burns were so serious that she would need skin grafts. Hours of surgery and seven days of care in the hospital passed before Liebeck was released to recuperate at her daughter's home in Santa Fe. The coffee, it turns out, was more than 180 degrees— at least 20 degrees hotter than the typical restaurant cup. McDonald's brewed it that way for the simple reason that it tasted better, but the risk was clear. When Liebeck was scalded that morning, the fast-food giant had already received some seven hundred complaints of mild to severe coffee burns and settled injury claims for more than $500,000 in total.

It was no surprise, then, that Liebeck sued as well. And two years later, when an Albuquerque jury awarded her almost $2.9 million in compensatory and punitive damages, public outrage jump-started the congressional assault on litigation.[13] It made no difference that the evidence against McDonald's was powerful, that the judge would cut the award to $640,000, or that Liebeck would settle for even less. Lawyers were financial pillars of the Democratic Party, and Republicans considered bashing them essential to GOP fortunes. Whatever more pressing concerns Americans had, went the logic, voters could still be persuaded that lawsuit reform was a good thing.[14] "It was like the hot fudge sundae of American politics," Edward Lazarus, a consultant to the trial lawyers' association at the time, later said, a tasty lagniappe in a meat-and-potatoes agenda.

A month after the August 1994 McDonald's verdict, the US House Republican Conference and one of its leaders, Newt Gingrich, unveiled the "Contract with America," a ten-point manifesto that included two proposals aimed at closing the courthouse doors. One touted stricter standards for suing over dangerous products, caps on the amount of money victims could recover in lawsuits, and "loser pays"—a rule designed to elevate the risk of bringing suits and therefore sharply cut the number filed by requiring losers to pay the winners' legal fees. The other proposal called for stiffer mandatory sentences and fewer opportunities to challenge a death sentence.[15] The first proposal did not pass but led the following year to a law that made it far harder for shareholders to sue fraudsters and corporate cheats. Called the Private Securities Litigation Reform Act, the law essentially said that a ripped-off investor would be bounced from court unless he could specify the how and who and why of an alleged scam from the moment he filed his complaint—a high standard that almost no other type of plaintiff had to meet.[16] The act was a major victory for corporate America and a continuation of efforts begun in the 1970s by Lewis Powell and his Supreme Court colleagues and the US Chamber of Commerce to protect big business from its own shareholders.

The second proposal helped prompt even more draconian measures. In April 1995 its tough-on-crime supporters received a horrific sort of boost: the bombing of the Oklahoma City federal building by Timothy McVeigh and Terry Nichols, a tragedy that killed 168 people and galvanized the nation against terrorism.[17] Congress would respond with legislation cracking down on terrorists, and lawmakers with law-and-order agendas stuffed the bill with peripheral measures like limits on federal judges' power to second-guess state or federal convictions—especially ones that carried the death penalty. The Antiterrorism and Effective Death Penalty Act of 1996 tightened deadlines for challenging imprisonment as unconstitutional, narrowed the grounds for doing so, and limited even wrongly convicted death-row inmates to essentially two shots at overturning their sentences.[18] Among a national swath of judges, lawyers, and criminal justice advocates, the law soon drew the ignominious distinction of being one of the worst statutes ever passed by Congress.

The greatest legal impact of the "Contract with America" may have been to give states the moral and political cover to bring the civil justice system to heel. That was important because states were where most of the action was. The vast majority of cases, especially those involving slips and falls and car wrecks and fraud and defective products (so-called "torts") are handled in state courts and governed by state law. So changes in state law, measures like caps on damages or limits on who can be sued, determine how most cases play out. Those changes can also matter for cases in federal court. When a lawsuit based on state law—like most tort suits—is filed in federal court, or moved there from state court, it is generally still governed by state law (although federal procedures apply). So Congress can impose limits on federal cases and courts, but states can constrain state lawsuits *and* in many cases federal lawsuits.[19] In Mississippi, however, the message of the "Contract with America" was surprisingly slow to break through.

Judicial Hellholes

On a morning in February 1994, Neal M. Cohen, a Washington public relations executive, held forth before a crowd of lobbyists gathered to share the tricks of their trade at the pastel-posh Colony Beach and Tennis Resort in Longboat Key, Florida. Cohen entertained his audience with tales that touted the success of a then new and increasingly popular tactic: grassroots lobbying, the practice of recruiting nonprofits, small businesses, and other sympathetic characters to say nice things about legislation that a lobbyist's true client—often a decidedly unsympathetic corporation—wanted to see enacted.[20]

Cohen warmed to one story in particular. The year before, a group called M-FAIR (Mississippians for a Fair Legal System) hired him to stir up support for a bill that would curb product liability suits, claims of injury from defective products. M-FAIR members included a variety of businesses, but its primary financial backers were among the most vilified corporations imaginable: tobacco companies, led by R. J. Reynolds Tobacco Company. M-FAIR had over the past several years helped elect state legislators friendly to its antilawsuit agenda, but bills M-FAIR supported had so far fallen short of passage. Then Cohen went to work. He blitzed the state with ads disparaging "greedy" lawyers. Billboards blared stark messages like "Fairness, Yes. Greed, No," and included an 800 number for recruiting new M-FAIR members. Cohen hired a professor to conduct a study that found the state spent more money on lawsuits than on education.[21]

Cohen boasted to the Florida crowd that his efforts brought "1,500 Mississippians mixed in with who our clients were," the tobacco companies, and caught the trial lawyers "completely by surprise." So they "caved in," he said. "We had divided them from the victims, and the media took our side, and their money became radioactive."[22] The result was Mississippi's first law constraining product liability cases, a legislative feat that Kirk Fordice, the state's first Republican governor since Reconstruction, praised as a major reform on behalf of business for Mississippi.[23] Fordice had exaggerated a bit. The new law had been heavily negotiated with the trial lawyers, and it essentially codified past decisions of the state Supreme Court, preserving the legal status quo. There might have been value in putting the rules in a statute, just to make sure the state's high court didn't do something crazy someday like make it even easier to sue over defective products, but beyond that this was no major reform.

As if to make the point, later in 1993, former employees of the Ingalls Shipyard in Pascagoula, Mississippi, won a major trial against distributors of products containing asbestos.[24] That same year,

Clarksdale lawyer Mike Lewis sat down for breakfast in Greenville with his friends Mike Moore, the attorney general of Mississippi, and Dickie Scruggs, who by this time had made a fortune in the asbestos-lawsuit industry. Moore pitched an idea that had first occurred to him while returning from a visit with his secretary's mother, a heavy smoker who was dying from lung disease: Why not sue tobacco companies for all the public money states were spending on caring for people like her? With all three now intrigued by the prospect, Scruggs told his co-counsel in a Gulf Coast trial, high-powered South Carolina attorney Ron Motley. "Motley immediately caught on to it," Scruggs remembered, "and I almost had to strap him down to his chair, he was ready to get up and file that afternoon."[25]

In May 1994, Mississippi would sue thirteen cigarette makers, seeking to recover the costs of caring for state residents with smoking-related diseases. By 1997, after whistleblower Jeffrey Wigand had given a televised interview to *60 Minutes* and thirty-nine states had joined Mississippi in suing tobacco companies, the case settled for $368.5 billion to be paid over twenty-five years.[26] Though Congress never gave its required approval of the settlement, Mississippi alone came away with $3.4 billion for its efforts.[27] The trial lawyers, collectively a big-money lobby skilled at backroom politics in that small state, seemed well in control, despite pressure from Washington. Forces were at play, though, that the lawyer lobby could not overcome. One was the US Supreme Court. The justices were beginning to turn their attention to punitive damages—awards designed to punish wrongdoers beyond a plaintiff's actual losses. Their size and the potential for winning them could justify hiring a lawyer and bringing a case that would otherwise not be worth the time and expense, but the problem was that the amount of punitives sometimes seemed far out of line with the actual damages. The court circled around the issue in 1989, 1991, and 1996 decisions, and in 2003 it ruled that punitive damages should generally not exceed "single-digit multipliers" of actual damages.[28] Though seemingly reasonable, the new rule could nonetheless keep some victims from seeking redress in court—and for a large corporation, make lawsuits over egregious behavior a manageable cost of doing business.

The Supreme Court presented a far more serious and immediate threat to trial lawyers and people's rights by promoting an alternative to litigation: mandatory arbitration, a private system of resolving disputes without laws or juries or constitutional protections. The basis of the justices' love affair with the process was the Federal Arbitration Act, a 1925 law aimed at requiring courts to enforce any arbitration provision in a "maritime transaction or a contract evidencing a transaction involving commerce."[29] The law's authors and supporters said they intended it to apply only to "merchants" in contract disputes rather than to, say, consumers.[30] For the next sixty years the nation's courts honored that intent. But by the mid-1970s the fear of an explosion in litigation had gripped the federal judiciary, feeding its desire to clear dockets by forcing cases out of court.[31]

In 1983, without explanation, the Supreme Court declared that the arbitration act had created a "liberal federal policy favoring arbitration agreements," meaning they should be upheld whenever possible.[32] The pronouncement marked a startling change in the high court's thinking, and the new policy soon drew criticism from its own members, including Justice Sandra Day O'Connor, who said the court "utterly fails to recognize the clear congressional intent underlying" the Federal Arbitration Act.[33] More and more businesses and professionals seized on the policy to force workers and consumers to agree, often unwittingly, to resolve any disputes in arbitration. And the justices repeatedly invoked the policy as they expanded mandatory arbitration throughout the nation's commercial life—even when civil rights were at stake. In 1991, for example, the Supreme Court ruled 7 to 2 that Robert Gilmer, a sixty-two-year-old financial services manager replaced by his twenty-eight-year-old protégé, must take his age discrimination case to arbitration. Gilmer had argued that the many deficiencies of the process—often-biased panels, limited discovery, no written opinions, the fact that his employer had forced it on him—made it unfair. The court dismissed Gilmer's objections, saying they were "far out of step with our current strong endorsement of the federal statutes favoring this method of resolving disputes."[34]

Still, Gilmer had a point. Arbitrations often require high filing fees, sometimes thousands of dollars. They lack the procedural safeguards of court, and limited awards can make hiring a lawyer difficult. Arbitrators don't have to be lawyers or in many cases even follow the law or justify their rulings. Their decisions are confidential and final. And then there is the repeat-player problem—since companies are generally involved in far more disputes than individuals are, arbitrators have an incentive to favor them in hopes of getting repeat business. Yet over the more than thirty years since Gilmer lost his case, the Supreme Court has continued to extend the reach of mandatory arbitration to block people from going to court.

The biggest factor working against trial lawyers in Mississippi, however, may have been their own success. In 1998 a jury in Holmes County, just north of Yazoo City, stunned Mississippians with a $145 million verdict against Ford Motor Company.[35] The next year, a jury in Jefferson County, south of Jackson along the Mississippi River, returned a verdict of $150 million in favor of five people, four of whom had claimed that the diet drug fen-phen caused them heart problems. After the verdict the drug's manufacturer, American Home Products, agreed to settle about fourteen hundred similar cases in the state.[36] Yet according to the company, it still faced some ten thousand claims in Jefferson County alone, which curiously had only about eighty-five hundred residents, with five hundred of those claims from people living in Maine, Hawaii, and other states. Many of those plaintiffs had been able to keep their cases in the county because they sued at least one company located there, often the area's lone pharmacy, Bankston Drug Store, in Fayette. "It's crazy," said Hilda T. Bankston, whose family owned the store from 1971 to 1999. "Our only role is that my husband filled prescriptions correctly. But we've been bombarded with lawsuits by everybody and their cousin."[37]

Bankston and her husband were not found liable, but the fen-phen verdict exposed another troubling aspect of the state's rules governing lawsuits: In a process called "joinder," a lawyer could combine in one lawsuit clients from all over the country with similar claims and file it in a Mississippi county where juries almost invariably delivered hefty awards. In an unfortunate bit of boasting, Dickie Scruggs would call these counties "magic jurisdictions," and topping the list were Holmes, Jefferson, and Claiborne.[38] The counties shared another characteristic: Their residents were overwhelmingly Black.[39] The conventional wisdom maintained that, compared with white juries, Black juries found in favor of plaintiffs more often and delivered consistently higher awards. It seemed logical that downtrodden minorities might favor ordinary people over powerful corporations, but studies have found little support for that phenomenon, while seeing a correlation between poverty and both more frequent plaintiffs' victories and, to a marginal degree, higher jury awards.[40] Some people concluded at the time that these sorts of jurors were just prone to being bamboozled. "In some venues in our state, including Jefferson County, plaintiffs are prospering off the lack of education of the juries," said George Dale, the state insurance commissioner. The mayor of Fayette, Rogers King, insisted that there were "fairly intelligent people in this area" and that its juries were "fair," but the national forces arrayed against lawyers and lawsuits found the poor Black counties of Mississippi irresistible targets.[41]

A major reckoning came on December 12, 2001, when the St. Paul Companies, the fourth largest US insurer of businesses, announced that it would no longer offer medical malpractice insurance. The decision applied nationally, but in Mississippi, where more than four hundred doctors would lose coverage, it was taken personally. Flyers and posters warning of "lawsuit abuse in Mississippi's courts" began to appear on the end tables and walls of physicians' and hospitals' waiting rooms across the state, and attorneys themselves would become targets of hate.[42] At some point during the rising furor, the young son of trial lawyer David Baria tripped on the bleachers at school and split open his scalp. He was rushed to a local emergency room for stitches, and his mother, Marci Baria, who was also a lawyer and the daughter of a physician, met him there. The doctor on duty soon learned that his young patient's last name was Baria. "Is that David Baria's son?" Baria recalls the doctor asking. "I wouldn't touch him with a ten-foot pole." Another doctor was quickly found, but the story stayed with Marci. "I thought it was pretty disgusting," she said.

The thing of it was that the medical profession's rage seemed largely misplaced. There was little doubt that rates for malpractice coverage and the number of claims against doctors were rising in Mississippi but no evidence that lawsuits were the primary cause. Other possibilities—policies underpriced because of competition among insurers, actuarial mistakes, investment losses in the 2001 stock market downturn, increased medical costs, more injuries and maladies, more doctors and so more claims—were largely dismissed or ignored by medical professionals and their allies in business and politics. Some lawyers and the outsize fees that financed their ostentatious lifestyles deserved opprobrium, especially in a state perennially among the nation's poorest. Yet targeting attorneys and the ostensibly misguided jurors who let them have their way seemed more a matter of opportunism than merit.[43]

This was the message that Reeves and his three colleagues sweating in a Cessna that August morning in 2002 aimed to convey personally and urgently to the Mississippians on their route. Reeves had left the US attorney's office the year before and, along with Pigott and Cliff Johnson, a younger lawyer in the office, and a fourth attorney formed a firm that did all kinds of work—representing injury victims, white-collar criminals, underpaid workers, and the occasional business or utility. A firm specialty, though, was related to the anti-health-care fraud effort that Pigott had made a priority as US attorney: representing whistleblowers against dodgy health-care providers. Lawsuits, Reeves knew, were often an effective way to hold bad doctors accountable, and his experience gave weight to what he had to say.

The first stop on the barnstorming tour: Greenville. Baria, as the trial lawyers' association president-elect, took the lead, telling the small crowd of reporters and attorneys and the attorneys' political allies gathered before the Mid-Delta Regional Airport terminal: "Today we hope we can tone down the hysteria and concentrate on the facts." Here in the Delta near his Yazoo City roots, Reeves stepped up to offer the "facts" of how "we trust the right to a jury," a right "premised on everyday citizens being able to understand and appreciate" the need to provide redress to the victims of wrongdoing. After Greenville it was on to the other towns, where the four lawyers took turns making their case, and it was not always well received. One doctor told a reporter that without limits on lawsuits "you're going to have people die from lack of medical care."[44] These were hard convictions to dislodge, cemented more firmly in people's minds with the harsh assessments of big-money organizations from out of state. In 2002 the American Tort Reform Association, a national business group that advocated for the squelching of lawsuits, released the first issue of what would become an annual provocation. The report included Jefferson, Claiborne, and Copiah counties among the nation's judicial "hellholes," places where "equal justice for all" had been forgotten.[45] The designation was meant to highlight how businesses sued in these counties could not get a fair shake, but it came across as offensively ironic for an area that had long been a true hellhole for its many Black residents, some the descendants of enslaved men and women, when they had sought even a modicum of justice, let alone equal justice.

The four lawyers' jaunt across the state of Mississippi seemed in danger of falling short of its hoped-for impact—even among one-time allies. On the morning of August 23, 2002, Governor Ronnie Musgrave, an attorney and Democrat and recipient of substantial trial-lawyer backing, made a serious miscalculation. While assuming the support of lawyers would remain rock solid, he thought he could also attract the support of businesses with a gesture of conciliation. He would convene a special session of the state legislature to consider the business proposals.[46] The reaction from the lawyers was predictable. Verbally and politically, "he got the shit kicked out of him," said one prominent attorney. The special session started on September 5 and lasted eighty-three days, the longest in Mississippi history. On most of those days Reeves or one of his partners would sit with the trial lawyers on one side of the old Supreme Court chambers, their adversaries on the opposite side, shouts and derisive laughter sometimes marring a veneer of cordiality as the House committee responsible for considering limits on lawsuits heard testimony.

Most of the action occurred behind closed doors, though, with the warring voices no less harsh for their molasses drawls. After the first thirty days the trial lawyers' supporters acceded to legislation that in medical malpractice cases capped at $500,000 so-called noneconomic damages for things like pain and suffering, shielded certain defendants from those damages, and made it harder to sue drug prescribers.[47] After eighty-three days they agreed to a bill limiting where plaintiffs could sue, cracking down on advertising by out-of-state attorneys, and authorizing a fine for filing frivolous cases. In the end, further wrangling seemed counterproductive. House Speaker Tim Ford said he feared the lengthy deadlock "was damaging the House."[48] Others were less high-minded. "I will be glad to see this place in my taillights in my rear-view mirror," said Rep. John Moore, a Republican leader from tiny Pearl, Mississippi.[49]

As it happened, the fighting was far from over. Just two years later, the legislature would be back at it, imposing further constraints on victims' access to court and the amount of damages they could recover there. The new law came easier this time, helped along by a new Republican governor, Haley Barbour, who had staked his campaign on the business benefits of reforming civil justice.[50] Whether the measures had the desired effect would long be disputed, but their impact on lawyers and the people who hired them was clear. "They affected us all," Reeves recalls. "There were lots of cases, good cases, we could no longer afford to take on," mostly because of the limits on recoveries.

Yeah, He Stumped Him

As the political skirmishes played out between trial lawyers and business interests, Democrats and Republicans, an alarming case landed in the offices of Pigott, Reeves, Johnson & Minor. It was a case that would touch on Reeves's past, shape his future, and confirm to him yet again how hard it was becoming for a target of clear wrongdoing to seek satisfaction in court. Around suppertime on July 22, 2005, Damalas Bouldin, a young Black man who worked maintenance at a semi-pro baseball park, was heading north on Route 49 toward his home in Mendenhall, Mississippi. He was tired, a little high, and something about the way his car moved down the road caused a highway patrolman to give chase. Bouldin slowed to the right, as if he were pulling to a stop, then thought better of it and gunned the accelerator. The officer did not request assistance, but he radioed word of the pursuit, and before long cars from the state department of transportation and the Simpson County sheriff's office had fallen in line behind him.[51]

Meanwhile, Jimmy Charles "Jimbo" Sullivan, the newly elected Mendenhall police chief, had just sat down to dinner with his wife and two fellow officers at the Country Fisherman restaurant near Route 49 when his dispatcher pinged his cellphone to say there was a car chase headed his way. Sullivan did not hesitate. "We're pulling out," he told the dispatcher. With Sullivan and his wife in one car and the two officers in a second, they reached the road in time to see Bouldin and the police cruisers, lights pulsing, on the horizon. They pulled in behind as the procession flashed by, bringing to five the number of vehicles in pursuit of Bouldin. Within a few miles, now surrounded by cop cars, Bouldin pulled a U-turn and swung into the southbound lane, but it was over. He sat in his car and waited, his hands above his head. "Open the door!" someone screamed. Bouldin froze. "I was too afraid to put my hands down because I didn't want to get shot," he said later in a deposition.[52]

The back door opened behind him, and he felt a gun against his head. It was Sullivan's. An arm wrapped around his neck and pulled him from the car and onto the ground, face down. One man sat on his ankles. A second man kneeled on his back and handcuffed his wrists. Bouldin lay motionless, eyes closed and praying that he would not get shot, as screams and sirens echoed around him. Then Sullivan approached. The police chief lifted his foot and stomped down hard on Bouldin's head. He lifted his foot again and stomped again. And again. And again. At least five times Sullivan stomped on Bouldin's head, adding an occasional kick. A state trooper stood on the trunk of his cruiser, waiving his flashlight and yelling at Sullivan to stop. Blood began to flow from Bouldin's mouth and chin. Another trooper ran to his car for bandages. When it was over, after the cops had thrown Bouldin onto the hood of a car and wrenched his arm up behind his back and finally called an ambulance, the two officers who had been with Sullivan earlier at the Country Fisherman restaurant walked back to their car.

"Where did all that blood come from that was on the ground?" asked one.

"Man, Jimbo stumped the shit out of that guy," the other replied.

"Do what?"

"Yeah, he stumped him."

"What the hell did he do that for?"

"I don't know."[53]

Bouldin would spend the next three days in the hospital. Gashes on his chin and face were stitched, a split tooth was repaired, his neck was wrapped in a brace, and a cocktail of painkillers was administered to numb his throbbing arm and head. Police officers came and went, asking for his statement. They charged him with speeding, possessing marijuana, driving under the influence, and failing to yield to an emergency vehicle.

Through friends Bouldin found a local lawyer, who eventually referred the case to Reeves. "It was a bad case," Reeves said. "It was totally unjustifiable what this police officer did." Yet he knew too well what Bouldin was up against. As a young lawyer at Phelps Dunbar, Reeves had been on the other side, defending errant cops and blind-eyed cities, and suing them for this sort of behavior was near futile. He also believed that Sullivan deserved severe punishment, and that's where his and his partners' connections at the US attorney's office in Jackson came in handy. Though qualified immunity protected police in civil cases, it did not apply in criminal prosecutions. On July 19, 2006, Reeves sued Sullivan and the City of Mendenhall and Simpson County on Bouldin's behalf, but he also "made sure that the federal authorities knew" about the details of the incident.[54] In late January 2009 prosecutors filed charges, and Sullivan pleaded guilty in exchange for a deal that would require him to serve twenty-seven months in prison. In April a federal judge sentenced him to thirty months, increasing the sentence because he had only grudgingly accepted responsibility.[55]

As is often true when criminal and civil cases are filed, Bouldin's lawsuit was put on hold while the prosecution of Sullivan played out. The hold was lifted after Sullivan pleaded guilty, and representing the City of Mendenhall were Reeves's former colleagues at Phelps Dunbar, who were well versed in the rules of the game. Even though the city admitted that the former police chief's "assault of the Plaintiff [Bouldin] was an inhumane, cowardice act that should not have occurred," Mendenhall could be held liable only if Sullivan had been following a "policy or custom" of the municipality in kicking hell out of the victim. To the extent a policy existed at all, it barred Sullivan from joining the chase and having his wife in the car. Reeves countered that as the chief of police, Sullivan himself was the policymaker on pursuits and car stops, but the argument failed.[56] In April 2011 the federal judge dismissed all claims against Mendenhall and Sullivan, at least to the extent he was acting in his official capacity. The claims against him in his personal capacity survived and were settled for a small amount.

It would be unfair to say that Bouldin came away with almost nothing, however. The various charges against him were dismissed, although he agreed to plead guilty to driving without car insurance. The lawsuit drew widespread attention to the racist abuses of law enforcement in Mississippi—and to the sorry state of the law on suing cops—even though the case yielded Bouldin no money. And the criminal case against Sullivan ensured that he would spend substantial time in jail—no small feat anywhere in America, let alone in the Deep South. "We hope other law enforcement officials will learn from this prosecution that you cannot violate the civil rights of citizens of this country," Reeves said after Sullivan pleaded guilty. "It is 2009, not 1959."[57]

. . .

It was also early days for a historic presidency, a week after Barack Obama became the nation's first African American president. In

Mississippi the man who had Obama's ear was Bennie Thompson, and he was acutely aware of the opportunities that all the newly vacant federal offices presented for other Black people. Reeves had kept in touch with the congressman and would from time to time run into him at fundraisers and meetings of the Magnolia Bar Association. On one such occasion Reeves approached his powerful and well-connected friend with a broad smile and glad hand and casually mentioned that he thought that he, Reeves, might make a good US attorney. "But I want to remind you," Reeves continued, maybe pushing his luck, "that there's a vacancy on the federal court in Jackson."

5   *What a Judge Does*

"You will be very lonely. It's the nature of the job." Jed Rakoff pondered this nugget of advice and quickly concluded that the earnest psychologist at the front of the bright-white classroom in Richmond, Virginia, did not know what he was talking about. Jed Rakoff lonely? The gregarious and curious and tons-of-friends Jed Rakoff? Please. As the day wore on and the speakers arrived and departed, the advice kept coming. "You have to live with yourself" and "It all depends on your personality" and "Here's what your health insurance looks like." If the lessons sounded mundane, their aims were nonetheless ambitious: to prepare the new judges assembled that April day in 1996 for an honored and influential but sometimes lonely life of public service, to convey the nuts and bolts and occasional frustrations of moving cases through a federal trial court. The lessons were the essence of what was officially known as the weeklong Phase One Orientation Seminar for Newly Appointed District Judges. Or, as it was fondly called, "baby judge school."[1]

Rakoff sat among the dozen or so other jurists because he had made it, although as often happens, there was a hitch along the way. In 1995 he applied for a judgeship and was invited to interview before a committee of litigators, professors, and journalists assembled by the then senior senator from New York, Daniel Patrick Moynihan, who would select the eventual nominee. Rakoff aced that preliminary interview, then spoke with Moynihan, and rather than judicial philosophy or anything related to judging, the two went on and on about India, where Moynihan had served as the US ambassador, and Mahatma Gandhi, about whom Rakoff had written his master's thesis. Rakoff got the nod from the senator and survived his hearing before the Senate Judiciary Committee, when in December, with the government mired in a shutdown and President Bill Clinton and House Speaker Newt Gingrich sniping over the federal budget, his nomination stalled.

Just before Christmas, Rakoff took his family on vacation to Steamboat Springs, Colorado, and called Moynihan's office periodically for any news. It did not look good. The Senate had decided to resume voting on judicial nominations, but Rakoff, his name starting with R, was far down the alphabetical list. Finally, just before the New Year, with Congress about to adjourn, word came that the nomination looked dead. Rakoff took the news hard, but as is his habit, he willed his disappointment behind him. He went skiing for the day and planned a family dinner. That night, as he waited in his rented SUV to go to the restaurant, his wife and three daughters went back inside the condo for extra sweaters. Minutes later, they returned and surrounded the car. While in the condo, they had answered the phone, and on the line had been a member of Moynihan's staff. The Senate had voted after all. "You're a judge!" they screamed as they bounced around the car.

What exactly did that mean? Rakoff, a sophisticated litigator who had appeared in court hundreds of times and witnessed the good and bad of judging, thought he knew. And he did, at least in a general way. In the hierarchy of the federal courts, a district judge like Rakoff was about to be is near the bottom, just one of forty-four district court judges in the Southern District of New York and of more than 660 across the nation.[2] Above them sit the thirteen active judges of the Second Circuit, who are among the almost 180 judges that serve on thirteen US courts of appeals.[3] Above them are the nine justices of the US Supreme Court. Helping these roughly 860 jurists is a small army of supporting players, from security officers to US marshals to docket clerks, courtroom clerks, and law clerks.[4]

The workload is mind-boggling. A typical trial judge may handle more than 1,000 cases a year. In the twelve months ending June 30, 2024, more than 430,000 new cases landed in district courts and almost 40,000 in appeals courts.[5] The Supreme Court grandees issued a leisurely sixty opinions during their October 2023 term.[6] Those almost half a million cases delved into every aspect of American life: broken promises, damaged belongings, clever rip-offs, lost jobs, company secrets, trampled rights, technical breaches of arcane rules, crimes ranging from the horrific to the inconsequential. Rakoff understood this, yet like all new judges, he did not necessarily know how to *do* the job. That's why in 1967 the Federal Judicial Center, the education and research agency for the federal courts, launched baby judge school. Even then, critics worried that the system was getting overloaded, that "lazy" judges were creating backlogs and a "crisis in the courts" was brewing.[7] The solution, many concluded, was "systems management" and teaching new judges about "docket management"—finding ways to pick up the pace in court. By the 1990s, with the US Chamber of Commerce and GOP politicians and insurance companies warning that the crisis was becoming a disaster for the nation's competitive standing, docket management took on the tone of a holy crusade.

In baby judge school, according to some judges, the training at the time emphasized how to move cases out of court rather than how to hear and decide them. In a lecture on handling civil rights lawsuits, the instructor began with some advice. "Here's how to get rid of those cases!" recalled Nancy Gertner, a former US district judge in Boston who attended the course in 1994. As for opinions, they were to be avoided as too time-consuming. "The message I heard then," said Gertner, "and from trainers later on was, if you wrote an opinion, you failed." Mark Bennett, who left the district court bench in 2019 and attended a different session in 1994, had a similar experience. "There was a tremendous emphasis on case management and how to move cases rather than on how to manage trials," he recalled. "I thought I was a trial judge." The lessons were of a piece with the recommendations emerging from the Judicial Conference of the United States—the federal courts' governing body, headed by then US chief justice William Rehnquist. Its 1995 report, "Long Range Plan for the Federal Courts," stressed using "alternative dispute resolution techniques" in "private forums" like arbitration, tightening discovery, and settling cases.[8]

Rakoff remembered lots of discussion in his 1996 course about case management but nothing about getting rid of cases or avoiding written opinions. And much of what he did remember learning proved spot-on. As he would discover after officially taking the bench on March 1, 1996, being a judge *was* sometimes lonely, and that surprised him. Part of the reason may have been, at least initially, that he was first posted in his court's White Plains, New York, division, away from Manhattan's invigorating hubbub. Yet even friendships were somehow different. "The old joke is, when you go on the bench, you suddenly develop a great sense of humor, and you know that because everyone laughs at your jokes," he said. "But the other side of that is, you know that people are treating you differently not because of the merits but because you're a judge."

Rakoff felt lucky because, unlike some of his colleagues, he had a family to ease the feeling of isolation. He drew great comfort from Ann, his wife of, at that time, twenty-two years, and his three young daughters—Jena, Elana, and Keira. Like other judges, he also had a sort of family at work, his law clerks—the two (and later three) recent and invariably brilliant law school graduates who drafted memos and fielded his calls and absorbed his teachings for a year. They were especially important during his first year on the bench as Rakoff was getting his chambers up and running. His first clerk, Rachel Fleishman, interviewed his secretary for him, arranged to get furniture for his office, and helped generally with logistics, in addition to researching the law and writing memos and all the substantive chores demanded of a law clerk. She and her co-clerk usually worked from 8:00 in the morning to 10:00 at night. (The next year Rakoff hired a third clerk to ease the load.)

The long hours and need to rely on each other typically lead judges and clerks to develop close and enduring relationships. Rakoff brought a remarkable warmth to the work. "This is a person with real emotional intelligence," said Fleishman. Even in court, Rakoff has fun with his clerks. During a hearing, one clerk passed him a note asking that he put a question to Robert F. Kennedy Jr., who was there representing an environmental group. The clerk just wanted to hear him speak. "Mr. Kennedy, we haven't heard anything from you," the judge said a few minutes later. "Is there anything that you would like to add?" After listening to Kennedy vamp for a bit, Rakoff nodded subtly to the clerk across the courtroom, who smiled and nodded back. "What I do for my clerks," the judge laughed on their way back to chambers.

A second thing that surprised Rakoff about the job was how many difficult issues a trial judge routinely faces. "You'd be amazed at how many cases raise issues that no one else has decided," he said. That creates a degree of leeway and responsibility that some judges avoid by ducking tough calls. Not Rakoff. "The other side of that coin is that's turned out to be one of the thrilling parts of the job," he added. "We get the first crack. You know, the Supreme Court gets the last crack, and you can get reversed, and I've certainly been reversed, but nevertheless, the first person to take a look at this issue is us little trial judges, and that is such a thrill." Yet his enthusiasm, which has allowed him to seek facts and resolve questions that might otherwise have gone unresolved, has also led to trouble.

Perilously Close to Simple Murder

On a morning in July 2000, Rakoff arrived at his chambers on the thirteenth floor of the Daniel Patrick Moynihan United States Courthouse in Manhattan, entering his wood-paneled office through the shadowed entrance in the corner of the back wall, the elevator reserved for judges just outside. It was dead quiet. On the right stood his desk, its heavy glass top cluttered with papers, a snow globe with a tiny photo of Rakoff himself inside, a baseball with the sun-faded signature of Yankees ace relief pitcher Mariano Rivera, and other mementos collected over his four years on the bench. Beyond it a wall of windows looked west over the paved confines of Foley Square and beneath the windows stood an electronic keyboard that Rakoff used to compose songs for courthouse follies and other extravaganzas—a reminder of his long-retired ambition to write Broadway musicals. To the left and straight ahead, floor-to-ceiling shelves brimmed with fading photos—his wife, his three daughters, his mother, his father's bar mitzvah, the judges and lawyers who had served as his mentors—along with tomes on the law and politics and framed poems and lyrics he wrote for the weddings and birthdays of friends.

One can imagine Rakoff barely pausing before heading to the compact kitchen off the reception area in search of a cup of Starbucks dark coffee, the first of maybe eight—creamer, four Splenda—that he would consume in the course of a day. His clerks would leave a stack of papers—briefs, complaints, memoranda—in an inbox just outside his office, and on this morning, caffeine elixir in hand, Rakoff tucked the top document under his arm, went back to his desk, and began to read. The document told the story of Alan Quinones, one of nine recently indicted heroin and cocaine dealers in the Bronx. It was a horrific tale. When Quinones was growing up, his mother had a Valium addiction, five kids under the age of five, and a habit of playing the numbers just to pay for food. Quinones's father, illiterate and unemployed, took to the streets to escape with drugs and alcohol. The family lived in shelters and welfare hotels and apartments—more than ten before Quinones was twelve. In this chaotic and brutal world, Quinones grew up and began to provide for his family, the one he already had and the one he would try to create. There may have been something noble about this had he not done it in a destructive and criminal way: through the drug trade. And unfortunately he was good at it.

In the late 1990s he built a cocaine operation that moved the drug from a wholesaler in Florida to his apartment in the Bronx. There was also the heroin side of the business that Quinones ran out of the apartment of his girlfriend, Janet Soto. He procured heroin from various sources, and either he or his chief lieutenant, Diego Rodriguez, sold it on consignment to vendors who parceled it out in $100 packets to managers and then runners for sale on the streets. In this operation there were rules that barred selling during "school hours"—between 1:00 and 3:00 p.m.—and tainting the product and stealing and using counterfeit money and, especially, snitching. "Snitches get stitches" was the expression; they got beaten or even killed.

In March 1999 one of Quinones's vendors, Edwin Santiago, introduced him to a man who twice bought small packets of heroin directly from Quinones and, after the second purchase, arrested him. The man was an undercover police officer, and Santiago, it was now clear, was a snitch. Quinones, out on bail, went after him, telling compatriots he was going "to put Santiago's head in a box." He and two accomplices lured Santiago to Soto's apartment, threw him to the floor, handcuffed him, hogtied him, spit in his face, beat him, and finally suffocated him with duct tape that covered his nose and mouth. After dragging the body outside, Quinones's henchmen doused it with gasoline and set it on fire. They used a shopping cart to wheel the charred remains to a van, drove them to a vacant lot, and dumped them in the mud. On July 20, 2000, prosecutors indicted ten people in the case on racketeering and narcotics charges and four, including Quinones, on charges of murder.[9]

Rakoff had as a prosecutor encountered grisly crimes before, and Santiago was far from a sympathetic character. Yet this one gnawed at him. The bludgeoning. The fire. It might be a death penalty case, an uncommon occurrence even in state court—where most criminal cases end up—but a possibility so rare in federal court that it had been years since any judge in the Southern District of New York had heard one. Rakoff wasn't keen on even thinking about whether he would be the next, and at least for a while, he could put the issue out of his mind. Over the next fifteen months all ten defendants but three—Quinones, Rodriguez, and Soto—pleaded guilty to various crimes, removing them from the case. Meanwhile, with the threat of a death sentence looming over their clients, lawyers for the remaining three engaged in long and intense meetings with prosecutors to argue that capital punishment would not be justified. Many of the meetings occurred at the US Justice Department in Washington, DC, where Attorney General John Ashcroft, a staunch proponent of the death penalty, had in about a dozen cases already overruled US attorneys who had decided not to seek capital punishment. In this case, against the recommendation of the US attorney's office in Manhattan, Ashcroft would do it again.[10]

On October 26, 2001, at a pretrial conference in Rakoff's courtroom, prosecutors announced that they would try for a sentence of death. Rakoff's first response was to set a schedule for the parties to submit death-penalty-related motions. It was his second response that startled most everyone in the courtroom—and later many outside of it too. "I will tell you one issue that I would think might be helpful to the court to have briefed," he began. Rakoff noted that there had been many cases of innocent people being convicted—and perhaps even put to death. "So I guess the question that that would lead any reasonable person to ask is[:] is a form of penalty that precludes forever rectification of err[or]s that go to actual innocence a form of penalty that accords with the Constitution?"[11] In other words, was capital punishment illegal? The obvious answer: No. Since it had reinstated the death penalty in 1976, the Supreme Court had ruled time and again, and in the face of persistent challenges, that executing eligible criminals passed constitutional muster.[12] So the obvious question: Why was Rakoff, a district court judge, even asking?

A big reason was DNA testing. In 1987, New York lawyers Barry Scheck and Peter Neufeld used basic detective work—ferreting out faulty witness testimony and contradictory blood-test results—to persuade a judge to overturn the rape conviction of Marion Coakley, a manual laborer in the Bronx with an IQ under 80.[13] After an Illinois lawyer relied on DNA tests for the first time to exonerate someone unjustly convicted, in that case alleged rapist Gary Dotson, Scheck and Neufeld recognized the power of this sort of evidence and took more cases on behalf of the wrongly accused.[14] Their success bred demand, and in 1992 they determined that a criminal justice system so flawed that it was ruining (and in some cases ending) the lives of an unknown number of innocent people cried out for a systematic and organized response. The Innocence Project was born.[15] By the time the Quinones case landed in Rakoff's courtroom, scores of death-row inmates had been found "factually innocent"—at least a dozen by DNA testing—through the efforts of the Innocence Project and similar organizations that had emerged around the nation. To the judge, "this was mind blowing."[16] As a prosecutor and later a defense lawyer, Rakoff had taken to heart the words of celebrated Judge Learned Hand: "Our procedure has always been haunted by the ghost of the innocent man convicted. It is an unreal dream." Rakoff figured that "maybe once in a blue moon we might make a mistake, but boy, is it rare. Hah! Little did I know."

Still, in the face of Supreme Court precedent, it seemed hardly the place of a trial judge to question whether the death penalty was constitutional—or even to raise the issue when none of the lawyers had. Rakoff disagreed. He believed a good judge spoke up when the law diverged from justice, when circumstances had changed so much that a statute or case law no longer made sense. He also believed that there was nothing unique about his view. England and then early America had a strong tradition of common law judging—questioning precedent that could lead to bad results.[17] That approach faded quickly, with US judges constrained by legislation and the role of courts under the Constitution, but it made a lot of sense to Rakoff, especially in a capital case.

Another factor was at play. It was the Antiterrorism and Effective Death Penalty Act, the 1996 law that sharply narrowed the ability of federal judges to second-guess convictions and limited access to court for even wrongly convicted death-row inmates challenging their sentences.[18] Those sorts of restrictions made it imperative for judges and juries to get it right the first time, before condemning anyone to die. In any event, Rakoff knew he was going out on a limb, and he would be cautious. Late in the evening shortly after the pretrial conference, alone in the hush of his office, the judge stood facing his tall bookcases, pulling down heavy volumes, *U.S. Reports*, the official compilation of Supreme Court opinions. What he was looking for were cases where the guilt of murderers sentenced to death was in doubt. He found five. The next night, ten more. Over the following weeks, he came up with more than thirty, instructing his clerks to research the details by day. Then he found it: a 1993 case that, the more Rakoff looked at it, the more he turned it over in his mind, persuaded him that a majority of justices then on the Supreme Court believed putting an innocent person to death—and consequently erasing any hope of fixing the tragic mistake—offended the Constitution. It was not a straightforward conclusion, but piecing together the justices' opinions and using his own creativity gave Rakoff enough to make an argument.

It went something like this: In 1982 a Texas jury convicted and sentenced forty-three-year-old Leonel Herrera to death for murdering two police officers. He appealed his conviction and lost, then filed a state habeas corpus petition—basically a claim that he was unconstitutionally imprisoned and should be released—and it was denied. Herrera then filed a habeas petition in federal court, and it was also denied. Yet in 1992, ten years after his sentencing, he filed a second federal habeas petition based on purportedly new evidence of his actual innocence—his brother was really the killer, Herrera said—and the Supreme Court turned him down.[19] Yet the justices seemed to struggle with the case, and they issued the kind of fragmented opinions that can trip up anyone trying to make sense of them. Chief Justice William Rehnquist wrote for the majority, with four other justices joining him, including Sandra Day O'Connor, who wrote a separate concurring opinion, which Anthony Kennedy joined. Antonin Scalia also wrote a concurring opinion, which Clarence Thomas joined. Byron White wrote an opinion concurring in the judgment, which nobody joined. And Harry Blackmun wrote a fiery dissent, which John Paul Stevens and David Souter joined, but only in part. What their collected works amounted to was a 6–3 ruling that evidence of actual innocence was not ordinarily enough to entitle a prisoner to a new hearing.

There was wiggle room in the decision, however, and Rakoff found it. Even the chief justice had entertained the idea, "for the sake of argument," that "a truly persuasive demonstration of 'actual innocence' made after trial would render the execution of a defendant unconstitutional."[20] Blackmun took the extraordinary approach of reading his dissent from the bench, and he sounded appalled. "Nothing could be . . . more shocking to the conscience," he said, "than to execute a person who is actually innocent." It "comes perilously close to simple murder."[21] The revelation for Rakoff, though, came with O'Connor's opinion, which Kennedy joined. The two had signed on to the majority, but the very first sentence of this separate opinion said: "I cannot disagree with the fundamental legal principle that executing the innocent is inconsistent with the Constitution."[22]

So there it was—three justices in dissent (Blackmun, Stevens, and Souter), plus two justices (O'Connor and Kennedy) concurring, equaled five of nine justices saying capital punishment for an innocent person would be unconstitutional. It wasn't an actual ruling, but given a case that squarely raised the issue, couldn't it be? The strong possibility of putting innocent people to death, Rakoff concluded, made capital punishment unconstitutional. Even then the judge trod cautiously. His theory needed testing, and there was skepticism. "Initially, all three of my law clerks said, 'Oh, it's totally wrong,'" Rakoff recalled. Yet as they worked through a draft opinion with him, they came around. The weight of the evidence was just too compelling.

When the draft was finished, it was clear and simple and maybe even persuasive. Despite the high standard of proof and procedural rules and opportunities for appeal and other safeguards of the criminal justice system, the draft argued, innocent people had been condemned to death and possibly executed. DNA testing made this so far beyond dispute that it could surely provide the kind of "truly persuasive demonstration" of innocence that Rehnquist had hypothetically been looking for in Herrera's case. But if the government ignored that tragic fact, if it cut short people's chance to show that they did not commit a crime, wasn't that, to put it mildly, unfair—in legal terms, a violation of their right to the process they were reasonably due under the Constitution? Sure, the Fifth Amendment contemplates capital punishment—it talks about not depriving anyone "of life . . . without due process of law"—but no one in 1791 and relatively few even in 1991 dreamed of DNA testing or other means of proving innocence so easily and definitively. Accounting for the evolving state of science and moral awareness, the draft concluded, there was no way that the death penalty could be constitutional.

And yet Rakoff was cautious still. As a reality check he did something that he had never done before and hasn't done since. He ventured across the courthouse and ran the opinion past another judge, Leonard Sand, twenty-five years his senior and a jurist with the kind of solid judgment and taste for bold decisions that the younger man admired. "Am I completely off the wall here?" Rakoff asked. "Is this beyond what a judge should be doing?" Sand said no. Next, Rakoff approached someone else whose judgment he trusted: his younger brother Todd, a professor at Harvard Law School. "I said to him," Rakoff recalled, "don't tell me whether you agree or disagree, just tell me whether you think this is a plausible legal theory, one that is not crazy, or whether I'm missing something." Todd took two days to respond but also told his brother the opinion's reasoning was sound. Even that was not enough to ease Rakoff's mind completely. He wanted to give the government another shot at poking holes in his logic. At a hearing in March 2002, having read the parties' briefs, one side telling him in effect that he was a legal genius and the other that he was nuts, the judge conceded: "I appreciate the fact that this issue is somewhat novel." A month later, Rakoff released his opinion but with a condition: There would be one more round of briefing before his final decision.

Almost lost in the back-and-forth over the death penalty was the actual case before him. Of the ten original defendants, Quinones and Rodriguez still awaited trial, while Soto, Quinones's girlfriend, had recently joined the other seven in entering a guilty plea. On a sweltering day in June 2002, she and her lawyer appeared before the judge to be sentenced—twenty years in exchange for admitting that she had conspired to commit murder. Before Rakoff officially pronounced her punishment, though, the mother of the murder victim, Edwin Santiago, rose to speak. She turned to address Soto. "You have no idea the pain and agony you have caused me," she began. "You took away my firstborn son." As Rakoff listened, a sorrow inside him began to stir; it was the closest he would come to crying on the bench. When Santiago's mother was finished and before she sat down, he told her something that he had never shared with the world and preferred to avoid discussing even with his closest friends. "Let me say," he began, "that I understand more fully than you might realize the pain you feel."[23]

He Deserved to Rot in Hell

In the small hours of a winter morning in 1985, the brittle ring of a telephone broke the silence at Rakoff's home in suburban Larchmont, New York. He and his wife and daughters asleep upstairs failed to hear it. A few hours later, at about 7:00 a.m., the phone rang again. Rakoff answered. It was Todd Rakoff, Jed's brother. He said he had terrible news. Their older brother, Jan, was dead. Murdered. The details were still spotty.

Jan had been living in the Philippines, working with the government to develop schools based on his innovative theories of education. Jan's relationship with Jed had had its ups and downs, but when they last saw each other just a few months before, Jed was struck by how upbeat his brother seemed. Jan's theories were gaining recognition, and he was apparently in love, living at the time in Hawaii with a young man named Tai. The world was finally turning his way, deservedly so, given that he was considered the most brilliant member of the family. Now, at the age of forty-four, Jan was dead. How could it have happened?

Jan had been in Manila and was in his bungalow in a gated community one evening with a young male prostitute. The two quarreled over payment. At some point the prostitute grabbed an ice pick and some sort of iron pipe and bludgeoned and stabbed Jan to death. He then set the bungalow on fire to try to cover the deed, but a security guard saw him fleeing and grabbed him. By morning, the killer had delivered a written confession to the police.

After hearing of Jan's murder, Rakoff got off the phone with Todd, called their mother, and made plans to leave for his boyhood home in Germantown. There they would meet and try to console each other and make arrangements for Jan's funeral. His death was traumatic for the entire family, of course, but Doris Rakoff had it especially hard. She had lost her husband of more than two decades just a few years before, and it would have been understandable if she had felt overwhelmed, rendered helpless by her grief. Instead, she faced the moment of crisis with poise and strength, focusing on the logistics of what had to be done in a way that amazed Rakoff. He took it as a model of how to act, how to be. He resolved that he too would not let the horror of his brother's violent death throw his wife or his children or his work off stride. His resolve would soon be tested. When Jan's body arrived in Philadelphia a few days later, his face was so battered and torn that Rakoff could hardly recognize it. The image rattled him, giving him nightmares for years to come. When he thought about the man who had done this to his brother, Rakoff wanted him dead. "The guy deserved to rot in hell," he recalled thinking.

That would not happen, at least not yet. The Manila police "lost" the murderer's confession, and he seemed on his way to freedom before an American diplomat produced a copy and pressed the prosecution forward. Even then, the dysfunctional and probably corrupt system of justice in the Philippines at the time found a way to give the guy a break—a plea deal that landed him in jail for three years. The anger, the absolute fury that Rakoff felt about his brother's death and this travesty of justice, kept him silent about the episode—until that day almost two decades later when he spoke to Edwin Santiago's mother from the bench. "Twenty years ago," Rakoff told her, "my older brother was murdered in cold blood."[24] It was a spontaneous reaction, perhaps a kind of release from the pain that he had kept inside for so long. Yet as much as his personal experience might demand it, and as clear as the evidence was of Quinones's guilt, Rakoff could not be dissuaded from his belief that it was unconstitutional to impose an irrevocable sentence that might result in the execution of any innocent person. On July 1 he issued a final decision that left no doubt where he stood. Execution under the federal death penalty law "is tantamount to foreseeable, state-sponsored murder of innocent human beings," Rakoff concluded.[25]

Press reaction was swift, blunt, and more than a little skeptical, delivered sometimes in admiration but often with caustic disdain. "The heart of [Rakoff's] reasoning is unassailable," wrote *Newsday* in an editorial.[26] The *New York Times* seemed no less impressed—"a cogent, powerful argument that all members of Congress—indeed, all Americans—should contemplate"—but warned of a reversal on appeal.[27] Yet under the headline "Run for Office, Judge," the *Wall Street Journal* probably spoke for many when it advised that "if Judge Rakoff wants to vote against the death penalty, he ought to resign from the bench and run for Congress or the state legislature, where the Founders thought such debates belonged."[28] What the critics may have been underestimating was the novelty of the ruling. Rakoff's argument was not the typical one that capital punishment was cruel or unusual, but a simpler appeal to logic that even anti-death-penalty activists had never publicly made. Putting people to death who could now, unlike a few years before, be proven innocent with unprecedented certainty was not a matter for legislation but a fundamental issue of fair, constitutional process. "I've been thinking about this issue in a serious way for at least twenty years," esteemed constitutional law professor Laurence Tribe told the *New York Times*, "and this is the first, fresh, new, and convincing argument that I've seen."[29]

For the US Court of Appeals in New York, known as the Second Circuit, the argument was none of those things. Prosecutors appealed Rakoff's ruling, and the higher court made swift work of it, issuing an opinion reversing the decision less than four months later. Writing for all three judges on the court panel, Jose Cabranes noted that "opponents of capital punishment 'began to argue that innocent people were often executed by mistake' as early as the mid-Nineteenth Century." Yet, he went on, "the Supreme Court has upheld state and federal statutes providing for capital punishment for over two hundred years . . . despite a clear recognition of the possibility that, because our judicial system—indeed, any judicial system—is fallible, innocent people might be executed and, therefore, lose any opportunity for exoneration." In any event, Cabranes concluded, "if the well-settled law on this issue is to change, that is a change that only the Supreme Court is authorized to make."[30]

Rakoff was disappointed but not entirely surprised, given how often challenges to capital punishment had failed. Yet he said "I never thought that my chances were zero because I thought I was right." In fact, he was hoping that even if the Second Circuit reversed him, the case would get to the Supreme Court, where he would "have a built-in ally," Justice O'Connor, on whose opinion in the *Herrera* case his theory turned. "I think it's totally correct to this day," he said. Still, Rakoff knew he was taking risks. One was political. Striking down the death penalty then, when crime rates were coming down but still relatively high, was like a Republican now supporting gun control or abortion—it probably doomed any aspirations for higher office. After he issued his initial decision back in April, Rakoff went home and told his wife, Ann.

"There goes any chance I had of going up on the Second Circuit," he said.

"Well, you're doing the right thing," she responded.

The other risk was not really a risk at all, certainly in his mind. It was that the public and legal scholars and maybe other judges would criticize him harshly, see him as a rogue judge, irresponsible for defying the Supreme Court. "That was not—and still is not—the law," said University of Texas Law School professor Lucas Powe of Rakoff's theory. "Judges have the duty to follow Supreme Court rulings."

Rakoff would agree, of course, but there's an argument that he was not so much defying the court as counting votes—five justices suggested in the *Herrera* case that executing an innocent person was unconstitutional. Besides, he explained, "I certainly would not agree that I should do it on a regular basis, and this is the only case I have done it, partly in my mind because of the stakes. Death is different, as they say. . . . I just thought, I'll throw it out there, and we'll see what the adversarial system does."

At the heart of the matter is the proper role of a district court judge. The *Wall Street Journal* editorial writers and a host of other people believed Rakoff had gone well beyond that role—as did the three Second Circuit judges who reversed his decision. Yet even on that court there was sympathy for his attempt to push the law in a new direction. "I wish there were more judges who were good enough to do that well," said Guido Calabresi, a senior judge on the Second Circuit. "We use those judges [to help develop the law]. There are situations where the possibility of change is real, and the Supreme Court used to welcome that sort of decision."

. . .

Quinones's case would finally go to trial on June 15, 2004. Rakoff would have to live with the Second Circuit's ruling, but still he found ways to express his dissatisfaction with the state of the law. During voir dire, the process of questioning potential jurors to see whether they are fit to serve, one potential juror said she had supported the death penalty until she began working in prisons as a lay minister. Though she met plenty of inmates who had committed horrific crimes, she was told some eloquent stories of redemption. "I know too many converted prisoners," she said. "I don't want to be in a place of God."

Rakoff had to excuse her because the law at the time barred jurors who strongly favored or opposed the death penalty from serving in a capital case. After she left, though, he turned to the lawyers to express his displeasure. "I think the Supreme Court has got this whole process completely wrong," he said, stressing that thoughtful people like her were exactly the sort who should be on a jury. "They come together, they reason together, they often change their mind or modify their views. They take very seriously, in my experience, the court's instructions, put aside their views and decide a case on the law." He paused and added: "In a matter as serious as this, I just think that it is a filthy business."

In the end, after a month of proceedings and ten days of deliberations, the jury convicted Quinones and his co-defendant of murdering Santiago and running a heroin and cocaine gang. The next day, on July 29, jurors reconvened to consider whether to impose the death penalty. Finally, on August 5, 2004, they reached a decision on the sentence: life in prison without parole.

6 *Opening the Courthouse Doors*

Jonathan Manuelito had been talking shit all day, and Reno Roy Russell had heard enough. The two cousins wobbled along the edge of Route 36 near Upper Fruitland, New Mexico, scuffing the baked dirt as they walked, too drunk on wine to notice the tangerine sun setting across the scrubby high desert of Navajo land. As they neared a cattle guard, a few rows of iron pipe spanning the road, Reno turned bleary-eyed to Jonathan, dreadlocked and at 250 pounds more than twice his size, and delivered a shove. His cousin tumbled into an irrigation ditch and in an instant Reno was on him, slashing with the knife he carried in his pocket, inflicting more than a dozen cuts to Jonathan's face, scalp, stomach, and hand. Reno rose and stretched his arms above his head like a prizefighter defiant in triumph and ambled off, his baggy white pants splattered with blood.

Later that evening in July 2004, after receiving a 911 call about a man sprawled in a ditch, Navajo Nation police officer Karletta Tso found Jonathan, bloodied but conscious, and rushed him to the county hospital. Jonathan was released within hours, and a few weeks later Reno was in custody, facing federal charges.[1] That they were federal charges rather than state or even tribal ones was not surprising but troubling nonetheless. In 1885 the US government had seized jurisdiction over most crimes on Indian reservations but failed to provide the courthouses, judges, prosecutors, or services necessary to handle them.[2] Rather than answer to officials who shared their culture and traditions and lived and worked among them, Native people dealt with strangers often hundreds of miles away. When punishment came down from a federal court for what almost anywhere else in the country would be a state crime—theft, fighting, setting a building on fire—it typically brought a harsher sentence, with no chance of parole.

For Reno Russell, an eighteen-year-old still in high school, that could mean eight years in prison rather than a probable one-year suspended sentence and probation in state court. A lot might depend on the judge who heard his case. As it happened, that judge would be Martha Vázquez. And in Reno Russell, rather than a criminal in need of punishment Vázquez saw a young man who could help his people. She had become a US district court judge in 1993, nominated by President Bill Clinton and approved without controversy in the Senate. The strong feeling among lawyers and especially Democrats in New Mexico was that it was past time—time for the first woman on the federal bench in the state, time for Vázquez as an accomplished attorney, and time for a Latina, especially a Mexican American. "Ten years before, I can't imagine her being tapped," said Todd Wertheim, a partner at Vázquez's old law firm.

The reason it had taken so long had much to do with the history of New Mexico, where blatant discrimination following US conquest of the territory in the Mexican-American War led many Mexicans—often of Indian, Spanish, and African heritage—to stress their Spanish roots, a choice that might allow them to be seen as "white" and entitled to the rights that the status conveyed.[3] Though no longer lawful, discrimination persisted well past Vázquez's arrival in the state in the 1970s. "I came to New Mexico at a time when being called Mexican was a bad word," she recalled. "I was so stunned by that. Even Mexican food was called Spanish food."[4] Vázquez's elevation to the bench brought honor and pride to her and the Santa Fe bar, but at first the job was grueling. Her four children were ages three, five, seven, and nine at the time, and during her confirmation hearings Senator Dianne Feinstein worried aloud about Vázquez's role as both a mother and judge. It is "one of the most difficult tasks for a woman," the senator and parent of a daughter said. "How do you raise a family and spend long hours at whatever your profession or vocation is."[5] Vázquez's husband, also a lawyer, shared the task of child-rearing equally, Vázquez assured the senator, but it would be too rarely true. The job required that on weekdays she sit occasionally on the bench in Las Cruces, New Mexico, about 285 miles south of Santa Fe, for three months at a time, with visits home on weekends. It left Vázquez often unable to keep her side of the child-rearing bargain, and it took its toll on her children and eventually her marriage.

Then, in October 1995, Vázquez got a death penalty case. Like almost all cases, it was randomly assigned, but it felt as if the universe had singled her out for a test of stamina. There were twenty-three defendants, members of the infamously brutal Sureño 13, a gang with origins in Southern California and ambitions to expand a crack cocaine empire into Albuquerque, New Mexico, through murder and violence so terrifying that competitors could only succumb. Over more than two years, prosecutors claimed, the gang collectively committed at least seven murders and engaged in countless drug transactions that amounted to a vast and well-organized conspiracy. For three of the defendants the charges could result in death sentences.

A decade before, Vázquez had tried a potential death penalty case as a public defender, helping to save Modesto Martinez from a murder conviction, so she knew how intense and draining the experience could be. But nothing prepared her for the awesome responsibility of handling a capital case as a new judge with young children, a heavy caseload, and an arduous travel schedule. The tasks and minutiae were mind-boggling. Vázquez had to appoint, at public expense, two lawyers for each defendant and track vouchers to ensure they were paid. She had to sift through hundreds of pleadings and a list of 650 exhibits and 250 proposed witnesses. She had to sever the defendants' cases into six groups. Jury selection started and stopped. Opening arguments were postponed. Her rulings were appealed to the Tenth Circuit three times before a trial could even start.

To deal with the mounting stress, Vázquez went running through Santa Fe's streets twice each day, once in the morning and again at lunch. She began to have head-splitting migraines. She was exhausted and withered to near skin and bones. "I felt very alone during that time in my life," she recalled, "because I hadn't gotten close to my colleagues, and I didn't have my former colleagues to talk to about that case. It was extremely isolating, and it was extremely difficult."[6] Mercifully, the defendants eventually pleaded guilty, one by one, and by June 1999, almost four years after the case had started, each of the last three—the murderers eligible for the death penalty—cut deals to spend decades in prison rather than risk execution.[7] During it all, Vázquez's other cases did not stop, the meth busts, the shootings, the rapes and domestic assaults, the often horrific transgressions that demanded hearings and sentencings and evenings of wading through documents. In fact, Vázquez's court was by some measures about the busiest in the United States, receiving in 2000 more new cases than all but six of the nation's ninety-four federal district courts, and most of the matters were criminal.[8] More recently, the District of New Mexico has ranked as high as first in the number of cases filed. A big reason is the flood of immigration-related matters, especially in courts near the border with Mexico. But another major factor derives from the law that imposed on Vázquez and other federal judges responsibility for many crimes occurring on Indian lands.

Like so much early legislation covering Native Americans, the Major Crimes Act of 1885 persisted on the books as an embarrassing remnant of bad policy and racist intentions.[9] The Constitution says Congress oversees the connection between Indian tribes and Washington, and in 1831 the Supreme Court articulated the relationship as that "of a ward to his guardian."[10] As late as 1883, in the Crow Dog case, the notion that federal law would impose on Native Americans rules that are "opposed to the traditions of their history, to the habits of their lives, to the strongest prejudices of their savage nature" struck the court's majority as fundamentally wrong.[11] The tribes had their own systems of criminal justice, traditional courts based on mostly unwritten laws and customs typically enforced by religious leaders and chiefs who determined guilt and fashioned remedies aimed at restitution—an effort to somehow make up for what a victim had lost.[12] Yet Congress passed the Major Crimes Act out of the belief that it just would not do to leave punishment for, say, murder to tribal law, "which is no law at all," as one of the bill's backers, Representative Byron M. Cutcheon of Michigan, put it. He stressed that Indians "will be civilized a great deal sooner by being put under such [criminal] laws and taught to regard life and the personal property of others."[13] That seemed especially important given what Congress had in mind for Native Americans.

Westward expansion and the desire for Indian lands prompted the "pulverizing," as Theodore Roosevelt put it, of the territory the government held in trust and its sale as private property—a process given the deceptively sterile term "allotment."[14] The General Allotment Act of 1887, known as the Dawes Act after its sponsor, Senator Henry L. Dawes of Massachusetts, directed the feds to parcel out land, usually 80 or 160 acres, to each member of a tribe and hold it in trust for twenty-five years before granting that member title. The point was to break up reservations and bring Native Americans into white society and more directly under legal control but also to open Indian territory to white settlement. All might go more smoothly with federal law enforcement ensuring that the "savages" behaved.

Allotment was a disaster for Native Americans. After the trusts expired, their property fell subject to state and local taxes, which many could not afford to pay, and so they lost their land. Any property not allotted became in the eyes of the government "surplus land," available to homesteaders who swarmed in like locusts. From 1887 to 1934 the territory where millions of Native Americans had made their home for millennia dwindled from 138 million acres to 48 million, and the enormity of the government's mistake at last became apparent.[15] A 1928 study—the *Meriam Report* (conducted by what is now the Brookings Institution)—had found that the fantasy of turning Indians into yeoman farmers tilling the soil and hauling their products to market had failed, bringing instead deep poverty, suffering, and discontent. In 1934, with the Indian Reorganization Act, allotment ended, and the remaining reservations, a fragment of their former size, survived.[16]

With them continued the exclusive reign of federal law over Native Americans—even though it was constitutionally suspect and intended to be temporary. So why federal law and not, say, the laws of the states where reservations were located? Easy, said the Supreme Court: Indians and state residents were often the "deadliest enemies." The former "owe no allegiance to the States, and receive from them no protection."[17] What's left, according to lawyers Troy Eid and Carrie Covington Doyle, is a separate and unequal system of criminal law that "discriminates invidiously in how it is currently funded and in the way it dispenses justice—if not for perpetrators . . . then for Native American victims of violent crime."[18]

That system is invariably as strange and distant as a foreign land to many Native Americans. There is no federal courthouse on an Indian reservation. For someone like Reno Roy Russell in the Navajo Nation, an expanse as large as West Virginia, the nearest federal courthouse, in Santa Fe, is over 170 miles away. Getting there by car—assuming you have one and can afford the gas—takes more than four hours. The scheduled bus takes almost eight. What's more, prospective jurors are selected from voter rolls, and many Indians are not registered to vote. So the chances that Native American witnesses, victims, or defendants will see a jury of their peers attempt to deliver justice are vanishingly slim.[19]

Perhaps the greatest unfairness of forcing Native Americans to answer for their crimes in federal rather than state courts, however, is the severity of the punishments they face. Federal prison sentences last on average twice as long as state sentences for similar offenses—largely because of the sentencing guidelines—and they don't provide for parole, an early exit from incarceration. It's even worse for juveniles, generally children under the age of eighteen. Federal law requires transferring serious felonies from tribal to federal jurisdiction, meaning Native Americans make up the largest chunk of kids in federal detention and most federal cases involving juveniles. An enormous number of them are sentenced as adults, far more than would be in state court.[20]

The sentencing system—its disparities for Native Americans but also the frigid indifference of federal guidelines and mandatory minimums to any human qualities of the accused—often infuriated Vázquez. Her brother Ricardo's severe punishment accounted for some of her reaction, but as a judge she would sometimes feel like a vending machine, a dispenser of packaged penalties designed by formula rather than human flesh and blood. From the get-go, she resisted, taking an approach that seemed true to the resolve that had motivated her ascension to the bench: Do better than the cruel insensitivity Judge Real had shown her brother.

Less than a year into Vázquez's tenure, Geneva Gallegos, a shy and poorly educated woman barely eighteen years old, came before the judge to face charges that she had intended to help her boyfriend of six weeks distribute 50 grams of crack cocaine found in their apartment. Her boyfriend was more than twice her age and a drug dealer so accomplished that he could afford to send his daughter to Notre Dame for college. Gallegos feared him and especially the possibility that, if she failed to comply with his demands, he might deny her a share of the profits that supported her six-year-old daughter and elderly parents. As she headed toward trial, her father, a traditional Hispanic man, suffered a debilitating heart attack. After Gallegos was convicted, she faced a mandatory minimum sentence of ten years. Her predicament—parents and a child who were totally dependent on her—led Vázquez to cite Gallegos's naivete, clean record, and minor role in the crime to depart from the prescribed penalty and sentence her to less than three years. But there was no leeway, no appetite among prosecutors to give Gallegos a break—or acquiesce to the startling behavior of a judge so unwilling to conform. They appealed, and the US Court of Appeals for the Tenth Circuit rejected Vázquez's decision, ordering her to try again.[21]

It was not Vázquez's only run-in with the court directly above her, a tribunal of about twenty judges who are often viewed collectively as conservative—Supreme Court justice Neil Gorsuch sat on the court in its home base of Denver, Colorado—and preside over cases from Oklahoma, Kansas, New Mexico, Colorado, Wyoming, and Utah, plus pieces of Yellowstone National Park in Montana and Idaho. It was not from a lack of respect.[22] At times, Vázquez was grateful that the court was there. During a criminal trial very early in her career, she realized that the prosecution's case contained so many holes that it should probably not reach the jury. But when defense lawyers asked her for a judgment as a matter of law, to end the case because no reasonable jury could find the evidence sufficient to convict their client, she declined, because she feared that her instinct to grant the request derived from a pro-defendant bias she might have developed as a former public defender. The jury delivered a guilty verdict, the defense lawyers appealed, and the appeals court reversed, finding that she should have dismissed the case. "That was the best lesson for me," Vázquez recalled. "Thank God there's a court of appeals. It is an important safety net to have, and I'm grateful for another set of eyes to review my decisions."[23]

Yet when determining sentences, Vázquez refused to stay within the mandatory guidelines so often that reversals by the Tenth Circuit seemed almost routine. Defense lawyers and more than a few judges who chafed under the guidelines' callous constraints admired her courage and believed it could help push the courts above to improve—to loosen those constraints and allow more compassionate sentencing. But to some prosecutors and appeals court judges, it seemed an act of rebellion incompatible with her role as a judge, and she caught criticism for it. "You could argue that it [her resistance] was the best thing that ever happened to the federal courts, or the worst thing that ever happened to Martha Vázquez," given the Tenth Circuit's harsh reactions, said Michael Stout, a Santa Fe lawyer and former colleague of Vázquez's in the state public defender's office. It was surely more the former than the latter, though. Life tenure on the bench means criticism, even from a higher court, lacks much bite, and besides, in the end, events would largely vindicate Vázquez's views of the sentencing guidelines.

They're All Drunk

On July 21, 2004, the day before Reno Roy Russell knifed his cousin in a Shiprock ditch, federal prosecutors asked the US Supreme Court to review the unrelated case of a drug dealer named Freddie Joe Booker. Local Wisconsin police had in 2003 arrested Booker for stashing 112 grams of crack cocaine in the basement of a friend's house, and he was later convicted by a jury of possessing and intending to distribute the crack and sentenced to thirty years in prison. The mandatory guidelines called for a penalty of about twenty years, but the judge—not the jury—found that Booker had probably sold a lot more crack and tried to obstruct justice, factors that bumped his minimum guidelines penalty to thirty years. The judge's decision to base the extra ten years on unproven accusations, Booker believed, violated his constitutional right to have a jury establish his guilt beyond a reasonable doubt. An appeals court agreed, and the government asked the Supreme Court to weigh in. Less than two weeks later—a blink of an eye for the justices—they took the case.[24]

Booker's appeal did not at the time have anything to do with Russell. Yet a Supreme Court case involving the sentencing guidelines would grab the attention of any defense lawyer or prosecutor practicing in federal court, and when the attorney Alonzo Padilla arrived at the detention center in Albuquerque to meet Russell, it was on his mind. Padilla, an assistant federal public defender who wore a wearied calm earned from too many clients and too little time, was appointed to represent Russell. What he saw at first surprised him: a slight, quiet, Navajo teenager who, he had been led to believe, somehow beat the hell out of a massive older cousin. After the two conversed—"overall, a good kid," Padilla remembered thinking—the lawyer figured he could go to trial and sell a case of self-defense. Besides, the cousin, still in the hospital, seemed to bear no hard feelings against Russell. Yet there was still the matter of harsh federal charges—assault with a dangerous weapon resulting in serious bodily harm—that, if Russell were found guilty, could under the guidelines put him in prison for about eight years with no parole. And if the concept of being tried by a jury of your peers had any value, a guilty verdict might be no small risk, given how few Native Americans were allowed to sit on juries and the prejudice that those accused of crimes often faced. The chances a white jury might see Russell—admittedly blind drunk and bellicose when he attacked his cousin—as a stereotype were real. Padilla and Russell would take their chances nonetheless.

By the time the court's computer system randomly spun the case to Vázquez's docket in October, she had been struggling for years to find ways of getting more Native Americans on juries. During a trial she held when she first became a judge, a court security officer told her that he had noticed at the lunch break that the one Native American on the jury had been sitting in his battered truck eating a single slice of white bread, apparently because he could not afford anything more. Soon after, Vázquez arranged for jurors to receive, in advance and in cash, the forty dollars a day they would normally be paid after the trial. With this small gesture, she hoped, people, and especially Native Americans, might be more willing to serve on juries because they were better able to afford it. Anything, she believed, was worth a try.

That's because with jury service might come understanding and then trust and, for everyone, a fairer and more accessible system of federal justice—the principle animating the Sixth Amendment's guarantee of a trial by a jury that reflected the community. Again, when Vázquez first went on the bench, how far her court was from that ideal soon became startlingly clear. The chief judge at the time described a letter he had received from a member of an all-white jury in a trial involving a crime in Indian country. The letter reported that during deliberations one juror had said of a Native American witness, "you can't believe these Indians because they're all drunk."[25] The conversation made an impression on Vázquez, not so much because of the juror's cruel ignorance but because of the chief judge's apparent failure to respond to it.

In 2003, as the senior active jurist on her court, Vázquez became chief judge, gaining authority over the policies and administration of the entire US district court in New Mexico—her chance to do what prior chiefs had failed to do: open the courts to more Native Americans. An easy fix might be to expand the jury pool, which in New Mexico consisted of American citizens eighteen years old or older, picked every two years from a list of registered voters.[26] That was an obvious problem. If you weren't registered to vote, you wouldn't get picked, and about a third of voting-age Native Americans weren't (and still aren't) on the voter rolls, for a host of reasons. Many on reservations lack an official street address or are homeless, making proof of residence difficult. Spotty internet service often rules out registering online. In-person registration offices are impossibly far away. Registering to vote is just too damned hard.[27]

Vázquez created a Jury Plan Task Force to consider options. One possibility that she had already proposed to Native American leaders was to supplement lists of registered voters with the names of people enrolled in tribes. A second option involved adding the names of people with drivers' licenses or government identification cards. That's what the New Mexico state courts had done, and the result had been a far more diverse pool. Yet in a 2004 preliminary report the task force recommended against both ideas. It feared that Vázquez's first proposal "might well violate the equal protection of the laws because it is race based." As for using drivers' license or ID card information, that might include in the pool people who for some reason had no interest in serving on a jury, the task force argued, and besides, it would create more work for court clerks than they wanted to take on. Any changes to the jury pool were subject to approval by all the court's judges, and they accepted the task force's recommendations, voting to do essentially nothing.[28]

It was frustrating but, in Vázquez's mind, not surprising, given most of her colleagues' ideology. Native Americans and other minorities tended to vote Democratic and, on juries, to side with the downtrodden and victims of corporate wrongdoing, and to award higher verdicts. "I had to be very careful that this wasn't seen as an effort to increase the voter pool for the Democratic Party," she explained. "Most of my colleagues were Republicans who had practiced at defense law firms, representing insurance companies." For a judge with a more modest view of her role, that might have been the end of it. For Vázquez, it gave truth to the proverb that if you want something done right, or even at all, you should do it yourself.

Opening the Courthouse Doors [139]

A Feast of Sorts

In the gray dawn of a December morning in 2003, the cozy smell of cookies baking pervaded the kitchen at Vázquez's home. In the oven were *biscochitos*, a buttery concoction of cinnamon and orange and crushed anise seeds that had been declared in 1989 the official cookie of New Mexico. After the treats were done, the judge arranged them, carefully wrapped, on a tray she carried that day to the small kitchen in her chambers, where they took their place beside a pot of mutton stew and traditional Native American bread. It was a feast of sorts, not for lawyers or clerks or anyone else in chambers, but for a couple of dozen or so children—girls younger than eighteen sentenced to live under close watch at a federal detention facility just outside of town. As in prior years, the judge and her clerks would visit the facility later that day. This year's visit, though, would be special. Vázquez had asked the president of the Navajo Nation, Joe Shirley Jr., to attend the event and speak with the children, and he had agreed.

A lean figure with graying hair swept back from his broad and leathered brow, Shirley showed up with a surprise guest: a beautiful young woman recently crowned Miss Navajo Nation. The two spoke with all the children, whose faces were fixed in expressions of awe, and then with the Native American children separately. With a warmth and poise that the judge found moving, Shirley told them about the pride of being a Native American. "I was so impressed with that man," Vázquez said. When it was over, after about three hours, the judge and Navajo president talked and soon found common ground in their concern over the gap between her world—the culture of the federal criminal justice system—and life in Indian country. She told Shirley that she wanted his help in trying to close that gap, and he agreed.

Over the following year, Vázquez and Shirley made radio commercials together, she speaking in English and he in Navajo, that told of the importance and purpose of jury service. Early on Saturday mornings, Vázquez would drive hundreds of miles to Crownpoint or Shiprock to walk among the flea-market stalls where Native Americans sold silver jewelry and homemade food. She would hand to the proprietors and browsers slim leaflets her clerk's office had prepared about how to register to vote, when to cast a ballot, where to report a crime or show up for jury duty or attend to the other tasks of civic participation. It did not seem enough, though. Just *telling* people these things would do little to address a broader problem, the foreignness of a faraway judicial process that could demand their presence and affect their lives as unpredictably as a passing thunderstorm. How to show them what her court did, how it could help them—how it *looked*? With the case of Reno Roy Russell, Vázquez saw her chance.

Bless Her Heart

On an afternoon in November 2004, the phone rang in Joe Shirley's office. It was Vázquez, and she had yet another idea. She wanted to bring her court to Navajo land. Would he help? The pitch was simple. She would find a case involving a young Navajo accused of a crime serious enough to draw notice and perhaps merit a trial but not so serious as to be exceptional. Bringing her court to a reservation for the trial would show his people what so few had ever seen, teach them how the legal process worked, and burnish his image as the man who brought them justice. It was an easy sell. "After she talked to me about what she was doing, I wanted to make it happen, too," Shirley said. "I thought, bless her heart."

There was a problem, though. As she read the law, holding a federal trial outside her district courthouse might technically be illegal. But Vázquez was careful. After receiving Shirley's support, the two also gained permission from Lawrence Morgan, speaker of the Navajo Nation Tribal Council, the Nation's legislative branch, and from

Herb Yazzie, the Nation's chief justice. She would also have to get prosecutors, Russell and his lawyers, and potential jurors and witnesses to agree, and the logistics might be a nightmare. Security, for one, was no small consideration in a federal judiciary where, even in 2005, the number of threats against courtroom officials and especially judges was rising.[29] Court reporters and clerks and all the other players in a trial would have to be transported to Shiprock and housed there. And the publicity—what would be the point of a judicial showcase if no one came to watch? But these were matters for later. First, Vázquez needed the right case, and she knew who could help her find it.

Assistant US Attorney Miles Hanisee was an affable and loquacious prosecutor whom Vázquez had come to respect for his long experience with cases in Indian country. Late on a spring afternoon in 2005, Hanisee received a message at his Albuquerque office that the chambers of Judge Martha Vázquez were on the line. The young prosecutor was swamped with work, but "when it's a federal judge, you take the call," he said. Vázquez told him about her plans and a particular case on her docket that she thought might work—the Russell case. She asked him to check it out. He felt so honored to be asked that he agreed instantly, forgetting that as a line prosecutor he resided near the bottom of a long chain of command that went through his supervisor and the US attorney for the District of New Mexico and ultimately to the US attorney general in Washington, DC. Within the hour Hanisee called Vázquez back, agreed with the judge that the Russell case would work well, suggested some possible trial dates, and hung up the phone, thinking how fun it would be to try a case in Shiprock. That night, at about 9:00 p.m., he received another call, this time at home. It was his supervisor. "What the hell are you thinking!" the supervisor bellowed. "This is not how things work!" Eventually, after enough feathers had been unruffled and higher-ups consulted, Hanisee was allowed to proceed.

Vindication

On January 25, 2005, after more than five months of motions and responses, briefs and reply briefs, oral arguments and sometimes contentious deliberations, the US Supreme Court released to the world its decision in the case of Freddie Joe Booker.[30] It was, in tabloid vernacular, a blockbuster. The sentencing guidelines, the court ruled, should be treated as "advisory" rather than as "binding requirements." The court cleaved the decision in two. The first part accepted Booker's contention that the guidelines violated his right to a jury trial because they directed a judge to increase his sentence based on unproven facts. The second part provided the solution: make the guidelines nonbinding. Judges would still have to take the guidelines into account when crafting a punishment, which could be reviewed on appeal for "reasonableness," whatever that might mean, but sentencing again became a matter of discretion for judges.

For Russell, the decision represented hope. If he were found guilty, it would be easier for a judge to show leniency—maybe a sentence closer to what he would probably get were he tried in state court. For Hanisee and other federal prosecutors, the decision seemed wrongheaded. In a press release the Justice Department warned that "the fairness, consistency and accountability that were the hallmarks of the [sentencing guidelines] are in serious jeopardy."[31] Hanisee explained: "We thought that if person A commits crime number 1, and then person B commits crime number 1, then their sentences should be same." He would change his view after entering private practice and then becoming a state appeals court judge, but at the time, he said, "I was not able to understand that the fact that the crimes were the same didn't make the defendants the same." For Padilla, Russell's lawyer, the practical impact of the decision was surprisingly mixed. It would increase his guilty clients' chances of receiving punishments fairly tailored to them and not just their crimes, but it would also put a greater burden on him and other defense lawyers. How thoroughly they dug into their clients' lives to portray them as real people with hard problems—often poverty, mental illness, broken families—deserving of mercy would matter more than ever. And judges like Vázquez, *especially* Vázquez, were rarely satisfied that they had dug deeply enough.

Finally, for Vázquez, the *Booker* decision represented a sort of vindication. "I cried," she said about the moment in her chambers when she first heard from a clerk what the Supreme Court had done. "I was getting appealed on almost every single [sentencing] decision . . . and after *Booker*, there was finally a sense that there's justice in our legal system." Not every judge shared her reaction. Many had grown comfortable in the guidelines straitjacket, content with how it simplified the otherwise demanding task of determining the fate of another human being and reduced their chances of being reversed. Vázquez, of course, had long resisted the guidelines, and now she was freer, if not completely free, to impose penalties she believed were just.

Over the following months, her plans for the Shiprock trial fell into place with remarkable ease. One reason was the authority she wielded as the chief judge of the district. The clerk's office—the manager of records and court dockets and all things logistical—and the marshal's office, which took care of security, answered to her and showed her great deference. According to Vázquez, "We just announced what we were doing and said, make it a point to be there." Another reason was Joe Shirley's enthusiasm for the project. He arranged for the courtroom in Shiprock, drummed up support among Navajo officials, committed to being there himself, and spread the word among the community and the news media. He wanted the event to make a splash. Maybe the biggest reason the run-up to the trial went smoothly was that unlike Shirley, the judge kept it quiet. She didn't ask permission, she didn't spread the word—she didn't tell other judges.

Originally scheduled for May, the trial was pushed back because Russell was a senior at Kirtland Central High School in Shiprock and did not want to miss the last three weeks of school before graduation. An October date was delayed because Padilla was starting a murder trial then and still had to arrange with his ex-wife for childcare while he was in Shiprock at Russell's trial. Finally, the trial was set for December 13, 2005.[32] There was still the matter of picking the jury. The parties agreed to do it in Albuquerque, on December 6, enough time to arrange for buses and reserve rooms at the Best Western hotel near Shiprock, where jurors would stay. Even though the prospective jurors were drawn from twenty-two counties across northern New Mexico, few were Native Americans, and as it turned out, no Native American was selected. That was the point, at least in Vázquez's mind: a stark message that if they wanted a role in determining their people's fate in court, Native Americans needed to sit on juries.

. . .

In the biting cold of a clear December morning in 2005, twelve jurors and two alternates stepped from a bus in front of the Navajo Nation district courthouse, a modest one-story building of beige, vertically striated stone that had until then hosted only the disputes of the Indigenous population. At the door they were greeted with smiles and gestures toward a screening device operated by US marshals and then to a windowless room. Through a side entrance, Martha Vázquez, pulling a box of files resting on a wheely cart, walked with her clerk and courtroom deputy to the office that the local district judge had vacated for them. There, on a desk, the judge had left Vázquez a gift: a crystal Lenox goblet welcoming one nation's judge to the chambers of another. Vázquez paused and smiled before donning her robe and heading to the courtroom.

Opening the Courthouse Doors [145]

It was a small and simple room, with white-painted walls and low ceilings, lacking the grandeur of Vázquez's own court. At 9:20 a.m., when her deputy called for all to rise and the judge took the bench and gazed down, Vázquez saw the prosecutor, Miles Hanisee, seated at a table to her right and, at a table to her left, Alonzo Padilla and the diminutive figure of his client, Reno Roy Russell. In the first row of benches behind them were Joe Shirley and several Native American dignitaries, Russell's mother and father, and other members of his family. Near them, pens poised, sat reporters from the *Farmington Daily Times* and the *Navajo Times*. The remaining seats, maybe two dozen in all, were crammed with friends and the merely curious, some waving and smiling at Russell and his family. The room hummed with festive anticipation. Joe Shirley had done his job. Vázquez welcomed the gathering, introduced Shirley and the lawyers, and explained the purpose of the trial and how it would play out. A Navajo interpreter translated her words and would translate those of the lawyers and witnesses to come, with earphones available to anyone who wanted to listen; English fluency was not a prerequisite to a fair hearing. Then Vázquez's deputy called in the jury and, with a rap of the judge's gavel, the proceedings turned sharply serious.

Over the next two days the trial took as typical a path as circumstances allowed. People in the audience came and went, staying the few minutes required to see what the fuss was about before vacating their seats for others, and the movement and sounds of people brushing politely past each other were distracting. Yet the lawyers pressed on, Hanisee and then Padilla summarizing their cases in opening statements, and Hanisee calling the first of his six witnesses. Manuelito testified about what had happened that July day the year before, doctors testified about his injuries, police testified about their investigation. The evidence that seemed to pique the most interest was a pair of white pants found burned in a barrel in Russell's backyard. They were Russell's pants, and the prosecutor argued that the defendant had set them afire to cover up his crime—damning evidence of guilt. But Russell's lawyer elicited a different interpretation. At 4:00 p.m., Padilla put Russell on the stand. The teenager said he had acted in self-defense, and as for the pants, he had burned them because he was afraid that his mother would scold him harshly for ruining them with splatters of blood.

The next day, when the trial resumed shortly after 10:00 a.m., Padilla made much of this in his closing argument. He told a story of how his teenage daughter had accidentally put a hole in her bedroom wall and covered it with a poster. Years later, he discovered the hole as he was preparing to paint her room. Like his daughter, Padilla argued, Russell was just an innocent kid more afraid of his mother than the legal consequences of a simple fight with his drunken and much bigger cousin. Shortly before noon, the jury filed out of the courtroom to deliberate. The onlookers dispersed, some to their homes, others across the street to the Nataani Nez Restaurant for fry bread and lamb stew. The audience had thinned significantly when, at about 3:30 that afternoon, word came that the jury had reached a verdict.

There was doubt in the air as the jurors settled in their seats. Did they see Russell as a criminal hardened in a culture they knew little about and deserving of punishment for using a knife against someone who had angered him? Or was he the kid of Padilla's telling, a teenager still scared of his mother who engaged in an unfortunate tussle with his cousin? After the judge asked the foreman whether the jurors had reached a verdict, and after the foreman said they had, the answer was finally revealed. Guilty. But there was a twist. Russell was guilty not of the felony assaults with which he was charged, but of the lesser crimes of two simple assaults—misdemeanors whose consequences were relatively minor. Russell would walk out of the Shiprock courtroom that day to go about his business under "supervised release," the watchful eyes of his parents and his bosses at the Pizza Hut in Farmington.[33] His sentencing would not come until the following May, back in Santa Fe before Judge Vázquez. As it turned out, the federal guidelines did not apply because the crimes were misdemeanors, so she was free to treat him as she saw fit, and that was with a penalty of one year of probation. As long as he behaved himself, he would be a free man.

. . .

The larger question of the federal trial, what it meant as almost certainly the first held on Indian land, was harder to answer. Vázquez's assessment was disarmingly modest. "My objective was a pretty humble objective," she explained. "I wanted people to see it and not be intimidated by it." In the immediate aftermath, she said, "I really didn't think it had an impact. I have been more surprised about the impact since then." In fact, moving her court to Indian country for a jury trial prompted other judges to do the same. In 2010 a federal judge in California began holding twice-a-month sessions at the Mendocino County reservation of the Hopland Band of Pomo Indians, citing Vázquez's success in showing Native Americans how the courts work and saving them from onerous travel and expense.[34] Several other judges—federal and state, in Arizona and elsewhere—have since held court on Indian lands.

Yet Vázquez remained unimpressed. "I am disappointed that our jury panel is the same," she said, pointing out that it still lacks a significant number of Native Americans. "It's as if we are only here to serve our own communities, and we don't think about that, we still make it almost impossible for certain parts of our nation to be heard" in court. The Navajo leaders involved—Herb Yazzie and Joe Shirley—were more generous in their assessments. Yazzie said he continued to marvel at the audacity and value of what Vázquez had done, stressing that it demonstrated how there could be "a better relationship between the US government and the Navajo Nation," given that "there's a sad, confusing history between the two." As for Shirley, he scoffed at the suggestion that the trial might not have had an impact. "For us Navajos, it doesn't matter if there are 430,000 of us today, we still think of ourselves as family," he said. At the trial of a member of that family like Russell, "when there are grandpas involved, grandmas involved, parents and sisters and brothers involved, possibly aunts and uncles watching, to me, that has a big impact on the accused. It shows him that we are watching, that it is going to be a fair trial."

7   *You Will Be Heard*

When Carlton Reeves began to practice law at the Phelps Dunbar firm in Mississippi, the senior partners there would upon occasion stretch back in their chairs and spin a story or two about the early days of going to court in Jackson. It was the "old Mississippi" in their telling, the one of all-white juries and persistent racism and a few judges whom lawyers would struggle to treat with a tongue-held tone of respect. Maybe the most notorious of those jurists, and a favorite topic of the lawyers' stories, was W. Harold Cox. Cox came to the public's attention in 1961 as President Kennedy's nominee to the federal district court in Jackson. He was by many accounts a skilled lawyer, a strict and proper man of tall build and graying hair and, by then, sixty years of age. He neither smoked nor drank and was said to order men in elevators to doff their hats in the presence of ladies.[1]

Not coincidentally, Cox was also a close friend in law school with Mississippi's James Eastland, among the US Senate's hardest of hard-core opponents of desegregation. Once on the bench, Cox be-

---

One of the cases discussed in this chapter involves the horrific murder of a Black man. The racial slur used in that case will disturb many readers. But to understand the context of both the murder and the case, it is, as Judge Reeves stressed, necessary to say that word.

haved in ways that may have at first warmed the senator's heart but later embarrassed even him.[2] When faced with a case involving the mass registration of Black people to vote, Cox said, "Who is telling these niggers they can get in line and push people around, acting like a bunch of chimpanzees?"[3] The judge opined that Black demonstrators "ought to be in the movies instead of being registered to vote."[4] In a letter to a US Justice Department official, Cox complained, "I spend most of the time fooling around with lousy cases brought before me by your department in the civil rights field and I do not intend to turn my docket to your department for your political advancement."[5] Civil rights advocates and members of Congress called for his impeachment from almost the moment he arrived on the bench, but Cox survived it all, remaining a judge until his death in 1988.

The story about Cox that Reeves remembered best was how the judge would hold his weekly "motion day," the time when lawyers with cases before him would gather around a long conference table in his chambers to argue for excluding evidence or ordering more depositions or whatever their request might be. After one lawyer finished and left, the other lawyers would move a seat closer to the judge at the end of the table. When an attorney representing a Japanese client finally got his turn, he asked the judge for more time to prepare his case. Cox stared at the attorney and roared, "I will give you as much time as the Japs gave us at Pearl Harbor!"

In 1982, Cox became a senior judge, a status of semiretirement that allowed him to receive his salary yet reduce his caseload and, more significant, opened a spot on the court for a new judge. That judge was William Barbour, cousin and law partner of future Mississippi governor Haley Barbour. A graduate of Princeton University and accomplished lawyer in Yazoo City, William Barbour brought dignity to the seat, but reminders of Cox's racism were never far away. Behind a judge's bench in the courthouse where Barbour sat, recently covered by a heavy black curtain, was a mural that depicted barefooted African Americans picking cotton and strumming a banjo for their white masters.[6] On February 4, 2006, Barbour took senior status, creating an opening on the court in Jackson yet again. It would take a few years, but in 2010 the seat that for two decades had been held by Harold Cox—the man whom Roy Wilkins, the executive secretary of the NAACP, had once described as "another strand in their [African Americans'] barbed wire fence, another cross over their weary shoulders and another rock in the road up which their young people must struggle"—would finally be filled by a new and different sort of judge.[7] In a twist of cosmic justice, that new judge would be a Black man. That man was Carlton Reeves.

A Great Day

On a Friday afternoon in late December 2010, the phone rang in the downtown Jackson office of Will Bardwell Esq. Bardwell, a boyish-looking lawyer nearing thirty, with sandy hair and black-rimmed glasses and an open, friendly manner, answered. On the line was a woman named Twana Summers. She told Bardwell that there was going to be a little swearing-in ceremony for Reeves on the upcoming Thursday, a small gathering of family and close friends at the James O. Eastland Federal Courthouse downtown. Would he like to come? Bardwell said of course. Reeves had chosen Summers as his first courtroom deputy and Bardwell as his first clerk, and after two precarious years of picking up contract work as a lawyer just starting out, Bardwell felt good about being included among the judge's family and close friends.

On the appointed day, Bardwell pulled open the heavy doors to the main courtroom and beheld an astonishing sight. Far from a small gathering, it was a conglomeration of maybe a hundred or more men and women—Black and white, nearing retirement and just starting out, lawyers and politicians and business leaders, parents and cousins and siblings—attired in dark suits and muted dresses and crammed together so tightly that many were forced to stand. At the front was Reeves, his right hand raised, his left hand on a Bible that his wife Lora held, their daughter Chanda by her side. After he repeated the oath delivered to him by the chief judge of the court, he turned to the applauding crowd, his grin broad and eyes as wide as saucers, and started to share his thoughts.

"This is a great day," Reeves began. His voice cracked, his eyes welled up, he began again. "This is a great day." He went on for a while and then offered a prediction that was unexpected but surely accurate. "I will not like some of the decisions I will make," he said, stressing that the law can lead to rulings that are fundamentally unfair.[8] It is a point that he would emphasize—and explain with patience and clarity—time and again in his toughest opinions to come. Those opinions would become his hallmark, his opportunities to teach the public why sometimes an outcome should by all rights not be the outcome and how, although he is required to follow it, the law should change.

That was the nub of it, Reeves's desire for those opportunities for public engagement, a big reason he had approached Congressman Bennie Thompson that evening in 2009 at a Jackson fundraiser. He might have gotten them earlier, possibly right after William Barbour stepped aside in 2006, had the president at the time been a Democrat. As it happened, President George Bush nominated several white lawyers who failed to gain enough support in the Senate, and by the time Reeves filled the seat, it had been vacant for almost five years.[9] During that time American law had changed in a way that would make the job of judges like Reeves—those who wanted people to have easier and broader access to court—both harder and more urgent. In a sense the leaders who shared the views that had animated the Southern Manifesto, people like Strom Thurmond and Olin Johnston and Senator Sam Ervin and even Harold Cox, the people who believed that federal courts should mostly butt out of their neighbors' way of life, had won.

To see how they had won, consider that the manifesto had argued that *Brown v. Board of Education* was wrongly decided and an abuse of the Supreme Court's power. Yet as Justin Driver, a professor at Yale Law School, has explained, opposition to *Brown* became less about trying to get it reversed or overridden by a constitutional amendment than about defining what it said.[10] In *Briggs v. Elliott*, one of the five cases that the Supreme Court reviewed together with *Brown* and then returned to lower courts for them to reconsider in light of that landmark decision, a South Carolina district court put its own spin on *Brown*.[11] That court insisted that "the Constitution . . . does not require integration. . . . It merely forbids the use of governmental power to enforce segregation," an interpretation growing popular in conservative circles at the time.[12] Senator Ervin, an astute lawyer as well as a savvy politician, picked up on the South Carolina court's words, telling the *New Orleans Times-Picayune* in 1956 that while *Brown* was "deplorable," it was "not as drastic as many people think."[13] Seven years later, the implication—that school desegregation could be voluntary—became explicit in a congressional hearing where the senator forced US attorney general Robert Kennedy to admit: "You could make an argument along those lines."[14] As Ervin would later write in his autobiography, *Brown* had actually been decided correctly, but its ruling only required "the States to ignore the race of school children in assigning them to their public schools."[15]

The view seemed far afield of where constitutional law actually stood at the time, but a generation later things shifted again. In 2007, as Reeves was serving as president of the Magnolia Bar Association and opposing yet another white man's nomination to the Fifth Circuit Court of Appeals, the Supreme Court startled the nation with a decision that sided squarely with Ervin's position. "The way to stop discrimination on the basis of race is to stop discriminating on the basis of race," wrote Chief Justice John Roberts for the plurality in a 5–4 decision striking down school-district plans in Seattle, Washington, and Louisville, Kentucky, that assigned students to public schools based on race. Before the court barred the practice in *Brown*, "schoolchildren were told where they could and could not go to school based on the color of their skin," wrote Roberts, and so stopping the practice again was a vindication of *Brown*.[16]

This interpretation may have been news to Reeves—as it probably would have been to the original supporters of *Brown*. It was, sadly, also evidence of a backward slide in people's ability to enforce their rights in court, to gain access to the better schools and maybe the better jobs and places to live. After half a century of what looked like progress on race, it felt to many as if the nation was back where it had been in the 1950s. And as Reeves would soon discover, nowhere was that feeling stronger than in Mississippi.

Let's Go Do Justice

Reeves may not have fully sensed the weight of expectations on him until he attended an event in Jackson early in 2011. It was a party celebrating the fiftieth anniversary of the Freedom Rides, civil rights forays into the Deep South that aimed to compel compliance with court rulings desegregating interstate buses. As he circulated around the room, he kept running into more than a few people, many of them Black lawyers, who had appeared before Judge Cox, and they recounted stories, some hilarious, some horrifying, about the mistreatment they had endured. They said Cox's court had "felt like a hostile place, like foreign soil to many," Reeves recalled, "and I felt that they were kindred spirits. I felt a sense of duty and an obligation from my connection with these people and the things they had sacrificed, culminating in my being on the court. The face of justice, mine, was very different from the one they had seen back then."

You Will Be Heard [155]

The memory of one man in particular, though, stuck with Reeves. He was Lawrence Guyot, a Black civil rights activist who had been savagely beaten and jailed repeatedly while leading protests on behalf of Black people and voting rights in Mississippi during the 1960s. Guyot on occasion had been hauled before Cox. He had also been imprisoned for a spell at Mississippi's Parchman Farm, an infamously cruel penitentiary where, after guards had thrashed him severely, he refused to eat for seventeen days in protest, losing one hundred pounds.[17] When Guyot saw Reeves, he approached and, dispensing with any formalities, just hugged him. Almost seventy-three at the time and graying and struggling with diabetes and the damage from several heart attacks, Guyot laughed and chatted and awed the judge with his encouragement and gracious manner. Guyot died the following year.

Reeves had a lot to live up to. Initially the going was slow. His first official day as a judge was a holiday. His first few weeks, he had no cases. Then, barely six months into the job, he had to pack up his chambers and move to a new courthouse, six stories of gleaming glass and beige stone and walls of sweeping curves—just five blocks south but a world away from the dark and antiquated confines of the James O. Eastland Courthouse and all its namesake stood for. It was in this new place that Reeves found his footing. In March 2011 he had received one of his first cases, a criminal matter charging a young man named Jonatan Lopez with possessing and intending to distribute 5 kilograms of cocaine found in his car during a traffic stop on Interstate 20.[18]

It looked routine, a typical drug case that is usually resolved quickly after a defense lawyer maneuvers for the best deal he can. One tactic is to try to have the evidence—the drugs—suppressed as illegally seized. This Lopez's lawyer attempted to do in a perfunctory motion that landed on Reeves's docket in early August. Without providing much detail, the motion argued that stopping Lopez for improper lane changes did not justify asking for and receiving his permission to search the car, where the cocaine was found. The lawyer did not request a hearing on his motion, but Reeves sensed trouble. He knew that cops liked to call I-20 a drug corridor where just about any nonwhite person driving along the route warranted scrutiny. Reeves wanted to know more about what had happened to Lopez, to hold a hearing, and he asked Bardwell to research the law of search and seizure in preparation.

Three weeks later, Reeves ascended to the bench in his courtroom, a bright and airy chamber, and asked Lopez to please stand. The accused drug dealer was there with his lawyer on one side and on the other, an interpreter—a figure whose presence highlighted a telling factor in the case: Lopez barely spoke English. "If at any time you don't understand something," Reeves gently counseled the defendant, "please advise . . . the court so that we can make sure you understand what is happening." Minutes later, the prosecutor called to the witness stand Sergeant Andy "Ski" Matuszewski, the deputy sheriff who had pulled Lopez over on I-20.

Matuszewski had been well prepared. With uncanny specificity he recounted every moment of his encounter with Lopez that day and why he had done what he had done. As he watched from his cruiser on the side of the road, Matuszewski testified, Lopez's car changed to a lane farthest from him while traveling well below the speed limit (or so Matuszewski assumed; he didn't have a speed gun). Lopez, unmistakably Latino, looked tense as he drove by, his hands on the steering wheel at the 10:00 and 2:00 positions. The windows of his car were up, even though he was sweating. When Matuszewski pulled out and drove slowly by him, Lopez did not even offer a glance. Finally, after Lopez began following a truck too closely and changed lanes without signaling, Matuszewski punched on the cruiser's flashing lights and pulled him over.

All of this behavior, the deputy testified, was "different than what I'm used to seeing from the normal motoring public, so it caught my attention." Matuszewski said that behavior continued. When asked for his driver's license, registration, and proof of insurance, Lopez fumbled nervously with the glove-compartment latch to get them. The driver's license was from Mexico. The car was registered under a different name, and Lopez said it was his cousin's vehicle, then said later it was a friend's. Matuszewski called the information into headquarters, and it checked out, so he told Lopez he would issue him only a warning.

Then things got complicated. The deputy asked, *Is there anything in the vehicle?* Lopez nodded and said yes. The deputy then asked, *Is there anything illegal in the car?* Lopez again nodded and said yes. Finally, speaking in Spanish, the deputy asked, *Are there drugs or narcotics in the car?* Lopez said, *Oh, no, no, no.* The deputy then asked, in English, *So you don't mind if we check?* In testimony the deputy said he understood Lopez to respond, *That's fine.* With two partners whom he had called to the scene, Matuszewski commenced to feel between seats and pry open panels inside the car and soon found the cocaine.

Listening to the testimony and the subsequent cross-examination by Lopez's lawyer, Reeves was appalled. "I felt a real sense that this officer was making stuff up," he said. "Here's a Hispanic-looking guy stopped because he was sweating profusely, would not look [the officer] in the eye, his hands on the steering wheel in a 10 and 2 position, his window's up—how do you see him sweating? What is wrong with a driver focusing on the road?" The question was what the judge would do about it. He figured that, "outlandish" as Matuszewski's initial suspicions were, the bit about driving too close behind another vehicle and the failure to signal a lane change probably justified the stop. It was what happened later—the belief that Lopez had consented to the search despite the obvious language barrier—that bothered Reeves. He would grant Lopez's motion to suppress, but how? Would he just write a short opinion explaining his logic and leave it at that? Or did this case deserve something more?

When the judge handed Bardwell a draft of the opinion a week or two after the hearing, the clerk was in awe. It did not merely throw out the cocaine as evidence because Lopez barely understood English and could not have consented to the search, the opinion reached back into history to explain why his consent was essential, why the Fourth Amendment to the Constitution prohibited illegal searches and seizures, and it did this in words of compassion and eloquence that lawyers and eventually the public would learn were typical of Reeves's writing.

"Less than three years after the most notable of the Nuremberg Trials," the judge began his analysis, "wherein he served as chief prosecutor against one of the gravest atrocities ever exacted upon the human race, Justice Robert H. Jackson wrote that the guarantees established by the Fourth Amendment 'are not mere second-class rights but belong in the catalog of indispensable freedoms. Among deprivations of rights, none is so effective in cowing a population, crushing the spirit of the individual and putting terror in every heart. Uncontrolled search and seizure is one of the first and most effective weapons in the arsenal of every arbitrary government.'" Reeves continued: "Moreover, Justice Jackson noted aptly that 'the right to be secure against searches and seizures is one of the most difficult to protect. Since the officers are themselves the chief invaders, there is no enforcement outside of court.' This Court cannot overstate the seriousness with which it carries that duty."[19]

There would be other, higher-profile opinions, ones with more elegant passages on weightier issues in more consequential cases. Here, though, was the first signal that Reeves would use his position as a US district court judge to teach Americans from whence their freedoms derived and why they mattered but also to let it be known to people whose concerns the courts had often dismissed—in this case Latinos, in later cases Black people and women and LGBTQ individuals—that, in his court at least, they would be welcomed and heard and *included*, no matter how small their cases. In Bardwell's mind, the Lopez case was emblematic of what set Reeves apart. "I don't know that you would have gotten that level of curiosity about a mundane case from just any judge," he said. When he was a clerk, Bardwell continued, "I don't think that a day went by when he didn't say, *Let's go do justice*." It was a noble-sounding sentiment that might actually mean something in Mississippi, where in the dark days of Judge Cox and his ilk there was so much justice that needed to be done. What would surprise Reeves, though, what would soon break his heart, was the realization that those days were far from a distant memory.

Jafrica

At a farm in Puckett, Mississippi, just east of Jackson, in July 2011, Deryl Dedmon and nine of his high school friends gathered around a bonfire to celebrate his eighteenth birthday. Dedmon, blue-eyed and boyish with a swoop of fair hair across his brow, was at first all swagger and jest. But as the beer flowed and the warm night wore on, he veered into griping about his troubles with a girl and the theft of his wallet the night before. Then his laughter turned to shouting—and a horrifying appeal to hate. Let's go "fuck with some niggers!" Dedmon whooped.[20]

It was what they did for fun. Over the past four months Dedmon and his friends had driven their trucks into Jackson—"Jafrica," they called it—and pelted Black pedestrians with beer bottles, beaten a drunken Black man near a golf course, accelerated straight at a Black woman crossing the street before swerving at the last moment, and stopped at a sporting goods store to buy a slingshot for shooting ball bearings at Black people passing on the sidewalk. That night at the farm, they picked up the empty beer bottles and in two vehicles—a white Jeep Cherokee and Dedmon's green Ford F-250 pickup—drove the fifteen minutes to Jackson and took the Ellis Avenue exit off Route I-20 west of downtown. It was just after 4:00 a.m.

Kirk Montgomery, Dedmon's best friend and the driver of the Jeep, saw James Craig Anderson first. It was in the parking lot of the Metro Inn on Ellis Avenue, and Anderson, a slight African American man in his late forties, was fiddling with the handle of his orange Chevy Avalanche, having apparently lost his keys. Montgomery called Dedmon on the phone: "Get over here." When Dedmon showed up a few minutes later, he jumped out of his pickup and shouted, "Nigger, get away from my truck!"

One of the teenagers dropped Anderson to the ground with a punch to his face. Dedmon jumped on Anderson and pummeled him with his fists. He then stole Anderson's wallet and the group drove off, yelling "white power!" As Dedmon was about to turn onto the road, though, his headlights caught Anderson stumbling to his feet. Dedmon backed up, aimed the pickup at Anderson, and gassed it, running him over. Later, as he drove away, he boasted by phone to his friends in the Jeep that he "ran that nigger over!" Little did Dedmon and his buddies know that the vicious assault and fatal hit-and-run had been caught on a motel security camera.[21]

Even in Mississippi, with its long history of horrific beatings and lynchings of African Americans, people were shocked. The director of the ACLU in the state called it "a cowardly act of violence that reminds us of the racial hatred that continues to plague the South."[22] When CNN broadcast the tape from the motel security camera, the disgust went national. Civil rights leader Gerald Rose in Atlanta said he "shed tears" when he saw the video. "That could have been me or it could have been my sons. . . . I can't believe stuff like this is going on in the year 2011."[23] The *New York Times*, CBS News, and dozens of other news organizations covered the incident with unnerved intensity. Protestors gathered outside the federal courthouse in

Jackson, holding signs with messages like "James Craig Anderson, Our Loving Brother Stolen By Hate, We Will Not Forget!!!"[24]

Reeves saw the coverage and protests, could not miss them, as they came literally to the door of his place of work. He would feel as shocked and disgusted as anyone at what had happened, yet his mind would also go back to a specific time and place of personal import. It was that sunny day in June 1971, that last day of first grade in Miss Thornton's class at Annie Ellis school in Yazoo City, the day memorialized in a faded photo of kids, Black and white. Reeves remembered that those kids had not learned about hate or racism, and he wondered how these other kids, "these genteel, God-fearing, God-loving" ones who had taken Anderson's life, had gone so wrong.[25]

Hinds County state prosecutors moved quickly, charging Dedmon with capital murder and a hate crime and one of his friends, John Aaron Rice, with murder, later reduced to assault.[26] Charges of varying severity against five of the other teenagers would soon follow. Meanwhile, lawyers from the US Justice Department prepared to file federal hate-crime charges. In March 2012 the cases came to a head in a flurry of legal moves. First, on March 21, Dedmon pleaded guilty to the state charges and was sentenced to two consecutive life terms in prison.[27] That same day, federal prosecutors filed their initial case—charges against Dedmon, Rice, and a third teenager, Dylan Wade Butler, of committing and conspiring to commit a hate crime. The criminal information reciting the charges encompassed not only Anderson's murder but also the prior assaults on Black people during nighttime trips to "Jafrica." The next day, March 22, the three accused men appeared before Reeves to answer the federal charges with guilty pleas.

The choice of Reeves to handle the case seemed suspiciously apt. He was not the only Black judge on the court—Henry Wingate had been appointed in 1985—but much in his experience and sense of history raised expectations among those who knew him well that he might articulate a redeeming lesson in an utterly senseless crime. Reeves had in fact gotten the matter in the usual, mundane way: his name drawn from a stack of one hundred light-blue index cards—twenty-two for each of the four active judges on the court, twelve for the one senior judge—that had been shuffled by hand and then attached with one binder ring through holes in the upper left corner. As each case came in, the card on top was flipped over, revealing the new card with the name of the judge who would get the case. This antiquated process would soon be computerized, but at the time it ensured that the assignment was random and at least in theory could not be gamed by people seeking a particular judge or by judges wanting to hear a particular case.

The three teenagers having confessed their guilt, about all that was left for Reeves to do was to determine their sentences. He would be guided by the Matthew Shepard and James Byrd Jr. Hate Crimes Prevention Act of 2009, the law under which they had been convicted.[28] It was named for the gay college student—Shepard—who had been tortured and killed in Wyoming in 1998, and Byrd, a Black father of three who in the same year had been beaten and then chained to the rear of a pickup truck that dragged and tore his body apart over the course of a three-mile drive.[29] Yet the Anderson case was the first under the statute to involve a murder, and prosecutors took particular care investigating it, making sure they could charge everyone who was culpable and show how effective the new law could be against violence from racial hate. That meant the sentencing of the first three teenagers would be delayed for almost three years. As it turned out, for the guilty parties as well as the American public, Reeves made the occasion worth the wait.

Somewhat lost in the Anderson case was that James Anderson had been not only a Black man but also a gay man. Forty-seven when he died, Anderson had lived with his partner, James Bradfield, for seventeen years and helped to raise the four-year-old, De'Mariouz, for whom Bradfield was the legal guardian. The little family lived in a modest three-bedroom house with a manicured lawn near woods in Jackson, attending on Sundays the First Hyde Park Missionary Baptist Church, where Anderson was the lead tenor in the choir. Warm and friendly and skilled around the kitchen and the garden, Anderson worked at a Nissan auto assembly plant. Bradfield, a tall and thickly built man who was more guarded and organized than Anderson, liked to take the three of them on trips around the country when he was off from his job at an airplane-parts assembly plant. Barred by law from marrying, the couple affirmed the bond between them by traveling to New Orleans and speaking vows to each other over dinner at a French Quarter hotel.[30]

They kept a low profile and lived in many ways a typical suburban life, and there was no evidence that Dedmon or his six friends suspected Anderson was gay. Yet they were known to bully gay kids around town in Brandon, Mississippi, the suburb where they lived, and virulent discrimination against LGBTQ people had long pervaded Mississippi culture.[31] During the civil rights battles of the 1960s, Ku Klux Klan missives made the hatred overt, calling "Communists, homosexuals, and Jews, fornicators and liberals and angry blacks—infidels all," wrote historian John Howard. By 1965, "homosexuality was linked to the specter of racial justice—what white authorities understood as the most serious threat to the status quo."[32] People like James Anderson, though, found themselves forced to navigate a complicated identity as both Black and gay in the Deep South. They faced animosity from whites but also from Black people, whose history of demeaning LGBTQ people was long and harsh. In choosing members of the Freedom Riders, civil rights leader James Farmer felt compelled to reject "Communists, homosexuals, drug addicts" because "they knew that if they found anything to throw at us, they would throw it."[33] Bayard Rustin, the close adviser to Martin Luther King Jr. and esteemed organizer of civil rights protests that included the 1963 March on Washington for Jobs and Freedom, was belittled by colleagues "put off by [his] homosexuality."[34]

Reeves did not have to consider the issue of Anderson's sexual orientation and the discrimination that it may have provoked because legally it was irrelevant to the case; federal prosecutors had charged Dedmon and his crowd with race-based crimes. But, in another context and only a few months after the Anderson case landed before him, the judge would for the first time face the issue squarely.

It Needed to Be Said

On a bright Tuesday morning in March 2014, Rebecca Bickett and Andrea Sanders collected their cash and driver's licenses and headed to the Hinds County Courthouse in downtown Jackson. Already gathering in front on the plaza of early-spring grass were dozens of other same-sex couples who, after Bickett and Sanders joined them, walked slowly in a wide circle and sang and held hands and listened as a young preacher prayed: "We gather today to celebrate love and to resist laws we believe to be immoral and also unconstitutional." After a while, the crowd following, Bickett and Sanders and four other couples went inside and, television cameras rolling, approached a white-haired woman behind the counter at the circuit clerk's office.[35]

"We'd like to apply for a marriage license."

"Okay, I need to see both your IDs."

Moments later, the clerk delivered the anticipated response: license denied.

The orchestrated effort to join in holy matrimony began a historic (and, for a court case, remarkably quick) process to bring Mississippi into the twenty-first century with most other states and strike down its ban on gay marriage. Bickett and Sanders would become two of four lead plaintiffs in the process, the public names on the legal documents that would bring that process to a successful conclusion.

Bickett and Sanders had been together for ten years. In 2010 they sealed their bond with a commitment ceremony beneath the grand Friendship Oak on the Gulf campus of the University of Southern Mississippi, from which Bickett had earned her degree. In 2013 the couple adopted twin boys on the day they were born, though only Bickett was considered by law to be a parent. They worried about one day having to tell their boys why the state considered their family lesser than others, about doctors not recognizing Sanders as their mother during an emergency, about a host of other legal complications they could not imagine. They wanted to be married.

The other couple that would join them in the case was Jocelyn Pritchett and Carla Webb. They had been born and raised in Mississippi and lived together there for eleven years, and in 2008 and 2012, Pritchett gave birth to their two sons. She and Webb had married in 2013, though in Maine, where they had spent vacations and gay marriage was legal. The State of Mississippi did not recognize their marriage, and the frustration of having to file business and personal taxes as individuals and explain to strangers why their kids had two mothers was wearing them down. They also wanted, believed that they had the right, to be married.

On October 20, 2014, Bickett, Sanders, Pritchett, Webb, and a gay rights organization—the Campaign for Southern Equality—filed a lawsuit in Jackson federal court seeking a preliminary injunction, the legal mechanism for blocking Mississippi's anti-gay-marriage law.[36] The claim they made was based on a statute that so many other lawsuits in the state's past had relied on but that had rarely if ever been used to protect the rights of gay men or lesbians or other members of Mississippi's LGBTQ community. It was Section 1983, the law that prohibited state officials from violating people's constitutional rights and had its origins in Reconstruction. The claim the women made was that the Mississippi Constitution's and a state statute's ban on gay marriages ran afoul of the US Constitution's guarantee of equal treatment and due process. The thing of it was, thirty-one states and the District of Columbia, from Oklahoma to Massachusetts to West Virginia, had by that time allowed same-sex couples to marry, suggesting the chances that Mississippi's law could survive the legal challenge were slim.[37]

Dozens of federal courts had already ruled that bans on matrimony between same-sex couples *did* violate their rights to equal treatment and due process and *were* wrong for all the reasons that these four women said they were wrong. Unless the federal judge who would be assigned their case intended to go against this trend and the legal and cultural forces propelling it, there seemed little that he or she might do beyond the boilerplate of blocking the Mississippi ban for the reasons stated. This was the situation that faced Reeves, the judge whose name appeared on the blue index card to which the court clerk downstairs had flipped the evening before. He would hear the case, and within a few days he was ready to talk with his law clerks about it.

When they gathered in Reeves's office on a late October morning, he told them he really didn't know how he was going to rule. "I didn't believe him," recalled Keith French, one of Reeves's clerks at the time. "He says, 'I want to see what you guys think. This is going to be a great opportunity to teach my law clerks, to see how you are going to solve a case that is going to impact the nation.'" The judge already had an idea of how he wanted to frame his opinion, to go beyond a judge's usual constraints of just applying the law to the facts and announcing a decision. He wanted to explain the history behind the state's ban on gay marriage and the discrimination against LGBTQ individuals more broadly, an effort that he believed might help all people, not just lawyers, better understand why the law must surely change in a fundamental way. Reeves did not yet know that history, though, and piled high on his desk were books, volumes like Mississippi historian John Howard's *Men Like That* and *Gaylaw: Challenging the Apartheid of the Closet* by William Eskridge, an eminent professor who had taught at the University of Virginia Law School when Reeves was there. He passed out the books to his clerks, asking them to read them as well as the slew of cases and other materials that had dealt with the issues and their history. French noticed that some passages in the books had already been underlined by the judge.

About three weeks later, on November 12, Reeves held a hearing on the request for a preliminary injunction—and the courtroom was packed, so packed that a second chamber and closed-circuit TV were required to accommodate everyone who wanted to watch. The lawyers alone numbered no fewer than ten, including several from New York and North Carolina. As the judge took the bench, settled into his dark brown high-backed chair, and welcomed the crowd, he seemed a bit astonished. "Welcome to the Southern District of Mississippi," Reeves said with a smile. "It's nice to have a full courtroom."[38]

First up was the women's attorney, Roberta Kaplan, a formidable high-decibel presence whom a client once described as eating bullies for lunch.[39] Though long a combative litigator in New York, she had become nationally known the year before for her landmark Supreme Court victory on behalf of Edith Windsor, the gay-rights activist who had challenged the federal Defense of Marriage Act's definition of marriage as "between one man and one woman."[40] On this issue Kaplan knew her stuff cold.

There is a pace to proceedings when Reeves presides. It is deliberate and unhurried, the judge often pausing for long stretches in thought or to read a document, the side of his jaw propped in his palm or his hands steepled to his chin. He invariably responds "No problem" when a lawyer apologizes for whatever. When he asks a question or makes a comment, it is typically incisive and delivered with arresting calm. Kaplan began her argument by saying, "It's good to be down here in Mississippi," adding that she had a "tendency to speak very, very fast," which, depending on the circumstances, could be a good or bad thing. "No, it's never a good thing for our court reporter," Reeves responded. Point made.

For the better part of an entire day the hearing played out, and it never seemed much of a contest. Kaplan presented her argument crisply, clearly. Gay couples were suffering harm in Mississippi "every single day" solely because they were gay. All her clients were asking was "to be treated like everyone else." Gay people could not change who they were, being gay did not affect their ability to contribute to society, they had long suffered discrimination, and only the courts could fix their predicament—all factors requiring Mississippi to show an exceedingly persuasive justification for its law, which it could not do, said Kaplan. The state could not even show that the law was rationally related to a legitimate government interest—the lowest level of legal justification—because it was clearly motivated by mere dislike and moral disapproval of gay people.

Reeves's occasional questions to Kaplan went largely to history. Was there evidence of long-standing gay discrimination in Mississippi? Plenty, she said, and went through it. Didn't gay people have the political power to effect change without the courts, given the lightning speed at which their movement had progressed compared with the Black civil rights movement? Maybe, though courts should still strike down laws that discriminate against gay people, Black people, or women. Should the Fourteenth Amendment—the rights to equal treatment and due process—apply when its authors had no notion of gay people or gay marriage in 1868? Absolutely, and nor did those authors envision desegregation of public facilities or marriage between Black and white people. After an intense couple of hours, Kaplan was finished. There was a break, and then state deputy attorney general Justin Matheny took his turn. It did not go well. Reeves allowed him to meander for a while, trying to nail down the motivation for the marriage ban, and then zeroing in on the case's heart.

"So what is the state's rational basis for saying that same-sex couples cannot marry," the judge asked, "that we will not recognize same-sex couples who are married from other states, and we will further burden same-sex couples and prohibit them from adopting children, children they can provide for, children who they love? All a child wants is to be loved. They don't care by whom or what. All they want is to be nurtured and loved." The basis, Matheny replied, was the state's desire for "responsible procreation" and "stable families." It didn't take much to shoot that down. What about old people or prisoners or infertile couples—they can marry but not procreate. "How legitimate then is procreation?" asked Reeves. There seemed no good answer to this—or to the dozens more questions Reeves directed Matheny's way. After the deputy attorney general stumbled through the rest of his argument, after Kaplan responded and the court broke for lunch, the lawyers argued about whether any decision Reeves reached could be put on hold, and the hearing was done.

Less than two weeks later, the opinion was out, seventy-two pages of facts and law and history and stories of people told with patience, simplicity, some humor, a voice of easy rhythm, and a striking degree of empathy for those who were sure to take hard the conclusions it would reach.[41] "The majority of Mississippians disapprove of same-sex marriage," Reeves wrote. Referring to a voter-adopted amendment to the state Constitution, he continued: "This court does not believe that the 86% of Mississippians who voted against same-sex marriage in 2004 did so with malice, bigotry, or hatred in their hearts. Many were simply trying to preserve their view of what a marriage should be, whether by religion or tradition. They deserve an explanation as to why same-sex marriage is now sweeping the country." Reeves then asked his readers—ordinary people, he hoped, as much as learned lawyers—seven questions, from

Can gay and lesbian citizens love? to *Can gay and lesbian citizens help make their children good and productive citizens?* to *Without the right to marry, are gay and lesbian citizens subjected to humiliation and indignity?* That the answer to each was yes, Reeves continued, led him to "the inescapable conclusion that same-sex couples should be allowed to share in the benefits, and burdens, for better or for worse, of marriage."

Most remarkable about the opinion was its deep recounting of history—an approach first evident in the Lopez car-stop case but pervasive here. In one twelve-page section came the stories of lobotomies and sterilization of homosexual "perverts," criminal penalties and bans against entering the country for being gay, "conversion therapy" and FBI surveillance and Mississippi Sovereign Commission harassment of gay congressmen, teachers, and civil rights lawyers. But it was the story of civil rights organizer Bayard Rustin that captured Reeves's focus, a depressing tale of a talented and honorable man whose tormentors were both Black and white—a startling fact that the judge had not appreciated fully before his research. As Reeves wrote, "Rustin's story speaks to the long tradition of Americans from all walks of life uniting to discriminate against homosexuals. It did not matter if one was liberal or conservative, segregationist or civil rights leader, Democrat or Republican; homosexuals were 'the other.'"[42]

Near the end of the opinion, Reeves wrote a telling passage about his role as a judge. An argument persuasive to many at the time, including the US Court of Appeals for the Sixth Circuit, and one gaining prevalence now, is that judges should step aside and let progress play out through the democratic process in legislatures. "The undersigned sees the judicial role differently," he wrote. "It is difficult to see how gay and lesbian Mississippians can depend on the political process to provide them any timely relief. And while they wait and see how the political process will play out, their legal rights and those of their children will continue to be denied."[43] As it happened, those gay and lesbian Mississippians would have to wait a good while longer. The state's appeal of Reeves's ruling delayed its enforcement until the following July, and by then the US Supreme Court had issued its landmark 5-4 decision, in *Obergefell v. Hodges*, striking down bans on same-sex marriage.[44]

Reeves's opinion, as powerful as it was, may have seemed superfluous and gotten lost in the wake of the high court's words. Nonetheless, the judge believed that what he had written was important, especially the bit about discrimination by Black Americans. "One of the things that I wanted to make sure people understood," he explained later, "was that gays and lesbians . . . had a unique set of people discriminating against them; the Black community was very hard on the gay community. . . . It needed to be said."

Something Savage Unleashed

On January 15, 2015, as the same-sex marriage decision stalled in the court of appeals, the last two of the ten teenagers involved in the racist rampages that ended with the murder of James Craig Anderson pleaded guilty to hate crimes. With the investigation and pleas done, Reeves could finally sentence the first three teenagers who confessed their guilt—Dedmon, Butler, and John Rice.[45]

Ask trial court judges what part of their job is most difficult, and many will say sentencing, determining the fate of the people who come before them. The presentencing report, prepared by the federal probation office, is a detailed compilation of a defendant's background and record, often thorough and rich with information, and the sentencing guidelines themselves can ease uncertainty over an appropriate punishment. Reeves tended to rely heavily on both. Arriving at sentences for the three teenagers, though, proved surprisingly contentious. Prosecutors wanted to make a splash of sorts with the first murder case under the Shepard–Byrd Act and pushed for punishments that would give the act weight and draw notice. The defense lawyers stressed their clients' youth and capacity for reform. So-called in-camera hearings—ones closed to the public—were held to hash out the differences.

"I thought about what it was I could say that would benefit these kids," the judge recalled. "I was thinking about the year we were in, where we had been, and wondered how these kids could be before me for this type of crime. . . . You do want to give those persons some sense of hope, but I did want them to understand the significant toll that they had placed on our state, that they did not have the right to take away *my* Mississippi." Reeves wrote what he wanted to say by hand, and it was only the day before the hearing that he shared it with his clerks. They were startled, especially by his use of a certain word. That word was "nigger." *Do you really think you ought to say that word?*, they asked. *It is* necessary *to say that word*, he responded.

On a cold gray morning in February 2015, the teenagers, in shackles and red prison jumpsuits, and their lawyers and three attorneys from the US government appeared before the judge. A somber hush settled across the courtroom and the many friends and relatives of either Anderson or the defendants and the dozen or so members of the media crowding the five rows of benches in back. Like a typical sentencing, this one followed a script. The defendants confirmed that their lawyers had represented them well and had shared with them the presentencing reports. The judge repeated the charges against them and confirmed their pleas of guilt. Victim impact statements were read—Anderson's sister spoke of "tears and grief so heavy, our hearts can hardly bear," and James Bradfield, Anderson's partner, in court but so upset that he needed a prosecutor to stand by his side and read his statement, told the defendants that "there's no room on earth for people like you." The judge then confirmed the range of possible sentences he could impose under criminal statutes and the guidelines and called for the defendants to speak if they wanted. Each expressed remorse, shame, sorrow, and apologies for the grief they had caused.[46]

Then, in a gentle voice, Reeves allowed the three teenagers to sit down, because "this statement is a little long." He began to read. He started, of course, with history. How his former professor had written that Mississippi "evokes strong reactions from those who live here and from those who do not," and how another author had written that "there is something different about Mississippi, something almost unspeakably primal and vicious; something savage unleashed there that has yet to come to rest." Reeves continued: "Mississippi has expressed its savagery in a number of ways throughout its history." He mentioned slavery as "the cruelest" but also, "a close second," its "infatuation with lynchings." They were public rituals, "carnival-like," which took place occasionally in states around the nation but nowhere more often than in what he called "that scar on the map of America," the Deep South.

"How could hate, fear, or whatever it was, transform genteel, God-fearing, God-loving Mississippians into mindless murderers and sadistic torturers?" Reeves asked. He wondered the same thing "about the events which bring us here together today. Those crimes of the past as well as these have so damaged the psyche and reputation of this great state." He continued: "You see, Mississippi soil has been stained with the blood of folk whose names have become synonymous with the civil rights movement." He mentioned Emmett Till and Medgar Evers and others, well known and obscure. "On June 26, 2011, four days short of his birthday, the blood of James Anderson was added to Mississippi soil." The common denominator in all these killings, Reeves explained, was not merely that most of the victims were Black, but that the last thing they saw was "the inhumanity of racism. The last thing that each felt was the audacity and agony of hate, senseless hate: crippling, maiming its victims and finally taking away their lives."

Mississippi had since tried to reform itself, to pull itself "from the abyss of moral depravity it once so proudly floundered in," but these three young men before him today had "ripped off the scab of the healing scars of Mississippi causing her, our Mississippi, to bleed again. A toxic mix of alcohol, foolishness, and unadulterated hatred caused these young people to resurrect a nightmarish specter of lynchings and lynch mobs from the Mississippi we long to forget," Reeves said. "This was a 2011 version of the nigger hunts." And the thing that "is so disturbing and so shocking and even so numbing is that these nigger hunts were perpetrated by our children"—a subtle reference to that photo of his first-grade class. In answering the question that he had asked near the beginning of his statement, the judge said: "The simple fact is that what turned these children, these kids, these young adults into criminal defendants was their joint decision to act on racial hatred. . . . Echoes of Mississippi's past. White Power. Nigger . . . the nuclear bomb of racial epithets."

Reeves continued: "The sadness of this day also has an element of irony to it." Almost every official involved with the case—from the mayor and district attorney of Jackson to the US attorney general to the judge himself—was Black. That represented progress, Reeves argued. "You see, today we take another step away from Mississippi's tortured past."

Ending with an acknowledgment that the defendants had told the world what they had done—"It is ugly. It is painful. It is sad. And it is criminal"—Reeves pronounced the sentences for each of them: seven years in prison for Butler, eight and a half years for Rice, and fifty years for Dedmon. Yet justice "will not be complete unless these defendants use the remainder of their lives to learn from this experience and fully commit to making a positive difference in the New Mississippi. And, finally, the court wishes that the defendants also can find peace." Within hours, the judge's speech had exploded on social media and been reported by CNN and NPR. Surprised by the reaction, Reeves became a public hero of sorts, asked to speak at the nation's top law schools and made the subject of admiring opinion pieces in the *Washington Post* and the *Atlantic*.[47]

. . .

People throughout the country had finally heard Reeves's voice, and he would share it again with them often, in opinions on questions small as well as large, on everything from religious complaints against gay marriage to cases challenging Mississippi's display of the Confederate flag. He would be reversed on appeal in some of these cases, and in several others he would find himself unable under the law to reach the decision he believed was just—but he would always explain why. Yet to come was a personal tragedy—and his ruling in a case that would be the most consequential for the nation in almost fifty years.

8 Neither Admit nor Deny

The sight of rain skimming across the plate-glass windows overlooking Manhattan from the heights of Merrill Lynch's midtown offices prompted John Thain to clap shut his briefcase, lift his suit coat from the back of a chair, and head for home. It was about 5:00 p.m. on a Friday in September 2008, and he wanted to beat the traffic back to his ten-acre estate in suburban Rye, New York.[1] Lean and chiseled with a rod-stiff way about him, the fifty-two-year-old financier had presided over the investment bank for nine months, a brief but demanding period that had left him feeling entitled to spend some time with his wife and the youngest of their four children on a stormy evening.[2] Thain's progress out the door was halted by the pulsing light and soft beep of a phone. It was Terry Checki, executive vice president of the New York Federal Reserve Bank. Checki was friendly but terse: "Be at the Fed at 6:00."

Thain could guess what was up. Word had it that the foundering investment bank Lehman Brothers was short on cash and headed for collapse. The call reminded him of the one that had summoned him in 1998, when he was a senior banker at Goldman Sachs, to help devise a bailout for hedge fund Long-Term Capital Management. Thain arrived alone at the Fed's cavernous offices downtown to find gathered in a conference room US treasury secretary Henry Paulson,

New York Fed boss Timothy Geithner, and the CEOs of the largest banks in New York. Paulson and Geithner got to the point: *Lehman is in serious trouble, probably can't open for business on Monday. We're here to find a solution before disaster strikes the economy. Oh,* Paulson added with characteristic bluntness, *the federal government is not going to put in a dime to help.*

Thain was taken aback. He glanced across the table at JPMorgan's Jamie Dimon and Goldman's Lloyd Blankfein and could tell they shared his surprise. Their options had suddenly narrowed. In March the Fed and Dimon's bank had stepped in to save investment firm Bear Stearns, and Thain reckoned that the pressure was on, maybe from Congress, to avoid another Wall Street handout. He had also heard that Bank of America (BofA) and Barclays were sniffing around as potential Lehman saviors. As the group continued discussions on Saturday morning, its members realized Lehman would need as much as $25 billion, an enormous sum even for them. And as the chances for the bank's survival began to fade, a terrifying question tugged at Thain: *What do I do about Merrill Lynch?* Merrill had, like so many banks, larded its books with mortgage-related securities that were losing value as the housing bust played out. He had directed the unloading of hundreds of millions of dollars' worth, but their continued decline sapped the bank of capital and liquidity. If Lehman went down, financing might dry up, and Merrill could be back in this same room next week.

During a late-morning break, Thain took the elevator down to the sidewalk on Liberty Street, pulled out his BlackBerry, and dialed Bank of America CEO Kenneth Lewis at his home near Charlotte, North Carolina.[3] "Ken, I think we should talk about a strategic arrangement," the Merrill boss said. "I'd like to do that," Lewis responded. "I can be in New York in a couple of hours. Meet me at our corporate apartment in the Time Warner Center at 2:30."[4]

Over the next thirty-six hours the two chief executives alone, and then with their staffs and lawyers, concocted a $50 billion merger. Thain wanted BofA to take a 9.9 percent stake in Merrill and provide financing. Lewis wanted 100 percent. Lewis prevailed. Thain liked being Merrill's CEO and didn't want to lose his job. Lewis assured him he would have a big role at BofA. Thain demanded guarantees that BofA wouldn't pull out if Merrill's finances deteriorated. That was okay with Lewis. And the bonuses—Thain wanted to pay up to $4.5 billion in bonuses before closing so that his top lieutenants wouldn't walk out the door. Agreed, said Lewis, so long as his people could approve any payments. By Sunday evening Thain had a deal for $29 a share—not bad for a company whose stock was at $17 and sliding.[5]

Then things deteriorated further. Merrill lost about $7 billion in October, $5 billion in November, and another $5 billion in December. Lewis, threatening to squelch the deal, extracted another $20 billion from the federal government. None of this was publicly revealed until Bank of America reported its fourth-quarter results in January 2009, long after the December 5 shareholder vote to approve the merger. Also disclosed for the first time in that quarterly report: the nearly $4.5 billion in bonuses.[6] Public outrage erupted. By September 2008, when Thain received the call on that rainy Friday afternoon, the sudden and widespread default of dirt-cheap mortgages and bewilderingly complex debt securities was already bringing the US economy to its knees. The unemployment rate had almost doubled since December 2007.[7] The Dow Jones Industrial Average had plummeted nearly 17 percent.[8] Pension plans and 401(k)s and aspirations for retirement had shriveled to insignificance. Across America, millions of ordinary people were bitter, out of work, and desperate for relief.

At Bank of America, newly merged with Merrill Lynch, it was Thain who would take the fall. As usual, though, it was shareholders who would pay the price.

A Façade of Enforcement

On a Sunday in August 2009, the kind of gently warming morning that beckoned New Yorkers to the beach or a backyard lawn chair, Jed Rakoff could not wait to get to his office. He arrived on the thirteenth floor of the Daniel Patrick Moynihan United States Courthouse and entered his spacious chambers. There was a ritual of sorts for the judge's clerks. On Friday evenings they would leave a stack of papers—briefs, complaints, memoranda—on the faded blue sofa just inside his office, hoping there were enough to keep him busy until Monday. On this Sunday morning Rakoff retrieved a cup of his beloved coffee from the chambers kitchen, picked up the document on top, and began to read.

It was the story of the Merrill deal with Bank of America and the alleged cover-up: the attempt to keep shareholders in the dark about multi-billion-dollar bonuses and losses that taxpayers would ultimately pay. The SEC had sued for fraud, seizing the chance to prove itself a fierce regulator rather than the toothless watchdog on duty when banks and financiers ruined the economy. The parties had agreed to settle and, on August 3, 2009, filed their agreement in federal court for approval.[9] Rakoff read the thirteen-page document again. And again. He couldn't quite believe it. Not only did the settlement call for a penalty of $33 million—oddly small for a $130 billion institution near the heart of the financial crisis—but it allowed the bank to avoid saying what it or, more to the point, any of its executives had done wrong.[10] Worse, he realized that BofA shareholders were being cheated twice. First, they had approved the merger while apparently unaware of the bonuses or the $17 billion of losses at Merrill. Now, they—and not the bank's bosses or the financial geniuses who had run Merrill into the ground—were being asked to pay the price. Rakoff wondered: Could he reject the arrangement and order the parties to do better? That would be unusual, to say the least. If they refused, what then? Could he just order them to trial? That would be unheard of. Rakoff decided that he would do what he typically did when he needed more facts. He would on short notice summon the parties to a public hearing in court.

The following Tuesday, August 10, just after 9:30 a.m., Rakoff and the clerk assigned to the case headed from chambers to the courtroom one flight up. On the bench his mood quickly darkened. The lawyer for the SEC, David Rosenfeld, began the hearing by recounting the history of the Bank of America settlement, but his voice was so soft that Rakoff motioned him toward a microphone on a podium by the jury box. Before long, the judge interrupted.[11]

"What you are saying, if I understand it, is that Bank of America and Merrill effectively lied to their shareholders about a highly material matter."

"What we are saying—" Rosenfeld started to reply.

Rakoff cut in. "Is that right?"

"That is essentially correct. We are saying they made representations—"

"So who at Bank of America and Merrill was responsible for that?"

"We have not alleged any individual misconduct."

"Did this happen," Rakoff continued, incredulous, "was this some sort of *government* that performed these actions or were there human beings that wrote these documents?"

"There were indeed human rogues who wrote these documents," Rosenfeld said.

Then came Rakoff's obvious but not so easily answered question: "So who were they?" Law firms, came the first response. After further and not so gentle probing came the names of the two executives who had negotiated the merger provisions. After a few more questions, the SEC lawyers revealed that the two chief executives—Thain at Merrill and Lewis at Bank of America—had signed off on the proxy

Neither Admit nor Deny [181]

statement, the public document that described the important terms of the deal but failed to mention the bonuses. None of these people had been named in the settlement agreement, let alone accused of deceiving shareholders.

"Why isn't this a grossly unfair amount?" said Rakoff of the $33 million penalty. "Why shouldn't it be a much larger amount, an amount to come from the individual persons who were responsible for orchestrating this misleading proxy?"[12]

Having finished his exasperating back-and-forth with the SEC lawyer, Rakoff turned to the bank's attorney, Lewis Liman, the son of Arthur Liman, legendary litigator and chief Senate counsel during the Iran-Contra affair. Noting that the bank had neither admitted nor denied the SEC's allegations in the settlement agreement, the judge asked, "I would like to know . . . do you admit it or deny it?"

Liman demurred, saying he didn't want to violate the agreement, but the judge told him to answer anyhow. "Your honor," said Liman, "the Bank of America's position is that it did not violate the proxy law or any other federal securities law."[13]

Rakoff then moved on to the amount of the bonuses. "Did the Wall Street people expect to be paid big bonuses in years when their companies lost $27 billion?" After explaining that much of the money was spread among thirty-nine thousand workers who received an average of $91,000 each, Liman said that "there are people who are paid a lot of money, but we are talking about payments that are spread out over a lot of employees."

The judge smiled. "I am glad you think that $91,000 is not a lot of money," he said. "I wish . . . an average American was making anything like $91,000."[14] Throughout the hearing, the lawyers sounded perplexed at Rakoff's probing, expecting that in the end he would simply conform to decades of practice and approve the settlement. Instead, on September 14, 2009, the judge issued a scathing opinion that called the agreement "a contrivance designed to provide the

S.E.C. with the façade of enforcement and the management of the bank with a quick resolution of an embarrassing inquiry." Rakoff was particularly incensed that the SEC hadn't pointed the finger at any of the executives or lawyers responsible for the bank's cover-up. The parties could do better, he figured, and he ordered them "to have this case ready to be tried on February 1, 2010."[15]

In the following days, as the judge's actions hit the news, the letters and words of praise poured in. A doctor wrote: "Finally, a jurist who lives up to our highest aspirations for our judges and our judicial system." From Massachusetts came a letter saying only Rakoff had "had the courage to stand up to the abusers!" His clerks were in awe, with one telling him, "Wow, you are cooler than Derek Jeter!" Achieving celebrity was not necessarily Rakoff's ambition, though plenty in the judge's background suggested that public accolades were welcome. What mattered for Rakoff—and what would largely propel his handling of cases related to the 2008 financial crisis—flickered in the barbed humor of his comment to Liman about the $91,000 that was considered not a lot of money on Wall Street but a dream salary in many American households. Prospering in the face of a financial disaster, especially one that may have been *your own damned fault*, while the less fortunate took the losses exemplified an abuse of wealth and swaggering power that undermined democracy and any notion of fairness. It was oligarchy, and it grated on Rakoff.

"When I was growing up, everyone was becoming middle class, and the difference between what a CEO and an average employee earned was something like forty times" and narrowing, he said. "We were all very proud of that. It was an example of democracy working, not just in the political sense but in the economic sense, and that was great. It was part of what made us proud to be Americans." Rakoff did not have "animosity toward Wall Street," stressed his friend from college, Robert Putnam, the political scientist and author of *Bowling Alone*. "I do think Jed is upset about the growing inequality, but his stance is not from animosity or resentment; he does believe things are out of kilter. . . . He has a good sense of what fits with the fundamental values of fairness, a really deep, grounded sense of what is fair."

That sense would not always fit easily with the law, or the growing constraints on what a judge could do to promote what he believed was right and served democracy. As much as anyone, though, and particularly over the following decade, Rakoff would push against those limits, trying within the bounds of the law and logic to impose the accountability on banks—and on bankers and other individuals—that so many Americans expected. Companies did not commit crimes, as the truism went while Rakoff was a prosecutor, people did, and Rakoff believed that the individuals responsible for the apparent wrongdoing in the Bank of America case deserved to be identified and pay the price. That they were not even mentioned seemed an artifact of a misguided preference for efficiency. Pursuing individuals was hard. It took time and money and thorough investigation. And individuals accused of wrongdoing tended to fight back, often all the way to trial. It was easier for an overworked agency staff to target companies, which were typically eager to settle, pay money, and promise to do better.

The bank had also refused to say what, exactly, it had done—not what it had done wrong, but what it had *done*—in Rakoff's mind a troubling consequence of the neither-admit-nor-deny deal with the devil that SEC enforcement chief Stanley Sporkin had made back in the 1970s. Worse, in the court hearing, Liman had said the bank denied violating any laws, leaving Rakoff not knowing what to think. So how could he possibly approve the settlement? If Liman was correct, $33 million was an unjustified penalty that the bank shouldn't have to pay. If the SEC was correct, if the bank had lied to its shareholders about paying $3.6 billion in bonuses, a $33 million penalty was not nearly enough.

Rakoff would try to use his one point of leverage—the legal requirement that he approve the settlement—to extract answers. The SEC and the bank would try to satisfy him. It would not be easy. The two law firms the Bank of America had relied on so far—Wachtell, Lipton, Rosen & Katz to negotiate the deal, and Liman's firm, Cleary Gottlieb Steen & Hamilton, to handle the SEC—appeared to have misjudged Rakoff. They had understandably advised the bank that most information about its dealings with lawyers on the Merrill acquisition were cloaked with the attorney-client privilege. Since the judge demanded more facts, however, the bank would have to waive the privilege and disclose some of that information. There was also the emerging threat of a shareholder class action challenging the transaction, a possibility the lawyers seemed to have underestimated. As a result, the bank hired new counsel—the nine-hundred-lawyer firm Paul, Weiss, Rifkind, Wharton & Garrison and its chairman, Brad Karp.

The choice of Karp made a lot of sense. For starters, he looked the part—a savvy advocate with a winning grin who wore Brioni suits and Hermès ties and spoke with a coiled enthusiasm that left scant room for pauses or doubt. More important, his legal skills were formidable. He had an enviable record of steering Citigroup, JPMorgan, and a host of other financial behemoths from the kind of trouble that could tank a stock price. With Karp in the lead, the discussions shifted to how to placate Rakoff. The amount of the penalty would certainly have to rise, because $33 million wasn't going to do it. The bank could also propose some kind of "corporate therapeutics," internal safeguards that might assure the judge that this sort of thing would never happen again. Pinning the blame on an individual was probably a nonstarter, unless one of the lawyers wanted to offer up himself or Edward O'Keefe, serving as Bank of America's general counsel since his predecessor's unceremonious ouster a year earlier. All agreed to wait and see what the SEC had in mind.

By December 2009, after several marathon negotiating sessions, the bank and the SEC were close on a new agreement. They had decided that BofA would pay a penalty of $150 million, and various independent auditors and consultants would police its future disclosures. There would be a detailed statement of facts that did not amount to an admission of wrongdoing. On one point, though, the bank refused to budge: No individual—let alone CEO Ken Lewis—could be named as a defendant in the suit. The SEC lawyers eventually conceded the point, and the parties had a deal. Yet soon a new player would knock their plans awry.

Half-Baked Justice

On the morning of February 4, 2010, a torrent of camera clicks washed through the large room at 28 Liberty Street in lower Manhattan as the New York attorney general strode to the podium. His meaty face stern, his barrel chest puffed out, Andrew Cuomo raised his right palm to quiet the crowd. He announced that his office, a persistent Wall Street pest and thorn in the SEC's side, had just sued Bank of America and two of its officers for fraud. "This was an arrogant scheme hatched by the bank's top executives who believed they could play by their own set of rules," Cuomo said.[16]

The complaint covered much of the same ground as the SEC's lawsuit, but the big difference was that it named individuals. It also claimed that Timothy Mayopoulos, Bank of America general counsel, had recommended telling shareholders about Merrill's losses and planned bonuses before they voted on the acquisition. He had been overruled and, just four days after the vote, fired.[17] The new details were lurid and potentially damning—although, in the view of BofA and the SEC, totally unsubstantiated. "That complaint was written by a psycho," commented an attorney for the bank. "Typical grandstanding," said an SEC lawyer. Sure, attorneys and accountants had talked about disclosing the losses and bonuses, they explained, but for a $130 billion bank, the total just wasn't "material"—meaning large enough for investors to care. Besides, at the time of the transaction, there was at least a chance the losses would shrink before quarterly reports were due. As for Mayopoulos, his ouster had nothing to do with the disclosure issue. The bank said it had merely needed to give his job temporarily to Brian Moynihan, who was being groomed as the next CEO and might have otherwise left the bank. The SEC, meanwhile, said it had found no evidence to contradict the bank's explanations.

Hours after Cuomo announced his lawsuit, the SEC and Bank of America submitted the new version of their settlement to Rakoff, and almost immediately the judge set a hearing for February 8.[18] That was typical Rakoff—keep a case moving at breakneck speed—a practice that annoyed litigants generally and, in this rancorous case, irritated the lawyers further. The day of the hearing, Rakoff zeroed in on the discrepancies between what Cuomo and the SEC had alleged against the bank.

"Are you in disagreement, then, with the attorney general's conclusions?" he asked George Canellos, head of the SEC's New York office at the time.

"Let me be a little bit roundabout in saying . . . ," the lawyer responded.

"It won't be unheard of in this litigation," said Rakoff.[19]

Canellos argued that while the attorney general was making mere allegations, the SEC had actual evidence. For Rakoff, however, that wasn't enough. He wanted to *see* that evidence—from everyone involved—an extraordinary demand from a judge whose job was simply to okay a settlement. In the following days, he got what he wanted. As Rakoff read the new material, Cuomo's case at first seemed compelling: Mayopoulos, the bank's general counsel, had been fired *one day* after trying to urge disclosure of the unexpectedly high losses—and escorted by guards out of the building. Yet Cuomo offered nothing to show *why* Mayopoulos had been fired. For its part, the SEC had done no better, failing to come up with any evidence for the bank's contention that Mayopoulos had been ousted simply to make room for Moynihan.

In the end Rakoff found it hard to believe either version, putting him at a crossroads. He could reject the bank's settlement and force the parties to trial—scheduled to begin in less than two weeks. Or he could comply with legal precedent that suggested he had to defer to the SEC's judgment, despite the open questions. It was a very tough call. "I didn't know how far to push it," he said later, "coupled with I wasn't sure where the legal line was drawn. I did feel that . . . they had made a good faith attempt to meet me at least halfway. I wasn't totally satisfied with it, but I know now, I didn't know then, that there was a big internal debate, between the lawyers . . . as to whether to take me up on appeal when I turned down the [first] settlement."

On February 22, 2010, Rakoff issued his opinion. In his typical way, and unlike many judges, he kept it short and engaging and avoided lengthy legal citations.[20] He wrote that if it were solely up to him, he "would reject the settlement as inadequate and misguided," but he acknowledged his obligation to show deference to the agency. More important in his view was his duty not to impose his own preferences but to show restraint. Rakoff continued: "In the words of a great former Justice of the Supreme Court, Harlan Fiske Stone, 'the only check upon our own exercise of power is our own sense of self-restraint.'" He approved the settlement, "while shaking [his] head" and calling it "half-baked justice at best." When Rakoff showed the opinion to his wife, Ann, that night, she nodded in approval but then looked up with a mischievous smile. "What do you know about baking?"

You Haven't Answered My Question

It would not be long before Rakoff would get another chance—in a strikingly similar case—to test the boundaries of a judge's self-restraint when faced with the misdeeds of Wall Street. It is fair to say that the case began in October 2006, on a trading floor in New York almost half the size of a football field. Computer screens glowed with brightly colored numbers and graphs, and the flags of Brazil and Korea and a host of other nations engaged in global finance hung from the ceiling. The taut murmur of voices and clacking of keyboards filled the room, punctuated with occasional bursts of shouting and profanity.[21]

In the room sat traders of collateralized debt obligations (CDOs) at Citigroup. On this fall morning the value of those insanely intricate conglomerations of mortgages were down. A lot. And Citi still owned tens of billions of dollars' worth. In a voice of controlled panic, one trader passed the word to a bond salesman at the bank, Sohail Khan, that they needed to short some stuff—presidents, constellations, that sort of thing. Translation: The trader wanted to bet against certain CDOs, named after constellations and US presidents, that were packed with mortgages near default. By bundling them into an even more complex security—a synthetic CDO squared—and then wagering that it would fail, Citigroup could squeeze some profit from deals going bad before other investors wised up.

Khan and the traders then told Brian Stoker, at the tender age of thirty-five the fabricator of perhaps more CDOs than anyone else at the bank. Stoker knew the drill. He would ask an independent firm—Credit Suisse Alternative Capital (CSAC)—to pick the CDOs for the new security, giving the process a veneer of credibility. This time, though, he and his colleagues would persuade CSAC to include the ones that they wanted to short. Those CDOs appeared reasonably safe, but unknown to CSAC, Citi believed they were toxic. Then

Stoker put a target on his back. He sent an email to his bosses explaining what he had done and warning: "Don't tell CSAC." The arrangement was not necessarily illegal but from an investor's point of view could look like fraud: not disclosing something—Citi's low opinion of the CDOs—that they would want to know before they parted with their money. As it turned out, on February 28, 2007, fifteen banks, hedge funds, and asset managers put almost $1 billion into the synthetic CDO squared. By November 2007 the "top of the line" security, as Stoker had touted it, was in default. Investors lost hundreds of millions of dollars. Citi, however, earned about $160 million in fees and trading profit. Stoker chalked it up as another win.[22]

It wasn't long, though, before the SEC, as part of a broader crackdown on banks in the CDO business, got wind of the transaction and called in Citigroup's lawyers—including Brad Karp—for a chat. During the meeting early in 2011, Karp made clear that he didn't think much of the agency's suggestions that the bank had committed fraud. First, Citi ultimately *lost* $30 billion on CDOs—proof, he argued, that it didn't know any better than its customers which would rise or fall in value. Second, the SEC seemed to be relying on essentially one email: Stoker's "Don't tell CSAC" missive.

As negotiations between Citi and the SEC stretched over months, and with no agreement in sight, Karp played an ace. He showed up with his partner, Theodore Wells, among the nation's most celebrated trial lawyers. The message was clear: Citi was prepared to battle to the end. The SEC had neither the resources nor the talent to go up against that kind of firepower, and so in early October 2011 it agreed to a compromise. The bank would pay $285 million to settle the case but instead of fraud would accept an accusation of mere negligence—the sin of being sloppy.[23]

The most consequential aspect of the settlement was again a term that was missing: any admission of misconduct. For the moment, though, the bank and the SEC had a deal, and as the parties congratulated each other for ending the case simply, quietly, and without interference from the courts, one of the lawyers delivered a jocular piece of professional advice to the attorneys at the SEC: *File the case in Washington, DC, rather than New York; you cannot risk its landing before Rakoff.*

A Legal Hero for Our Time

"Whose street? Our street! Whose street? Our street!" The shrill chant echoed through the swarm of protestors walking south on Centre Street, along Foley Square, in lower Manhattan. Crudely lettered cardboard signs—"No more greed. No more war" and "Shit is fucked up and bullshit"—bobbed above their heads. To their left, a raucous crowd covered the gray stone steps below the massive pillars of the state Supreme Court building and spilled to the sidewalks below. Across Centre Street in Thomas Paine Park, circling a fifty-foot black-granite shaft intended to symbolize freedom but now suggesting a middle finger thrust into the sky, a scruffy cast of thousands chanted and played trumpets and tubas and thumped white plastic tubs as hundreds of cops with batons and navy NYPD caps moved warily among them.[24]

As Citi and the SEC were wrapping up their agreement, the lefty anticorporate movement known as Occupy Wall Street was marching from its base in Zuccotti Park downtown to Foley Square some twenty blocks north, galvanized by the arrest of seven hundred protestors for blocking the roadway on the Brooklyn Bridge four days earlier.[25] Watching the show from behind a metal-rail barrier along Centre Street were two of Rakoff's clerks—Caleb Hayes-Deats and Matt Shahabian. They were doing their best to look inconspicuous, a tall order for anyone there in a suit and tie, determined to heed Rakoff's admonition of "watch, don't join!" More than idle curiosity had prompted the clerks to walk the block from the federal courthouse to the demonstration. The day before, on October 4, 2011, the protestors detained at the Brooklyn Bridge had sued the city for false arrest, and the complaint had landed before Rakoff. Hayes-Deats had been assigned the case and wanted to get a feel for the people and spirit behind it.

A few days later, though, a second case arrived in chambers. With the Occupy Wall Street lawsuit, it formed a serendipitous pair, dual challenges to money and power—and a financial institution that had helped fuel the protestors' ire. It was the SEC's lawsuit against Citigroup, and almost instantly the rumors began to fly.[26] How had the judge snagged a *third* lawsuit aimed at reining in Wall Street? The press and much of the legal establishment suspected without evidence that Rakoff had fixed "the wheel"—the supposedly random system of assigning cases to federal judges—so that he could be at the center of yet another bank-driven drama.

The Occupy Wall Street suit had barely begun, and the judge turned first to the settlement that the SEC had reached with Citigroup. As Rakoff read the complaint, his initial optimism turned to chagrin. The SEC had sued an individual—Brian Stoker—so that was good. Yet despite the fraud described in the complaint, the bank had admitted nothing. It and the SEC obviously assumed that Rakoff would again be their rubber stamp.[27] Several nights later, the phone finally silent, his clerks gone home, Rakoff swiveled to his computer and typed a list of nine questions. The first: "Why should the Court impose a judgment in a case in which the S.E.C. alleges a serious securities fraud but the defendant neither admits nor denies wrongdoing?" The second: "Is there an overriding public interest in determining whether the S.E.C.'s charges are true?"

As Rakoff saw it, his paramount task in every case was to make sure that the truth came out. Yet for a decade he had been told that he could not always do that, could not even venture into certain areas of the law. Just the year before, the Second Circuit had barred him from ordering foreign officials to pay taxes on offices used for purposes other than diplomacy. Foreign affairs, the court said, were none of his business.[28] In fact, the Supreme Court had—mistakenly, in his view—put a host of issues largely beyond the reach of judges: police misconduct, because cops needed leeway to do their jobs; war, because the Constitution gave Congress and the executive the power to wage war; national security, because it involved secrets inappropriate for airing in court; politics, because the courts were supposed to be apolitical—and, under a 1984 case called *Chevron v. Natural Resources Defense Council*, interpretations of law by administrative agencies like the SEC because regulators were the supposed experts in their fields.[29] In a broad sense that was what Rakoff was up against now: the SEC's presumption that he owed deference to its determinations on, say, whether to settle cases. But to him, deference—like the war and national security and politics exceptions—was just an excuse for ducking cases. He had had enough. After finishing his list, Rakoff wrote: "The parties should be prepared to answer these questions in detail at the November 9 hearing."

On the appointed day, the judge put his black robe over a gray suit and a bright tie and, with his three young law clerks in tow, mounted the flight of metal stairs to the so-called robing room. "This is going to be fun!" he said on the way up. His deputy rapped hard on the door to the courtroom and bellowed "All rise!" In the majestic chamber top attorneys and moneyed bankers packed the rows of pews to the left. Regulators up from Washington sat among them in sober clumps of twos and threes. On the right, in the jury box, reporters scribbled in their notebooks. Dozens of late arrivals leaned against the walls, drawing nervous glances from marshals positioned at the door. All were there to see whether a bank at the heart of the 2008 financial crisis would finally be held accountable for the pain it had caused America.

Rakoff climbed the three steps to his massive wooden bench, eased into a high-backed black chair, and took a sip of coffee from a

Styrofoam cup. "So I'm reminded," he began, "of Humphrey Bogart's famous comment in *Casablanca*, 'Of all the joints in the world, you chose to come here.' But I'm delighted to have you all." It was a subtle reference, largely lost on the crowd, to the lawyers' probable chagrin at having to face him again so soon after the Bank of America ordeal. Rakoff then thanked Citi and the SEC for having answered his questions and explained that he had a few more. At the top of the list: Could he consider the "public interest" in deciding whether to approve their settlement?

Rakoff turned to Matthew Martens, the lawyer for the SEC. Martens, lean and clean-cut as a farm boy, rose from behind the long table facing the bench and offered a circuitous response. Rakoff cut him off. "You haven't answered my question," the judge growled softly, peering down at the lawyer through rimless glasses. Martens shot a glance at his notes, maybe a little nervous but poised. The thirty-eight-year-old attorney had been valedictorian of his law school class, clerked for US chief justice William Rehnquist, prosecuted scores of criminals for the Justice Department—and wrangled with more than his fair share of difficult judges.

Yet now, as chief litigation counsel for the SEC, Martens had the job of defending what to many others seemed indefensible—a suspiciously lenient settlement with Citigroup. What's more, the notion that Rakoff could reject this kind of closed-door bargain as not serving the public interest seemed outlandish, a clear breach of legal precedent, and Martens hesitated to respond. No federal judge in memory had blocked an SEC settlement. "As I read the case law," Martens began, "as I read the courts as saying—the Second Circuit, the Supreme Court, other circuits—as collectively saying . . ." He paused, wary of sounding evasive. "The appropriate standard for the court to apply is one of whether the settlement is fair, adequate, and reasonable." The answer was oblique but its meaning clear: The public interest had little to do with it. All that mattered was what the courts had done in the past. And what the courts had almost always done was defer to the government and the banks.

Yet Rakoff pressed the point. "So if I were to find that [the settlement] still disserved the public interest . . . should I refuse" to approve it? "Your answer is no." Correct, Martens responded. "It's an interesting position," Rakoff said, indicating his disappointment with a slightly theatrical sigh. "I'm supposed to exercise my power, but not my judgment." The judge quickly shifted topics. "I'm not sure why this practice—admittedly a practice that has existed for many decades—of accepting a settlement in which the defendant neither admits nor denies liability makes any sense when we are talking about a public agency like the SEC." Rakoff believed that approving the SEC's settlement with Citigroup, a deal that provided the people with no insight into what had happened, would not only offend his instincts, it would make him, like so many judges before him, complicit in hiding the truth. He stared down at Martens. "Does not the SEC, of all agencies," he asked with quiet and rising intensity, "have an interest in establishing what the truth is . . . what the facts are?"

Martens insisted that the public *does* know what the facts are.

"Why?" Rakoff shot back. "Because you say they are the facts, but the other side does not admit them?"

Martens pushed on. "Citi has agreed to pay a substantial sum of money in response to our allegations," he said, "and they have not denied the allegations. We don't believe in that instance that the public is left wondering what occurred in this case."

"Let's find out," said Rakoff, turning to Karp, Citigroup's lawyer, who had been sitting quietly at the other end of the table from Martens. "Let me ask Mr. Karp. Do you admit the allegations?"

Karp rose, buttoned his suit jacket, and responded in a steady voice: "We do not admit the allegations, your honor." He turned to sit, paused, and rose again. "But if it's any consolation, we do not deny them." The crowd burst into laughter, relishing the release. Even Rakoff cackled.

"I understand that," the judge responded, his competitive instinct compelling him to try answering a good quip with a better one. "And I won't get cute and ask you what percentage of Citigroup's net worth is $95 million because I don't have a microscope with me."

The hearing continued for another ten minutes or so—Rakoff thrusting, Martens and Karp parrying. Eventually, the judge eased up: "I'm not going to rule today, I want to think about all this." When it was over, he descended from the bench and exited through a side door, his three clerks and court deputy trailing. The crowd erupted in a frenetic buzz, speculating about what Rakoff would do. It was almost unthinkable that he might reject the settlement, although he had come close in the Bank of America case. They did not have to wait long.

Rakoff and his three clerks had barely entered the back stairwell when they started chattering about what had happened. "I guess they finally decided to send a hotshot lawyer," the judge laughed, voicing his opinion that Martens had performed better than the SEC attorneys who had bumbled through the hearing on the Bank of America settlement.

Rakoff hadn't made up his mind on what to do, but he was frustrated at Martens's responses. "I was a little ticked," he said later. "I did think he was equivocating." Back in chambers, Rakoff discussed the hearing with Aaron Scherzer, one of his clerks, and as they talked, the SEC's position that it was not his job to determine what was in the public interest—a bold thing to tell a federal judge—rankled. A softer approach, something like, *You do have a role in determining the public interest, and here's why the settlement qualifies*, might have swayed him. He decided that he would reject the settlement, but this would be a collaborative effort, more so than in most cases. The judge would take the first whack at an opinion, as he typically did in the most important matters. His opinions often came back to his clerks typed but also annotated with scrawl so indecipherable that they had to call the judge's deputy to interpret. Clerks would insert legal citations and sometimes an attempt at the kind of joke that often appeared in Rakoff's opinions. "Nice try, that's a good one," Rakoff would respond in the rewrite. "But here's a better one."

In the Citi case the process continued for weeks. On the Sunday before Thanksgiving the judge sent the penultimate draft to all three clerks, eager for their input on an opinion that he knew would draw intense public scrutiny and maybe an appeal. Early on the Monday after Thanksgiving, with a click on the "File" button of the court docket system, the final fifteen-page opinion flew into the ether and landed in the offices of the SEC and Paul Weiss with a thud.

"Finally, in any case like this that touches on the transparency of financial markets whose gyrations have so depressed our economy and debilitated our lives, there is an overriding public interest in knowing the truth," the judge wrote. "In much of the world, propaganda reigns, and truth is confined to secretive, fearful whispers. Even in our nation, apologists for suppressing or obscuring the truth may always be found. But the SEC, of all agencies, has a duty, inherent in its statutory mission, to see that the truth emerges; and if it fails to do so, this court must not, in the name of deference or convenience, grant judicial enforcement to the agency's contrivances."[30] Rakoff rejected the settlement and ordered the parties to trial.

Wall Street and its defenders were shocked. Citi itself offered only the sterile words of PR: "We respectfully disagree with the court's ruling." The rest of America—journalists, lawmakers, Midwestern wage-earners—delighted at the news that a powerful public figure, a dignified federal judge no less, had confronted the banks with deeds and not just words. "Judge Jed Rakoff is furious," the *New York Times* declared in an editorial. "He should be. We all should be."[31] Senator Chuck Grassley, a conservative Republican, praised Rakoff for rejecting a "settle and slap-on-the-wrist approach."[32] *Rolling Stone* called the judge a "legal hero for our time."[33] And hundreds of grateful Americans phoned and wrote to the judge's chambers to express their joy and admiration. "Rakoff for president!" said a teacher from Minnesota. "Wisconsin loves you, judge!" a woman exclaimed in a voicemail. A retiree from Florida even sent a box of chocolates, prompting a debate in chambers about the ethics of accepting gifts.

Karp had of course been in this bind before: different bank, similar issue, same obstinate judge. Something else was different as well. In the two years since Bank of America had slipped Rakoff's grasp, as the hordes of Occupy Wall Street demonstrators who were walking and drumming and shouting in a unified roar made obvious, public anger had swelled over the government's failure to punish banks for their transgressions. Citigroup, facing heavy losses, felt intense pressure to avoid more public scrutiny.

In at least some parts of the legal world, the consensus seemed to be that Rakoff was right on this one. The betting was that a renegotiation would result in a settlement to the judge's liking. But the SEC had other ideas. "We believe the district court committed legal error by announcing a new and unprecedented standard that inadvertently harms investors by depriving them of substantial, certain and immediate benefits," said the agency's head of enforcement, Robert Khuzami, in a lengthy written statement on December 15, 2011.[34] The SEC had appealed, joined four days later by Citigroup. They had done more than just appeal, though. They had sought what's known as "mandamus," a blunt and potentially demeaning command for the judge to approve the settlement. It was almost as if they wanted to embarrass Rakoff. And it would get worse.

Two days after Christmas, in a call with the lawyers for the SEC and Citi, Rakoff said he wasn't inclined to grant their request to delay the trial of the Citigroup case during the appeal. In fact, he didn't think they even *had* a right to appeal. What he didn't know, and what the lawyers didn't tell him, was that only a couple of hours earlier they had gone over his head and asked the Second Circuit for the delay—known as a "stay." Minutes after the call ended, the Second Circuit agreed in a preliminary ruling to put the trial on hold. Literally one minute after that, Rakoff issued his own opinion rejecting any postponement—oblivious to what the Second Circuit had just done. When he found out two days later, he pounded out an order. It accused the SEC and Citigroup of "materially misleading the court" and demanded that they confess their offense to the Second Circuit.

A Nasty Jab

On an icy afternoon in mid-January 2012, Rakoff and Hayes-Deats sat before a computer and watched as a shaky video played on the screen. It showed a police officer yelling into a bullhorn, a mass of people chanting—"Take the bridge!" and "Whose streets? Our streets!"—and clapping and blowing whistles around him. "I am ordering you to leave this roadway now," said the cop, barely audible above the din. He turned to join a line of officers walking across the Brooklyn Bridge. The crowd followed, apparently confused. Suddenly the police turned. They surrounded the protestors with orange netting and arrested them one by one.[35]

The judge and his clerk were preparing to hear New York City's motion to dismiss the false-arrest lawsuit. Rakoff reckoned he would deny the motion, being sympathetic to the demonstrators' argument that they had honestly misinterpreted the cops' instructions. But something else bothered him. The motion was based on the defense of qualified immunity, the argument that the police could not be second-guessed in court for doing their jobs. In other words, as in the Citigroup case, Rakoff was being told that he had no business passing judgment on an executive agency's conduct. And also as in the Citigroup case, the judge was not inclined to go along.

Before he had a chance to issue a ruling, the Second Circuit came down with the decision that Rakoff had been half-dreading, half-eager to see: the final word on the stay in the Citi case. In a scathing opinion, the appellate judges officially postponed the trial and suggested that, when they got around to hearing the full appeal two years later, Rakoff would lose. "It is not the proper function of federal courts to dictate policy to executive administrative agencies," the court scolded. Rakoff took it hard, calling it a "nasty jab" from three judges he had considered friends.[36]

Two months later, he would offer a public response of sorts—a clear statement of his principles. It came in the first two sentences of his thirty-page opinion denying New York City's motion to dismiss the Occupy Wall Street lawsuit. He was referring to the arrested protestors, but for anyone who knew him at all, there was little doubt that he was also talking about himself. "What a huge debt this nation owes to its 'troublemakers,'" he wrote. "From Thomas Paine to Martin Luther King, Jr., they have forced us to focus on problems we would prefer to downplay or ignore."[37]

I Have Always Loved Juries

It was a muggy morning in July 2012 when Rakoff's deputy clerk, Linda Kotowski, performed her ritual rap on the courtroom door and commanded all to rise. The judge swept through and mounted three steps to a black high-backed chair behind his bench and gazed at the crowd before him. The trial of Citi itself was on hold, but the trial of its sacrificial lamb, Brian Stoker, was about to start, and though the courtroom was not as crowded, the scene resembled the one that had unfolded nine months before, when the judge had first grilled the bank and the SEC about their settlement. This time, Martens's staff attorney, Jeffrey Infelise, represented the agency and at the long table behind him sat a defense lawyer every bit as formidable and well-known as Karp: a tough, experienced Vietnam War veteran from San Francisco named John Keker.

In a sense this was Rakoff's hedge against the Second Circuit. Because no matter what the appeals court ultimately ruled, he would get his way: a full accounting of the facts. He turned his chair to the right and addressed the jury. "In most countries in the world," he began, "civil cases are decided by judges or, of course, in some countries, by dictators. But under our Constitution, we think that the determination of justice, the determination of the truth, the determination of what is the fair and just result in any given case, is too important to be left to anyone but citizens like yourselves drawn from all walks of life who come together, who reason together, and who decide, if they can, on a verdict."[38] It was obvious from his unabashedly over-the-top tone that Rakoff adored trials, a process that he believed was unmatched in its ability to reveal the truth. He presided over as many as twelve trials a year, far more than any other jurist in the Manhattan federal courthouse.

Stoker would get his day in court, but as Rakoff watched the ten-day trial unfold, he began to wince. Infelise and his colleagues at the SEC were getting killed. From day one Keker hammered the point that hedge funds and similar investors in Citi's CDO could not have been surprised by what Stoker and the bank had done. He led the first two witnesses through the intricacies of CDOs and asked them again and again, "And investors know that, don't they?" As he was inflicting this line of questioning on the third witness, a lightbulb went off in Infelise's head. "I'm going to object!" he cried.

"Sustained," said Rakoff. The judge leaned forward, hands clasped. "I've been sitting here all afternoon wondering when someone would object to that question . . . because no witness can testify as to what someone [else] did or did not know."[39] It went downhill from there for the SEC. When Keker insisted on asking his own witnesses leading questions—an evidentiary no-no—Rakoff chided Infelise for failing to object. When the SEC lawyer introduced what he considered his smoking gun, Stoker's "Don't tell CSAC" email, Keker countered with dozens of emails from the banker telling his bosses exactly what he was doing. The message was clear: Stoker wasn't the villain here. The true villains, if any, were the bank's senior managing directors who each walked away with millions of dollars but were far enough removed from the deal's nitty-gritty that their responses of "I don't recall" were enough to keep them safe.

The judge tried to compensate for the SEC lawyers' shortcomings by giving them an additional fifteen minutes of closing argument, but by then it was too late. On July 31, 2012, after deliberating for just a few hours, the jury found in Stoker's favor. With the decision, though, came a surprise: a note from the jury. "This verdict," it said, "should not deter the SEC from continuing to investigate the financial industry, review current regulations and modify existing regulations as necessary."[40] What jurors think matters enormously to Rakoff. He views them as the collective voice of reality, and he is "absurdly kind" to them, said Austin King, one of Rakoff's former clerks. "If he could, he would cook them breakfast every morning." Now, this jury was telling the judge that Citi's behavior was appalling, even though the SEC had tried the wrong guy.

This had never happened to Rakoff. As far as he knew, it had never happened to any judge. When he returned to his chambers, he stopped by to chat with his clerks and, in his understated way, let loose. "I have always loved juries," he said. "Now I *really* love juries!"

Nothing but Sour Grapes

The Thurgood Marshall United States Courthouse dominates the east side of Foley Square, its columned granite façade and thirty-seven-floor tower an intimidating monument to the law. Inside, up the bronze-framed elevators, across green- and black-veined marble floors, through massive oak doors, and into the hush of heavy carpets and carved-wood walls and ceilings, the courtrooms of the Second Circuit await. On this morning in February 2013 three judges—two seated behind an enormous bench, a third appearing on a television monitor—glanced at papers and adjusted their chairs. Before them sat scores of lawyers and bankers and journalists, pens poised. Scores more watched a monitor in an overflow room. Finally, the only case of the day was called: *Securities and Exchange Commission v. Citigroup Capital Markets*. The Second Circuit was hearing arguments on Rakoff's ruling of more than two years before, the one rejecting Citi's settlement, and from the start it was clear that this was a difficult case.[41]

Seconds into the SEC lawyer's opening screed about Rakoff's unreasonable demands, Judge Rosemary Pooler cut in. "The district court [Rakoff] said he did not have enough information," she said. "Could you help me with that?" The lawyer continued to expound on the "proper scope" of Rakoff's authority when the two other judges steered him back to the question. *Why didn't you just give him more information, as you had in the Bank of America case?* After a few minutes of bobbing and weaving, the lawyer landed on the heart of the problem: the power struggle between the SEC and the courts. Referring to whether Rakoff could question the amount of money Citi would pay in the settlement, the SEC attorney said that is, "frankly, not something for the court's proper consideration."[42]

Just as it seemed things might be going Rakoff's way, Judge Raymond Lohier went to work. "Why in the world," he asked, would a "judge try to, more or less, control a ... process where there's a federal executive agency that has made its determination with vastly more facts available to it than the district court that this is a fair, adequate and reasonable settlement that's in the public interest?" Rusty Wing, Rakoff's old friend from the US attorney's office, was representing him—or more accurately his court—in the Citi appeal. He tried to explain again to Lohier that Rakoff wasn't attempting to control the process but merely asking for more facts. As Wing had written in his court papers, judges "would be effectively reduced to potted plants" if the Second Circuit sided with the SEC and Citigroup.

"It's an obvious concern about separation of powers," said Lohier. On one side was the executive—of which the SEC was a part—and its discretion to enforce the law. On the other side were the courts and their ability to make judgments based on facts. The hangup here was, how many facts were enough? In Rakoff's mind it was not a close question. If the executive branch or anyone else appeared in his courtroom to seek his judgment, he would be the one to decide how many facts were enough. On the most important and difficult issues—Who was responsible for the financial crisis? What was the role of the banks and the people who ran them?—that might well require a trial. He did not get one in the Bank of America case and, the Stoker trial aside, it looked as if he might not get one in the Citigroup case either.

On June 4, 2014, the Second Circuit came down with its decision.[43] The harshness of the language was enough to make even this judge cringe. "Trials are primarily about the truth," the court pronounced. Settlements "are primarily about pragmatism," a way for the parties to "manage risk." Rakoff would have to approve the settlement. Then came Lohier's concurring opinion. In the last line he referred to Rakoff as "the very able and distinguished district judge," the judicial equivalent of an elbow to the ribs.[44] The insult wasn't lost on King, who called the opinion "blistering." Though barely out of law school, he and Rakoff's other two clerks were steeped in the history between their boss and the Second Circuit in general. There was occasional tension, to be sure, but also respect. The appeals court often invited Rakoff to sit on panels in temporary need of another judge, and its chief judge—Robert Katzmann at the time—was one of Rakoff's closest friends. In fact, the two jurists often hired clerks jointly, with most working for a year with Rakoff before moving to Katzmann's chambers.

The decision nonetheless highlighted constraints on the power of a federal judge that Rakoff would try to overcome but could not. The first was fundamental, the constitutional separation of powers, which was in part behind the Second Circuit's, and particularly Lohier's, concern about Rakoff's substituting his judgment for that of another branch. The second constraint was related to the Supreme Court–created rule that administrative agencies got the final say on interpreting statutes and other matters so long as their interpretation was reasonable because they were the experts in their fields. Citing the Supreme Court opinion in *Chevron*, Judge Rosemary Pooler wrote for the court in the Citi decision: "The job of determining whether the proposed S.E.C. consent decree best serves the public interest, however, rests squarely with the S.E.C., and its decision merits significant deference." Rakoff would have to approve the settlement.

In the end the judge would not submit quietly. On August 5, 2014, Rakoff issued his opinion, making sure to take a final dig at his bosses. "That Court has now fixed the menu," he wrote, "leaving this Court with nothing but sour grapes."[45] The Citigroup case would not be the last time that the judge and the appeals court would clash, and Rakoff being Rakoff, it was not beyond the realm of possibility that he would find a way to get the better of his bosses.

9   *No Life Wasted*

By twos and threes the men would come most every morning to look. The 2001 Chevy Tahoe is nice, they might say, though a bit rusted for the price. Maybe the Mercedes, that 1999 SUV? Yeah, too much, was the message their sheepish smiles conveyed. The 2002 Nissan Altima, then, under one hundred thousand miles and only $8,000. A pause, a test drive, a bit of haggling, then handshakes all around.

    David Rivera, owner of David's Auto Mart, a neighborhood institution on a bleak corner lot amid the trailer parks and warehouses scattered across the flat terrain of southeastern Santa Fe, would invite the men back to his pink adobe office to seal the deal. They would pull out their cash—almost always cash, because so many were day laborers, often undocumented immigrants who could not risk the exposure that might befall them if they tried to open checking accounts. And credit? Not from any sort of financial institution, but that's where Rivera could help. He would provide financing without interest in exchange for a modest bump-up in the price of a used car, a third of the purchase price down, and payments every week. He did it because it was good business but also because he knew these people—if not personally then at least in a cultural way—and for them he filled a need.

Rivera was of their world. He was born in Chihuahua, Mexico. His father died when he was twelve, and he moved to the States when he was fifteen, first to Texas, where he graduated from high school, then to Santa Fe, where he worked in restaurants for seven dollars an hour. He became a naturalized citizen in 1998. In 2007 he took a two-day training course that qualified him for a license to run a used-car lot. He took business classes at a local community college.[1]

Rivera's commercial methods were old-school but, as best anyone could tell, honest and transparent. He did well, selling about twenty cars each month. For each sale, instead of using a spreadsheet or accounting software, he would write the customer's name and the terms of the sale on a three-by-five index card, noting the payments as they came in. He reported all his income and paid taxes on it. Yet his lack of financial sophistication led him to make a mistake. Rivera had heard somewhere, couldn't recall exactly where, that if you deposited more than $10,000 in cash at one time, the government would be notified, which sounded like something that one might want to avoid. So for a few years he deposited the cash his customers had given him—a total of more than $2 million—into several banks, in amounts less than $10,000 each.

This raised a bright red flag for federal prosecutors. On December 15, 2010, they charged him with eleven counts of "structuring"— trying to short-circuit the requirement that banks report cash deposits over $10,000, a rule designed to detect possible money laundering by, say, drug traffickers or terrorists.[2] Rivera was neither, but his interference with the banks' reporting obligations was itself a crime, and it exposed him not only to a possible prison term but also to forfeiture, a legal process allowing the government to seize any money or property related to the crime. In a ruinously tight spot, Rivera cut a deal. In exchange for prosecutors' promise not to seek a prison term, he agreed to plead guilty to ten of eleven counts of structuring and to forfeit more than $520,000 and ten cars.[3] He stood a good chance of staying out of prison and keeping his business, but losing the money would hurt.

On Valentine's Day in 2011, Martha Vázquez got the case for sentencing.[4] She put aside time for Rivera and prosecutors to work out the details of their deal, and when it was done, she reviewed the plea agreement, the presentencing report, and the briefs of each side and scheduled a hearing for early the next year. This case bothered her, maybe more than most cases did. In the way that Rivera knew his customers, Vázquez knew Rivera. He reminded her of her father, who had been undocumented, and of her other relatives who had come to this country, found work, were paid weekly, and spoke English with thick accents. They operated in a separate world that transacted business in cash and avoided the suspicions or outright discrimination they risked when dealing with financial institutions. They achieved success in that world, joining an economic middle class and gaining respect and maybe some influence, living lives of value. "I was really taken with him," Vázquez said of Rivera. "He was a simple man, an uneducated man, but he had a nice house, all that money in the bank, and the government wanted to take it away. I just didn't think it was right."

What often seems wrong, or at least unfair, is forfeiture.[5] It has been around since the nation's founding and can serve a compelling purpose—depriving drug dealers, white-collar fraudsters, or any other criminals of their ill-gotten gains. There are two types of forfeiture: criminal, where the assets that a convicted criminal received from a crime are seized, and civil, where the seized assets are somehow related to a crime—even if their owner has never been charged. While the target of criminal forfeiture is the person and his property, civil forfeiture amounts to a lawsuit against property alone, and it is especially prone to abuse. Horror stories abound of people, say, losing their car after loaning it to a friend who is caught speeding and found to have a handgun or some pot.[6] When threatened with criminal charges if they don't give up their cash or property, suspects, even those who are innocent, tend to fold and let the authorities take pretty much whatever they want.

Rivera's case involved both types of forfeiture. The government relied on the criminal kind to take the cash and cars it claimed were the proceeds of Rivera's crime—structuring—but also said it would use civil forfeiture to get any other cash it thought was related. Whatever Vázquez thought about the amount seized, there didn't seem much she could do about it. Forfeiture was mandatory under the statute Rivera had violated, and besides, he and prosecutors had an agreement, and in that agreement Rivera had waived any arguments he might have for contesting it. The judge could reject the deal, of course, but no one was asking for that. In the eyes of Rivera's lawyer, it was a very good deal—no jail time in exchange for a bunch of cash.

Still, it did not sit right with Vázquez. She postponed the first sentencing hearing and asked the lawyers for briefs on whether the cash seized was clearly connected to Rivera's alleged crime and, if so, whether it was excessive. What came back was curious. Prosecutors let slip that only about $170,000 of the more than $520,000 seized was actually connected to the ten charges Rivera had pleaded guilty to. Rivera's lawyer stressed that he did not seek to overturn the plea agreement but nonetheless suggested the seized amount might be an "excessive fine" under the Constitution's Eighth Amendment. Vázquez saw an opening.

On September 6, 2012, Rivera appeared before the judge for sentencing. As she typically does, she asked Rivera about himself—his background, his family, his hopes and plans. Stocky, with a shy smile, he spoke in a quiet and heavily accented voice about how proud he was of where he had come from and his success in providing for his family. "I detected he was someone with no ill will at all, innocent, naive, very well liked by the community," Vázquez recalled. "There was no proof that his money had come from drug trafficking, it just raised a question because of all of the cash."

At the end of the hearing, Vázquez rejected the plea agreement. Her reasoning was simple. Even though Rivera's lawyer had not even made the argument, it was clear that the amount of cash Rivera had agreed to give up was excessive, and unconstitutionally so. Only about $170,000 was tied to his crime, and what *was* that crime, really? He had deposited money earned legally, honestly, and not in the service of any unlawful activity. He had caused no harm. According to a 1998 Supreme Court decision, facts like those could not justify a significant fine, or perhaps any fine at all.[7] So the judge saw two options: try to change the deal Rivera and the government had agreed to—a move that would probably be improper—or impose a sentence she believed violated the Constitution. She decided to do neither, so the deal was off.[8] Rather than go through a third sentencing hearing, prosecutors dismissed the charges against Rivera in exchange for "pretrial diversion," essentially his agreement not to structure any more deposits.[9] They also sued to keep the money they had seized—more than $520,000—and ended up cutting a deal with Rivera to retain $300,000. Rivera and David's Auto Mart are still in business, serving their community in Santa Fe on the corner of Lopez Lane and Airport Road.

The government would not always accede so easily to Vázquez's point of view, and sometimes she knew she would lose. In those cases the purpose of taking a controversial stand on the law was not necessarily to succeed immediately but over time, when the judge's push from below might persuade the courts above to conclude that she was correct. It was a patient, occasionally futile, often controversial approach to resisting the growing constraints on judicial power. But sometimes, with the help of a clever attorney, the course of the law was on Vázquez's side.

I Knew That I Would Be Reversed

At the federal public defender's office in Albuquerque, they kept a list. By March 2016 the list had grown to more than fifty entries, fifty clients whom the office had represented, fifty times that an agent of the federal Drug Enforcement Agency—a man named Jarrell Perry—had gone down to the local Greyhound station and met a bus that was passing through town so that he could conduct a search. Fifty times Perry had used the same routine: Wait for the bus to arrive, watch the passengers file off, cast an eye over the luggage and tags as the bus was washed and serviced, board the bus, then greet the passengers one by one as they filed back on and ask whether he could search them and, depending on their response and attitude, their luggage.

On one of those fifty occasions, the bus that Perry awaited was due to arrive from Claremont, California, at 9:55 a.m. on March 10, 2016. It carried a passenger named Ollisha Easley. Easley, age thirty-four at the time, was struggling. A Black mother and the sole provider for her children and extended family, she lived in Louisville, Kentucky, and earned the minimum wage at a local chain restaurant. It was not enough. So when a friend put her in touch with a woman who was offering a job, Easley jumped at the chance. She would earn $1,000, said the woman, for flying to Ontario, California, and returning to Louisville on a Greyhound bus, expenses paid. The woman did not explain the purpose of the trip, and Easley did not ask.[10]

Perry had prepared for the arrival of this particular bus. He had reviewed a passenger list obtained from Greyhound and noticed two names—Ollisha Easley and Denise Moore—with the same reservation number and one piece of checked baggage each. After the bus arrived, Perry went through his routine and, while examining the passengers' luggage, noticed two suitcases with tags, each displaying one of the women's names. As the passengers filed back on to the bus, Perry continued his routine, asking them where they were headed and whether they would consent to a search. All said yes, but it soon became apparent that the agent was treating certain passengers differently: Most passengers who were actually searched had Hispanic-sounding last names or were, in Easley's case, Black. After searching Easley, Perry pulled the two bags he had noticed before and asked her whether they were hers. Easley said only the one with her name on it; the other she had never seen. Deciding that bag had been abandoned, the agent cut it open and found it filled with methamphetamine.

Easley was arrested and pressured to confess, on the way to the DEA office and after she arrived. *You face ten years to life*, she was told. *You need to be selfish, think of your kids, give up the drug suppliers, you need to help yourself.* This went on for hours before Perry finally read Easley her Miranda rights and recorded a formal interview. After a bit of back and forth about how long it might take to get a lawyer, Easley described her travels from Kentucky and the woman who gave her the suitcase. On March 23, Easley was charged with possessing and intending to distribute 500 grams of meth.[11]

After assistant public defender Brian Pori was assigned Easley's case, he almost had to laugh. In his mind it was yet another Jarrell Perry special, another of scores of encounters at the Albuquerque bus station between invariably poor Latino or Black passengers and this bully of a white cop who would miraculously discover drugs. Pori had been at the job for decades, and he had handled so many cases involving Perry that he could almost call him a friend—*almost* but not quite, and especially not after the pattern behind the agent's arrests began to emerge. "How is it you always seem to find the one person with drugs?" Pori asked him once. "I have a sixth sense," Perry said, according to Pori. The truth was that Perry seemed to engage in fishing. He often lacked a warrant—court affirmation of probable cause to search—and relied instead on asking unsuspecting passengers for consent, a request that one could reasonably assume none but the most self-assured would deny. Minority passengers rarely fit that description, and so they became the agent's targets.

The behavior offended Pori, a balding, gray-bearded true believer who grew up among alcoholics and abusers and fell into addiction and recovery himself. He managed to graduate from Yale Law School and received job offers from Wall Street law firms before devoting his life to defending indigents who had been criminally accused. In Pori's view what Perry was doing constituted an illegal search and seizure under the Constitution's Fourth Amendment. The law in that area had developed into one of those fuzzy consider-all-the-circumstances situations. Things got especially complicated if a police officer believed a warrantless search was okay because a person consented to it. The big factor then was whether the consent was voluntary. Facts that could suggest that consent *was* voluntary included asking for permission in a public place in a polite tone with others around so the "reasonable" person felt free to say no and leave. It truly did depend on the "totality of the circumstances," as courts liked to say, and understandably the police sometimes got it wrong.[12]

Pori's take was that the "consent" Perry allegedly obtained from people like Easley—Black people and other minorities—was involuntary. "Look, if a man is confronting you on a bus and says I need you to consent, you're only going to say *no, you can't have it* if you're a white guy," Pori explained. On May 23 he filed a motion on Easley's behalf to exclude as evidence the drugs Perry had seized and the statements Easley had made while in custody.[13] The case had landed before Vázquez, and she set a hearing on the motion for August 24.

When Perry took the stand that day in the grand confines of the judge's mid-nineteenth-century courtroom in Santa Fe, he came with a history, not only with Pori but also with Vázquez. Perry's searches had been challenged in federal court a number of times and were often upheld but sometimes found flawed enough to throw out the evidence they had yielded. As Vázquez listened to Perry's testimony and watched the video he had recorded of the encounter, she noticed that he had asked most passengers on the bus a few perfunctory questions (*where are you coming from, where are you going, would you consent to a search?*) but seemed to question Latinos more closely (*may I see your ticket and ID?*) while actually searching them. He even knifed into the sole of a Latino man's shoe to see if it concealed drugs. Would any person of color—particularly Easley, the only Black person on the bus—feel free to say no to this man?

After the hearing, Vázquez took her time, more than a year, writing an opinion that would grant or reject the motion to suppress. The judge wanted to be careful. She wanted to be sure. She wanted to read everything—that was her mantra, "read everything." It was not a complicated case, it was not on its face even an important case to anyone other than the defendant. But Vázquez wanted to make it more than that; she wanted to see whether she could change what she believed to be a profound flaw in the law surrounding searches. She knew that what she planned to write would be controversial, and she wanted to get it right.

The opinion began in a simple acknowledgment of the ubiquity but also quotidian nature of the task before her: "This Motion concerns a warrantless bus sweep and its fallout—one of many warrantless sweeps that have come before this Court and courts across the country." It continued through the facts and the legal standards and the arguments of the lawyers and ticked through the countless factors that courts had considered in determining whether consent to a search had been voluntary. Then, this: "However, in considering the totality of the circumstances . . . the Court finds that a reasonable person in Ms. Easley's position would not have felt free to terminate the encounter" with Perry. She explained why. Everyone else on the bus had consented to a search, Perry had suggested they might all be in danger if they didn't consent because he was checking the bus "for security," and he hadn't told Easley she could refuse consent. But maybe the most persuasive reason that Easley felt compelled to consent, Vázquez continued, was also the simplest and most disturbing: She was a Black woman, and "through everyday experiences, people of color are conditioned to presume that asserting their constitutional rights in a police encounter will increase their likelihood of physical harm or arrest."[14]

Although the judge cited scholarly articles for her conclusion, she lacked legal precedent—a court decision that had factored in a person's race to decide whether a police search was consensual. So she drew on an analogy: age. The US Supreme Court had ruled in a 2011 case that it was a "common sense" reality that a child might agree to answer a cop's questions when an adult would feel free to decline.[15] Vázquez was not comparing Black people to children in any way other than that they too had an objective trait that made them less likely to challenge a cop's request; it was the color of their skin—and hundreds of years of history had cruelly taught them that saying no was dangerous. Refusing to acknowledge race as part of the context in a police encounter was in a sense to deny Black people's access to equal justice, to close the courthouse door on an argument for why a police search was wrong. Vázquez hoped to pry that door open.

"I knew that I would be reversed, and fast," she conceded. The appeals court did not disappoint. On January 19, 2019, a unanimous three-judge panel refused to allow suppression of the evidence against Easley, ruling that a "reasonable person in her position would have felt free to terminate her encounter with the police and refuse to cooperate."[16] In December, Easley pleaded guilty. In August 2021 she was sentenced to prison for just shy of six years. "There is no doubt in my mind that any person of color who has an encounter with law enforcement is affected by their race," Vázquez said later. "I don't think any person honestly believes that race is not a factor. And it behooves the district courts to bring these matters to the attention of higher courts even if they are going to be reversed."

No Life Wasted [215]

This had pretty much been the story of Vázquez's life as a judge to this point, often banging her head against the proverbial wall that was the Tenth Circuit and losing, being reversed and told to stop pestering the higher-ups with rulings that seemed born more of hope than established law and to try again. Yet she would not stop, it was not in her nature or sense of a judge's purpose. And while she was still handling Easley's case, another extraordinary matter landed on her docket.

The Luckiest Guy in the History of Bank Robberies

Show me your hands! Show me your fucking hands! They had tried to be nice, tried to engage in civil conversation with this dumbass stoner stumbling down the Albuquerque sidewalk on a day late in January 2016, chin tucked to his chest against the cold, hands jammed into the pockets of his coat, determined in his heroin haze to act as if he were invisible and they were not even there. But the cops were getting impatient. Nervous. They feared that this whoever-he-was—this moron who like a cartoon character had minutes before slammed his van into a wall and then bounced it off a utility pole that sparked into flames and continued to drive until his vehicle jumped a curb and collided with a fire hydrant that stopped it cold—was carrying a gun. Now the situation had escalated, and the officers reached for their holstered weapons.

Show me your hands! Finally, slowly, the man pulled his hands from his pockets and held them out to his sides as if to find his balance. The cops grabbed him, searched him, cuffed him, took a loaded .22-caliber pistol out of his right pocket, and returned to the station with the man in the back seat.[17] His name was Marc Dutch, and he needed a lawyer, a really good one. He got lucky: the public defender's office assigned Brian Pori to his case. Pori knew cops, had respected cops since his days as a public defender in high-crime

Oakland, California, had taught him how dangerous their job could be. He also believed, after hearing what Dutch had done, that these cops in Albuquerque would have been 100 percent justified in taking Dutch out with a bullet.

"Thank you for not killing my client," Pori told the police officers involved.

Over the following months, he grew surprisingly fond of Dutch. It would be too much to say that he saw himself in his client, but it would also not be so very far from the truth. Both men had come from hard backgrounds of abuse and alcoholism and had fallen into addiction themselves, and yet there was a determinative difference: Dutch had failed to find his way out. His life had been chaotic beyond even Pori's belief. In 1987, when Dutch was four and living in Santa Fe, his father, who was bipolar, inflicted on him and his older brother the punishment of drinking beer until they were sick. At five, Dutch noticed with sobbing terror that his father imbibed all the time and would beat his mother senseless. At ten, he watched his mother flee for Illinois and his father take on the habit of smoking crack. At eleven, he got a paper route and used his earnings of twenty-five dollars a day to buy his father more crack. From thirteen to twenty, he bounced back and forth between his father's and mother's homes, smoking crack with his father, being assaulted and hit by a car while at his mother's, drinking and smoking pot every day and getting addicted to methamphetamine and becoming homeless and remaining awake for days on end and having a nervous breakdown and being convicted of felony assault after brawling with roommates over a gun.

Then Dutch decided to rob banks. In 2005, while out of his mind on meth and crack, he pursued a two-week spree of heists at three savings and loans in Santa Fe and was convicted and sent to a federal penitentiary in Indiana. Released in 2010 and living again in Santa Fe, Dutch continued on a course of violent madness—more drugs, more crimes—until in 2015 he began to turn his life around. A buddy from prison got him a job with a construction company, Dutch became a supervisor, and he gained friends and respect and stayed clean as a member of Narcotics Anonymous.

Early in January 2016, at the end of a long work week, he received from his boss the usual envelope of cash for the employees Dutch supervised. This time, instead of paying them, Dutch drove to a casino and gambled through the night, blowing all the cash on blackjack. It was enough to throw him into a funk and back on meth and heroin. On January 27 he prepared to do a speedball—consecutive shots of the depressant heroin and the stimulant meth—but after injecting the heroin and not the meth, he took off in his van through the streets of Albuquerque and within blocks hit the wall that was his first stop on the way to his arrest and introduction to Brian Pori.[18]

There seemed at first not much that the lawyer could do for Dutch; he was going to jail, no way around it. He faced state charges of drunk driving, leaving the scene of an accident, and possessing meth and a gun, and he had obviously violated his probation and parole. Yeah, he was in trouble. The feds would surely nail him too—a felon in possession of a firearm and ammunition would get anywhere between seventy and eighty-seven months in prison under the sentencing guidelines. The best Dutch could probably hope for was a plea bargain and a judge who would look upon him with compassion, though God knows his long record of fuckups had left him a poor candidate for sympathy.

Pori handled the state charges simply enough, and Dutch's guilty plea put him in state prison. The federal case, however, would be tougher. Not only was Dutch a felon with a gun, he was in the eyes of Uncle Sam a career criminal—convicted in federal court of committing three violent bank robberies in 2005. In 1984, during the Reagan administration's tough-on-crime campaign, Congress had enacted the Armed Career Criminal Act to deal with concerns that a relatively few career criminals commit most offenses.[19] The act imposed especially harsh punishment on those miscreants, a mandatory sentence that would keep them behind bars for a very long time: fifteen years. There was no room for a clever lawyer or a compassionate judge to concoct a lesser sentence.[20]

Yet Dutch seemed to get lucky again. The spin of the court clerk's wheel had put his case in the hands of Judge Vázquez. Pori played up the tragic circumstances of Dutch's so-called childhood—it was a good legal strategy, but it also mattered to Pori. He too had been through similar if far less extreme horrors and knew them to be surmountable. None of that, though, would affect the problem of the career criminal act, so Pori raised a longshot argument. To qualify for sentencing under the act, someone must have committed at least three crimes on separate "occasions" rather than during a single episode. Dutch hadn't done that, Pori explained. Instead, he had robbed three banks in one continuous spree while whacked out on meth and zero sleep, with no mental ability to stop between each robbery and consciously decide to go on to the next.

Vázquez bought the argument, concluding that the government had not met its burden of proving that the bank robberies had occurred on different occasions. She would not apply the career criminal act to Dutch but instead would sentence him to only five years in prison, below the guideline range, because of his drug addiction, his mental illness, and his "very difficult and painful childhood." She also ordered a heavy dose of drug treatment and testing—in prison and during a three-year period of supervised release. "I have great faith in you," she told Dutch during his sentencing hearing on October 12, 2017. "I believe that you can do this. . . . Don't give up, Mr. Dutch, I believe that you will do well."[21] Maybe he would have done well, had the Tenth Circuit given him the chance. The government appealed Dutch's sentence, insisting that he was exactly the kind of person that the career criminal act was meant to cover, and in a terse and testy opinion the appeals court agreed. Of course Dutch had the mental ability to stop between each of the bank robberies, the court wrote, ordering Vázquez to "vacate" Dutch's sentence and "resentence him consistent with this order and judgment."[22]

There seemed no doubt that Dutch would soon be headed to prison for at least fifteen years, but Pori refused to concede. Aside from the lawyer's persistence, two things were going for Dutch. One was the ambiguity of the word "occurrence" in the Armed Career Criminal Act. The other was the sloppiness of the prosecutors and judge who had put Dutch behind bars for both committing and "aiding and abetting" the three bank robberies in 2005. It gets complicated, but essentially nothing in the record from that case made clear what crimes Dutch had actually done. Had he held up three banks or, say, "aided and abetted" three robberies with a single act like loaning his accomplices a car—in which case Dutch had committed a crime on only one "occasion" rather than three? It may have been the technicality of all technicalities, but under the career criminal act, it could matter. Pori gave the argument a shot.

On August 29, 2019, Vázquez held a second sentencing hearing, and at first it did not go well for Dutch. The Tenth Circuit had issued its order, and not even she was inclined to question it. Dutch would have to do the fifteen years, but she wanted to give him hope, and for the next twenty minutes or so she spoke to him from the bench like a stern friend. As the judge prepared to pronounce the sentence and wrap up the hearing, she asked Pori whether he had anything to add. He didn't really, nothing that he hadn't already said, but he figured, what the hell. Stumbling a bit, Pori repeated his argument about the Armed Career Criminal Act.

"Well, I tend to agree with you," Vázquez said, "but we were both considered to be wrong by the Tenth Circuit."

"This was an okiedoke opinion," Pori responded, referring to the document the appeals court had issued.

"A what?"

"An okiedoke; you know, run through it and don't publish it and achieve what you want to achieve by fiat." Wary of making things worse, Pori doggedly plowed on, trying to articulate what he had come to believe was no longer a mere technicality but a matter of fairness and principle. Sparring at times with the prosecutor, and with Vázquez listening intently, Pori sensed the momentum turning like a slack tide.

"Okay, I hate to inconvenience all of you, but I need to review this a little bit more, then," Vázquez interrupted. "I need to give this some more thought."[23]

It did not make any difference at first. Almost a month later they were back in court, with the judge ascending the bench carrying a script that dutifully carried out the Tenth Circuit's order and imposed on Dutch a sentence of fifteen years. Pori would not let up, however, and as Vázquez turned his arguments over again in her mind, she found it impossible to refute. "I completely understand what my place is in the judiciary," said the judge. "I have utmost respect for the position that I hold and that is held by the Court of Appeals." Yet she could not in good conscience impose on Dutch the draconian punishment that the government requested and the higher court demanded. Her original sentence of five years would stand. As Dutch and Pori stood before Vázquez, they burst into sobs and tears. The government appealed yet again, and of course the Tenth Circuit judges—testy before but furious now—ordered Vázquez yet again to comply with their orders.[24]

The rule-bound, frighteningly formal, black-robed bureaucracy of the federal judiciary may leave little room for serendipity. Even so, it does happen. And as Vázquez prepared to sentence Dutch again, this time to the full fifteen years, a Georgia inmate without a lawyer asked the US Supreme Court to hear a case that raised an issue that was remarkably similar to the one that the judge had been struggling with. In 1997 the inmate, William Dale Wooden, pleaded guilty to ten counts of burglary for robbing ten separate storage units in a single night. Almost two decades later a court decided that the crime spree qualified him for sentencing under the Armed Career Criminal Act as a felon in possession of a firearm when he was caught with a hunting rifle in his house. Like Dutch, Wooden argued that the ten burglaries had occurred on a single "occasion," and like the Tenth Circuit, the Court of Appeals for the Sixth Circuit rejected that view of the law, ruling that it was enough for the ten burglaries to have happened at separate times.[25]

When the Supreme Court agreed, on February 22, 2021, to hear Wooden's case, all bets were off in Dutch's case. Depending on how the court ruled, it could mean nothing for Dutch or change the course of his life. Either way, putting off his sentencing seemed the prudent move, and so the parties waited. On March 7, 2022, Vázquez sat reading at her desk in chambers, preparing for a series of sentencing hearings scheduled back-to-back that morning. Dutch was helping wire lights for a Facebook facility in Los Lunas, New Mexico, as an apprentice electrician, a job he had been assigned while waiting on supervised release for his resentencing. Pori had left the public defender's office for private practice almost three years earlier and was working madly on a brief due the next day. It is unclear who heard first, but at some point that day all received the startling news they had long awaited—the word that the Supreme Court had issued its decision.[26]

Despite all the hypothetical musings during oral argument, despite the total uncertainty about how the court would come out, the justices had managed to agree on what the deceptively simple term "occasion" means. They had ruled in favor of Wooden, and the decision was unanimous, 9–0. Pori immediately called his client. "This Wooden thing is going to save your ass," he said. There would be more than a few legal formalities to come, sentencing memos and motions and consultations between the prosecutors and their bosses at the Justice Department in Washington, DC, but essentially Pori was correct.

As Vázquez had ruled in her first sentencing order, timing alone was not enough to determine an "occasion," the Supreme Court justices said in their *Wooden* opinion. Crimes committed at different times could still have occurred on one occasion if they took place near each other, in similar ways, in a short period, or as parts of one episode rather than tasks separated by substantial effort and reflection. The decision seemed broad enough to cover the circumstances of Dutch's bank robberies, and the sparse record of those robberies left prosecutors with a near impossible task if they tried to prove what Dutch had done. So they gave up.

On November 9, 2022, Vázquez imposed on Dutch her original sentence of five years. After decades of challenging the judges above her on the law, sometimes successfully, more often not, and on this occasion after severely testing their patience, she had won. With the help of a persistent lawyer, Vázquez had been proven right by the highest court in the land. It was not a moment for celebration, however. The point of it all had been to ensure that Dutch's life would not be wasted, lost in a system that could not deal with his afflictions. He deserved that, she believed, because he was trying to pull his life together and at times succeeding in doing so, and she wanted to give him that chance. She knew only too well what denying it to someone who deserved it—deserved it far more than Dutch did—looked like.

As Vázquez was struggling with Dutch's case, her brother, Ricardo, died in a Santa Fe hospital bed. He had been released from prison in 2013, and even then she could tell that the sunny and determined person she had admired and loved with all her heart was long gone. While incarcerated, he contracted colon and kidney cancer, had a kidney removed, suffered a heart attack, and received a level of medical care that might embarrass a third-world country. After his release Ricardo was rarely out of the hospital, and he no longer had much of a relationship with his children. His belongings—letters, photos, the small stuff he loved to have around—reside in boxes behind the doors of a tall wooden cabinet in Vázquez's office, and the judge can barely bring herself to look at them for the sadness that wells up. Yet, incongruously, she says the pain of witnessing her brother's demise was "a good experience for me as a judge. . . . I visited him in every prison where he was, and I saw what parents go through." She continues: "Everyone I sent to prison on mandatory minimums, they come out, and I see how unable they are to go to a mall, how crippled they are, how frightened by noises. Everything they lost because of a long federal prison sentence."[27]

. . .

As for Dutch, he is still a work in progress, at times his own worst enemy. Since his release under the strictest of supervision, he has relapsed into drug use, a serious violation of his parole. Even Pori's patience is wearing thin. "Oh my God, this guy is the luckiest fucking guy in the history of bank robberies," the lawyer says. "Every time he relapses, I fight for him, I say don't put him into custody, he's got a good job. He gets a Cadillac representation from me." For the moment, though, Vázquez has seen enough. On October 31, 2023, she ordered Dutch locked up for eight months, first in prison but only until a bed opened up at an inpatient drug-treatment center in Rio Rancho, New Mexico. The point is still to help him, not throw him away. Asked if her frustration with Dutch and the many people like him ever becomes too much, the judge goes quiet for a moment: "It's still unfinished business."

10 *Pure Gaslighting*

The plain truth of it was they were lying. A lot of voters knew it. At least some of the Mississippi lawmakers who had said aye to the bill probably knew it. Anyone who had been paying even casual attention to how the state of Mississippi had been treating women throughout its more than two-hundred-year history surely knew it. Yet no one—not the voters, not the lawmakers, not the attorneys who argued against it—was willing to suggest publicly that it was so. Except for Carlton Reeves.

On March 19, 2018, the Mississippi legislature enacted a law that banned abortions after fifteen weeks of pregnancy. The authors of the measure said that the justifications for it were simple—to protect "unborn life," yes, but more strikingly to protect women. "Abortion carries significant physical and psychological risks to the maternal patient," read the law's "findings of fact," and these risks rose "exponentially" with the age of the fetus. Among them were "blood clots; heavy bleeding or hemorrhage"; "laceration, tear, or other injury to the cervix"; and "injury to the bowel or bladder." Then there were the psychological harms: "depression; anxiety; substance abuse."[1] Evidence for any of these claims, and the fact that abortions were one of the safest medical procedures in the United States, was all but missing from these "findings of fact" because there had been no hearings on the measure, no public airing of whether it could withstand scrutiny of its claims, let alone its legal basis.

That scrutiny began the next day, though, when the Jackson Women's Health Organization, the last abortion clinic in Mississippi, asked Reeves to temporarily block the law from taking effect while they prepared for a more extensive challenge.[2] At a hastily arranged hearing that the clinic's lawyers joined by phone, the judge picked up quickly on the absence of evidence for the antiabortion law's claims. "So if they [the legislators] didn't have hearings," Reeves asked the state attorney defending the law, "how much deference should I give . . . any of the justifications that they set out, or their findings that they set out, in the statute?"[3] The state's lawyer said the judge should give them plenty of deference, but it was clear that Reeves was not persuaded. After noting that "a lot of stuff happens over there in the legislature that just should not happen, in ways that it should not happen," Reeves ended the hearing and that evening issued his decision. He pointed out that the Supreme Court had long held, from *Roe v. Wade* on, that the Constitution protects a woman's right "to have an abortion before viability" of the fetus—and fifteen weeks was clearly before viability—so the claim of Jackson Women's Health Organization and their patients that the Mississippi law was unconstitutional would almost certainly succeed; a temporary restraining order (TRO) was granted.[4]

Over the next several months, the judge and an ever-growing number of lawyers went back and forth over the legal mechanics of the litigation—setting the schedule, deciding what evidence to allow in, filing and responding to amended complaints—until on August 24, 2018, the clinic and its patients filed for summary judgment, a request that Reeves rule in their favor and block the antiabortion measure permanently without a trial because, in their view, the facts were undisputed and the law was on their side. On November 20 the judge came down with his decision.[5] It was, most everyone knew, an easy case, given the clarity of the Supreme Court precedents on abortion, among the best known of any in the nation's history. There was little doubt that Reeves would rule the Mississippi law unconstitutional and could not be enforced. The judge wrote as much in his opinion, but he asked an obvious question: "So, why are we here?"

Rejecting sophistry from the state's legislators like the ban wasn't really a "ban," Reeves revealed the truth as he saw it: The state had passed a law "it knew was unconstitutional to endorse a decades-long campaign . . . to ask the Supreme Court to overturn *Roe v. Wade*."[6] He scolded the lawmakers for pretending to care about women's health and the well-being of the unborn and minorities while the state led the nation in infant mortality, tolerated "alarming" poverty and maternal death rates, and curtailed health-care programs like Medicaid. In perhaps the opinion's most memorable phrase, he wrote: "The Mississippi Legislature's professed interest in 'women's health' is pure gaslighting."[7] It was, in other words, a lie.

Reeves went on to accuse legislators of perpetuating "the old Mississippi," the one that in 1968 became the last state to allow women to serve on juries, that systematically sterilized Black women against their will—getting a "Mississippi appendectomy," it was called.[8] The one that in 1984 became the last state to ratify the constitutional amendment guaranteeing women the right to vote. He recounted Mississippi's long history of denying its citizens' constitutional rights with segregated schools, prohibitions on same-sex marriage, limits on the rights of Black people to vote, and a "secret intelligence arm" that enforced racial discrimination. Far from helping women and minorities, Reeves wrote, the state still seemed "bent on controlling" them. Near the end of his opinion, almost as an aside, the judge revealed a bit about himself and his view of his role as a judge. "The fact that men, myself included, are determining how women may choose to manage their reproductive health is a sad irony not lost on the Court," he wrote. "As a man, who cannot get pregnant or seek an abortion, I can only imagine the anxiety and turmoil a woman might experience when she decides whether to terminate her pregnancy through an abortion."[9]

With three sisters—one a banker, another a corrections officer, the third an executive assistant—and a mother who had washed and folded laundry at the Yazoo Motel to support her seven children, Reeves had developed deep admiration for the strength of women and all that they endured. With his only child, his daughter, Chanda, living and working in Tennessee, Reeves called her almost every day, and together they shared their news and hopes and worries. It was his wife, though—Lora, the girl he had met as a kid in Yazoo City and the woman he had married as a new lawyer in 1990—who brought him to understand as best he could the goodness and burden of being a woman. Her memory now filled him with sadness perhaps as much as joy. In 2017, just before the abortion case came before him, she had succumbed to breast cancer and passed away. With Chanda, Lora and Reeves celebrated their twenty-seventh wedding anniversary on her last weekend alive. Asked about her death, pausing a long moment, he said quietly, "She was my world."

With Reeves's other family, his law clerks, he made sure to include women and their perspectives in his work. After the abortion opinion came out, he went on Twitter (now X) and saw that "somebody said, Ooh! Ooh! Ooh! It almost sounds like a woman wrote that!" He thought to himself, "Yes! A woman had a hand in writing it, yes, because one of my clerks was a female, and it was so important."[10] With the opinion Reeves gave evidence of his determination to help women choose freely the course of their lives and participate more fully in society, in democracy, without hypocrisy from the state or resistance from men. Through his decisions he had made similar efforts on behalf of Black people and gay people, and this was his chance to again use blunt and compelling prose to explain why women deserved better too.

As sometimes happens with Reeves on controversial issues, his opinion provoked morality-fueled indignation. Although the US Court of Appeals for the Fifth Circuit affirmed his decision a year later, as legal precedent compelled it to do, James Ho, among the court's most outspoken and conservative judges, took offense at Reeves's criticism of Mississippi's and the antiabortion movement's claims to protect women and Black people. In a concurring opinion, Ho cited surveys, articles, and legal briefs ostensibly proving that many if not most women had long viewed abortion as "women's oppression" and "an injustice against . . . female life." He relied heavily on a startling 2019 concurring opinion, by Supreme Court Justice Clarence Thomas, that condemned abortion as "a tool of the eugenics movement," used throughout American history to draw "the distinction between the fit and the unfit . . . along racial lines." History, Ho concluded, must also "infect" abortion proponents "with the taint of racism."[11]

Judge Ho largely missed Reeves's point—Mississippi could not credibly proclaim a desire to help women and Black people when it hindered them in so many ways—and Ho's history was far off the mark as well. In this case, however, the troubling question soon became whether any of it would matter at all.

. . .

It would be too much to say that Judge Reeves saw it coming, but by the time he held a status conference on a sweltering day in June 2021, he knew it was at least a possibility. On May 17 the Supreme Court had dropped the first surprise, granting Mississippi's request to consider the abortion case. Reeves held the conference to see whether a trial over making his injunction against the abortion ban permanent should wait until the justices ruled. An attorney for the Jackson Women's Health Organization opposed the idea. The law as it stood said a measure was unconstitutional if it put an "undue burden" on the right to abortion, and "we just don't think the standard is going to fundamentally change as a result of the current Supreme Court case," the attorney explained, and so delaying the trial would be unnecessary. Reeves was not so sure. "Why wouldn't it be prudent to just wait and see what they say?" The Supreme Court "took this case up for a reason," he said. "It's not a foregone conclusion that the court will not overturn its preexisting state of the law." The trial would be postponed.[12]

The second surprise from the Supreme Court came a year later. On May 2, 2022, a draft opinion overturning *Roe v. Wade*, the landmark 1973 decision establishing the right to abortion, was leaked to *Politico*.[13] Millions of Americans hoped and prayed that the draft was a fake. It was not. On June 24 the justices delivered their final surprise, a 6–3 decision that reversed the rulings of Reeves and the Fifth Circuit in the Mississippi case and ended the constitutional right to abortion. "*Roe* was egregiously wrong from the start," declared Justice Samuel A. Alito Jr. in the majority opinion.[14] Another man, another decision determining how women may choose to manage their reproductive health. The irony of abortion law that so worried Reeves was alive and thriving.

. . .

On a quiet August afternoon in the nation's capital, a wood-paneled hearing room on the second floor of the Thurgood Marshall Federal Judiciary Building began to fill in dribs and drabs with the denizens of court bureaucracy. The deputy general counsel of something-or-other chatted in animated whispers with a gray-suited colleague. A liaison to a congressional committee sat quietly holding file folders on her lap. An eager young microphone fiddler walked behind the dais to ensure that the sound system worked. As 3:00 p.m.

approached, guests of more distinguished appearance started to arrive—collars crisp, hair coiffed, creases sharp—conversing in muted tones or sitting lost in thought. Then, sensing a shift in the mood of the room, heads turned toward the door.

Making an entrance, wearing his A-game grin, was Carlton Reeves. He shook hands, slapped backs, tossed quips, paused to laugh, pointed to people across the way, and proceeded down the rows of chairs to greet every last individual who had made the effort to attend the meeting that he was about to lead. On May 11, 2022, President Biden had nominated Reeves to a position that at least on occasion could get a district court judge out from under the thumb of the courts above, a perch from which the compelling voice he had developed on the bench might reach a wider audience—and have a clearer impact. Supreme Court Justice Stephen Breyer had served, and so had Justice Ketanji Brown Jackson. The position was as a member of the US Sentencing Commission (created by Congress), and in Reeves's case not just a member but its chair—the first Black person to hold the job.[15]

Obscure to many Americans, the commission nonetheless wields far-reaching clout in the world of criminal justice. It is essentially the keeper of the sentencing guidelines, adding and subtracting and otherwise tweaking the rules that largely determine the punishments for breaking federal law. When the commission speaks, judges, prosecutors, defense lawyers, and certain members of Congress pay close attention. Since the commission's creation in 1984, its seven members—typically four from one political party, three from the other, depending on the president's affiliation—have generally delivered sentencing reforms in bursts of remarkably unified and bipartisan wisdom.[16] In 2007, for example, the commission voted unanimously to fix the 100-1 ratio problem, at long last lowering sentences for offenses involving crack cocaine, which had been the same as those for one hundred times the amount of powder cocaine. This problem had swept Black people into the nation's prisons at disproportionate rates. In 2014 the commission further reduced penalties for drug crimes, leading to the First Step Act, a sentencing overhaul that shortened certain mandatory prison terms, made the crack-cocaine reductions retroactive, and granted judges more sentencing discretion.[17]

Reeves says he doesn't know how he came to Biden's attention—he just received a call one day from the White House—but in the first four years of his six-year tenure, the commission has already shaken up federal sentencing in a host of ways. It has, for example, reduced sentences for prisoners with little or no history of committing crimes.[18] It has barred using criminal charges of which someone was acquitted to boost a sentence.[19] It has eased the standards for so-called "compassionate release"—the early discharge of, say, very old or terminally ill prisoners—including by allowing judges to free anyone who has served at least ten years of an "unusually long sentence" and, if sentenced under current law, would probably be out by now.[20] These changes have been remarkably controversial, each approved by the commission 4–3 along party lines: four Democratic members in favor, three Republicans opposed. This represents a dramatic break from the consensus and even unanimity often achieved by past versions of the commission, maybe a sign of a vastly more partisan Washington, DC, or simply an illustration of the principle that big changes provoke deep disagreement. That commission hearings have not broken out in figurative fist fights is at least a testament to the skills of the chair.

As the commission gathered on the morning of February 23, 2023, for the first public hearing of Reeves's tenure, he was gracious and warm and painstakingly polite. He introduced his fellow commissioners and thanked the proverbial little people, the commission employees who "played an essential role in making this day possible." The hearing focused on the changes to compassionate release, and fidgeting in the seats before him were dozens of witnesses—defense lawyers, federal prosecutors, academics, former felons who had done significant time. To put them at ease, Reeves promised that their "extensive journeys and preparation will be worth it. When you speak to the commission, you *will* be heard." That was the fundamental message he hoped to convey, repeated with rhythmic emphasis: *You will be heard.* He said it again to the people who had sent in written comments: "It does not matter if you sit in the halls of Congress or at the desk of a prison library.... When you speak to the commission, you will be heard because you *must* be heard."

Reeves stressed how little the commissioners—and he—knew from personal experience about the topics of the day, how the judges on the panel had "acquitted others of conduct, but we have never been acquitted," how "we've granted compassionate release from federal prison, but we have never had to apply for it." He introduced the first witness, and then he sat back and listened. It was surprising how patiently he listened. Throughout the day the other commissioners asked lots of questions, made frequent comments, and Reeves waited until they had had their say before asking questions of his own. It was in many ways an impressive performance—the first of many that would gain the respect of most everyone in the criminal justice system, including his fellow judges from places like Santa Fe. "Carlton Reeves is my hero," said Martha Vázquez. "He is truly my hero. Because he's creative and courageous, and it is not easy. I don't know how he does everything he's doing but we are so fortunate as a country to have him in that position."

After Reeves adjourned that first commission hearing at 5:00 p.m. and chatted with as many of the guests as he could, he made his way to the elevators and then his spacious corner office on the second floor. It was still early in the afternoon in Jackson, Mississippi, and Reeves said with a weary jocularity that betrayed the exhausting reality of his life: "I have to go do my second job." He picked up the phone and got back to the business of being a US district court judge.

11   *The Troublemaker Prevails*

On a crisp morning in April 2014 the Second Circuit prepared to hear oral arguments in the most consequential Wall Street insider-trading case to come before the courts in decades. A wave of recent prosecutions had felled scores of bankers and hedge fund managers caught trading on stolen corporate secrets, and the convictions and guilty pleas had burnished the reputation of Preet Bharara, the US attorney for the Southern District of New York, as the new sheriff of Wall Street. A few of those cases had been appealed, but essentially without success. That—and Bharara's perfect record of winning insider-trading prosecutions—was about to change.

Antonia Apps, the assistant US attorney representing Bharara's office in the case, had barely begun when Judge Barrington Parker, one of three judges hearing the appeal, began to pick apart her argument. Apps had been asserting that two hedge fund managers, Todd Newman and Anthony Chiasson, were properly convicted after trading on inside information that had passed through several intermediaries. Neither man had known where the financial secrets had originally come from, but Apps insisted that they were guilty anyhow—an astoundingly broad view of illegal trading. Finally, Parker erupted. "We sit in the financial capital of the word," he said, his baritone voice stirring the crowd. "And the amorphous theory that you've tried this case on gives precious little guidance to all of these institutions . . . out there who are trying to come up with some bright line rules about what can and what cannot be done. And your theory leaves all of these institutions at the mercy of the government."[1]

On December 10, 2014, the slim hope that the court would go Apps's way vanished. The Second Circuit reversed the convictions of Newman and Chiasson. In its opinion the court stressed that the traders couldn't be guilty because they didn't even know the source of the inside tips and, in a slap at Bharara's office, criticized the "doctrinal novelty of . . . recent insider trading prosecutions," suggesting that prosecutors had usurped the job of lawmakers by creating overly broad rules. Then the judges engaged in a little lawmaking of their own, fabricating a remarkably narrow requirement: Traders who had wrongly received corporate secrets could only be guilty if they made some kind of *payment*—something "of a pecuniary or similarly valuable nature"—for the secrets, even if they knew the information had been disclosed illegally.[2]

Jed Rakoff was not involved in the case, and when he got around to reading the opinion, his feelings about it were mixed. Bharara's office had for years been stretching the law on insider trading, grabbing headlines but doing real damage to legitimate traders' lives. Like a lot of people, Rakoff believed prosecutors sometimes overreached, engaging in dodgy behavior like piling on charges and extracting guilty pleas without meaningful review by, say, a court. In this case the prosecutors had "shot themselves in the foot," he would say later, because they probably would have won the case at trial anyhow.

Yet as the judge read further, he realized the Second Circuit had also gotten the law wrong. "It was a panel of great judges," Rakoff said, "and I had no idea why they did what they did" in creating the new rule. His clerks had some ideas, though. One suggested that the opinion was a cry for help, a request for Congress to define illegal insider trading—something Rakoff also believed should happen. He and his clerks recognized the risk the decision posed. It might allow stock market cheats to shower their relatives and friends with lucrative tips, so long as no one paid for the information. At the moment that was the law of the circuit, and there was nothing that Rakoff could do because, as he would tell his clerks for the umpteenth time, "I'm just a district court judge." As events would play out, however, that wasn't strictly true.

His Bosses' Equal

Early the following spring, Rakoff turned to the federal courts' case management system on his computer and clicked open an unfamiliar entry: *United States v. Salman*. It was unfamiliar in part because it was from California. Ever since 2010, when he turned sixty-seven and became a senior judge, Rakoff had been able to sit on appeals courts in other states, and the Ninth Circuit Court of Appeals in San Francisco had just invited him to join a three-judge panel in June. He had accepted, and as a small bonus he figured he could indulge his passion for baseball by watching the San Francisco Giants play at AT&T Park on San Francisco Bay. *Salman* was one of the cases the panel would hear. He began to read.[3]

The document told of a man named Maher Kara. In 1976, when Maher was four years old, he and his family moved from embattled Lebanon to San Francisco. Maher was bright and ambitious and the light of his parents' eyes. His brother, Michael, may have been even smarter but was deeply troubled. As they grew, both brothers studied hard, and Maher landed a job in Citigroup's health-care group, advising on mergers and financings, while Michael earned a biochemistry degree and studied toxicology. In time, Maher sought his brother's advice about drugs produced by companies that Maher followed for the bank. Then Michael asked probing questions of his own. After a while Maher had a disturbing thought: Was Michael trading on the information they discussed? Michael swore on his daughter's life that he was not. Still, Maher feared he was crossing a line by answering the questions, but his brother was "so persistent and so nagging," Maher would later testify, "that to get him off my back, I finally caved in."[4]

On July 6, 2011, Maher pleaded guilty to securities fraud. Michael had not only traded on the inside information his brother shared; he had also passed it along to Maher's brother-in-law, Bassam Salman, who had funneled thousands of dollars to an account held jointly by his sister-in-law and her husband, Karim Bayyouk. Bayyouk had then traded on the secrets, splitting the profit of almost $2 million with Salman. Everyone involved with the convoluted scheme pleaded guilty, except for Salman. At trial, Salman was convicted, despite arguing that he did not realize Michael's investment recommendations were based on confidential information. Then the Second Circuit issued its *Newman* decision—the one that snapped Bharara's string of victories—creating a new line of defense. In Salman's appeal he argued that Maher Kara hadn't been *paid* for passing secrets to Michael. Under the logic of *Newman*, Salman could not possibly be guilty of insider trading.[5]

When Rakoff finished reading, his eyes lit up, as he recognized the possibilities. The legal aspects of the matter aside, the reality was that time and again his bosses on the Second Circuit had overruled him—on the death penalty, on SEC settlements, on a host of issues. Yet they had gotten it wrong in *Newman*, an insider-trading decision. Here was another case that relied squarely on *Newman*, and he would help decide it. Except in this case, Rakoff would in a sense be his bosses' equal.

A Comeuppance?

At 10:00 a.m. on June 9, 2015, in a third-floor courtroom of the grand Beaux-Arts federal courthouse on a grimy corner of Seventh and

Mission Streets in San Francisco, Rakoff took the bench with two Ninth Circuit judges. One of the judges called the case of *United States v. Salman* for argument.[6] At first, Rakoff mostly listened, but near the end of the half-hour hearing, he asked the government's lawyer, Merry Jean Chan, whether *Newman* had been wrongly decided. Chan, who had clerked for a Second Circuit judge, slipped the question, stressing that the facts in *Newman* were dramatically different from those in *Salman*. Distinguishing *Newman* was a plausible way to uphold Salman's conviction—and avoid a collision with the Second Circuit. But a collision was nonetheless dead ahead.

Rakoff and his colleagues left the bench and gathered in the robing room just outside the court chamber, and within seconds they discovered that they were in complete agreement: Salman was guilty, and *Newman* had been wrongly decided. Morgan Christen, the senior judge, suggested to Rakoff that the case was a natural for him to write, and while a more modest visitor from New York might have suggested that one of the others draft the opinion—especially an opinion that might defy his home circuit—this *was* a natural for Rakoff. He was thrilled at the opportunity.

When he turned to the writing, he got quickly to the point: Salman's conviction satisfied all the elements of illegal insider trading. That could have—and many people, including judges, say *should* have—ended the matter. Yet to Rakoff's way of thinking, it would have been weird to leave it there and not address the *Newman* issue. "The Second Circuit," he explained later, "has always had a reputation of being the leading circuit in securities fraud cases. So it was not inappropriate to say, our sister circuit has taken the following view, but we disagree." Otherwise "everyone would be saying, well, why have they not said anything about *Newman*?" And so his opinion continued: "We would not lightly ignore the most recent ruling of our sister circuit in an area of law that it has frequently encountered." Then, simply: "We decline to follow it."[7]

There it was, a split between two circuit courts, the Second and the Ninth, on an issue of prime Wall Street importance, a situation that the US Supreme Court, if asked to consider it, could ignore no more easily than a Labrador would resist a pork chop. Yet the justices' desires are never certain, and before they might even review the case, Bassam Salman asked a larger group of Ninth Circuit judges to take a look. They declined. That started the clock on the ninety-day period when he could bring the case to the Supreme Court—file a petition for certiorari, it was called. The wait was on, and it continued for nearly three months. Then, in early November 2015, just before the ninety days would expire, an entry appeared on the Supreme Court's website: petition for writ of certiorari in *Salman v. United States*. The only question now was whether the court would agree to hear the case. Finally, on January 19, 2016, the justices gave their answer.

"Oh, this is going to be fun!" Rakoff exclaimed, seeing the notation "cert granted." The reaction was decidedly less cheerful at law offices across Manhattan. Defense attorneys *liked* what the Second Circuit had decided in the *Newman* case, *liked* the leeway it had given their clients to trade. Now, with *Salman* on the top court's docket, the decision was in danger. And immediately suspicions blossomed anew: As with the Occupy Wall Street lawsuit and the Citigroup settlement, Rakoff must have bypassed the wheel—this one in San Francisco, no less—somehow grabbing control of the *Salman* appeal to set up a dramatic conflict that would land in the nation's highest court. One defense lawyer was so upset that he demanded an accounting from the Ninth Circuit of how the case had been assigned, although his efforts unearthed no evidence of anything improper.

Down and across the alley from Rakoff's court, at least a few Second Circuit judges were furious too. They considered his opinion in *Salman* a guerrilla action, a blatant thumbing of his nose at them. Now, the prospect of a Supreme Court vindication for the clever jurist was beyond what they could stomach. Though none would admit it openly, they would welcome Rakoff's comeuppance.

Fann-tastic!

In the early morning chill of October 5, 2016, lawyers and curious onlookers arrived at One First Street in Washington, DC, and began to ascend an imposing staircase, forty-four steps in all, toward a double row of sixteen towering columns that supported a massive portico. They climbed past the tall candelabra, past the seated marble figures representing Law and Justice, and through the tall bronze doors of the Supreme Court of the United States. Inside the storied courtroom of heavy red drapes and ornately carved wood awaited a murmuring crowd of attorneys and journalists, watchful federal marshals, and at the front a pair of attorneys. One was Michael Dreeben, a wiry and bespectacled deputy solicitor general and veteran of scores of Supreme Court arguments. He was there to represent the government. To his left was Alexandra Shapiro, a brilliant litigator and appellate specialist who represented Bassam Salman.

Minutes later, at 10:00 a.m. sharp, to the marshal's sonorous cry of "Oyez! Oyez! Oyez!" eight black-robed justices of the US Supreme Court filed one by one to their places behind an enormous wing-shaped mahogany bench at the front of the chamber. Chief Justice John Roberts, seated on a high-backed chair at the center, said in his youthful-sounding tenor: "We'll hear argument first this morning in Case No. 15–628, *Salman v. United States*. Ms. Shapiro." Clearly, slowly, Shapiro started with a warning. The crime of insider trading was so ill-defined that no one, including her client, could be sure what was and was not allowed. That made it especially important to construe this crime—whose elements were not even described in a statute—narrowly, to restrict it "to its core." The Second Circuit had come up with a practical solution: that passing along company secrets to someone likely to trade on them was not illegal unless you somehow got *paid* for the secrets—and the justices should adopt that rule while reversing Salman's conviction. It was a sensible beginning. After all, the court had not heard an insider-trading case for twenty years and, in the interim, the law had become a mess. Why not take this once-in-a-generation opportunity to make a clear and simple rule?

The first question came from Justice Ruth Bader Ginsburg, in whose chambers Shapiro had clerked more than two decades before. What if, the eighty-three-year-old justice asked, a corporate insider traded on one of his company's secrets and gave the profits to his brother? Would he still be liable? "Yes, your honor," Shapiro said. Easy enough. But then Ginsburg pressed. So what's the difference between that and the situation where, instead of the profits, the insider—in this case, Maher Kara—just gives the secret to his brother, who then trades on it and makes the profit? Why wouldn't the brother be liable? Why create this rule, as the Second Circuit had done, that the brother is blameless unless he somehow paid the insider for the information?

Here's what Ginsburg was getting at: Under Supreme Court precedent, to be convicted of illegal insider trading, you had to have known that a company insider got some benefit from telling you a secret, and it's reasonable to assume that if the insider was a friend or relative, he received something valuable—if only the warm feeling of helping you, a person he loved or at least liked. After Shapiro explained the difference—"the securities transaction is complete when the insider trades"—Roberts chimed in. "Maybe I'm missing . . . the import of the question," said the chief justice, perplexed. "Are you suggesting that if two people get together, one of them has inside information and he says to the other person, why don't . . . you trade on that, and then you and I will split the proceeds, that's not covered" by the law?

"That is covered, your Honor," Shapiro said, apologizing for being unclear. She doubled down on her argument that no one should be found guilty for passing along secrets unless they were actually paid for the secrets. Before long, Justice Stephen Breyer interrupted, returning to Ginsburg's point that the benefit of doing a relative a favor was compensation enough. "To help a close family member is like helping yourself," he said. When Shapiro again pushed back, Justice Elena Kagan intervened sharply. "Ms. Shapiro, you're asking us to ignore some extremely specific language," she said, citing *Dirks v. SEC*, a 1983 precedent that suggested no payment was necessary between friends and relatives who shared corporate secrets. A bit later, the justice, a whip-smart lawyer and academic and the first female dean of Harvard Law School, went into professor mode with a hypothetical. "Let's suppose," Kagan said, "I would like to give a gift to a friend of mine, but it's just too expensive ... then I pass a coworker's desk, and I see a $100 bill sitting there, and I take the $100 bill; and now I can give a gift that I had wanted to give, but I couldn't. Now, have I benefitted from stealing the $100 bill?"

Shapiro conceded the point, acknowledging that a corporate secret was no different from the $100 bill but trying to distinguish her client's case. The questions came rapid-fire now. Justice Sonia Sotomayor tried to throw Shapiro a lifeline—"What other possibilities might there be?"—but she declined to take it, defending her initial position. The minutes were ticking by, and as her time nearly expired, she reserved her remaining minutes for rebuttal and sat down.[8]

"Mr. Dreeben," the chief justice said. Earlier in the year, Dreeben, a deputy solicitor general, had become only the second person to argue one hundred cases before the court—his first was a 1989 lawsuit in which Roberts, then in private practice, had represented the other side—and his sense of the justices' predilections was sharp.[9] Almost immediately he seemed to stake out an extreme position, suggesting that it was almost always illegal to share corporate secrets with anyone likely to trade on the information. No tangible benefit—not even the satisfaction of giving a friend a gift—was required. Predictably, the justices took exception, starting with Roberts. Surely, the chief justice said, it wasn't illegal to inadvertently reveal information in a casual conversation. Dreeben conceded that it wasn't, but that failed to satisfy Roberts. "It's kind of a hazy line to draw, isn't it," he asked, between a gift and casual chat. For Dreeben the distinction didn't much matter. The biggest question was whether someone had wrongfully revealed a company secret.

Justice Samuel Alito wasn't buying it. "It doesn't seem to me," he said, "that your argument is much more consistent with *Dirks* [the 1983 precedent] than Ms. Shapiro's." Dreeben insisted that it was, and his comfort with speaking bluntly but respectfully to the justices became apparent. He responded to their questions with phrases like "No, I did not say that" and "I'm trying to explain" and in several instances a flat "No." Still, Dreeben was not making much headway, and he knew when to ease up. As time was running out, he responded to Sotomayor that "if the court is more at home with the language actually used in *Dirks*, and wants to reaffirm it, it should do so." Was his concession enough to snatch a victory? By the time Roberts had thanked counsel and called the next matter, there was no way to know.[10]

Whatever the lawyers' worries that day, they were nothing compared with the anxiety rippling through the legal and financial worlds back in New York. There, the real issue wasn't about the meaning of benefits or gifts or friends or other legal esoterica. It was about whether bankers and traders and hedge fund titans could continue to reap the benefits of working their sources without fear of ending up in prison. It was about whether Preet Bharara and other prosecutors would see a host of insider-trading convictions and guilty pleas evaporate because of a change in the rules. And it was, to some, about whether Rakoff would prevail over the Second Circuit in a skirmish over the meaning of the law.

The Troublemaker Prevails [243]

As the argument before the Supreme Court was ending, the judge and his three clerks may have been engaged in their typical lunchtime bridge game, debating how the case would turn out. This Supreme Court was widely considered to favor business, but that could cut both ways. It could mean that the court would reverse Rakoff and support the Second Circuit's view that an overly broad law against insider trading unfairly ensnared innocent investors. Or it could mean that Rakoff would be upheld so that companies would be protected from rapacious traders exploiting corporate secrets. "I have learned from long experience," said the judge, "that you cannot predict what the court will do." In truth, he believed that the justices would see things his way. Maybe the decision would be 4-4, a result that still meant his ruling would stand. More likely, he could eke out a 5-3 majority. Either way, the answer would probably not come until spring.

On a December morning, though, Rakoff had barely hung up his parka and snapped on his computer before an alert flashed across the screen. The judge sprang from his chair, trotted on aging legs into the reception area, stopped at the door to his clerks' office, and cried, "Fann-tastic!" Almost immediately the phone began to ring. His old friends—even the defense lawyers who had been rooting for his reversal in the *Salman* case—called one after another to offer congratulations. Rakoff's clerks, ever aware of the formalities required in dealing with a federal judge, made an exception and patted him on the back. Finally, he received a phone call from his wife Ann that moved him close to tears. "I am so proud of you, Jed," she said.

. . .

The Supreme Court had issued its decision, and he had won. But the vote had not been 4-4 or even 5-3. It had in fact been unanimous: 8-0.[11] In retrospect, the outcome was predictable, as the justices' unanimity suggested. Yet the impact was extraordinary. The decision not only restored the law of insider trading but prompted an unprecedented rethinking of what that law should be. The Second Circuit would in later cases move even farther from its logic in the *Newman* opinion and closer to Rakoff's view, refining the rules to give traders, prosecutors, and judges more clarity about what they were allowed to do. Dozens of insider-trading convictions in danger of being reversed would stand. For the judge the impact from a personal point of view was even greater. The Supreme Court's decision allowed some vindication for him, ever the troublemaker, and his expansive view of the power of the federal courts.

Epilogue

On a drizzly Friday evening in January 2017, a generous slice of New York's legal elite drifted into the nineteenth-century neoclassical headquarters of the City Bar Association on West 44th Street and gathered for cocktails, sushi, and steamed dumplings on the second floor. The dim light and suits of navy and gray reflected the muted tone of the power assembling there: accomplished attorneys, esteemed judges, honored public officials, a moneyed banker or two. There was, however, no mistaking the center of this privileged universe. To one side of the darkly paneled room, a circle of maybe a dozen people spoke and nodded and loudly laughed with the slight figure in their midst. He was the honored guest of the evening's main event, a musical extravaganza titled "MacJed, or All's Well That Ends: The Life and Times of Jed Rakoff."

Shortly after 8:00 p.m. the celebration moved across the hall to a grander room of dark-wood wainscoting, portraits of Cyrus Vance and Ruth Bader Ginsburg and other legal luminaries on the wall, and a large stage to one side. Rakoff and his wife Ann sat front and center, witnesses to a rollicking skewering of his career. The show didn't miss much, making fun of his striking ambition (to the tune of *Fiddler on the Roof*'s "Tradition"), his marathon demands on his clerks ("Jed Isn't Easy"), and his appetite for publicity and harsh treatment of

Wall Street ("The Banker's Lament"). At the end Rakoff himself took the stage and warbled a song with lyrics he had composed the week before at the electronic keyboard in his office. It loosely followed the tune of *My Fair Lady*'s "You Did It," thanking the show's creators for roasting him without making him feel too bad. He was met with raucous applause.

Not many judges can attract an enormous crowd on an inclement Friday evening in January and revel in what seems genuine laughter and warmth. Many of these people came as old friends. But more were there out of simple respect for what Rakoff, as a lower-court judge among thousands of federal court judges, has dared accomplish on the bench. Though back in 2010 he had called Bank of America's agreement with the SEC "half-baked justice," Rakoff's opinion approving it was so harsh that plaintiffs' lawyers seized on its language to extract almost $2.5 billion over the merger with Merrill.[1] His insistence that executives rather than shareholders be punished for Bank of America's transgressions helped prompt the 2015 "Yates Memo," the Justice Department's policy of targeting individual wrongdoers rather than just the financial institutions and other companies they work for. Although the policy's enforcement was spotty at first and then weakened during the first Trump administration, it regained strength under President Biden after the Justice Department declared its restoration in 2021.[2] And Rakoff's calls for harsher punishment of financial institutions ultimately led prosecutors to extract massive fines and guilty pleas from JPMorgan, Barclays, and other global institutions for such offenses as manipulating foreign-exchange markets and the now-defunct London Interbank Offered Rate (LIBOR).

Citigroup's Second Circuit victory dashed hopes that federal judges could force banks into admissions, but the SEC got the message, at least at first, in 2013, when it started extracting mea culpas in egregious cases.[3] The commission has since retreated, although it makes occasional noises about cracking down again.[4] Rakoff inspired many of his colleagues to reject settlements in a variety of areas. In November 2018, for example, Judge William Pauley cited Rakoff in bouncing New York City's $1.2 billion settlement with the federal government over substandard public housing.[5] In February 2018, Judge Lewis Kaplan in New York denounced a deferred prosecution agreement with U.S. Bancorp as not serving "the interests of just punishment." In an echo of Rakoff's bitter acceptance of the Citigroup settlement, Kaplan said, "I'm obliged to swallow the pill, whether I like it or not."[6]

At an age when many Americans would have probably been content to call it a day, Rakoff has not let up. He continues to employ what a former clerk called his simple superpower of asking "why?" while challenging the overreaching Wall Street oligarchs and assorted other miscreants who have had the misfortune of finding themselves in his courtroom. He has been at it long enough that sometimes he gets to see some of his once heavily criticized views vindicated. On June 28, 2024, the US Supreme Court overturned the *Chevron* decision, holding that courts must "exercise their independent judgment in deciding whether an agency has acted within its statutory authority." Beyond Rakoff's determination to pass judgment on the Citigroup's settlement with the SEC, he has long criticized the *Chevron* doctrine in opinions, writings, and speeches. "So, all in all," he has said with satisfaction, "I think the Supreme Court got it right!"

I Love What I Do

Half an hour southwest of Santa Fe on US 25, about where Placer Mountain peaks to the distant east, Martha Vázquez steers her enormous white SUV on a gently downhill stretch through gray mist while arguing on the phone about why the court's budget cannot accommodate her request for real-time transcripts. "I'll buy the damn thing!" she responds in final frustration. The road is slick but the traffic sparse on this morning in March 2023, and in another half hour she is in the garage of the downtown Albuquerque federal courthouse, parking her unwieldy machine with the skill of a midtown Manhattan garage attendant. In a few minutes, her court deputy and a small plastic crate of documents perched on a wheely cart in tow, Vázquez is up the judges' elevator and sitting at a round table outside a courtroom, reviewing the records of the two people she is about to see.

They are ex-cons, men she or a colleague has sentenced to prison who are now out and trying to make a go of honest work and supervised living. One, Michael Kellerwood, did time at the Florence Supermax prison in Colorado for, most recently, arranging the murder of an inmate who questioned his authority as a Navajo gang leader. Vázquez reads a passage transcribed from a wiretap: "Fuck him," Kellerwood says. "In every yard, I'm the boss, every Diné [a word for the Navajo people] in here is under me." Other inmates were terrified of Kellerwood, but his own apparent despair was so intense that he tried to slit his throat. As the judge prepares for her latest meeting with him, her court deputy assures her: "Don't faint when you see him, he's in a suit and tie. He looks incredible."

Vázquez enters the spacious courtroom and sits at the head of a long wooden table, Kellerwood catty-corner to her left. To anyone who has never seen him before, he does, in a different sense, look incredible. Tattoos cover every inch of his face and neck and hands, the only parts of his body visible outside his roomy light-gray suit and white shirt with a collar too loose for his neck. Black hair slicked back, eyes dark and wary, Kellerwood adjusts his jacket and shifts in his seat, his compact body tense and never quite still. Vázquez fixes him with a smile. "Michael, it is good to see you. How are you?"

Kellerwood says he is okay. He says he works at a nonprofit that supports the families of prisoners. The judge leans toward him and gets down to business, taking notes: *What do you do? How many* hours? *How do you get along with the people there?* Vázquez pauses. "You look just amazing, you look really good!" she says with a surprising tone of affection.

"I *feel* good," he responds, nodding and his face brightening, the initial impression of menace falling away. The judge asks about his life at the home he shares with other former inmates. "We talk to each other, we help each other. I like it. I feel welcome," he says.

"You really take my breath away," Vázquez says. When she asks about his ambitions, Kellerwood mentions staying clean but also going to school.

Then he brings up his tattoos. "If I have school behind me, maybe they see past the tattoos. People see me now and they go, 'Whoa!'" He throws his arms back in mock surprise.

"We can help with the tattoos," Vázquez says. "It hurts, but . . ."

"I've thought about it, but I'm not ready. They're too much of my life. I don't . . . yeah."

Vázquez presses gently. "I don't want you to feel your face is keeping people away from you. I want you to have options. So think about it, because it makes an impression, and we don't like our defendants to be locked in their houses."

Kellerwood then gets to a simple truth that Vázquez hears so often from people who are trying to make their way after prison. "I was somebody in there, and out here, I'm nobody, just a guy, you know?" he says, sounding not so much bitter as realistic, maybe even optimistic. "When I first got out, I would see a cop, and I would stop and pat myself down. Now, I just walk by and say, 'Hi, officer!' You know?"

Vázquez does not know, of course, how Kellerwood or anyone else she has seen pass through her courtroom over thirty years will turn out. He has slipped already once, visiting a drug-addicted girlfriend in Arizona and testing positive upon his return to Albuquerque. Vázquez refuses to see his life wasted, though, just as she has refused to give up on anyone—not David Rivera, not Ollisha Easley, not even

Marc Dutch. The strain of delving so deeply into these people's lives, of caring what happens to them sometimes more than they do themselves, feels exhausting to the judge, and it seems to be taking its toll. After her conversation with Kellerwood, she gets lunch at her favorite Albuquerque restaurant, Duran's Pharmacy, a kitschy place of souvenirs and the local version of Mexican food. She has not made a decision about staying on the bench beyond another year. It is a thought she has shared before. Maybe, after two divorces and family not seen and necessary daily attention to an aging parent, it is time to take care of herself.

"I am seriously thinking about trying to be the grandmother that my mother was," she says. "I have eight grandchildren, and I don't want to wait until I'm eighty or ninety. I want to be able to have an influence on them, to be able to impart the things that are important to me to their lives." She continues: "What I see in my cases that breaks my heart is that so many of the people that come before me don't have that.... It is so sad for me. It is not going to be easy for me to leave. I love what I do."[7]

Small Victories

It is September 2023, and a quiet, young Black man, short and heavy and wearing a beard and thick dreadlocks, stands before Carlton Reeves in a red jumpsuit, the attire of incarceration. The judge has arrived late to the bench, and he is reading, trying to catch up, and after a long pause, he says, "I do apologize for the delay."

Reeves has seen this man, Timothy Liddell, before, in 2020, when the judge sentenced him to about four months in prison for possessing a machine gun, after crediting him with the time he had already served on state charges. It was, in the scheme of things, a minor crime, but Liddell has violated the conditions of his sentence by testing positive for marijuana and traveling to Starkville, Mississippi, farther than allowed, and he now faces another five to eleven months behind bars. It is easy to imagine that this man reminds Reeves of some of the young Black men he grew up with.

"We had a conversation before, and we are having one again," the judge begins. "You are going to have to do whatever you can to stay away from marijuana. You have a baby on the way, you have many people who are depending on you—including yourself. Promise me you won't use it, promise me you won't possess it, promise me you won't distribute it." Reeves pauses and fixes his gaze on Liddell, waiting. "I'm *asking* you for a *promise*. Can you do that? Can you do that for me?" Liddell says he can. "I want you to stand by those promises," the judge says. "I want you to do well. I want you to move on with your life. You have a *child* coming . . ." and his voice trails off. Reeves sentences Liddell to time served and another eighteen months of supervised release. His aim is not necessarily to be lenient with people like Liddell, and it is not just to ensure that they have chances to move on with their lives. It is also, Reeves says, "to stand up for the judiciary," to remind the Liddells of the world "that the courts belong to them. I want them to feel like, if they had to do it over again, at the end of the day they would come back to *this* court, before *this* judge, to give them the confidence that *this* judge has treated *this* case with the most attention and in as impartial a way as he could."

There is every reason to believe that Reeves succeeds in this effort, and it is a meaningful if small victory at a moment when so much of the nation—on the right and the left—seems to have lost faith in the federal courts. Trump and MAGA world continue, of course, to rail madly against the "rigged" judicial system that has tried but largely failed to hold accountable this current and former president and the rioters who invaded the Capitol on January 6 and otherwise tried to undermine our constitutional framework. Decades of conservative efforts to narrow access to justice and constrain judicial authority persist, shielding corporations and hiding the truth and the wrongdoing of the powerful while eroding people's rights and their ability to vindicate those rights in court. Frustration on the left builds as judges act in confounding and seemingly political ways. It is the Supreme Court that draws liberals' greatest ire with decisions like the reversal of *Roe v. Wade*, prompting calls for limiting justices' tenure and narrowing the types of cases they can hear.

Much of the criticism is understandable and even justified, but it gives short shrift to the lessons that these three judges—Carlton Reeves, Jed Rakoff, Martha Vázquez—have for decades been teaching us. First, almost all the action, the legal wrangling that matters in people's lives, occurs in courtrooms like theirs and never reaches the lofty confines of the Supreme Court or even the chambers of appeals court judges. If ordinary Americans are to receive legal redress, it will probably come in these lower courts, and closing their doors while constraining the ability of judges to help deprives people of their due. Second, there are shocking exceptions, and no one ascends to the bench without political views, but federal trial judges—with lifetime tenure, the duty to base their decisions on law, and a safety net of at least two layers of appellate judges to catch their mistakes—are less vulnerable than elected officials to the influence of financial backers and political sponsors and far likelier to act with independence and courage and within the limits of the law. In so many cases their demand for facts and public scrutiny of the powerful has created hope and provoked action when too many public officials and institutions have averted their eyes.

Third, diversity on the bench matters. Vázquez's background as the daughter of Mexican immigrants fuels her drive to help outsiders and the deeply troubled gain or recover lives of value and security. Reeves's experiences as a Black man from Yazoo City animate his efforts to include everyone in our system of legal rights and democracy regardless of race or gender or sexual orientation. Even Rakoff, in a sense, contributes to this diversity. His status as an establishment insider of rare independence and confidence allows him to stand up to institutional power and Wall Street oligarchs with credibility and extraordinary impact. An effective judiciary that fulfills its constitutional role requires judges with experiences and perspectives broad enough to allow them to understand why a Black man fears a cop, why a woman does not say no to her boss, why an immigrant deals in cash and avoids banks—and why no executive or financial institution is ever too big or influential to go unchallenged. Yet as of August 1, 2024, after almost four years of the Biden administration's efforts to make the US judiciary more diverse, the 1,457 sitting federal judges were overwhelmingly male (67 percent) and white (74 percent).[8]

Even engaged and courageous jurists of varied experiences and backgrounds, however, cannot do their jobs when overloaded with cases and bound by wrongheaded laws. The number of federal judges has lagged far behind the growth in their responsibilities and the nation's population. Since 1990, the US population has increased almost 35 percent while the number of federal judges has risen slightly more than 3 percent.[9] There's a simple if costly fix: Congress could provide for more judges, more courtrooms, and more judicial resources. There's an equally straightforward way to restore people's ability to vindicate their rights. Again, it depends on Congress: abolishing qualified immunity, giving judges more leeway in sentencing, loosening the strict standard for stating a claim, and making a host of other reforms. But the judiciary needs to change in a more fundamental way. For much of the nation's history and especially over the past six decades, lawmakers and presidents on the left and right have thundered at the courts for assorted ills, largely because judges are such easy targets.

Alexander Hamilton admitted as much when he wrote in *Federalist No. 78* that the judiciary is the "weakest" and "least dangerous" branch, having "neither FORCE nor WILL, but merely judgment."[10] Even with life tenure, few judges have been willing to speak publicly, wary of tipping their hands on how they may decide cases or, worse, becoming targets of violence. Serious threats against federal judges more than doubled between October 1, 2020, and September 30, 2023, from 224 to 457.[11] Yet ethics rules encourage judges to speak publicly in the service of educating people about "the administration of justice," and that surely includes explaining why judges are not "unhinged" or "haters" or "terrible persons" as the forty-fifth (and forty-seventh) president would have us believe.[12] The occasional stilted statement from, say, Chief Justice John Roberts about how "we do not have Obama judges or Trump judges" is not enough or even true.[13] Judges need to give as good as they get.

. • .

On an April afternoon in 2019, as Carlton Reeves bear-hugged the dean and ambled to a podium at the University of Virginia Law School to receive its highest honor, the hundreds of students and teachers seated before him could not have known what was coming. He grinned his big grin and laughed and pointed at the crowd and revealed that it was his fifty-fifth birthday. He said it was the first in years that he had spent without his late wife, the words catching in his throat, and he gave a shout-out to his daughter and a younger sister and to all the people who had helped him over the years. He was honored. He was joyous. And then he began his remarks.[14]

The words were typically tough but uplifting as Reeves spoke of justice and Mississippi and the nation's history of race. About halfway through, however, his voice rose and hardened as he mentioned a "great assault on our judiciary." This attack included the crude language of then former president Trump, Reeves said, but it was more—it was personal. "The proof is in *my* mailbox," he said. "In countless letters of hatred I've been called a 'piece of garbage,' 'an arrogant pompous piece of shit,' 'a disgrace,' an 'asshole . . . [who] will burn in

Epilogue [255]

hell,' and the 'embodiment of Satan himself.' . . . The deliverers of hate who send these messages aim to bully and scare judges who look like me from the judiciary." He continued: "The slander and falsehoods thrown at courts today, are not those of a critic, seeking to improve the judiciary's search for truth. They are words of an attacker, seeking to distort and twist that search toward falsehood."

Before ending his remarks, Reeves delivered the simple message that Chief Justice John Roberts and so many other jurists have lacked the courage to send: "To fulfill the Constitution's promise to establish justice, 'We the People' need to defend the judiciary."

Acknowledgments

I owe great thanks to the scores of people who helped me navigate and understand as best I could the world of a federal judge. They include law clerks, scholars, attorneys, court deputies, people sued or charged with crimes, and friends of judges or judges themselves. Many of them I agreed not to name. Many more will go unmentioned because it would be impossible to name them all, and for that I apologize.

In New Mexico, Dominique Fenton, Nora McDonnell, Jackie Davis, Linda Zieba-Romero, and Toni Cowden welcomed me to Judge Vázquez's court with generosity and trust. Thank you also to Andrew Hayt of the National Archives and lawyer Mark Heaney in Los Angeles for ferreting out essential documents relating to Vázquez's cases. In Mississippi, Twana Summers provided invaluable help as Judge Reeves's assistant, and I am grateful to Patricia Bennett at Mississippi College School of Law, Jo G Pritchard and especially Gloria-Elayne Owens for showing me Yazoo City, and David Rae Morris for connecting me with Pritchard and Owens. In New York, more people than I can or am allowed to mention guided me in and around Judge Rakoff's court, and so I will just thank the judge's deputy clerk, Linda Kotowski, for all her help.

I am grateful to John C. Coffee Jr. at Columbia Law School for his support and wisdom, and to editor Maura Roessner for believing in this book and helping to make it real. I am especially indebted to Lincoln Caplan—colleague, boss, teacher, and friend—for his encouragement, insight, generosity, and skill at working through ideas.

Finally, thank you to my wife, Joanna Hendon, and my daughter, Carolyn, whom I love and depend on in more ways than I can say.

Notes

Prologue

1. The facts of the case are set forth in Clarence Jamison v. Town of Pelahatchie et al, No. 16-cv-00595-CWR-LRA, PACER (S.D. Miss. 2016).
2. Lizette Alvarez and Cara Buckley, "Zimmerman Is Acquitted in Trayvon Martin Killing," *New York Times*, July 13, 2013.
3. Jelani Cobb, "The Matter of Black Lives," *New Yorker*, March 6, 2016.
4. McLendon said at his deposition that Jamison simply consented.
5. McLendon denies saying this.
6. Bouldin v. City of Mendenhall, Mississippi et al, No. 06-cv-00399-HTW-LRA PACER (S.D. Miss. 2006).
7. Pierson v. Ray, 386 U.S. 547 (1967).
8. Ramirez v. Martinez, 716 F.3d 369 (5th Cir. 2013).
9. Mitch Smith, "Minnesota Officer Acquitted in Killing of Philando Castile," *New York Times*, June 16, 2017; Richard A. Oppel Jr., Derrick Bryson Taylor, and Nicholas Bogel-Burroughs, "What To Know about Breonna Taylor's Death," *New York Times*, December 13, 2023; "How George Floyd Died, and What Happened Next," *New York Times*, July 29, 2022.
10. Jamison v. McClendon, 476 F. Supp. 3d 386 (S.D. Miss. Aug. 2020).
11. Law, "Theory of Judicial Power and Judicial Review," 723.
12. Brown v. Board of Education, 347 U.S. 483 (1954); "Declaration of Constitutional Principles," 102 Cong. Rec. 4459–61 (1956).
13. Snyder, *Democratic Justice*.
14. Bickel, *Least Dangerous Branch*.
15. Ely, *Democracy and Distrust*.

16. Barker, "Thurgood Marshall, the Law, and the System"; Ginsburg, Hartnett, and Williams, *My Own Words*.

17. Fishkin and Forbath, *Anti-Oligarchy Constitution*.

Chapter 1

1. Bolton, *Hardest Deal of All*.
2. Alexander v. Holmes County Board of Education, 396 U.S. 19 (1969).
3. Morris, *Yazoo*, 15–16.
4. "Theodore Gilmore Bilbo," by David G. Sansing, April 13, 2018, *Mississippi Encyclopedia*, https://mississippiencyclopedia.org/entries/theodore-gilmore-bilbo/.
5. Civil Rights Act of 1964, 42 U.S.C. Section 2000(a).
6. Quoted in Walton, *Mississippi*, 174.
7. "Former County Supervisor Dies in Mississippi House Fire," AP, January 16, 2023, https://apnews.com/article/mississippi-fires-8a6d5a48dc6ece09f56c4e0d8e6072a9.
8. Nancy K. Bristow, "50 Years after the Jackson State Killings, America's Crisis of Racial Injustice Continues—and Shows the Danger of Forgetting," *Time*, May 15, 2020.
9. Quoted in Walton, *Mississippi*, 180.
10. Brown v. Board of Education (Brown II), 349 U.S. 294, 301 (1955).
11. Harper v. Virginia Board of Elections, 383 U.S. 663 (1966).
12. Jones v. Mayer, 392 U.S. 409 (1968).
13. Heart of Atlanta Motel, Inc. v. United States, 379 U.S. 241 (1964).
14. Browder v. Gayle, 142 F. Supp. 707 (M.D. Ala. 1956).
15. "Frank M. Johnson, Jr.," by Jack Bass, *Encyclopedia of Alabama*, https://encyclopediaofalabama.org/article/frank-m-johnson-jr/.
16. Jack Bass, "John Minor Wisdom, Appeals Court Judge Who Helped to End Segregation, Dies at 93," *New York Times*, May 16, 1999; Nina Totenberg, "Elbert Tuttle, Quiet Civil Rights 'Revolutionary'," *NPR.org*, October 5, 2011, www.npr.org/2011/10/05/140948689/elbert-tuttle-quiet-civil-rights-revolutionary; Bruce Lambert, "John R. Brown, 83, Federal Judge Who Ordered Integration in South," *New York Times*, January 27, 1993; Jack Bass, "He Made the Right Enemies," *Washington Post*, January 29, 1983.
17. Prigg v. Pennsylvania, 41 U.S. 539 (1842).
18. Dred Scott v. Sandford, 60 U.S. 393 (1857).

19. Abraham Lincoln, "First Inaugural Address," March 4, 1861, Avalon Project, Lilian Goldman Law Library, Yale Law School, www.loc.gov/resource/mal.0773800/?st=text#.

20. Ex parte Merryman, 17 F. Cas. 144 (No. 9487) (C.C.D. Md., Taney, Circuit Justice 1861); Noah Feldman, "This Is the Story of How Lincoln Broke the U.S. Constitution," *New York Times*, November 2, 2021.

21. Plessy v. Ferguson, 163 U.S. 537 (1896).

22. On laws setting minimum wages and maximum hours for workers, see Roediger and Foner, *Our Own Time*, 81-122.

23. Fishkin and Forbath, *Anti-Oligarchy Constitution*, 145-47.

24. Fishkin and Forbath, *Anti-Oligarchy Constitution*.

25. Fishkin and Forbath, *Anti-Oligarchy Constitution*.

26. Lochner v. New York, 198 U.S. 45 (1905).

27. Gillman, "How Political Parties Can Use the Courts"; Fishkin and Forbath, *Anti-Oligarchy Constitution*, 147.

28. *Lochner*, at 75.

29. Hoffer, Hoffer, and Hull, *Federal Courts*.

30. Hoffer, Hoffer, and Hull, *Federal Courts*, 294-95.

31. West Coast Hotel Co. v. Parrish, 300 U.S. 379 (1937).

32. *West Coast Hotel Co.*, at 391.

33. Barrett, "Attribution Time."

34. Johnson, "Willis Van Devanter"; Fishkin and Forbath, *Anti-Oligarchy Constitution*, 307-18.

35. United States v. Carolene Products Co., 304 U.S. 144 (1938).

36. John Kyle Day, "The Southern Manifesto: Making Opposition to the Civil Rights Movement" (PhD dissertation, University of Missouri, 2006).

37. Day, "Southern Manifesto," 400.

38. Driver, "Supremacies and the Southern Manifesto," 1054.

39. Quoted in William S. White, "Ruling to Figure in '54 Campaign," *New York Times*, May 18, 1954.

40. "The Nation: The Master of the Maze," *Time*, November 7, 1977.

41. Thomas Chadwick (Johnston's press secretary), interview by Herbert J. Hartsook, June 26, 1995, Oral History Project, South Carolina Political Collections, University of South Carolina.

42. Driver, "Supremacies and the Southern Manifesto," 1061.

43. Heath, *To Face Down Dixie*, 34-43.

44. Heath, *To Face Down Dixie*, 63, 244-46.

45. Heath, *To Face Down Dixie*, 40.
46. Heath, *To Face Down Dixie*, 61–76.
47. Heath, *To Face Down Dixie*, 72–73.
48. "Johnston's Death Is Likely to Bring Political Struggles in South Carolina," *New York Times*, April 19, 1965; Heath, *To Face Down Dixie*, 117–36.
49. Pierson v. Ray, 386 U.S. 547 (1967), at 555.
50. Powe, *Warren Court*.
51. Tom Charles Huston, interview by Tim Naftali, the Richard Nixon Presidential Library and Museum, April 30, 2008.
52. Christopher Saunders, "How We Got Here: The Education of Tom Charles Huston," *The Avocado*, June 8, 2019, https://the-avocado.org/2019/06/08/how-we-got-here-the-education-of-tom-charles-huston/.
53. Christopher Lydon, "Conservative Architect of Security Plan Tom Charles Huston," *New York Times*, May 24, 1973.
54. Goldman, *Picking Federal Judges*, 205–207.
55. Sheldon Goldman, "Judicial Confirmation Wars: Ideology and the Battle for the Federal Courts," *University of Richmond Law Review* 39, no. 3 (2005): 879.
56. Robert B. Semple Jr., "Warren E. Burger Named Chief Justice by Nixon," *New York Times*, May 22, 1969.
57. Powe, *Warren Court*, 482–83.
58. As quoted in Linda Greenhouse, "Warren E. Burger Is Dead at 87; Was Chief Justice for 17 Years," *New York Times*, June 26, 1995.
59. Roe v. Wade, 410 U.S. 113 (1973).
60. Bivens v. Six Unknown Named Agents of Federal Bureau of Narcotics, 403 U.S. 388 (1971).
61. Bush v. Lucas, 462 U.S. 367 (1983); United States v. Stanley, 483 U.S. 669 (1987); Chemerinsky, *Closing the Courthouse Door*, 70–71.
62. Imbler v. Pachtman, 424 U.S. 409 (1976).
63. Briscoe v. LaHue, 460 U.S. 325 (1983).
64. Scheuer v. Rhodes, 416 U.S. 232 (1974).
65. United States v. Richardson, 418 U.S. 166 (1974).
66. Davis v. United States, 411 U.S. 233 (1973); Francis v. Henderson, 425 U.S. 536 (1976); Wainwright v. Sykes, 433 U.S. 72 (1977).
67. Griswold v. Connecticut, 381 U.S. 479 (1965); Bowers v. Hardwick, 478 U.S. 186 (1986); Graetz and Greenhouse, *Burger Court*, 244–67.
68. Baker v. Nelson, 409 U.S. 810 (1972); Doe v. Commonwealth's Attorney for the City of Richmond, 403 F. Supp. 1199 (1975), affirmed, 425 U.S. 901 (1976); Graetz and Greenhouse, *Burger Court*, chapter 8.

69. Goldman, *Picking Federal Judges*, 200–11.

70. "Ronald Reagan's 1980 Neshoba County Fair speech," transcribed by Stanley Dearman, *The Neshoba Democrat*, April 8, 2021.

71. William Raspberry, "Reagan's Race Legacy," *Washington Post*, June 14, 2004.

72. Mobile v. Bolden, 446 U.S. 55 (1980).

73. Pub. L. No. 97–205, 96 Stat. 131 (1982).

74. Martin Luther King Jr. Federal Legal Holiday, Pub. L. No. 98-144, 97 Stat. 917 (1983); Steven V. Roberts, "King Holiday Faces a Filibuster," *New York Times*, October 4, 1983; Emily Wagster Pettus, "Mississippi's MLK-Lee Holiday Persists after Decades," *Jackson Clarion-Ledger*, April 2, 2017.

75. Abraham Lincoln, "The Dred Scott Decision," June 26, 1857, The Freeman Institute, www.freemaninstitute.com/lincoln.htm

Chapter 2

1. McCann, *On the Inside*; Peter Kihss, "44-Story Plunge Kills Head of United Brands," *New York Times*, February 4, 1975.

2. Cohen, *Fish That Ate the Whale*; Mary Bralove, "Was Eli Black's Suicide Caused by Tensions of Conflicting Worlds?" *Wall Street Journal*, February 14, 1975.

3. Lucinda Franks, "The 4-Year Odyssey of Jane Alpert, from Revolutionary Bomber to Feminist," *New York Times*, January 14, 1975.

4. McCann, *On the Inside*, 121; Briloff, "Accounting Practices," 612.

5. Mary Bralove, "At United Brands Co., Fight for Control Came after Honduran Payoff," *Wall Street Journal*, May 7, 1975.

6. Bralove, "At United Brands Co."

7. Bralove, "At United Brands Co."

8. Kenneth Bacon, "United Brands Bribe Cover-Up Charged by SEC," *Wall Street Journal*, May 21, 1975.

9. Bralove, "At United Brands Co."

10. Robert Cole, "S.E.C Suit Links a Honduras Bribe to United Brands," *New York Times*, April 10, 1975.

11. Cole, "S.E.C Suit Links a Honduras Bribe."

12. Rosenfeld, "Civil Penalties."

13. Levine and Herlihy, "Father of Enforcement."

14. 18 U.S.C. Section 1343.

15. Rakoff, "Federal Mail Fraud Statute."

16. New York Central & Hudson River Railroad Co. v. United States, 212 U.S. 481 (1909).

17. Arnold H. Lubasch, "Guilty Plea in Foreign Bribe Case," *New York Times*, July 20, 1978.

18. Shultz v. Wheaton Glass Company, 421 F.2d 259 (3d Cir. 1970).

19. Mayer, *Dark Money*; Graetz and Greenhouse, *Burger Court*, 237–40 and fn95.

20. Lewis F. Powell Jr., "The Memo," August 23, 1971, Washington and Lee University School of Law Scholarly Commons, https://scholarlycommons.law.wlu.edu/powellmemo/1/.

21. US Chamber of Commerce, Chamber Litigation Center, accessed March 15, 2024, www.uschamber.com/program/us-chamber-litigation-center; Pilaar, "Making of the Supreme Court Bar."

22. Flood v. Kuhn, 407 U.S. 258 (1972); Virginia State Board of Pharmacy v. Virginia Citizens Consumer Council, Inc., 425 U.S. 748 (1976); Citizens United v. Federal Election Commission, 558 U.S. 310 (2010); Graetz and Greenhouse, *Burger Court*, chapter 11 and fn95.

23. In re Cady Roberts & Co., 40 S.E.C. 907 (1961).

24. J.I. Case Co. v. Borak, 377 U.S. 426 (1964).

25. SEC v. Texas Gulf Sulphur Co., 401 F.2d 833 (2d Cir. 1968).

26. Pritchard, "Justice Lewis F. Powell, Jr.," 863–66.

27. Eisen v. Carlisle & Jacquelin, 417 U.S. 156 (1974).

28. "The Law: Taking Mass from Class," *Time*, June 10, 1974.

29. Blue Chip Stamps v. Manor Drug Stores, 421 U.S. 723 (1975).

30. Pritchard, "Justice Lewis F. Powell, Jr.," fn139.

31. Ernst & Ernst v. Hochfelder, 425 U.S. 185 (1976).

32. TSC Industries, Inc. v. Northway, Inc., 426 U.S. 438 (1976).

33. Santa Fe Industries, Inc. v. Green, 430 U.S. 462 (1977).

34. United Housing Foundation v. Forman, 421 U.S. 837 (1975); International Brotherhood of Teamsters v. Daniel, 439 U.S. 551 (1979).

35. Arnold H. Lubasch, "Guilty Plea in Foreign Bribe Case," *New York Times*, July 20, 1978.

36. 15 U.S.C. Section 78dd-1, et seq.

37. "Address of Edwin Meese III Before the Palm Beach County Bar Association, February 10, 1986," NCJRS Virtual Library, www.ojp.gov/ncjrs/virtual-library/abstracts/address-edwin-meese-iii-palm-beach-county-bar-association-february.

38. Hoffer, Hoffer, and Hull, *Federal Courts*, 403–4.

39. Steven V. Roberts, "Meese and Reagan: The Anatomy of a Friendship," *New York Times*, April 3, 1988.

40. Will Haun, "The Philosopher in Action: A Tribute to the Hon. Edwin Meese III," *Federalist Society Review* 13, no. 1, (2012): 6.

41. Teles, "Transformative Bureaucracy."

42. Haun, "Philosopher in Action."

43. "About Us," Federalist Society, accessed March 15, 2024, https://fedsoc.org/about-us.

44. Lynette Clemetson, "Meese's Influence Looms in Today's Judicial Wars," *New York Times*, August 17, 2005.

45. David Montgomery, "Conquerors of the Court," *Washington Post Magazine*, January 2, 2019.

Chapter 3

1. U.S. v. Vazquez, 977 F.2d 594 (9th Cir. 1992); further details of Ricardo Vázquez's case are set forth in U.S. v. Fernando Mendez et. al., No. 90-cr-613-R (C.D. Cal. 1990).

2. "How Notre Dame Admitted Undergraduate Women 50 Years Ago," University of Notre Dame, accessed March 17, 2024, https://50goldenyears.nd.edu/news-and-features/almost-mary-ed-near-merger-ended-with-notre-dame-welcoming-women-50-years-ago/.

3. Michael L. Stout, "True Believers and the Road to Hell, Hon. Martha Vazquez," interview with Vázquez, June 8, 2021, YouTube, https://mlstoutlaw.com/home/true-believers-and-the-road-to-hell/hon-martha-vazquez/.

4. David Colker, "Reies Lopez Tijerina Dies at 88; Chicano Rights Movement Leader," *Los Angeles Times*, January 22, 2015.

5. Karslake and Townsend, "Definite Sentencing in New Mexico."

6. Karslake and Townsend, "Definite Sentencing in New Mexico," fn17.

7. Office of the New Mexico Attorney General, "Report of the Attorney General on the February 2 and 3, 1980, Riot at the Penitentiary of New Mexico," June 1980.

8. Michael Tonry, "Mandatory Penalties," *Crime and Justice* 16 (1992): 251.

9. Hagan, *Who Are the Criminals?*, 11.

10. Hagan, *Who Are the Criminals?*, 17.

11. Hagan, *Who Are the Criminals?*.

12. Pub. L. No. 98-473, 98 Stat. 1988.

13. Hoffer, Hoffer, and Hull, *Federal Courts*, 433.

14. U.S. Sentencing Commission, "Supplementary Report on the Initial Sentencing Guidelines and Policy Statements," 19 (1987); Stith and Cabranes, *Fear of Judging: Sentencing Guidelines in the Federal Courts*, 35-77.

15. Dorany Pineda, "Manuel L. Real, Judge Who Helped Desegregate Southern California Schools, Dies at 95," *Los Angeles Times*, July 1, 2019; Henry Weinstein, "Impeachment Inquiry of Judge Sought," *Los Angeles Times*, July 18, 2006.

16. U.S. v. Mendez et al., No. 90-cr-00613-R, Declaration of Mark Heaney, October 5, 1990 (C.D. Cal. 1990).

17. *Vazquez*.

18. US Sentencing Commission, *Guidelines Manual* (incorporating guideline amendments effective November 1, 1991).

19. *Vazquez*.

Chapter 4

1. Sylvain Metz, "Residents Fond of Bush's Message, Tone," *Jackson Clarion-Ledger*, August 8, 2002.

2. Nash and Taggart, *Mississippi Politics*.

3. Gertner, "Pope & John Lecture," 428.

4. Daniels, "Question of Jury Competence," 284-86.

5. Department of Justice, "Report of the Tort Policy Working Group on the Causes, Extent and Policy Implications of the Current Crisis in Insurance Availability and Affordability" February 1986.

6. J. David Cummins and Patricia M. Danzon, "Price, Financial Quality, and Capital Flows in Insurance Markets," *Journal of Financial Intermediation* 6, no. 1 (1997): 3-38.

7. Daniels, "Question of Jury Competence," 308.

8. Manzer, "1986 Tort Reform Legislation."

9. "Civil Jury Trials Halted in Most U.S. Courts," *New York Times*, June 19, 1986.

10. 28 U.S.C. Sections 471-82 (1994); James S. Kakalik et al., "Just, Speedy, and Inexpensive? An Evaluation of Judicial Case Management under the CJRA," Rand Research Brief, 1996.

11. Longan, "Congress, the Courts, and the Long Range Plan," 630-36.

12. 28 U.S.C. Sections 1441-1453; Federal Rules of Civil Procedure 81(c); Erie Railroad v. Tompkins, 304 U.S. 64 (1938).

13. Forell, "McTorts"; Andrea Gerlin, "A Matter of Degree: How a Jury Decided That a Coffee Spill Is Worth $2.9 Million," *Wall Street Journal*, September 1,

1994; Hilary Stout, "Retro Report: Scalded by Coffee, Then News Media," *New York Times*, October 21, 2013.

14. Alessandra Stanley, "The 1992 Campaign: Issues—Tort Reform; Selling Voters on Bush, As Nemesis of Lawyers," *New York Times*, August 31, 1992.

15. "The Republican 'Contract with America,'" Oxford University Press, 1994, https://global.oup.com/us/companion.websites/9780195385168/resources /chapter6/contract/america.pdf.

16. 15 U.S.C. Section 78u-4.

17. Federal Bureau of Investigation, "Oklahoma City Bombing," accessed March 17, 2024, www.fbi.gov/history/famous-cases/oklahoma-city-bombing.

18. Pub. L. No. 104-132, 110 Stat. 1214. President Clinton signed the Antiterrorism and Effective Death Penalty Act (AEDPA) on April 24, 1996.

19. Allen, "A Survey and Some Commentary," 921-22.

20. Jane Fritsch, "Sometimes, Lobbyists Strive To Keep Public in the Dark," *New York Times*, March 19, 1996.

21. Fritsch, "Sometimes, Lobbyists Strive"; Nash and Taggart, *Mississippi Politics*, 294-97.

22. Fritsch, "Sometimes Lobbyists Strive."

23. Nash and Taggart, *Mississippi Politics*, 296.

24. Reuters, "3 Guilty in Asbestos Trial," *New York Times*, August 7, 1992.

25. Nash and Taggart, *Mississippi Politics*, 262.

26. Nash and Taggart, *Mississippi Politics*, 266.

27. Wilkie, *Fall of the House of Zeus*.

28. BFI, Inc. v. Kelco Disposal, Inc., 492 U.S. 257 (1989); Pacific Mutual Life Insurance Co. v. Haslip, 499 U.S. 1 (1991); BMW of North America, Inc. v. Gore, 517 U.S. 559 (1996); State Farm Mutual v. Campbell, 538 U.S. 408 (2003).

29. 9 U.S.C. Section 2.

30. Szalai, "Exploring the Federal Arbitration Act."

31. Reynolds Holding, "Private Justice / Millions Are Losing Their Legal Rights / Supreme Court Forces Disputes from Court to Arbitration—A System with No Laws," *San Francisco Chronicle*, October 7, 2001.

32. Moses H. Cone Memorial Hospital v. Mercury Construction Corporation, 460 U.S. 1 (1983).

33. Southland Corp. v. Keating, 465 U.S. 1, 25, 36 (1984) (O'Connor, J., dissenting).

34. Gilmer v. Interstate/Johnson Lane Corp., 500 U.S. 20 (1991).

35. "Record Jury Awards in '98 Include One from Miss.," *Jackson Clarion-Ledger*, January 8, 1999.

36. David S. Morrow, "American Home to Settle Some 1,400 Fen-Phen Suits," *New York Times*, December 23, 1999.

37. Robert Pear, "Mississippi Gaining as Lawsuit Mecca," *New York Times*, August 20, 2021.

38. Nelson D. Schwartz, "Court Intrigue for the King of Torts," *New York Times*, December 9, 2007; Hanlon and Smetak, "Asbestos Changes," 525.

39. "Mississippi Black Population Percentage by County," *IndexMundi*, accessed March 18, 2024, www.indexmundi.com/facts/united-states/quick-facts/mississippi/black-population-percentage#chart.counties.

40. Gifford and Jones, "Keeping Cases from Black Juries," 588–96.

41. Pear, "Mississippi Gaining."

42. Nash and Taggart, *Mississippi Politics*, 299.

43. Vidmar and Brown, "Tort Reform."

44. Amy Redwine, "Lawyers Take to the Air in Tort Reform," *Delta Democrat Times*, August 14, 2002.

45. Report, American Tort Reform Association, "Bringing Justice to Judicial Hellholes," 10 (2002), www.judicialhellholes.org/wp-content/uploads/2010/12/JH2002.pdf.

46. Nash and Taggart, *Mississippi Politics*, 289.

47. Mark A. Behrens, "Medical Liability Reform," *Obstetrics & Gynecology* 118, no. 2 (2011): 335–39.

48. Nash and Taggart, *Mississippi Politics*, 301.

49. Travers Mackel, "Legislature Adjourns; Tort Reform Bill Headed to the Governor," station WLBT, November 26, 2002.

50. Nash and Taggart, *Mississippi Politics*, 301.

51. The facts of the case are set forth in Bouldin v. City of Mendenhall, Mississippi, et al., No. 06-cv-399 HTW-LRA, PACER (S.D. Miss. 2006).

52. *Bouldin*, Bouldin deposition, 55.

53. *Bouldin*, Noland deposition, 71–72.

54. *Bouldin*, Summary Judgment Order, April 28, 2011, 2.

55. Jimmie E. Gates, "Ex-Mendenhall Chief Gets More Prison Time," *Hattiesburg American*, April 17, 2009.

56. *Bouldin*, Plaintiff's Memorandum of Authorities.

57. Jimmie E. Gates, "Ex-Chief Gets 30 Months in Prison," *Jackson Clarion Ledger*, April 18, 2009.

Chapter 5

1. Administrative Office of the US Courts, "Baby Judges School Jump Starts Learning Process," *The Third Branch* 37, no. 8 (2005). Associated Press, "Baby Judges School Is Underway for New Federal Judicial Appointees," CBSnews.com, February 7, 2018, www.cbsnews.com/news/baby-judges-school-is-underway-for-new-federal-judicial-appointees.

2. "Judges of the Southern District of New York," accessed September 6, 2024, www.nysd.uscourts.gov/judges.

3. United States Court of Appeals for the Second Circuit, "About the Court," accessed January 16, 2025, www.ca2.uscourts.gov/about_the_court.html.

4. Administrative Office of the US Courts, United States Courts, "Authorized Judgeships," accessed September 6, 2024, www.uscourts.gov/sites/default/files/allauth.pdf.

5. Administrative Office of the US Courts, United States Courts, "United States District Courts—National Judicial Caseload Profile," accessed January 16, 2025, www.uscourts.gov/sites/default/files/data_tables/fcms_na_distprofile0630.2024.pdf; "US Court of Appeals—Judicial Caseload Profile," accessed January 16, 2025. www.uscourts.gov/sites/default/files/data_tables/fcms_na_appprofile0630.2024.pdf.

6. "Supreme Court cases, October term 2023-2024," *Ballotpedia*, accessed September 6, 2024, https://ballotpedia.org/Supreme_Court_cases,_October_term_2023-2024.

7. Resnik, "Managerial Judges."

8. "Long Range Plan for the Federal Courts," Judicial Conference of the United States, 134, December 1995.

9. United States v. Quinones, No. 00-cr-761 PACER (S.D.N.Y. 2002); see also Burt, "The Importance of Storytelling at All Stages of a Capital Case"; Julia Preston, "Witness Gives Details of Life As Drug Dealer," *New York Times*, July 12, 2004; Julia Preston, "2 Are Convicted in US Trial; Death Penalty To Be Weighed," *New York Times*, July 28, 2004.

10. Dan Eggen, "Ashcroft Aggressively Pursues Death Penalty," *Washington Post*, June 30, 2002.

11. US v. Quinones, 313 F.3d 49, 53-54 (2d Cir. 2002).

12. Gregg v. Georgia, 428 U.S. 153 (1976).

13. "The Innocence Project: A Short History Since 1983," Blackpast.org, accessed March 18, 2024, www.blackpast.org/african-american-history

/perspectives-african-american-history/innocence-project-short-history-1983/.

14. Rob Warden, "First DNA Exoneration," Bluhm Legal Clinic, Center on Wrongful Convictions, Northwest University Pritzker School of Law, accessed January 16, 2025, www.law.northwestern.edu/legalclinic/wrongfulconvictions/exonerations/il/gary-dotson.html.

15. Innocence Project, "About," Innocenceproject.org, accessed March 18, 2024, https://innocenceproject.org/about/.

16. Cohen, *Blindfolds Off*, chapter 10.

17. Devins and Klein, "The Vanishing Common Law Judge?," 595–631.

18. Pub. L. No. 104-132, 110 Stat. 1214.

19. Herrera v. Collins, 506 U.S. 390 (1993).

20. *Herrera*, 417.

21. *Herrera*, 446.

22. *Herrera*, 419.

23. Benjamin Weiser, "A Legal Quest against the Death Penalty," *New York Times*, January 2, 2005.

24. Weiser, "Legal Quest."

25. US v. Quinones, 205 F. Supp. 2d 256 (S.D.N.Y. 2002).

26. "To Spare Lives of the Innocent, End Death Penalty," editorial, *Newsday*, July 2, 2002.

27. "The Death of Innocents," editorial, *New York Times*, July 2, 2002.

28. "Run for Office, Judge," editorial, *Wall Street Journal*, July 3, 2002.

29. Tribe as quoted in Benjamin Weiser, "Manhattan Judge Finds Federal Death Law Unconstitutional," *New York Times*, July 2, 2002.

30. Cabranes in US v. Quinones, 313 F.3d 49, 53–54 (2d Cir. 2002).

Chapter 6

1. US v. Russell, No. 04-cr-01828-MV, PACER, Affidavit in Support of Arrest Warrant, August 18, 2004 (S.D.N.M. 2004).

2. Major Crimes Act, Chapter 341, Section 9, 23 Stat. 385 as amended, 18 U.S.C. Section 1153 (2006).

3. Gomez, *Manifest Destinies*.

4. Michael L. Stout, "True Believers and the Road to Hell, Hon. Martha Vazquez," interview with Vázquez, June 8, 2021, YouTube, https://mlstoutlaw.com/home/true-believers-and-the-road-to-hell/hon-martha-vazquez/.

5. *First Session on Confirmations of Appointees to the Federal Judiciary*, Sen. Comm. on the Judiciary, 103d Cong., 19 (1993) (Feinstein in testimony of Martha Vázquez to be US district judge).

6. Quoted in Stout, "True Believers."

7. Scott Sandlin, "Deal Fetches Trio Long Prison Terms," *Albuquerque Journal*, June 2, 1999.

8. Administrative Office of the US Courts, Federal Judicial Caseload Statistics, Table D, US District Courts—Criminal Cases Commenced, Terminated, and Pending during the 12-Month Periods Ending March 31, 2000, and 2001.

9. 18 U.S.C. Section 1153 (2006).

10. US Constitution, Art. I, Section 8, cl. 3; the Cherokee Nation v. the State of Georgia, 30 U.S. 1, 30 (1831).

11. Ex parte KAN-GI-SHUN-CA, 109 U.S. 556 (1883).

12. Creel, "Tribal Court Convictions."

13. Cutcheon as cited in Eid and Doyle, "Separate but Unequal," fn69, fn74.

14. Roosevelt as cited in Eid and Doyle, "Separate but Unequal," fn40; "Native American Ownership and Governance of Natural Resources," Natural Resources Revenue Data, US Department of the Interior, accessed January 16, 2025, https://revenuedata.doi.gov/how-revenue-works/native-american-ownership-governance/.

15. "Native American Ownership and Governance of Natural Resources."

16. Lewis Meriam, *The Problem of Indian Administration*, Report of a Survey Made at the Request of Honorable Hubert Work, Secretary of the Interior, The Brookings Institution, February 21, 1928.

17. United States v. Kagama, 118 U.S. 375, 384-85 (1886).

18. Eid and Doyle, "Separate but Unequal," 1095-96.

19. "Native Voter Impact: A Potent but Untapped Political Force," Native American Rights Fund, June 2020, https://vote.narf.org/wp-content/uploads/2020/06/obstacles_voter_impact_summary.pdf.

20. Eid and Doyle, "Separate but Unequal," fn164-68, fn170; Creel, "Tribal Court Convictions."

21. United States v. Geneva Gallegos, 129 F.3d 1140 (10th Cir. 1997).

22. The US Court of Appeals for the Tenth Circuit, "About the Court," accessed January 16, 2025, www.ca10.uscourts.gov/clerk/general-information.

23. Quoted in Stout, "True Believers."

24. United States v. Booker, 543 U.S. 220 (2005), the facts of the case are set forth at United States v. Booker, 2003 U.S. Dist. LEXIS 24609 (W.D. Wis. Sept. 5, 2003).

25. Recounted in Stout, "True Believers."

26. US District Court, District of New Mexico, "Juror Frequently Asked Questions," accessed March 18, 2024, www.nmd.uscourts.gov/juror-information/faq.

27. James Thomas Tucker, Jacqueline De Leon, and Dan McCool, "Obstacles at Every Turn: Barriers to Political Participation Faced by Native American Voters," Native American Rights Fund (2020).

28. David C. Iglesias and Stephen P. McCue, "Report of Jury Plan Task Force," draft as of July 6, 2004.

29. Deborah Sontag, "In Courts, Threats Have Become a Fact of Life," *New York Times*, March 20, 2005.

30. *Booker*, 543 U.S. 220.

31. US Department of Justice, "Fact Sheet: The Impact of United States v. Booker on Federal Sentencing," news release, March 15, 2006.

32. Valarie Lee, "Judicial History Made," *Navajo Times*, December 15, 2005.

33. *Russell*, Sentencing Memo.

34. "Federal Judge To Hold Court on Hopland Indian Reservation," Lake County News, June 23, 2010,

Chapter 7

1. "Judge in Rights Case: William Harold Cox," *New York Times*, February 26, 1965.

2. Bass, *Unlikely Heroes*, 164.

3. Quoted in Hustwit, *Integration Now*, chapter 4.

4. "W. Harold Cox, Federal Judge in Mississippi, Dies," *Washington Post*, February 27, 1988.

5. Quoted in "Judge in Rights Case."

6. Tyler Cleveland, "Preserving and Updating the Eastland Courthouse," *Jackson Free Press*, September 25, 2013 .

7. Quoted in Bass, *Unlikely Heroes*, 166.

8. Quoted in Jimmie E. Gates, "Reeves Takes Oath As U.S. District Judge," *Jackson Clarion-Ledger*, December 20, 2010.

9. Southwick, *The Nominee*.

10. Driver, "Supremacies."

11. Brown v. Board of Education, 349 U.S. 294 (1955).

12. Briggs v. Elliott, 132 F. Supp. 776 (E.D.S.C. 1955); Tushnet, "Significance of Brown."

13. Driver, "Supremacies," fn246.

14. James E. Clayton, "Sam and Bob Show Enters Fourth Week," *Washington Post*, August 9, 1963.

15. Ervin, *Preserving the Constitution*, 145-46.

16. Parents Involved in Community Schools v. Seattle School Dist. No. 1, 551 U.S. 701 (2007).

17. Douglas Martin, "Lawrence Guyot, Civil Rights Activist Who Bore the Fight's Scars, Dies at 73," *New York Times*, November 26, 2012.

18. The facts of the case are set forth in United States v. Jonatan Lopez, No. 11-cr-00005-CWR-FKB PACER, and 817 F. Supp. 2d 918 (S.D. Miss. 2011).

19. Reeves's opinion in *Lopez*, 817 F. Supp. 2d, 925.

20. United States v. Dylan Wade Butler et al., No. 12-cr-00034-CWR-FKB, PACER, Criminal Information, March 21, 2012 (S.D. Miss. 2012).

21. Albert Samaha, "'This Is What They Did For Fun': The Story of a Modern-Day Lynching," *Buzz Feed News*, November 18, 2015, www.buzzfeednews.com/article/albertsamaha/this-is-what-they-did-for-fun-a-modern-day-lynching-in-missi.

22. Holbrook Mohr, "Internet War of Words Breaks out in Miss. Killing," *NBCnews.com*, August 13, 2011, www.nbcnews.com/id/wbna44131756#.

23. Quoted in Associated Press, "Mississippi Killing Sparks Internet War of Words; Did Case Involve Race?," *AL.com*, August 13, 2011, www.al.com/wire/2011/08/mississippi_killing_sparks_int.html.

24. Samaha, "This Is What They Did for Fun."

25. *US v. Butler*, Sentencing Hearing transcript, September 24, 2015.

26. Scott Bronstein and Drew Griffin, "Mississippi Teen Pleads Not Guilty in Hate Crime Case," *CNN.com*, September 30, 2011, www.cnn.com/2011/09/30/justice/mississippi-hate-crime/index.html.

27. Scott Bronstein and Drew Griffin, "Life Sentence in Mississippi Hate-Crime Case," *CNN.com*, March 22, 2012, www.cnn.com/2012/03/21/justice/mississippi-hate-crime/.

28. Matthew Shepard and James Byrd Jr. Hate Crimes Prevention Act of 2009, 18 U.S.C. Section 249.

29. Eliott C. McLaughlin, "There Are Two Names on the Federal Hate Crimes Law. One Is Matthew Shepard. The Other Is James Byrd Jr.," *CNN.com*, April 25, 2019, www.cnn.com/2019/04/24/us/james-byrd-hate-crime-legislation-john-king-execution/index.html.

30. Kim Severson, "Weighing Race and Hate in a Mississippi Killing," *New York Times*, August 22, 2011; Samaha, "This Is What They Did for Fun."

31. Lacey McLaughlin, "Divided We Fall: The Killing of James Craig Anderson," *Jackson Free Press*, October 5, 2011.

32. Howard, *Men Like That*, 142.

33. Quoted in Younge, *No Place Like Home*, 271.

34. Branch, *Parting the Waters*, 862.

35. "Gay Couples File for Marriage Licenses," WAPT (Jackson, Mississippi), March 25, 2014, www.wapt.com/article/gay-couples-file-for-marriage-licenses/1863117.

36. Campaign for Southern Equality, et al. v. Bryant et al., No. 14-cv-00818-CWR-LRA, PACER, Plaintiffs' Original Complaint, October 20, 2014 (S.D. Miss. 2014).

37. "Same-Sex Marriage, State by State," Pew Research Center, June 26, 2015, www.pewresearch.org/religion/2015/06/26/same-sex-marriage-state-by-state-1/.

38. *Campaign for Southern Equality v. Bryant*, Argument for Preliminary Injunction, transcript filed November 17, 2014.

39. David Lat, "'She Eats Bullies For Lunch': An Interview with Robbie Kaplan," *Original Jurisdiction*, November 2, 2022, https://davidlat.substack.com/p/she-eats-bullies-for-lunch-an-interview.

40. United States v. Windsor, 570 U.S. 744 (2013).

41. *Campaign for Southern Equality v. Bryant*, 64 F. Supp. 3d 906 (S.D. Miss. 2014).

42. Reeves's opinion in *Campaign for Southern Equality v. Bryant*, 933.

43. Reeves's opinion in *Campaign for Southern Equality v. Bryant*, 947-48.

44. Obergefell v. Hodges, 576 U.S 644 (2015).

45. Therese Apel, "Last of 10 Defendants in Hate Crime Case Plead Guilty," *Jackson Clarion-Ledger*, January 7, 2015.

46. *US v. Butler*, Sentencing Hearing transcript.

47. Emily Badger, "A Stunning Reckoning with Mississippi's Past, from a Black Judge Sentencing 3 White Men for a Lynching," *Washington Post*, February 18, 2015.

Chapter 8

1. James Doran, "Thain's Home Is His Castle," *New York Post*, November 18, 2007.

2. John Thain, interview by Michael Kirk, "Breaking the Bank," *Frontline*, PBS, April 17, 2009, www.pbs.org/wgbh/pages/frontline/breakingthebank/interviews/thain.html.

3. Ken Lewis, interview by Michael Kirk, "Breaking the Bank," *Frontline*, PBS, April 6, 2009, www.pbs.org/wgbh/pages/frontline/breakingthebank/interviews/lewis.html

4. Thain interview, "Breaking the Bank."

5. Thain interview, "Breaking the Bank"; Shawn Tully, "Divorce—Bank of America style," *CNN.com*, January 30, 2009, https://money.cnn.com/2009/01/30/news/companies/tully_bofa.fortune/index.htm?postversion=2009013007.

6. SEC v. Bank of America No. 09-cv-6829-JSR. PACER, Complaint (S.D.N.Y. 2002).

7. "The Recession of 2007-2009," US Bureau of Labor Statistics, February 2012, www.bls.gov/spotlight/2012/recession/pdf/recession_bls_spotlight.pdf.

8. "Dow Jones Industrial Average," *Yahoo!finance*, Historical Data, https://finance.yahoo.com/quote/%5EDJI/history?period1=1098763200&period2=1223265600&interval=1d&filter=history&frequency=1d.

9. *SEC v. Bank of America*, Complaint.

10. "Market Capitalization of Bank of America," *CompaniesMarketCap.com*, accessed August 23, 2024, https://companiesmarketcap.com/bank-of-america/marketcap/.

11. *SEC v. Bank of America*, hearing transcript, August 10, 2009.

12. *SEC v. Bank of America*, hearing transcript, 18-19.

13. *SEC v. Bank of America*, hearing transcript, 21-22.

14. *SEC v. Bank of America*, hearing transcript, 26-27.

15. *SEC v. Bank of America*, 653 F. Supp. 2d 507 (S.D.N.Y 2009).

16. "The New York State Attorney General Andrew M. Cuomo Files Fraud Charges Against Bank of America, Former CEO Kenneth Lewis, and Former CFO Joseph Price," press release, February 4, 2010.

17. Louise Story, "Cuomo Sues Bank of America, Even as It Settles with S.E.C.," *New York Times*, February 4, 2010; Louise Story, "Bank Firing of Counsel Is Examined," *New York Times*, September 8, 2009.

18. *SEC v. Bank of America*, Final Consent Judgment, February 4, 2010.

19. *SEC v. Bank of America*, hearing transcript, February 8, 2010, p. 7.

20. *SEC v. Bank of America*, Opinion and Order, February 22, 2010 (S.D.N.Y. 2010).

21. Julie Creswell and Eric Dash, "Citigroup: Above the Fray?," *New York Times*, September 20, 2008; Jonathan Randles, "Citigroup Battles Lehman in 'Tale of Two Citis' Trial," *Wall Street Journal*, May 2, 2017.

22. SEC v. Brian H. Stoker, No. 11-cv-07388-JSR, PACER, Complaint, October 19, 2011, Opinion, June 6, 2012 (S.D.N.Y. 2011).

23. SEC v. Citigroup, No. 11-cv-07387-JSR, PACER, Memorandum in Support of Proposed Settlement, October 19, 2011 (S.D.N.Y. 2011).

24. "Occupy Wall Street / Foley Square / NYC," October 5, 2011, YouTube video, www.youtube.com/watch?v=lOW36Zxk1Yg.

25. Garcia v. Bloomberg, No. 11-cv-6957-JSR, PACER, Opinion and Order, June 7, 2012 (S.D.N.Y. 2012).

26. *SEC v. Citigroup*, Complaint.

27. *SEC v. Citigroup*, Complaint.

28. Jed Rakoff, "Don't Count on the Courts," *New York Review of Books*, April 5, 2018.

29. Chevron v. Natural Resources Defense Council, 467 U.S. 837 (1984).

30. *SEC v. Citigroup*.

31. "The S.E.C.'s Enabling," editorial, *New York Times*, November 28, 2011.

32. Chuck Grassley, "SEC-Citigroup Settlement Rejected," press release, November 28, 2011.

33. Matt Taibbi, "Finally, a Judge Stands Up to Wall Street," *Rolling Stone*, November 10, 2011.

34. US Securities and Exchange Commission, "SEC Enforcement Director's Statement on Citigroup Case," press release, December 15, 2011.

35. "Occupy Wall Street Brooklyn Bridge Protest," October 1, 2011, YouTube video, www.youtube.com/watch?v=j8ZqfoOohgs.

36. *SEC v. Citigroup*, No. 11-5227, PACER, Opinion, March 15, 2012 (2d Cir. 2012).

37. Garcia v. Bloomberg, 865 F. Supp. 2d 478 (S.D.N.Y. 2012).

38. SEC v. Brian H. Stoker, No. 11-cv-07388-JSR, PACER, trial transcript, 7, July 16, 2012 (S.D.N.Y. 2011).

39. *SEC v. Brian H. Stoker*, trial transcript, 180.

40. Peter Lattman, "S.E.C. Gets Encouragement from Jury That Ruled against It," *New York Times*, August 3, 2012.

41. *SEC v. Citigroup*, No. 11-5227, argument transcript, 3, February 8, 2013.

42. *SEC v. Citigroup*, argument transcript, 9.

43. *SEC v. Citigroup*, 752 F.3d 285 (2d Cir. 2014).

44. *SEC v. Citigroup*, Concurring Opinion.

45. *SEC v. Citigroup*, 34 F. Supp. 3d 379 (S.D.N.Y. 2014).

Chapter 9

1. US v. Rivera, No. 10-cr-3348-MV, PACER, Memorandum Opinion and Order, October 11, 2012 (D.N.M. 2012).

2. *Rivera*, Indictment, December 15, 2010.

3. *Rivera*, Plea Agreement, August 12, 2011.

4. *Rivera*, Minute Order, February 14, 2011.

5. Federal Bureau of Investigation, "What We Investigate, Asset Forfeiture," accessed March 19, 2024, www.fbi.gov/investigate/white-collar-crime/asset-forfeiture.

6. Sarah Stillman, "Taken," *New Yorker*, August 5, 2013.

7. United States v. Bajakajian, 524 US 321 (1998).

8. *Rivera*, Memorandum Opinion and Order, October 11, 2012.

9. *Rivera*, Motion to Dismiss Indictment with Prejudice, June 23, 2026.

10. US v. Easley, 16-cr-01089-MV, Memorandum Opinion and Order, January 10, 2018 (D.N.M. 2018).

11. *Easley*, Memorandum Opinion and Order.

12. See United States v. Bostick, 501 U.S. 429 (1991); United States v. Easley, 293 F. Supp. 3d 1288, 1301–1303 (D.N.M. 2018).

13. *Easley*, Defendant's Motion to Suppress, May 23, 2016.

14. *Easley*, Memorandum Opinion and Order.

15. J.D.B. v. North Carolina, 564 U.S. 261 (2011).

16. United States v. Easley, 911 F.3d 1074 (10th Cir. 2018).

17. US v. Dutch, No. 16-cr-01424-MV, PACER, Defendant's Sentencing Memorandum, April 3, 2017, 14 (D.N.M. 2016).

18. *Dutch*, Defendant's Sentencing Memorandum.

19. Armed Career Criminal Act, 18 U.S.C. Section 924(e).

20. "Federal Armed Career Criminals: Prevalence, Patterns, and Pathways," US Sentencing Commission, March 2021.

21. *Dutch*, sentencing hearing transcript, 25, October 12, 2017.

22. United States v. Dutch, No. 17-2219, PACER (10th Cir. November 1, 2018).

23. Vázquez in *Dutch*, sentencing hearing transcript, 10, October 8, 2019.

24. United States v. Dutch, 978 F. 3d 1341 (10th Cir. 2020).

25. United States v. Wooden, 945 F. 3d 498 (6th Cir. 2019).

26. Wooden v. United States, 595 U.S. 360 (2022).

27. Michael L. Stout, "True Believers and the Road to Hell, Hon. Martha Vazquez," interview with Vázquez, June 8, 2021, YouTube, https://mlstoutlaw.com/home/true-believers-and-the-road-to-hell/hon-martha-vazquez/.

Chapter 10

1. Gestational Age Act, Mississippi Code Annotated, Section 41-41-191 (West, 2018).

2. Bracey Harris, "The Mississippi Abortion Clinic at the Center of the Supreme Court Fight Shuts Its Doors for Good," *NBC News*, July 6, 2022, www.nbcnews.com/news/us-news/mississippi-abortion-clinic-supreme-court-closes-rcna36906; Jackson Women's Health Organization v. Currier, No. 18-cv-00171-CWR-FKB, PACER, Complaint, March 19, 2018 (S.D. Miss., 2018).

3. Reeves in *Jackson Women's Health*, Hearing on the Motion for TRO transcript, 9, March 20, 2018.

4. *Jackson Women's Health*, Temporary Restraining Order, March 20, 2018.

5. Jackson Women's Health Organization v. Currier, 349 F. Supp. 3d 536 (S.D. Miss. 2018).

6. *Jackson Women's Health*, 349 F. Supp. 3d at 542.

7. *Jackson Women's Health*, 349 F. Supp. 3d at fn22.

8. Dobbs v. Jackson Women's Health Organization, No. 19-1392, Brief of Equal Protection Constitutional Law Scholars as amicus curiae, 32, September 20, 2021 (U.S. Supreme Court, 2022).

9. *Jackson Women's Health*, 349 F. Supp. 3d at 545.

10. "The Judicial Doctrine of Qualified Immunity and the Future of Police Reform," *The Appellate Project*, February 9, 2021, YouTube, comment at 44:22, www.youtube.com/watch?v=V491FZUblfA&t=3s.

11. Ho's concurring opinion in *Jackson Women's Health v. Dobbs*, 945 F. 3d 265 (5th Cir. 2019).

12. *Jackson Women's Health*, No. 18-cv-00171-CWR-FKB, Status Conference, June 4, 2021.

13. Josh Gerstein and Alexander Ward, "Supreme Court Has Voted To Overturn Abortion Rights, Draft Opinion Shows," *Politico*, May 2, 2022, www.politico.com/news/2022/05/02/supreme-court-abortion-draft-opinion-00029473.

14. Alito's opinion in *Dobbs v. Jackson Women's Health Organization*, 597 U.S. 215 (2022).

15. The White House, "President Biden Nominates Bipartisan Slate for the United States Sentencing Commission," press release, May 11, 2022.

16. US Sentencing Commission, "About," accessed January 16, 2025, www.ussc.gov/about-page.

17. Sadie Gurman, "Justice Department Set To Free 3,000 Prisoners as Criminal-Justice Overhaul Takes Hold," *Wall Street Journal*, July 19, 2019.

18. US Sentencing Commission, "2023 Amendments in Brief, Criminal History," accessed January 16, 2025, www.ussc.gov/sites/default/files/pdf/amendment-process/amendments-in-brief/AIB_821R.pdf.

19. US Sentencing Commission, "2024 Amendments in Brief, Acquitted Conduct," accessed January 16, 2025, www.ussc.gov/sites/default/files/pdf/amendment-process/amendments-in-brief/AIB_2024-acquitted-conduct.pdf.

20. US Sentencing Commission, "2023 Amendments in Brief, Reduction in Sentence," accessed January 16, 2025, www.ussc.gov/sites/default/files/pdf/amendment-process/amendments-in-brief/AIB_814.pdf.

Chapter 11

1. United States v. Newman, No. 13-1837, PACER, Oral Arguments transcript, 49, April 22, 2014 (2d Cir. 2013).

2. United States v. Newman, 773 F.3d 438 (2d Cir. 2014).

3. United States v. Salman, 792 F.3d 1087 (9th Cir. 2015).

4. Maher Kara quoted in Salman v. United States, No. 15-678, Brief for Petitioner, 11, May 6, 2016 (US Supreme Court, 2016).

5. *Salman*, Brief for Petitioner, 7-15.

6. United States v. Salman, No. 14-10204, Oral Argument, June 9, 2015 (9th Cir. 2015), www.ca9.uscourts.gov/media/video/?20150609/14-10204/.

7. United States v. Salman, 792 F.3d 1087, 1093 (9th Cir. 2015).

8. Salman v. United States, No. 15-628, Oral Argument transcript, October 5, 2016 (US Supreme Court, 2016).

9. "Dreeben Presents 100th Oral Argument before SCOTUS," *Member News*, American Law Institute, May 2, 2016.

10. *Salman*, No. 15-628, Oral Argument transcript.

11. Salman v. United States, 580 U.S. 420 (2016).

Epilogue

1. Jessica Silver-Greenberg and Susanne Craig, "Bank of America Settles Suit over Merrill for $2.43 Billion," *New York Times*, September 28, 2012.

2. Memorandum from Deputy US Attorney General Lisa Monaco, "Corporate Crime Advisory Group and Initial Revisions to Corporate Criminal Enforcement Policies," October 28, 2021, www.justice.gov/dag/file/1173651-0/dl?inline=.

3. Jean Eaglesham and Andrew Ackerman, "SEC Seeks Admissions of Fault," *Wall Street Journal*, June 18, 2013.

4. Gurbir S. Grewal, US Securities and Exchange Commissioner, "Remarks at SEC Speaks," October 13, 2021, www.sec.gov/newsroom/speeches-statements/grewal-sec-speaks-101321.

5. Luis Ferré-Sadurní and Benjamin Weiser, "Judge Rejects Deal To Overhaul City's Public Housing," *New York Times*, November 14, 2018.

6. Quoted in Bob Van Voris and Christian Berthelsen, "U.S. Bancorp Judge Slams Deals To Sidestep Criminal Prosecution," *Bloomberg.com*, February 22, 2018, www.bloomberg.com/news/articles/2018-02-22/u-s-bancorp-judge-slams-deals-to-sidestep-criminal-prosecution.

7. Quoted in Michael L. Stout, "True Believers and the Road to Hell, Hon. Martha Vazquez," interview with Vázquez, June 8, 2021, YouTube, https://mlstoutlaw.com/home/true-believers-and-the-road-to-hell/hon-martha-vazquez/.

8. "ABA Profile of the Legal Profession 2024," American Bar Association, accessed January 16, 2025, www.americanbar.org/news/profile-legal-profession/judges/.

9. Marc J. Perry and Paul J. Mackun, "Census 2000 Brief: Population Change and Distribution: 1990 to 2000," US Census Bureau, April 2001, www.census.gov/library/publications/2001/dec/c2kbr01-02.html; US Census Bureau, "Quick Facts," accessed January 16, 2025, www.census.gov/quickfacts/fact/table/US/PST045218; US Courts, "Authorized Judgeships," accessed January 16, 2025, www.uscourts.gov/sites/default/files/allauth.pdf.

10. *The Federalist Papers No. 78* (James Madison), ed. Lawrence Goldman (Oxford University Press, 2008).

11. Joseph Tanfani, Peter Eisler, and Ned Parker, "Exclusive: Threats to US Federal judges Double since 2021, Driven by Politics," Reuters, February 13, 2024, www.reuters.com/world/us/threats-us-federal-judges-double-since-2021-driven-by-politics-2024-02-13/.

12. US Courts, "Code of Conduct for United States Judges," Canon 4, accessed January 16, 2025, www.uscourts.gov/administration-policies/judiciary-policies/ethics-policies/code-conduct-united-states-judges.

13. Mark Sherman, "Roberts, Trump Spar in Extraordinary Scrap over Judges," Associated Press, November 21, 2018.

14. Carlton Reeves, "Defending the Judiciary: A Call for Justice, Truth and Diversity on the Bench," YouTube, April 11, 2019, University of Virginia School of Law, www.youtube.com/watch?v=BlvzpFVDBZw.

Bibliography

Unless otherwise specified, quotations throughout this book are from documents or the hundreds of people I interviewed, and dialogue comes from documents or the best recollections of the participants. In some cases sources agreed to speak with me on the condition that they not be named. They include lawyers who did not want to jeopardize their careers by speaking publicly about judges they appear before. They also include about a dozen US court of appeals judges who had served as US district court judges and who offered valuable perspectives on the role of a district court judge and efforts over recent decades to narrow that role. Dozens of current and former clerks for Judges Rakoff, Reeves, and Vázquez graciously agreed to speak with me on the record, although some information they shared about certain cases and discussions in chambers was not attributed to them because it was considered confidential.

Books

Bass, Jack. *Unlikely Heroes*. Simon & Schuster, 1981.
Bickel, Alexander M. *The Least Dangerous Branch: The Supreme Court at the Bar of Politics*. Yale University Press, 1986.
Bolton, Charles C. *The Hardest Deal of All: The Battle over School Integration in Mississippi, 1870–1980*. University Press of Mississippi, 2005.
Branch, Taylor. *Parting the Waters: America in the King Years, 1954–63*. Simon & Schuster, 1988.
Chemerinsky, Erwin. *Closing the Courthouse Door: How Your Constitutional Rights Became Unenforceable*. Yale University Press, 2017.
Cohen, Joel. *Blindfolds Off: Judges on How They Decide*. ABA Book Publishing, 2014.

Cohen, Rich. *The Fish That Ate the Whale: The Life and Times of America's Banana King*. Farrar Straus and Giroux, 2012.

Ely, John Hart. *Democracy and Distrust: A Theory of Judicial Review*. Harvard University Press, 1980.

Ervin, Sam J., Jr. *Preserving the Constitution*. The Michie Co., 1984.

Fishkin, Joseph, and William E. Forbath. *The Anti-Oligarchy Constitution: Reconstructing the Economic Foundations of American Democracy*. Harvard University Press, 2022.

Ginsburg, Ruth Bader, Mary Hartnett, and Wendy W. Williams. *My Own Words*. Simon & Schuster, 2016.

Goldman, Sheldon. *Picking Federal Judges: Lower Court Selection from Roosevelt through Reagan*. Yale University Press, 1999.

Gomez, Laura E. *Manifest Destinies: The Making of the Mexican American Race*. NYU Press, 2023.

Graetz, Michael J., and Linda Greenhouse. *The Burger Court and the Rise of the Judicial Right*. Simon & Schuster, 2016.

Hagan, John. *Who Are the Criminals? The Politics of Crime Policy from the Age of Roosevelt to the Age of Reagan*. Princeton University Press, 2012.

Heath, James O. *To Face Down Dixie: South Carolina's War on the Supreme Court in the Age of Civil Rights*. Louisiana State University Press, 2017.

Hoffer, Peter Charles, Williamjames Hull Hoffer, and N.E.H. Hull. *The Federal Courts: An Essential History*. Oxford University Press, 2016.

Howard, John. *Men Like That: A Southern Queer History*. University of Chicago Press, 2001.

Hustwit, William P. *Integration Now: Alexander v. Holmes and the End of Jim Crow Education*. University of North Carolina Press, 2019.

Mayer, Jane. *Dark Money: The Hidden History of the Billionaires behind the Rise of the Radical Right*. Doubleday, 2016.

McCann, Thomas. *On the Inside: A Story of Intrigue and Adventure on Wall Street, in Washington, and in the Jungles of Central America*. Quinlan Press, 1987.

Morris, Willie. *Yazoo: Integration in a Deep-Southern Town*. Harper's Magazine Press, 1971.

Nash, Jere, and Andy Taggart. *Mississippi Politics: The Struggle for Power, 1976–2008*. University Press of Mississippi, 2009.

Powe, Lucas A., Jr. *The Warren Court and American Politics*. Belknap Press, 2002.

Roediger, David R., and Philip S. Foner. *Our Own Time: A History of American Labor and the Working Day*. Verso, 1989.

Snyder, Brad. *Democratic Justice: Felix Frankfurter, the Supreme Court, and the Making of the Liberal Establishment*. W. W. Norton, 2022.

Southwick, Leslie H. *The Nominee: A Political and Spiritual Journey*. University Press of Mississippi, 2013.

Stith, Kate, and Jose Cabranes. *Fear of Judging: Sentencing Guidelines in the Federal Courts*. University of Chicago Press, 1998.

Walton, Anthony. *Mississippi: An American Journey*. Vintage Departures, 1996.

Wilkie, Curtis. *The Fall of the House of Zeus: The Rise and Ruin of America's Most Powerful Trial Lawyer*. Crown, 2010.

Younge, Gary. *No Place Like Home: A Black Briton's Journey through the American South*. University Press of Mississippi, 2002.

Journal Articles

Allen, Michael P. "A Survey and Some Commentary on Federal 'Tort Reform,'" *Akron Law Review* 39, no. 4 (2006): 909–41.

Barker, Lucius J. "Thurgood Marshall, the Law, and the System: Tenets of an Enduring Legacy," *Stanford Law Review* 44 (Summer 1992): 1237–47.

Barrett, John Q. "Attribution Time: Cal Tinney's 1937 Quip, 'A Switch in Time'll Save Nine,'" *Oklahoma Law Review* 73 (Winter 2021): 229–42.

Briloff, Abraham J. "Accounting Practices and the Merger Movement," *Notre Dame Law Review* 45, no. 4 (1970): 604–28.

Burt, Michael N. "The Importance of Storytelling at All Stages of a Capital Case," *University of Missouri-Kansas City Law Review* 77, no. 4 (2009): 877–920.

Creel, Barbara. "Tribal Court Convictions and the Federal Sentencing Guidelines: Respect for Tribal Courts and Tribal People in Federal Sentencing," *University of San Francisco Law Review* 45, no. 1 (2010): 37–92.

Daniels, Stephen. "The Question of Jury Competence and the Politics of Civil Justice Reform: Symbols, Rhetoric and Agenda-Building," *Law and Contemporary Problems* 52, no. 4 (1989): 269–310.

Devins, Neal, and David Klein. "The Vanishing Common Law Judge?" *University of Pennsylvania Law Review* 165, no. 3 (2017): 595–631.

Driver, Justin. "Supremacies and the Southern Manifesto," *Texas Law Review* 92, no. 5 (2014): 1053–135.

Eid, Troy A., and Carrie Covington Doyle. "Separate but Unequal: The Federal Criminal Justice System in Indian Country," *University of Colorado Law Review* 81, no. 4 (2010): 1068–117.

Forell, Caroline. "McTorts: The Social and Legal Impact of McDonald's Role in Tort Suits," *Loyola Consumer Law Review* 24, no. 2 (2011): 105-55.

Gertner, Nancy. "Pope & John Lecture: Opinions I Should Have Written," *Northwestern University Law Review* 110, no. 2 (2015): 423-38.

Gifford, Donald G., and Brian Jones. "Keeping Cases from Black Juries: An Empirical Analysis of How Race, Income Inequality, and Regional History Affect Tort Law," *Washington & Lee Law Review* 73, no. 2 (2016): 557-651.

Gillman, Howard. "How Political Parties Can Use the Courts to Advance Their Agendas: Federal Courts in the United States, 1875-1891," *American Political Science Review* 96, no. 3 (2002): 511-24.

Goldman, Sheldon. "Judicial Confirmation Wars: Ideology and the Battle for the Federal Courts," *University of Richmond Law Review* 39, no. 3 (2005): 871-908.

Hanlon, Patrick M., and Anne Smetak. "Asbestos Changes," *NYU Annual Survey of American Law* 62, no. 3 (2007): 525-606.

Johnson, Wallace H. "Willis Van Devanter—A Re-Examination," *Wyoming Law Review* 1, no. 1 (2001): 403-12.

Karslake, Allison Grace, and Kathleen Kennedy Townsend. "Definite Sentencing in New Mexico: The 1977 Criminal Sentencing Act," *New Mexico Law Review* 9, no. 1 (1979): 131-65.

Law, David S. "A Theory of Judicial Power and Judicial Review," *Georgetown Law Review* 97, no. 3 (2009): 723-802.

Levine, Theodore A., and Edward D. Herlihy. "The Father of Enforcement," *Securities Regulation Law Journal* 43, no. 1 (2015): 7-27.

Longan, Patrick E. "Congress, the Courts, and the Long Range Plan," *American University Law Review* 46, no. 3 (1997): 625-68.

Manzer, Nancy L. "1986 Tort Reform Legislation: A Systematic Evaluation of Caps on Damages and Limitations on Joint and Several Liability," *Cornell Law Review* 73, no. 3 (1988): 628-52.

Pilaar, Jeremy. "The Making of the Supreme Court Bar: How Business Created a Solicitor General for the Private Sector," *Michigan Law Review* (online), December 2018, https://michiganlawreview.org/the-making-of-the-supreme-court-bar/.

Pritchard, A. C. "Justice Lewis F. Powell, Jr., and the Counterrevolution in the Federal Securities Laws," *Duke Law Journal* 52, no. 5 (2003): 841-949.

Rakoff, Jed S. "The Federal Mail Fraud Statute (Part I)," *Duquesne Law Review* 18, no. 4 (1980): 771-822.

Resnik, Judith. "Managerial Judges," *Harvard Law Review* 96, no. 2 (1982): 374-448.

Rosenfeld, David. "Civil Penalties against Public Companies in SEC Enforcement Actions: An Empirical Analysis," *University of Pennsylvania Journal of Business Law* 22, no. 1 (2019): 135-208.

Szalai, Imre Stephen. "Exploring the Federal Arbitration Act through the Lens of History Symposium," *Journal of Dispute Resolution* 2016, no. 1 (2016): 116-39.

Teles, Steven M. "Transformative Bureaucracy: Reagan's Lawyers and the Dynamics of Political Investment," *Studies in American Political Development* 23, no.1 (2009).

Tushnet, Mark. "The Significance of Brown v. Board of Education," *Virginia Law Review* 80, no. 1 (1994): 173-84.

Vidmar, Neil, and Leigh Ann Brown. "Tort Reform and the Medical Liability Insurance Crisis in Mississippi: Diagnosing the Disease and Prescribing a Remedy," *Mississippi College Law Review* 22 no. 1 (2002): 9-46.

Federal Court Cases

US Supreme Court

Alexander v. Holmes County Board of Education, 396 U.S. 19 (1969)
Baker v. Nelson, 409 U.S. 810 (1972)
BFI, Inc. v. Kelco Disposal, Inc., 492 U.S. 257 (1989)
Bivens v. Six Unknown Named Agents of Federal Bureau of Narcotics, 403 U.S. 388 (1971)
Blue Chip Stamps v. Manor Drug Stores, 421 U.S. 723 (1975)
BMW of North America, Inc. v. Gore, 517 U.S. 559 (1996)
Bowers v. Hardwick, 478 U.S. 186 (1986)
Briscoe v. LaHue, 460 U.S. 325 (1983)
Brown v. Board of Education, 347 U.S. 483 (1954)
Brown v. Board of Education (Brown II), 349 U.S. 294 (1955)
Bush v. Lucas, 462 U.S. 367 (1983)
The Cherokee Nation v. the State of Georgia, 30 U.S. 1 (1831)
Chevron v. Natural Resources Defense Council, 467 U.S. 837 (1984)
Citizens United v. Federal Election Commission, 558 U.S. 310 (2010)
Davis v. United States, 411 U.S. 233 (1973)
Dobbs v. Jackson Women's Health Organization, 597 U.S. 215 (2022)
Dred Scott v. Sandford, 60 U.S. 393 (1857)
Eisen v. Carlisle & Jacquelin, 417 U.S. 156 (1974)
Erie Railroad v. Tompkins, 304 U.S. 64 (1938)

Ernst & Ernst v. Hochfelder, 425 U.S. 185 (1976)
Ex parte KAN-GI-SHUN-CA, 109 U.S. 556 (1883)
Flood v. Kuhn, 407 U.S. 258 (1972)
Francis v. Henderson, 425 U.S. 536 (1976)
Gilmer v. Interstate/Johnson Lane Corp., 500 U.S. 20 (1991)
Gregg v. Georgia, 428 U.S. 153 (1976)
Griswold v. Connecticut, 381 U.S. 479 (1965)
Harper v. Virginia Board of Elections, 383 U.S. 663 (1966)
Heart of Atlanta Motel, Inc. v. United States, 379 U.S. 241 (1964)
Herrera v. Collins, 506 U.S. 390 (1993)
Imbler v. Pachtman, 424 U.S. 409 (1976)
International Brotherhood of Teamsters v. Daniel, 439 U.S. 551 (1979)
J. D. B. v. North Carolina, 564 U.S. 261 (2011)
J.I. Case Co. v. Borak, 377 U.S. 426 (1964)
Jones v. Mayer, 392 U.S. 409 (1968)
Lochner v. New York, 198 U.S. 45 (1905)
Mobile v. Bolden, 446 U.S. 55 (1980)
Moses H. Cone Memorial Hospital v. Mercury Construction Corporation, 460 U.S. 1 (1983)
New York Central & Hudson River Railroad Co. v. United States, 212 U.S. 481 (1909)
Obergefell v. Hodges, 576 U.S 644 (2015)
Pacific Mutual Life Insurance Co. v. Haslip, 499 U.S. 1 (1991)
Parents Involved in Community Schools v. Seattle School Dist. No. 1, 551 U.S. 701 (2007)
Pierson v. Ray, 386 U.S. 547 (1967)
Plessy v. Ferguson, 163 U.S. 537 (1896)
Prigg v. Pennsylvania, 41 U.S. 539 (1842)
Roe v. Wade, 410 U.S. 113 (1973)
Salman v. United States, 580 U.S. 420 (2016)
Santa Fe Industries, Inc. v. Green, 430 U.S. 462 (1977)
Scheuer v. Rhodes, 416 U.S. 232 (1974)
Southland Corp. v. Keating, 465 U.S. 1, 25, 36 (1984) (O'Connor, J., dissenting)
State Farm Mutual v. Campbell, 538 U.S. 408 (2003)
TSC Industries, Inc. v. Northway, Inc., 426 U.S. 438 (1976)
United Housing Foundation v. Forman, 421 U.S. 837 (1975)
United States v. Bajakajian, 524 U.S. 321 (1998)
United States v. Booker, 543 U.S. 220 (2005)

United States v. Bostick, 501 U.S. 429 (1991)
United States v. Carolene Products Co., 304 U.S. 144 (1938)
United States v. Kagama, 118 U.S. 375 (1886)
United States v. Richardson, 418 U.S. 166 (1974)
United States v. Stanley, 483 U.S. 669 (1987)
United States v. Windsor, 570 U.S. 744 (2013)
Virginia State Board of Pharmacy v. Virginia Citizens Consumer Council, Inc., 425 U.S. 748 (1976)
Wainwright v. Sykes, 433 U.S. 72 (1977)
West Coast Hotel Co. v. Parrish, 300 U.S. 379 (1937)
Wooden v. United States, 595 U.S. 360 (2022)

US Courts of Appeals

Ex parte Merryman, 17 F. Cas. 144 (No. 9487) (C.C.D. Md., Taney, Circuit Justice 1861)
Jackson Women's Health v. Dobbs, 945 F.3d 265 (5th Cir. 2019)
Ramirez v. Martinez, 716 F.3d 369 (5th Cir. 2013)
SEC v. Citigroup, 752 F.3d 285 (2d Cir. 2014)
SEC v. Texas Gulf Sulphur Co., 401 F.2d 833 (2d Cir. 1968)
Shultz v. Wheaton Glass Company, 421 F.2d 259 (3d Cir. 1970)
United States v. Dutch, 978 F.3d 1341 (10th Cir. 2020)
United States v. Easley, 911 F.3d 1074 (10th Cir. 2018)
United States v. Geneva Gallegos, 129 F.3d 1140 (10th Cir. 1997)
United States v. Newman, 773 F.3d 438 (2d Cir. 2014)
United States v. Quinones, 313 F.3d 49 (2d Cir. 2002)
United States v. Salman, 792 F.3d 1087, 1093 (9th Cir. 2015)
United States v. Vazquez, 977 F.2d 594 (9th Cir. 1992)
United States v. Wooden, 945 F.3d 498 (6th Cir. 2019)

US District Courts

Briggs v. Elliott, 132 F. Supp. 776 (E.D.S.C. 1955)
Browder v. Gayle, 142 F. Supp. 707 (M.D. Ala. 1956)
Campaign for Southern Equality v. Bryant, 64 F. Supp. 3d 906 (S.D. Miss. 2014)
Doe v. Commonwealth's Attorney for the City of Richmond, 403 F. Supp. 1199 (1975), affirmed, 425 U.S. 901 (1976)
Garcia v. Bloomberg, 865 F. Supp. 2d 478 (S.D.N.Y. 2012)

Jackson Women's Health v. Currier, 349 F. Supp. 3d 536 (S.D. Miss. 2018)
Jamison v. McClendon, 476 F. Supp. 3d 386 (S.D. Miss. Aug. 2020)
SEC v. Bank of America, 653 F. Supp. 2d 507 (S.D.N.Y. 2009)
SEC v. Citigroup, 827 F. Supp. 2d 336 (S.D.N.Y. 2011)
United States v. Dylan Wade Butler et. al., No. 12-cr-00034-CWR-FKB, PACER (S.D. Miss. 2012)
United States v. Easley, 293 F. Supp. 3d 1288 (D.N.M. 2018)
United States v. Jonatan Lopez, 817 F. Supp. 2d 918 (S.D. Miss. 2011)
U.S. v. Quinones, 205 F. Supp. 2d 256 (S.D.N.Y. 2002)
U.S. v. Rivera, No. 10-cr-3348-MV, PACER (D.N.M. 2012)
U.S. v. Russell, No. 04-cr-01828-MV, PACER (S.D.N.M. 2004)

Index

abortion ban (Mississippi), challenge to (*Jackson Women's Health v. Currier* [S.D. Miss. 2018]): ban after fifteen weeks of pregnancy, 225; lack of evidence to back up claims of risks to mother's health, 225-26; Reeves granting temporary restraining order (TRO), 226; Reeves grants summary judgment, 226-27; Reeves postpones trial due to Supreme Court involvement, 229-30; as unconstitutional because fifteen weeks is before viability of the fetus, a determinative factor under Supreme Court precedent, 226-27
—REEVES'S OPINION: as informed by his deep admiration for the strength of women, 228; men's control over women perpetuated by the ban, 227-28, 230; pretending to care about women's health as a lie given how the state had been treating women throughout its history, 225, 227, 229; the state passed an unconstitutional law to ask the Supreme Court to overturn *Roe v. Wade*, 227

—HIGHER COURT DECISIONS: the Fifth Circuit affirming (with concurring opinion taking offense at Reeves' opinion and making inaccurate claims) (*Jackson Women's Health v. Dobbs* [5th Cir. 2019]), 229; the Supreme Court reversing the rulings and ending the constitutional right to abortion (*Dobbs* decision), 229, 230, 253
ACLU Mississippi: Reeves working summers during law school, 37; response to white supremacist murder of James Anderson, 161
age discrimination, Supreme Court requiring arbitration for, 98-99
Alexander v. Holmes County Board of Education (1969), 16, 30
Alito, Samuel A. (justice): on reversal of *Roe*, 230; and *Salman v. United States*, 243
Amendments. *See under* Constitution (US)
American Home Products, fen-phen diet drug, 99-100
Americans with Disabilities Act (1990), 89

American Tort Reform Association, 102–3
Anderson, James Craig: beating and murder of, 161–62, 172–75; as black gay man, 163–65, 173. *See also* Dedmon, Deryl, and hate-crime co-conspirators in murder of James Craig Anderson
Anderson, Reuben (justice of Mississippi Supreme Court), 37–38, 88, 91
animosity toward lawyers. *See* trial lawyers and lawsuits, animosity toward
Antiterrorism and Effective Death Penalty Act (1996), 94–95, 118, 267n18
Apodaca, Jerry, 72
appeals court. *See* Court of Appeals (US)
Apps, Antonia, 234–35
arbitration, mandatory, 98–99
Armed Career Criminal Act (1984): overview of passage and mandatory sentencing, 218–19; *Wooden* opinion of Supreme Court on meaning of single "occasion" (2022), 221–23. *See also* Dutch, Marc—and the Armed Career Criminal Act
asbestos lawsuits, 85, 96–97
Ashcroft, John, Attorney General, 116

Baker v. Nelson (1972), 35
"banana republics," 40
banana trade. *See* United Brands (once United Fruit Company)
Bank of America merger with Merrill Lynch (*SEC v. Bank of America* [S.D.N.Y. 2009]): CEO John Thain's realization of the need for, 177–78; CEO Kenneth Lewis and terms of agreement, 178–79; disclosure of bonuses paid ($4.5 billion) and further losses ($17 billion) withheld until after shareholder approval of merger (Dec. 2008), 179
—SEC LAWSUIT FOR FRAUD AND SETTLEMENT AGREEMENT: agreement terms, 180; basis of claim, nondisclosure of bonuses and losses as, 180, 181–82; "neither-admit-nor-deny" bargain allowed to BofA, 180, 182, 184; penalty amount as oddly small, 180, 182; Judge Rakoff assigned to approve the settlement, 180; Rakoff's belief that the individuals responsible for wrongdoing deserved to be identified and pay the price, 181–82, 183, 184; Rakoff's fact-finding hearing, 180–82; Rakoff's opinion on the settlement as providing a façade of enforcement, and celebrity resulting from, 182–83; "Yates Memo" prompted in part by (DOJ policy of targeting individuals rather than just corporations, 2015), 247
—SEC LAWSUIT SETTLEMENT RENEGOTIATION: BofA changing lawyers and working out new agreement with the SEC, 185–86; BofA's refusal to allow any individual to be named as defendant, 185, 186; hearing on, 187; New York Attorney General Andrew Cuomo announces lawsuit for fraud and names individuals, 186–87; penalty amount increased, 186; Rakoff's decision to comply with obligation to defer to SEC and accept the new settlement, 188;

Rakoff's opinion so harsh that plaintiff's lawyers seized on language to extract $2.5 billion, 247
Bankston, Hilda T., 99–100
Barbour, Haley (governor of Mississippi), 18, 104, 151
Barbour, Henry, 18
Barbour, William (judge), 20, 21, 151–52, 153; Judge Reeves eventually taking the same seat as, 152; Reeves's childhood interaction with, 20
Barclays, 247
Bardwell, Will, 152–53, 157, 159, 160
Baria, David, 84, 101, 102
Baria, Marci, 101
Barlow, Chuck, 89–90
baseball: Major League, antitrust exemption protected by Supreme Court, 57; Rakoff as fan of, 48, 236; Reeves and segregated Little League teams, 18
Bayyouk, Karim, 237
Bear Stearns, 178
Bennett, Mark (judge), 112
Bennett, Patricia, 21
BFI, Inc. v. Kelco Disposal, Inc. (1989), 97–98
Bharara, Preet, 234, 235, 237, 243
Bickel, Alexander, 10–11
Bickett, Rebecca, 165–66. *See also* same-sex marriage—lawsuit to strike down Mississippi ban (2014)
Biden, Joseph: appointing Reeves to US Sentencing Commission, 231, 232; and Civil Justice Reform Act (1990), 89; efforts to diversify the US judiciary, 254; judicial appointments, 231; and strengthening of "Yates Memo" targeting individual wrongdoers rather than just the companies they work for, 247
Bilbo, Theodore G., 17
Bingaman, Jeff, 83
Bivens v. Six Unknown Named Agents of Federal Bureau of Narcotics (1971), 33–34
Black, Eli: bribe paid to Honduras, 42–43, 44, 45; as CEO of United Brands (Chiquita bananas), 40–41; suicide of, 39–40, 41–42
Black Lives Matter movement, 2, 8
Blackmun, Harry (justice): appointment of, 34; dissenting in *Bivens*, 34; on executing the innocent as unconstitutional, 119, 120
Black people: discrimination against LGBTQ people among, 164–65, 171, 172; exclusion from society based on assumed historical facts that were really falsehoods (Lincoln), 38; free people not considered citizens (1857 Supreme Court), 23; Interstate 20 corridor and police routinely stopping, 2, 157; the Southern Manifesto claim of *Brown* as endangering, 28; systematic involuntary sterilization of Black women, 227; Justice Clarence Thomas's claim of abortion as endangering, 229. *See also* civil rights movement; Mississippi; police; police searches; racism; racist murders of Black people
Blankfein, Lloyd, 178
Blue Chip Stamps v. Manor Drug Stores (1975), 58
BMW of North America v. Gore (1996), 97–98
Bogart, Humphrey, 194
Booker, Freddie Joe, 136–37, 143–44

Bouldin, Damalas, police beating case (*Bouldin v. City of Mendenhall* [S.D. Miss. 2006]), 6, 104–7
Bowers v. Hardwick (1986), 35
Bradfield, James, partner of James Craig Anderson and father of De'Mariouz, 163–64, 173
Brandeis, Louis (justice), as defender of social justice, 25
Breyer, Stephen (justice), 231, 242
bribery: Foreign Corrupt Practices Act (1977), 59–60; by United Brands, and absence of anti-foreign bribery law, 44, 46. *See also* United Brands (once United Fruit Company)—criminal prosecution for Honduran bribe
Briggs v. Elliott (E.D.S.C. 1955), 154
Briscoe v. LaHue (1983), 34
Browder v. Gayle (M.D. Ala. 1956), 22
Brown, John Robert (judge), 22
Brown, Michael, 7
Brown v. Board of Education (1954): *Alexander v. Holmes County Board of Education* (1969) as order directing Mississippi to stop procrastinating, 16, 30; "all deliberate speed" *Brown II* (1955), interpretation as delaying desegregation, 21, 29, 30; *Briggs v. Elliott* (1955) interpreted as holding desegregation voluntary, 154; Thurgood Marshall as architect of, 30; Judge Manuel Real and desegregation of Pasadena school district, 78; and Reeves's attendance at integrated grade- and high-school, 15–16, 21, 27, 30, 162; the Roberts court striking down school desegregation plans (2007), 154–55; the Southern Manifesto as racist backlash to, 10–11, 28–29, 154

Brown v. Board of Education (Brown II) (1955), 21, 29, 30
Burger Court: approach of, as putting so many conditions on rights that they withered, 34; barring prisoners from claiming they should be released if they never mentioned the constitutional flaw at trial, 35; blocking Americans from using taxpayer status to challenge government conduct, 35; blocking rights for LGBTQ people, 35; formation of, 33–34; hundreds of opinions favoring business, 57; limitations attached to *Bivens*, 34; mandatory arbitration expanded (1983), 98. *See also* lawsuit limitations, Supreme Court; qualified immunity
Burger, Warren (chief justice): appointment of, 33; dissenting in *Bivens*, 33–34; imposing administrative regime on the federal courts rewarding speed, efficiency, and resolution of cases without trials, 35; as outspoken critic of the Warren Court (appeals court judge), 33
Bush, George W.: judicial nomination failures, 153; speech raising animosity toward trial lawyers, 85
Bush v. Lucas (1983), 34
bus station searches. *See* Easley, Ollisha, and race as factor in searches (*U.S. v. Easley* [D.N.M. 2018])
bus travel. *See* public accommodations—ban on segregation of
Butler, Dylan Wade, 162, 172–75. *See also* Dedmon, Deryl, and hate-crime co-conspirators in murder of

James Craig Anderson
Byers, Shirley, 37
Byrd, James, Jr., 163

Cabranes, Jose (judge), 124–25
Calabresi, Guido (judge), 126
Calhoun, John C., 28, 32
California, federal judges holding court sessions on Indian lands, 148
Campaign for Southern Equality v. Bryant (S.D. Miss. 2014). *See* same-sex marriage—lawsuit to strike down Mississippi ban (2014)
Campos, Santiago (judge), 83
Canellos, George, 187
Casablanca, 194
Castile, Philando, 6–7
Chamberlain, Wilt, 47
Chamber of Commerce (US): influence on the Supreme Court, 56–57; Lewis Powell's memo exhorting litigation by, 55–57, 86, 94. *See also* civil justice system, struggle over the purpose of
Chambers, Julius (Charlotte, NC), 37, 38
Chan, Merry Jean, 238
Checki, Terry, 177
The Cherokee Nation v. the State of Georgia (1831), 132
Chevron v. Natural Resources Defense Council (1984): deference of judges to interpretations of law by executive agencies (e.g., the SEC), 193, 205; overturned (2024), 248; the Second Circuit citing, in reversal of Rakoff decision to reject SEC settlement with Citigroup, 200, 203–5
Chiasson, Anthony. *See* insider trading—Newman case (*U.S. v. Newman* [2d Cir. 2014])
children: of same-sex couples, and the need to be married, 166, 170; Supreme Court finding as "common sense" that a child might agree to answer a cop's questions when an adult would feel free to decline (2011), 215. *See also* incarceration in federal facilities—of children (under age 18)
Christen, Morgan (judge), 238
CIA, toppling Guatemalan government (1954), 40
Citigroup alleged to have misled investors in defaulted mortgage-backed CDO (*SEC v. Citigroup* [S.D.N.Y. 2011]): agreement with SEC for settlement terms, 190–91; basis of claim, nondisclosure to investors of role Citigroup played in asset selection process or the short position taken in collateralized debt obligation (CDO), 189–90; "neither-admit-nor-deny" bargain, 190, 192, 195–96; public acclaim for Rakoff's rejection of settlement, 197–98; Judge Rakoff randomly assigned to approve the settlement, 192; Rakoff's decision not to defer to the SEC but to pursue the truth in the public interest, 192–93, 194–95, 196, 204; Rakoff's fact-finding hearing, 192, 193–96; Rakoff's opinion rejecting the settlement and ordering parties to trial, 196–98; Rakoff ordered to approve the settlement, final opinion (2014), 205; Rakoff's rejection of delay of trial during the appeal, overruled, 198–99, 200; Brian Stoker's creation of CDO and email

Citigroup alleged to have misled
investors *(continued)*
advising "Don't tell CSAC," 189–90,
202; Stoker sued as individual (*SEC
v. Brian H. Stoker* [S.D.N.Y. 2011]),
189–90, 192, 200–202
—APPEAL (*SEC V. CITIGROUP* [2D
CIR. 2014]): overview of SEC and
Citigroup seeking mandamus
command for Rakoff to approve
settlement, 198; concurrence
offering insult to Rakoff, 204;
deference to SEC as separation of
powers issue, 204, 205; reversing
Rakoff and demanding deference
to SEC, 200, 203–5; stay of trial
granted, 199, 200
citizenship, denied to free Blacks
(1857), 23
*Citizens United v. Federal Election
Commission* (2010), 57
Civil Justice Reform Act (1990), 89
civil justice system, struggle over the
purpose of: overview, 9–14, 86,
252–56; "budget deficit" rhetoric
preventing investment in, 89;
budget shortfalls in the 1990s and
cuts to number of judges, 89; Civil
Justice Reform Act (1990),
requiring courts to cut delays while
providing no new funding to
support, 89; Congress cutting
federal jurors' per-day fee and
suspension of civil jury trials
(1986), 88; as damaging the right of
Americans to seek legal redress, 86,
87–88, 101–3, 104, 252–53; "docket
management" pushed on judges,
111–12; Alexander Hamilton on
weakness of the judiciary as branch
of government, 254; "litigation
explosion" of frivolous lawsuits
claimed, 88–89; and the need for
judges to boldly stand up for the
judiciary, 252, 254–56; the number
of judges has not risen with US
population growth, 254; public
relations campaign blaming
lawyers and lawsuits for insurance
premium increases, 86–88; recent
climate on the left and right for
giving up on the courts, 11, 12–13,
252–53; the Southern Manifesto
view as having won, 153–55; and
state court vs. federal court
jurisdiction, 89–90; violence and
threats against judges, 22, 55, 142,
254–56. *See also* federal judiciary;
lawsuit limitations; Southern
Manifesto (declaration of war on
the federal courts); trial lawyers
and lawsuits, animosity toward
Civil Rights Act (1964): as amending
the Equal Pay Act (1963), 51–52;
continued segregation practices
following, 18; effects of, 22
Civil Rights Act (1991), 89
civil rights cases: as concern of the
Democratic Party, 92; Judge W.
Harold Cox's racist opinion of, 151;
mandatory arbitration enforced in,
98–99
civil rights movement: discrimination
against LGBTQ people in, 164–65,
171; Episcopal priests' "prayer
pilgrimage," 31; Freedom Riders,
155, 164; Lawrence Guyot's
appreciation of Reeves, 156; and
Justice Harlan Fiske Stone's
footnote 4 in *Carolene Products*
(1938), 26; March on Washington
for Jobs and Freedom (1963),

164–65; Ronald Reagan campaign speech giving wink of approval to Southern segregationists, 35–36. *See also* racial desegregation; voting rights

class action lawsuits: against tobacco companies, to recover public money states spent for health care, 85, 96–97; definition of, 57–58

—Supreme Court limits on: consumer groups as outraged by, 58; making banding together harder, 58. *See also* lawsuit limitations

Cleary Gottlieb Steen & Hamilton, 185

Clinton, William J.: budget wrangling and government shutdown, 110; judicial appointments, 129; signing the Antiterrorism and Effective Death Penalty Act (1996), 267n18; US Attorney appointments, 91–92; Vázquez's petition for clemency for her brother Ricardo, 83

Coakley, Marion, 117

Cohen, Neal M., 95–96

Cold War, 49

collateralized debt obligations (CDOs). *See* Citigroup alleged to have misled investors in defaulted mortgage-backed CDO (*SEC v. Citigroup* [S.D.N.Y. 2011])

common law tradition, and Rakoff's belief that precedent should be questioned if it could lead to bad results, 117–18

Congress (US): Civil Justice Reform Act (1990) requiring courts to cut expensive delays, and the pattern of passing pricey laws but refusing to pay for the soaring caseloads that result, 89; cutting federal jurors' per-day fee and suspension of civil jury trials (1986), 88; Indian tribes overseen by (US Constitution), 132; proposals for changes in laws and increases in funding to restore access to courts, 254. *See also* federal laws

Constitution (US): Fifth Amendment, on capital punishment, 120; Sixth Amendment guarantee of a trial by an impartial jury, 138; Eighth Amendment protection against "excessive fines," 209–10; Thirteenth, Fourteenth, and Fifteenth Amendment hopes, as crushed by white supremacist backlash, 7–8; fugitive slave clause, 23; Indian tribes and Washington, Congress given oversight of, 232; liberty protections for labor laws, 26; "originalism" theory, 61–62; the right's view of, as protecting property and rugged individualism, 12–13; separation of powers, 204, 205

—Fourth Amendment: prohibition on illegal searches and seizures as indispensable freedom, 158–59; search requirement for voluntary consent as dependent on the "totality of the circumstances," 213, 214–15

—Fourteenth Amendment: *Brown* claimed to have misread the right to equal treatment, 28; "freedom of contract" claimed to exist in, 25; "freedom of contract" overthrown, 26; hope of, as crushed by white supremacist backlash, 7–8; judicial denial of race as factor in police encounters as denial of equal

Index [295]

Constitution—Fourteenth
   Amendment *(continued)*
   treatment, 215; same-sex marriage
   bans as violating rights of equal
   treatment and due process, 166–67,
   169; "separate but equal" found not
   to violate, 23–24
consumer groups: outrage at limits on
   class action lawsuits, 58; Lewis
   Powell naming as threat to
   business, 56
corporate law practice: appealing jury
   awards as "excessive damages," 88;
   Rakoff and, 52, 60; removal of state
   court cases to federal courts as
   preference in, 89–90; as unfamiliar
   and suspect territory for Black
   lawyers (1991), 88. *See also* Reeves,
   Carlton (judge)—with Phelps
   Dunbar in corporate practice
corporations: companies may be held
   liable for the actions of a single
   employee (1909), 45–46; constitutional rights of, 24, 57; Southern
   District of New York policy of
   prosecuting actual people rather
   than, 45; "Yates Memo" policy
   targeting individual wrongdoers
   rather than just the companies they
   work for (2015), 247. *See also*
   Chamber of Commerce (US);
   civil justice system, struggle over
   the purpose of; financial crisis
   (2008); SEC (US Securities and
   Exchange Commission); securities
   laws
Costa Rica, and United Fruit
   Company/United Brands, 40, 41
Court of Appeals (US): number of
   judges, 110–11; three-judge panels
   typically hear cases, with a senior
   judge taking the lead, 51; workload,
   generally, 111
—Second Circuit: barring Rakoff
   from foreign affairs questions
   (2010), 192–93; courthouse of, 202–3;
   friendships and respect between
   Rakoff and, 204–5; insider trading
   violates federal securities laws
   (1968), 57; Rakoff's ruling that the
   death penalty is unconstitutional, reversal of (2002), 124–25, 126;
   tensions between Rakoff and, 200,
   204, 205. *See also* Citigroup alleged
   to have misled investors in defaulted
   mortgage-backed CDO—appeal
   (*SEC v. Citigroup* [2d Cir. 2014]);
   insider trading—Newman case (*U.S.
   v. Newman* [2d Cir. 2014])
—Fifth Circuit: affirming Reeves's
   decision on abortion ban as
   unconstitutional (2019), 229;
   Reeves's opposition to white male
   appointments to, 154; "the Four"
   judges ensuring desegregation
   went forward, 22, 55
—Sixth Circuit, preference for
   judges to step aside and let progress
   play out through legislative process,
   171
—Ninth Circuit: courtroom, 237–38;
   Rakoff invited to sit with, as senior
   judge, 236. *See also* insider
   trading—Salman case (*U.S. v.
   Salman* [9th Cir. 2015])
—Tenth Circuit: as collectively
   conservative, 135; reversals of
   Vázquez's sentences, 135, 136, 144,
   219–20, 221; reversals of Vázquez's
   sentences expected, taking
   controversial stands as form of
   resistance, 210, 214–16; the Sureño

13 death penalty case and appeals of pretrial rulings, 131; territory covered by, 135; Vázquez's gratitude to court as safety net, 135–36
—CASES: overview list with full citations, 287; *Ex parte Merryman* (C.C.D. Md., Taney, Circuit 1861), 23; *Jackson Women's Health v. Dobbs* (5th Cir. 2019), 229; *Ramirez v. Martinez* (5th Cir. 2013), 6; *SEC v. Texas Gulf Sulphur Co.* (2d Cir. 1968), 57; *Shultz v. Wheaton Glass Company* (3d Cir. 1970), 51–52; *U.S. v. Dutch* (10th Cir. 2020), 219–20, 221; *U.S. v. Easley* (10th Cir. 2018), 215; *U.S. v. Geneva Gallegos* (10th Cir. 1997), 135; *U.S. v. Quinones* (2d Cir. 2002), 116–17, 124–26; *U.S. v. Vazquez* (9th Cir. 1992), 80, 82–83; *U.S. v. Wooden* (6th Cir. 2019), 222. *See also* Citigroup alleged to have misled investors in defaulted mortgage-backed CDO—appeal (*SEC v. Citigroup* [2d Cir. 2014]); insider trading—Newman case (*U.S. v. Newman* [2d Cir. 2014]); insider trading—Salman case (*U.S. v. Salman* [9th Cir. 2015])
—JUDGES: John Robert Brown, 22; Warren Burger, 33; Jose Cabranes, 124–25; Guido Calabresi, 126; Morgan Christen, 238; Abraham Freedman, 50–52, 54–55; Learned Hand, 117; James Ho, 229; Robert Katzmann, 204–5; Raymond Lohier, 203–4, 205; Thurgood Marshall, 30; Barrington Parker, 234–35; Rosemary Pooler, 203, 205; Richard Rives, 22, 55; Simon Sobeloff, 29–30; Elbert Tuttle, 22; John Minor Wisdom, 22
COVID-19 lockdown, and police harassment of Black people, 7

Covington & Burling, 43
Cox, W. Harold (judge): appointment of, 30, 150; calls for impeachment of, 151; "motion day" of, 151; racism of, 150–52, 153–54, 155–56, 160; as senior judge, 151
Credit Suisse Alternative Capital (CSAC), 189–90, 202
Cribb, Kenneth, 61–62
Crow Dog case (1883), 132
CSAC (Credit Suisse Alternative Capital), 189–90, 202
Cuban Missile Crisis (1962), 49
Cuomo, Andrew, as NY attorney general, 186, 187–88
Cutcheon, Byron M., 132

Dale, George, 100
David's Auto Mart. *See* Rivera, David, forfeiture case (*U.S. v. Rivera* [D.N.M. 2012])
Davis v. United States (1973), 35
Dawes Act (General Allotment Act of 1887), 132–33
Dawes, Henry L., 132
Dean, Clyde, 4
death penalty: Antiterrorism and Effective Death Penalty Act (1996) limiting challenges to, 94–95, 118; Attorney General John Ashcroft's aggressive pursuit of, 116; DNA testing and scores of death-row inmates found to be "factually innocent," 117; juror candidates who strongly favored or opposed the death penalty barred from serving on (2004), 126–27; as rare among federal court cases, 116; workload on judges for cases involving, 130–31; wrongly convicted death-row inmates

death penalty *(continued)*
limited in challenges to, 94–95, 118. *See also* Quinones, Alan (and codefendant Diego Rodriguez)—Rakoff's ruling that the death penalty is unconstitutional
Debevoise & Plimpton (New York), 52
Dedmon, Deryl, and hate-crime co-conspirators in murder of James Craig Anderson (*U.S. v. Dylan Wade Butler et al.* [S.D. Miss. 2012]): James Anderson as Black gay man, 163–65; attack on and murder of James Anderson, 160–61; federal hate-crime charges and sentences, 162, 163, 165, 172–73, 175; guilty pleas, 162, 172; national news media response to, 161–62, 175–76; prior history of assaults on Black pedestrians, 160, 162; prior history of bullying of gay kids, 164; protest demonstrations following, 161–62; Judge Reeves as randomly assigned to case, 162–63; Reeves becoming a public hero in the wake of case, 175–76; Reeves on the irony of almost every official involved with the case being Black, 175; Reeves's personal response to, 162; Reeves's sentencing statement on history of racist savagery in Mississippi, 173, 174–76; state charges and sentences, 162, 163
Defense of Marriage Act, challenge to (2013), 168
democracy of opportunity: broadening of the middle class, 13, 83, 208, 253; constraints on the excessive money and power that creates oligarchy, 13, 38, 45–46, 50, 63, 183–84, 248, 253–54; definition of, 13; FDR's use of term, 13; inclusion of more people across all races and genders, 13–14, 38, 159–60, 251–52, 253; judges as advancing, 13–14, 253–54. *See also* Rakoff, Jed (judge); Reeves, Carlton (judge); Vázquez, Martha (judge)
Democratic Party: lawyers as financial pillars of, and Republican strategy of fueling animosity toward trial lawyers, 93, 103–4; in New Mexico, and Martha Vázquez appointment as federal judge, 129; and US Attorney Pigott's agenda in Mississippi, 92, 102
desegregation. *See* racial desegregation
Dimon, Jamie, 178
Dirks v. SEC (1983), 242, 243
discrimination: on age, Supreme Court requiring arbitration for, 98–99; in housing, banning of, 22; Jewish people experiencing, 47; sexism, girls discouraged from studying science as, 47. *See also* LGBTQ people—discrimination against; racial discrimination; voting rights
District Court (US): "baby judge school," 109, 111–12; diversity on the bench matters, 12, 253–54; "docket management" and avoidance of trials as expectation (1990s), 111–12; importance of lower courts for legal redress by ordinary Americans, 253; judges expected to defer to administrative agencies (See *Chevron v. Natural Resources Defense Council*); judges expected to follow Supreme Court precedents without question,

117–18, 124, 125–26; as less vulnerable than elected officials to influence of financial backers, 253; and Nixon/Burger Court era's cramped view of rights, 35; number of judges overall, 110–11; opinions, pressure to avoid writing, 111–12; Rakoff's belief that precedent should be questioned if it could lead to bad results (common law), 117–18; random assignment of judges to cases, 163; and Reeves's "judges are heroes," 22; separation of powers as constraint on, 204, 205; Vázquez taking controversial stands she knew would be reversed, as resistance, 210, 214–16; workload, generally, 111; workload in District of New Mexico as among highest, 131. *See also* Native American territories (Indian reservations)—as federal criminal law jurisdiction

—CASES: overview list with full citations, 287–88; *Bouldin v. City of Mendenhall* (S.D. Miss. 2006), 6, 104–7; *Briggs v. Elliott* (E.D.S.C. 1955), 154; *Browder v. Gayle* (M.D. Ala. 1956), 22; *Campaign for Southern Equality v. Bryant* (S.D. Miss. 2014), 165–72; *Doe v. Commonwealth's Attorney for the City of Richmond* (1976), 35; *Garcia v. Bloomberg* (S.D.N.Y. 2012), 191–92, 199–200; *SEC v. Brian H. Stoker* (S.D.N.Y. 2011), 189–90, 192, 200–202; *U.S. v. Fernando Mendez et al.* (C.D. Cal. 1990), 67–68, 77–82; *U.S. v. Jonatan Lopez* (S.D. Miss. 2011), 156–59. *See also* abortion ban (Mississippi), challenge to (*Jackson Women's Health v. Currier* [S.D. Miss. 2018]); Bank of America merger with Merrill Lynch (*SEC v. Bank of America* [S.D.N.Y. 2009]); Citigroup alleged to have misled investors in defaulted mortgage-backed CDO (*SEC v. Citigroup* [S.D.N.Y. 2011]); Dedmon, Deryl, and hate-crime co-conspirators in murder of James Craig Anderson (*U.S. v. Dylan Wade Butler et al.* [S.D. Miss. 2012]); Easley, Ollisha, and race as factor in searches (*U.S. v. Easley* [D.N.M. 2018]); Jamison, Clarence, lawsuit for damages due to police stop and search (*Jamison v. McClendon* [S.D. Miss. Aug. 2020]); Quinones, Alan (and codefendant Diego Rodriguez) (*U.S. v. Quinones* [S.D.N.Y. 2002]); Rivera, David, forfeiture case (*U.S. v. Rivera* [D.N.M. 2012]); Russell, Reno Roy (Navajo) (*U.S. v. Russell* [S.D.N.M. 2004])

—JUDGES: William Barbour, 20, 21, 151–52, 153; Mark Bennett, 112; Santiago Campos, 83; W. Harold Cox, 30, 150–52, 153–54, 155–56, 160; Nancy Gertner, 111–12; Frank M. Johnson, 22; Lewis Kaplan, 248; Morris Lasker, 52–55; William Pauley, 248; Milton Pollack, 54, 55; Leonard Sand, 121; Henry Wingate, 162. *See also* Rakoff, Jed (judge); Reeves, Carlton (judge); Vázquez, Martha (judge)

DNA testing: establishment of, and Innocence Project, 117; proving innocence easily and definitively, and Rakoff's ruling on death penalty as unconstitutional, 117, 120, 124

Dobbs v. Jackson Women's Health Organization (2022), 229, 230, 253
Doe v. Commonwealth's Attorney for the City of Richmond (1976), 35
Donatelli, Mark, 75
Dotson, Gary, 117
Doyle, Carrie Covington, 133
Dred Scott v. Sandford (1857), 23, 38
Dreeben, Michael, 240, 242–43
Driver, Justin, 154
Drug Enforcement Administration (DEA). *See* Easley, Ollisha, and race as factor in searches (*U.S. v. Easley* [D.N.M. 2018]); Vázquez, Ricardo (brother)—involvement in cocaine drug sting
drug laws: Congress passing antidrug statutes but refusing to pay for the soaring caseloads that result, 89; fix for 100:1 sentencing disparity between crack and powder cocaine offenses (2007), 231; further sentencing overhaul (2014, and 2019 First Step Act), 231–32; Rockefeller's draconian 1970s laws, prison overcrowding resulting from, 75–76
Dutch, Marc, and vindication of Judge Vázquez's tailoring of sentences to the individual (*U.S. v. Dutch* [D.N.M. 2016]): overview of 2016 drug relapse and arrest, 216–17, 218; background of severe childhood abuse, trauma, and drug use, 217–18, 219; federal charges as felon with a gun, sentence range for, 218; Narcotics Anonymous meetings, 218; public defender Brian Pori as lawyer, 216–17, 218–23, 224; rehabilitation and work history, 217–18, 222; relapse and new sentence to drug-treatment (2023), 224; state charges, guilty plea and sentencing, 218; Vázquez's commitment to ensure Dutch's life would not be wasted, 223, 224; Vázquez's original sentence of five years plus drug-treatment and probation, as final, 219, 221; Vázquez's sentencings repeatedly reversed or delayed, 220–22
—and the Armed Career Criminal Act: bank robberies as qualifying Dutch for (2005), 217, 218; bank robberies as single incident vs. three separate occasions, Pori raising question of, 219, 220–21; bank robberies, sloppiness of records as factor, 220, 223; government appeals of Vázquez's sentences and Tenth Circuit orders to resentence under, 219–20, 221; mandatory sentence of fifteen years for 2016 charges, 218–19, 220; Vázquez as repeatedly unable to bring herself to sentence Dutch under, 219, 220–21; the *Wooden* opinion of Supreme Court as vindication of Vázquez's position, 221–23

Easley, Ollisha, and race as factor in searches (*U.S. v. Easley* [D.N.M. 2018]): overview of DEA agent Jarrell Perry's routine at the Albuquerque bus station, 211–14; arrest of Easley and hours-long pressure to confess before reading her Miranda rights and recording a formal interview, 212; Easley as Black mother and sole provider for children and extended family who

[300] INDEX

got paid to take a trip, 211; federal charges of possession and intent to distribute meth, 212; list of more than fifty public defender's office clients for searches by Perry, 211; Perry asked all passengers if they would consent to a search, but most who were actually searched had Hispanic-sounding last names or were Black, 211-12; public defender Brian Pori and pattern of Perry's cases, filing motion to suppress, 212-13; Vázquez's hearing on the motion, 213-14; Vázquez's legal precedent by analogy of age (*J.D.B. v. North Carolina*), 215; Vázquez's opinion granting motion because any person of color who has an encounter with law enforcement is affected by their race, 214-15; Vázquez's reversal denying race as factor, as expected, 215-16; as warrantless bus sweeps that depend on voluntary consent by people of color, 212-15

Eastland, James: and appointment of Harold Cox to the Court of Appeals, 30, 150; and backlash against *Brown v. Board of Education*, 27, 28

"Ebony and Ivory" (Stevie Wonder and Paul McCartney), 19

Ehrlichman, John, 33, 35

Eid, Troy, 133

Eisenhower, Dwight, judicial appointments, 29, 30

Eisen v. Carlisle & Jacquelin (1974), 58

Ely, John Hart, 11

entrapment defense, factors in, 80, 83

environmental cases, as concern of the Democratic Party, 92

Environmental Protection Agency, creation of, 56

Equal Pay Act (1963), 51-52

Erie Railroad v. Tompkins (1938), 89

Ernst & Ernst v. Hochfelder (1976), 58

Ervin, Sam, 153-54

Eskridge, William, 168

ethics rules, encouraging judges to speak publicly to educate people, 255

Evers, Medgar, 174

ex parte conversations, 54

Ex parte KAN-GI-SHUN-CA (1883), 132

Ex parte Merryman (C.C.D. Md., Taney, Circuit 1861), 23

Farmer, James, 164

Father Knows Best (TV), 48-49

FBI surveillance, of LGBTQ people, 171

Federal Arbitration Act (1925), 98-99

federal courts: overview of best functions performed by, and constraints and blocks on access to, 9-14, 252-56; budget deficit rhetoric as blocking increased judges and resources for, 89; budget shortfalls in the early 1990s and cuts in number of judges, 89; Civil Justice Reform Act (1990) requiring courts to make plans to cut expensive delays while providing no funding to support, 89; consensus in DC as being overburdened, slow, and expensive, 88-89; removal of state court cases to, corporate defendants' preference for, 89-90; structure of, and number of judges, 110-11. *See also* civil justice system, struggle

Index [301]

federal courts *(continued)*
over the purpose of; Court of Appeals (US); District Court (US); federal judiciary; Native American territories (Indian reservations)—as federal criminal law jurisdiction; Supreme Court (US)

Federalist Society: current number of Supreme Court justices affiliated with, 62; founding of, 62; Edwin Meese seeking judicial candidates adhering to "originalism," 62

Federal Judicial Center, baby judge school, 109, 111–12

federal judiciary: attacks on judges, 252, 254–56; baby judge school, 109, 111–12; Congressional actions proposed to restore access to legal redress, 254; diversity on the bench matters, 12, 253–54; Alexander Hamilton on weakness as branch of government, 254; importance of lower courts for legal redress by ordinary Americans, 253; Judicial Conference recommendation for avoiding trials, 112; as less vulnerable than elected officials to influence of financial backers, 253; lifetime tenure of, 136, 253, 254–55; loneliness of judges, 109, 112, 131; the need for judges to boldly stand up for the judiciary, 252, 254–56; population of the US, number of judges has not risen with, 254; random assignment of judges to cases, 162–63, 163, 167, 180, 192, 239; senior status, 83, 151, 236; sentencing guidelines made nonbinding (with review) in *Booker* decision, mixed reactions to, 144; violence and threats against, 22, 55, 142, 254–56; workload of, generally, 111, 254. *See also* civil justice system, struggle over the purpose of; federal courts; federal laws

—SELECTION OF: Biden's efforts to increase diversity, and demographics of judges remain overwhelmingly white and male (2024), 254; Nixon selection process based on loyalty, 31–33, 56; Reagan/Meese selection process based on adherence to "originalism," 60–62; the Southern Manifesto and increasingly deferential judges, 29, 30; the Southern Manifesto and template of rancorous hearings over nominations, 29–30

federal laws: Americans with Disabilities Act (1990), 89; Antiterrorism and Effective Death Penalty Act (1996), 94–95, 118, 267n18; Civil Justice Reform Act (1990), 89; Civil Rights Act (1991), 89; Defense of Marriage Act, challenge to (2013), 168; Equal Pay Act (1963), 51–52; Federal Arbitration Act (1925), 98–99; First Step Act (2018), 231–32; Foreign Corrupt Practices Act (1977), 59–60; Fugitive Slave Act (1793), 23; General Allotment Act (1887 Dawes Act), 132–33; Indian Reorganization Act (1934), 133; Martin Luther King Jr., national holiday honoring (1983), 36; Major Crimes Act (1885), 128–29, 131–32; Matthew Shepard and James Byrd Jr. Hate Crimes Prevention Act (2009), 163, 172–73; Private Securities Litigation Reform Act (1995), 94; Sentencing Reform Act (1984), 76; Voting

Rights Act (1982), 36. *See also* Armed Career Criminal Act (1984); Civil Rights Act (1964); Section 1983 (1871 law barring violation of people's constitutional rights by state officials); securities laws federal officials, *Bivens* giving the right to sue for violations of constitutional protections, and Burger Court weakening of, 33–34
Feinstein, Dianne, 130
fen-phen diet drug, 99–100
Field, David Dudley, 24
Field, Stephen (justice), 24
financial crisis (2008): overview of economic effects, 179; Bear Stearns, 178; Lehman Brothers, 177–78; public anger over government's failure to punish banks for, 197–98; Rakoff as upset with the unfairness of oligarchs prospering from, 183–84. *See also* Bank of America merger with Merrill Lynch (*SEC v. Bank of America* [S.D.N.Y. 2009]); Citigroup alleged to have misled investors in defaulted mortgage-backed CDO (*SEC v. Citigroup* [S.D.N.Y. 2011]); Occupy Wall Street movement; SEC (US Securities and Exchange Commission)
First Step Act (2018), 231–32
Fishkin, Joseph, 13. *See also* democracy of opportunity
Fiske, Robert, 46
Fleishman, Rachel, 113
Flood v. Kuhn (1972), 57
Floyd, George, 6–7
Forbath, William, 13. *See also* democracy of opportunity
Fordice, Kirk, 96

Ford Motor Company, Mississippi verdict against, 99
Ford, Tim, 103
foreclosure crisis. *See* financial crisis (2008)
foreign affairs, district court judges ordered to stay out of, 192–93
Foreign Corrupt Practices Act (1977), 59–60
forfeiture: civil, 208–9; criminal, 208; as mandatory for violating "structuring" cash deposits statute, 207, 209. *See also* Rivera, David, forfeiture case (*U.S. v. Rivera* [D.N.M. 2012])
Foxx, Redd, 19–20
Francis v. Henderson (1976), 35
Frankfurter, Felix (justice), 10
Freedman, Abraham (judge), 50–52, 54–55
freedom of contract, overturning labor protection laws based on, 24–25
Freedom Riders, 155, 164
French, Keith, 167, 168
Fugitive Slave Act (1793), 23

Gallego, Geneva, 134–35
Gandhi, Mahatma, Rakoff's master's thesis on independence movement of, 50
Garcia v. Bloomberg (S.D.N.Y. 2012), 191–92, 199–200
Garner, Eric, 7
Garza, Alicia, 2
gay marriage. *See* same-sex marriage
Geithner, Timothy, 177–78
General Allotment Act (1887 Dawes Act), 132–33
George, Walter, 27–28
Gertner, Nancy (judge), 111–12

Index [303]

Gilbert & Sullivan, 47–48
Gilmer, Robert, age discrimination suit, 98–99
Gilmer v. Interstate/Johnson Lane Corp. (1991), 98–99
Gingrich, Newt, 94–95, 110
Ginsburg, Ruth Bader (justice): as civil rights lawyer pushing for federal courts to act when the political system would not, 11; clerks for, 241; portrait in the New York City Bar Association, 246; and *Salman v. United States*, 241, 242
Goldman Sachs, 177, 178
Gorsuch, Neil (justice), 135
Grassley, Chuck, 89, 98
Gregg v. Georgia (1976), 117
Griswold v. Connecticut (1965), 35
Guatemala: CIA toppling government of, United Fruit Company assistance (1954), 40; and United Fruit Company, 40
Guyot, Lawrence, 156

Haldeman, H. R., 33
Hamilton, Alexander, the judiciary as weakest branch of government, 254–55
Hand, Learned (judge), 117
Hanisee, Miles, 142–43, 146–47
Harper v. Virginia Board of Elections (1966), 22
Harvard Law School, Rakoff and, 50
Hayes-Deats, Caleb, 191–92, 199
health care: as embarrassingly bad in prisons, 223–24; Mississippi's abysmal record of disregard for the needs of women and minorities, 227. *See also* medical abuse
health-care fraud, as special focus of Brad Pigott, 92, 102

Heaney, Mark, 78, 79–80, 82, 83
Heart of Atlanta Motel, Inc. v. United States (1964), 22
Helms, Jesse, 36
Herrera v. Collins (1993), 118–20, 125, 126
Ho, James (judge), 229
Holmes, Oliver Wendell (justice), 25
homophobia. *See* LGBTQ people—discrimination against
Honduras: tax on banana exports, 41. *See also* United Brands (once United Fruit Company)—criminal prosecution for Honduran bribe
Hopland Band of Pomo Indians, 148
housing: judge citing Rakoff in rejecting NYC's settlement over substandard public housing, 248; shares in government-subsidized co-ops excluded from securities laws, 59
housing discrimination, banning of, 22
Howard, John, 164, 168
Hughes, Charles Evans (chief justice), 26
Huston, Tom Charles, and Nixon judicial selection method, 32–33, 61

Imbler v. Pachtman (1976), 34
immunity from lawsuits: absolute immunity of cops who lie on the stand, 34; absolute immunity of prosecutors who knowingly use perjured testimony, 34; of judges, 31; for state officials, generally, 34. *See also* qualified immunity
in-camera hearings, 173
incarceration in federal facilities: crippling effects of long-term sentencing after release, 223–24, 250; gangs, 249; health care as

embarrassingly bad in, 223–24; parole not possible, 129, 134; ratio problem of crack vs. powder cocaine, as disproportionately imprisoning Black people, 231; Vázquez and supervised release visits with ex-cons, 249–51. *See also* prison overcrowding and abusive conditions
—CHILDREN (UNDER AGE 18): largest portion Native, 134, 140; sentenced as adults, 134
Indian Reorganization Act (1934), 133
inequality, as political and economic crisis: the Nixon election and growing concern about, 50; oligarchy as resulting from, 12–13, 183–84. *See also* democracy of opportunity
Infelise, Jeffrey, 200–202
Ingalls Shipyard, asbestos liability, 96
injunctions, 43
Innocence Project, DNA testing and founding of, 117
in pari materia, 52
insider trading: Preet Bharara's approach as US Attorney, 234, 235, 237, 243; investors allowed to sue for securities fraud (Supreme Court, 1964), 57; SEC defining as improper (1961), 57; as violating federal securities laws (Second Circuit, 1968), 57
—NEWMAN CASE (*U.S. V. NEWMAN* [2D CIR. 2014]): overview reversing convictions of Todd Newman and Anthony Chiasson, 234–35; argued as defense in *Salman* (9th Cir.), 237, 238; argued as defense in *Salman* (Supreme Court), 240–42; circuit split created by Ninth Circuit ruling in *Salman*, 238–39; creates requirement of *payment* for corporate secrets to establish guilt, 235; Manhattan defense lawyers happy with, 239, 243; prosecutorial overreach criticized in opinion, 235; Rakoff accepting as current law of the circuit, 236; Rakoff's view as wrongly decided, 235–36, 237, 238; Supreme Court's ruling to affirm *Salman* and Second Circuit's response to, 245
—SALMAN CASE (*U.S. V. SALMAN* [9TH CIR. 2015]): overview of the facts resulting in conviction at trial of Bassam Salman, 236–37; arguments at hearing, 237–38; circuit split with the Second Circuit created by ruling, 238–39; *Newman* decision as defense in, 237, 238; Rakoff asked to write the unanimous opinion that all elements were met for illegal insider trading, and declined to follow *Newman*, 238; Rakoff invited to sit on panel as senior judge and assigned the case, 236, 239; Rakoff's belief that *Newman* was wrongly decided by the Second Circuit, 235–36, 237, 238; Salman's request for en banc review declined, 239
—SALMAN CASE (*SALMAN V. UNITED STATES* [2016]): anxiety while waiting for the decision, 243–44; certiori petition filed and granted, 239; decision affirming Ninth Circuit's ruling, 244–45; defendant Salman's lawyer (Shapiro) argues for *Newman* defense, 240–42; *Dirks v. SEC*

insider trading—*Salman v. United States (continued)*
personal-benefit precedent (1983), 241, 242, 243; government lawyer (Dreeben) argues no tangible benefit necessary for illegality, 240, 242–43; justices argue that to help a close family member is like helping yourself, 241–42, 243; Manhattan defense lawyers as unhappy with threat to *Newman*, 239, 243, 244; Second Circuit judges displeased with Rakoff's position, 239–40; the Second Circuit refining the rules in light of, 245; as vindication for Rakoff, 244, 245

Insurance Information Institute, 87

insurance premium increases: blamed on lawyers and lawsuits with little evidence, 85–86, 87–88, 100–101; reasons for, 86, 101; statistics showing, 87. *See also* medical malpractice insurance

International Brotherhood of Teamsters v. Daniel (1979), 59

Interstate 20 corridor, Black and Latino motorists routinely stopped on, 2, 157

Jackson, Ketanji Brown (justice), 231

Jackson, Mississippi: Episcopal priests' "prayer pilgrimage," arrests and prosecutions, 31; James O. Eastland Courthouse, 151–52, 156; Thad Cochran United States Courthouse, 5. *See also* Dedmon, Deryl, and hate-crime co-conspirators in murder of James Craig Anderson; US Attorney—Southern District of Mississippi

Jackson, Robert H. (justice), 159

Jackson State University: as historically Black institution, 20–21; police shooting of ten students (1970), 20–21, 34; Reeves as student and student leader in, 20–21, 27, 36, 37, 38

Jackson, Stonewall, 36

Jackson Women's Health v. Currier. See abortion ban (Mississippi), challenge to (*Jackson Women's Health v. Currier* [S.D. Miss. 2018])

Jackson Women's Health v. Dobbs (5th Cir. 2019), 229

Jamison, Clarence, lawsuit for damages due to police stop and search (*Jamison v. McClendon* [S.D. Miss. Aug. 2020]): aftereffects and damages requested, 4, 5; consent to search as coerced in context of police (and others) killing unarmed Black people, 2, 5, 6–7, 8; nonwhite motorists in the Interstate 20 corridor viewed as "fair game" by police, 2; reason given for stop, 3; Reeves as judge, and determination to do his best for, 5–7; Reeves's opinion reciting recent history of police killings and calling for end of qualified immunity, 7–9; Reeves's requirement to dismiss the lawsuit, 9; stop and search of car by Officer Nicholas McLendon, 1–4

J.D.B. v. North Carolina (2011), 215

Jewish people, religion as basis of denied admission to medical school, 47

J.I. Case Co. v. Borak (1964), 57

Johnson, Cliff, 102

Johnson, Frank M. (judge), 22

Johnson, Harvey, 42

Johnson, Lyndon: as president, judicial appointments, 30, 78; as senator, 27
Johnston, Olin: as author of the Southern Manifesto, 28-29; delaying the Sobeloff appointment to Court of Appeals, 29; delaying Thurgood Marshall appointment to Court of Appeals, 30; introducing bill giving district courts final say over school desegregation cases, 29; and new template for generations of rancorous judicial nomination hearings, 29-30; and views in Southern Manifesto as having won, 153-54
Jones v. Mayer (1968), 22
JPMorgan, 178, 247
judicial clerks, definition of, 50-51
Judicial Conference of the United States, 112
juries: Black juries stereotyped, but poverty shown as the factor increasing plaintiff's victories and awards, 100; guarantee of trial by jury that reflects the community, as right, 102, 138; large awards by, in public relations campaigns of animosity toward trial lawyers and lawsuits, 85, 88, 99-100; prejudices against Native Americans among jurors, 137, 138; Judge Rakoff addressing, in appreciation of, 201; Rakoff receiving note from, 202; women serving on, Mississippi as the last state to allow, 227. *See also* Native Americans on juries, Judge Martha Vázquez's work to increase numbers of
jurors, federal: Congress as cutting per-day fee paid to, and suspension of civil jury trials (1986), 88; and death penalty cases, those strongly favoring or opposing the death penalty barred from serving on (2004), 126-27
Justice Department (US): Attorney General John Ashcroft overruling US Attorneys who decided not to seek the death penalty, 116; Office of Legal Policy, and Meese's judge-picking machine, 61; Rakoff's calls for harsher punishment ultimately led to massive fines and guilty pleas, 247; stating lawsuits to be a major issue in the insurance premium increases, 87; "Yates Memo" policy targeting individual wrongdoers rather than just the companies they work for (2015), 247. *See also* US Attorney's Office

Kagan, Elena (justice), and *Salman v. United States*, 242
Kaplan, Lewis (judge), 248
Kaplan, Roberta, 168-69, 170
Kara, Maher, 236-37, 241
Kara, Michael, 236-37
Karp, Brad: and *SEC v. Bank of America* (2009), 185-86; and *SEC v. Citigroup* (2011), 190-91, 195-96, 198
Katzmann, Robert (judge), 204-5
Kean, Mike, 48
Keker, John, 201-2
Kellerwood, Michael, 249-51
Kennedy, Anthony (justice), on executing the innocent as unconstitutional, 119-20
Kennedy, John F.: beseeching Americans to ask what they could do for their country, 49; judicial appointments, 30, 150

Index [307]

Kennedy, Robert, as attorney general, 30, 154
Kennedy, Robert F., Jr., 113
Kennedy, Ted, mandatory sentencing law, 76
Kent State University, national guard shooting of four students, 34
Khan, Sohail, 189
Khuzami, Robert, 198
King, Austin, 202, 204
King, Martin Luther, Jr.: national holiday established to honor (1983), 36; Rakoff citing the debt owed to "troublemakers," 200; Bayard Rustin as close adviser to, 164–65
King, Rogers, 100
Kotowski, Linda, 200
Ku Klux Klan, 164
Kunstler, William, 56

labor laws: backlash to the Supreme Court's embrace of tycoons and big business, 25; Equal Pay Act (1963) amended by the Civil Rights Act (1964), 51–52; "freedom of contract" claimed to be violated by, 25; "freedom of contract" declared not to exist, 26; health and safety standards, 24; "liberty" declared to require protections of, 26; Lochner Era and overturning of, 24–25, 26; minimum wage and maximum hours, 24–25, 26; prohibitions on "yellow dog contracts" barring labor unions, 24
labor unions: Burger Court curtailing power of, 57; protection of right to organize, 24
language interpreters: need for, and the Jonatan Lopez illegal search case, 156–59; and the Russell case held on Navajo land, 146
Las Cruces, New Mexico, Judge Martha Vázquez's arduous travel for rotations in, 130
Lasker, Morris (judge), 52–55
Latino people: Interstate 20 corridor and police routinely stopping, 2, 157. *See also* Mexican Americans
lawsuit limitations: as damaging the constitutional right to seek legal redress, 86, 87–88, 101–3, 104. *See also* civil justice system, struggle over the purpose of; immunity from lawsuits; qualified immunity; trial lawyers and lawsuits, animosity toward
—FEDERAL LAWS: Antiterrorism and Effective Death Penalty Act (1996), 94–95, 118; Private Securities Litigation Reform Act (1995), 94; public outrage over the Liebeck jury award for McDonald's coffee injuries used to gain support for, 93; the Republican House Conference's "Contract with America" and, 94, 95
—STATE LAWS: adopted by majority of states in 1986, 87–88; effects of, as state courts handle the majority of cases, 95; federal lawsuits constrained by, 95; insurance industry public relations campaign leading to, 86–88; in Mississippi (2002 and 2004), 103–4; the Republican "Contract with America" as giving moral and political cover to, 95
—SUPREME COURT: overview, 57–58, 86; intention to cheat (scienter) ruled as requirement to sue for securities fraud (1976), 58;

mandatory arbitration, expansion of enforcement, 98–99; "material" fraud requirement (1976), 58–59; proof of lie or failure to disclose requirement, no duty to be fair (1977), 59; punitive damages lowered, making lawsuits a manageable cost of doing business, 97–98; securities anti-fraud laws not applicable to someone persuaded *not* to buy shares (1975), 58. *See also* class action lawsuits; securities laws
Lazarus, Edward, 93
Leach Wardell, 20
Leave It to Beaver (TV), 48–49
Lehman Brothers, 177–78
Lewis, Kenneth, 178–79, 181–82, 186
Lewis, Mike, 96–97
LGBTQ people: Burger Court refusal to acknowledge state laws criminalizing sodomy could be unconstitutional, 35; privacy right for intimate practices found not to apply to (*Bowers v. Hardwick*, 1986), 35. *See also* Anderson, James Craig; same-sex marriage
—DISCRIMINATION AGAINST: among Black people, 164–65, 171, 172; bullying of gay kids by Daryl Dedmon and friends, 164; history of, and arguments for court ruling to strike down same-sex marriage bans, 167–68, 169–72; history of virulent discrimination in Mississippi culture, 164–65, 169, 171; the Ku Klux Klan and, 164; medical abuse, 171; murder of Matthew Shepard, 163; personal damage inflicted by, 48
Liddell, Timothy, 251–52

Liebeck, Stella, McDonald's coffee injuries, 93
Liman, Arthur, 182
Liman, Lewis, 182–83, 184–85
Lincoln, Abraham: challenge to Supreme Court's undemocratic power, 23; on *Dred Scott* as based on assumed historical facts that were falsehoods, 38; suspension of habeas corpus by, 23
Lizalde, Lenny, 66
Lochner Era, 26
Lochner v. New York (1905), 24–25
Lohier, Raymond (judge), 203–4, 205
Long-Term Capital Management, 177
Lopez, General Oswaldo, 42
Lopez, Jonatan, motion to suppress due to illegal search (2011): the accused barely understood English and could not have consented to the search, 156–59; Judge Reeves's opinion elucidating the Fourth Amendment right against unreasonable search and seizure, 158–59
lynching and lynch mobs, Judge Reeves on Mississippi's infatuation with savagery of, 174–75

McCarthyism, 48
McDonald's coffee injuries (1994), 93
McLendon, Nicholas. *See* Jamison, Clarence, lawsuit for damages due to police stop and search (*Jamison v. McClendon* [S.D. Miss. Aug. 2020])
McVeigh, Timothy, 94
MAGA, attacks on the judicial system and judges, 252, 255–56
mail fraud, 44
Major Crimes Act (1885), 128–29, 131–32

mandamus, 198
mandatory arbitration, 98–99
Manila, Philippines, Jan Rakoff's murder, 122–23
Manuelito, Jonathan, fight with his cousin. *See* Russell, Reno Roy (Navajo) (*U.S. v. Russell* [S.D.N.M. 2004])
Marshall, Thurgood (justice): appointed as judge on US Court of Appeals, 30; as civil rights lawyer pushing for federal courts to act when the political system would not, 11; as lawyer for NAACP appearing before Supreme Court, 27, 30
Martens, Matthew, 194–96, 200–201
Martinez, Modesto, 73, 130
Martin, Trayvon, 2
Matheny, Justin, 169–70
Matthew, Dayna, 37
Matthew Shepard and James Byrd Jr. Hate Crimes Prevention Act (2009), 163, 172–73
Matuszewski, Andy "Ski," 157–58
Maxey, John L., 91
Mayopoulos, Timothy, 186–88
medical abuse: of LGBTQ people, 171; systematic involuntary sterilization of Black women ("Mississippi appendectomy"), 227
medical malpractice insurance: doctors blaming lawyers and lawsuits for increases in premiums and lack of coverage, 85, 87, 100–101; St. Paul Companies' announcement of no longer offering, 100–101
Meese, Edwin: "fear of crime" rhetoric of, 76; and the federal sentencing guidelines, 76; and Reagan judicial selection process based on adherence to "originalism," 61–62
Mendenhall, Mississippi, Damalas Bouldin police-violence case, 104–7
Merrill Lynch. *See* Bank of America merger with Merrill Lynch (*SEC v. Bank of America* [S.D.N.Y. 2009])
Mexican Americans: cash economies of, 206, 208; discrimination experienced by, 70–71, 72, 208; discrimination in Santa Fe, and Mexicans emphasizing their Spanish roots to avoid, 72–73, 129; faith in the US to treat them fairly, 70–71; work ethic of, 70–71, 208, 209–10
Mexican-American War, 129
M-FAIR (Mississippians for a Fair Legal System), 96
Mississippi: George W. Bush speech in, raising animosity toward trial lawyers, 85; Interstate 20 corridor, Black and Latino motorists routinely stopped on, 2, 157; Judge Reeves's sentencing statement on the history of racist savagery in, 173, 174–76; Magnolia Bar Association, 108, 154; MLK national holiday observed together with Robert E. Lee's birthday, 36; Parchman Farm (penitentiary), 156; Ronald Reagan campaign speech in, giving wink of approval to Southern segregationists, 35–36; tobacco company litigation launched by state attorney general (1994–1997), 85, 96–97; University of Mississippi (Ole Miss), Reeves refusing to attend, 21; women's health care as abysmal in, 227. *See also* discrimination;

Jackson, Mississippi; Mississippi laws; Mississippi Supreme Court; police; police searches; racial discrimination; racial segregation; racism; Reeves, Carlton (judge); trial lawyers and lawsuits, animosity toward—in Mississippi; US Attorney—Southern District of Mississippi

Mississippi laws: ban on same-sex marriage, 166-67, 170; "joinder" lawsuit rules, 100; limitations on lawsuits (2002 and 2004), 103-4; on product liability lawsuits, codifying status quo (1993), 96; women and minorities treated with disregard throughout the state's history, 225, 227, 229. *See also* abortion ban (Mississippi), challenge to (*Jackson Women's Health v. Currier*); same-sex marriage—lawsuit to strike down Mississippi ban (2014)

Mississippi Municipal League, 90

Mississippi Sovereign Commission, harassment of LGBTQ people, 171

Mississippi Supreme Court: Reuben Anderson as first African American justice of, Reeves clerking for, 37-38, 88, 91; campaign of animosity toward lawsuits and lawyers, and appeals to reduce "excessive damages," 88; constraints on product liability, codified into law, 96

Mitchell, Dennis, 21, 27

Mitchell, John, as former partner in Mudge, Rose, 60

Mobile v. Bolden (1980), 36

Montgomery, Alabama, banning of bus segregation, 22

Montgomery, Kirk, 161

Moore, Denise, 211

Moore, John, 103-4

Moore, Mike, 96-97

Morgan, Lawrence, 141-42

mortgage crisis. *See* financial crisis (2008)

Morvillo, Robert, 59

Moses H. Cone Memorial Hospital v. Mercury Construction Corporation (1983), 98

motions, judges directing a lawyer to make, 54

Motley, Ron, 97

Moynihan, Brian, 187, 188

Moynihan, Daniel Patrick (senator from New York): Rakoff applying for appointment as federal district judge, 62, 109-10; as US ambassador to India, 110

Mudge, Rose, Guthrie, Alexander & Ferdon, 60

Musgrave, Ronnie, 103

NAACP, 27, 152

Nader, Ralph: on limits on class action suits, 58; Lewis Powell naming as threat to business, 56

Narcotics Anonymous meetings, 218

national security, district court judges ordered to stay out of issues involving, 193

Native Americans on juries, Judge Martha Vázquez's work to increase numbers of: overview, 137-38; arranging for jurors to receive $40 per-day fee in advance and in cash, 138; exclusions due to registered voters as juror pool, many Indians aren't registered to vote, 134, 138-39; expansion of jury pool

Native Americans on juries *(continued)* suggested by including names of people with driver's licenses/ID cards (as per state courts), 139; expansion of jury pool suggested by using lists of enrolled tribe members, 139; Jury Plan Task Force created, Republican judges voting to keep status quo, 139; lack of Natives on juries means lack of jury of their peers, 134, 137, 138; leafletting at Native flea-markets, 141; prejudices against Natives among non-Native jurors and need for, 138; public service ads with Joe Shirley Jr. (Navajo Nation president), 140-41; and Russell trial moved to Navajo land, 145, 148. *See also* Native American territories (Indian reservations)—as federal criminal law jurisdiction

Native American territories (Indian reservations): allotment (breaking up into private property and opening to white settlement), 132-33; allotment ended (1934), and survival of fragment of former size, 133; and difficulties registering to vote, 139; tribal traditions of criminal justice recognized as valid by Supreme Court, 83

—AS FEDERAL CRIMINAL LAW JURISDICTION: children under age eighteen, in federal detention facilities and sentenced as adults, 134, 140; established via Major Crimes Act (1885), 128-29, 131-32; juries rarely have Native members, 134; lack of federal courthouses or services on reservations, 128-29, 133-34; parole not possible in federal system, 129, 134; as separate and unequal system of discriminatory criminal law, 133; severity of punishments as typically harsher than same crimes handled under state laws, 129, 134; state law control rejected by Supreme Court, 133; travel costs and times to federal court, 133-34; tribal traditions of criminal justice canceled by Congress, 132. *See also* Native Americans on juries, Judge Martha Vázquez's work to increase numbers of; Russell, Reno Roy (Navajo)—Judge Vázquez brings her court to Navajo land

Navajo Nation: annual visit by Judge Vázquez to federal detention center for girls under age eighteen, 140; distances and times to travel to courthouse, 133-34; federal juries rarely have any Native members, 134; severity of punishments faced by, 129, 134; Vázquez and supervised release visits with ex-cons, 249-51. *See also* Native Americans on juries, Judge Martha Vázquez's work to increase numbers of; Native American territories (Indian reservations); Russell, Reno Roy (Navajo)—Judge Vázquez brings her court to Navajo land; Shirley, Joe Jr. (president of Navajo Nation)

Nester, Kathy, 84

Neufeld, Peter, 117

New Deal, 26

Newman, Todd. *See* insider trading—Newman case (*U.S. v. Newman* [2d Cir. 2014])

New Mexico: discrimination in, Mexicans emphasizing their

Spanish roots to avoid, 72–73, 129; expansion of diversity in juror pool, 139; Penitentiary of New Mexico, riot due to overcrowding and abusive conditions in (1980), 74–75. *See also* Navajo Nation; New Mexico Law Office of the Public Defender; New Mexico sentencing guidelines (1979); Vázquez, Martha (judge)

New Mexico Law Office of the Public Defender: overview, 73, 77; defense of inmates in prison riot (1980), 74–75; list of more than fifty clients stopped and searched by the same DEA agent at the Albuquerque bus station, 211; Alonzo Padilla (and the Russell case), 137, 143–44, 145, 146–47. *See also* Pori, Brian (public defender); Vázquez, Martha (judge)—in public defender's office

New Mexico sentencing guidelines (1979): overview of choice left for judges, 73–74; extra time for use of a gun or other "deadly weapon," 74; as "get tough on criminals" approach, 74, 75; prison overcrowding and abusive conditions resulting from, 74; as spreading to most states and to national policy, 75; Vázquez as public defender still found wiggle room, 77. *See also* sentencing guidelines (federal)

news media: insurance industry public relations campaign against trial lawyers, 86–88; and Judge Vázquez bringing her court to Navajo land, 144, 146; and the racist hate-crime murder of James Anderson, 161–62, 175–76; reaction to Rakoff's rejection of Citigroup settlement with SEC, 197–98; reaction to Rakoff's ruling that the death penalty is unconstitutional, 124, 126. *See also* public relations industry

New York Central & Hudson River Railroad Co. v. United States (1909), 45–46

New York City: City Bar Association, 246; Daniel Patrick Moynihan United States Courthouse, 114, 180; judge citing Rakoff in rejecting settlement with federal government over substandard public housing, 248; Thurgood Marshall United States Courthouse, 202–3. *See also* financial crisis (2008); Rakoff, Jed (judge); US Attorney—Southern District of New York

New York Federal Reserve Bank, 177–78

Nichols, Terry, 94

Nixon, Richard M.: as former partner in Mudge, Rose, 60; as lawyer arguing before the Supreme Court, 31–32; as president, judicial selection process and appointments based on loyalty, 31–33, 56; as vice-president and presiding officer of the Senate, 27–28; Watergate, 20

Obama, Barack: judicial appointment of Carlton Reeves, 108, 153; Bennie Thompson and, 107–8

Obergefell v. Hodges (2015), 172

Occupy Wall Street movement, 191, 198; lawsuit against NYC for false arrest on Brooklyn Bridge (2012), 191–92, 199–200

O'Connor, Sandra Day (justice): criticizing expansion of mandatory arbitration, 98; on executing the innocent as unconstitutional, 119–20, 125
O'Keefe, Edward, 185
Oklahoma City federal building bombing (1995), 94
oligarchy as crisis of political and economic inequality, 12–13, 183–84. *See also* democracy of opportunity
O'Neill, Tip, 75
originalism, 61–62
Oxford University, Rakoff and, 50

Pacific Mutual Life Insurance Co. v. Haslip (1991), 97–98
Padilla, Alonzo, 137, 143–44, 145, 146–47
Paine, Thomas, 200
Panama, and banana trade, 41
Parents Involved in Community Schools v. Seattle School Dist. No. 1 (2007), 154–55
Parker, Barrington (judge), 234–35
Parks, Rosa, 22
parole not an option in the federal system, 129, 134
Pauley, William (judge), 248
Paulson, Henry, 177–78
Paul, Weiss, Rifkind, Wharton & Garrison, 185, 198
Peckham, Rufus (justice), 25
Pennsylvania. *See* Philadelphia; University of Pennsylvania
pension plans, excluded from securities laws, 59
Persico, Joseph, and "fear of crime," 75–76
Phelps Dunbar (law practice, Jackson): the Mississippi Municipal League as client of, 90, 107; Reeves on the respect among young partners for Black lawyers, 90–91; senior partners' stories about the "old Mississippi," 150. *See also* Reeves, Carlton (judge)—Phelps Dunbar in corporate practice
Philadelphia, Pennsylvania: white flight and, 48. *See also* Rakoff, Jed (judge)
Pierson v. Ray (1967), 6, 31
Pigott, Brad: background of, 91; as US Attorney, 91–92, 102
Pigott Reeves Johnson & Minor (Jackson): barnstorming tour to educate people about the need to preserve the right to legal redress in court, 84–86, 101–3; case of police violence against Damalas Bouldin, 104–7; connections at the US Attorney's office, 106; formation and client base of, 101–2; and the Mississippi legislature imposing constraints on people's right to sue for legal redress, 103–4
Plessy v. Ferguson (1896), 23–24
police: absolute immunity from lawsuits for lying on the witness stand, 34; civil forfeiture abuses and, 208–9; Occupy Wall Street's false-arrest lawsuit against (2012), 191–92, 199–200. *See also* police searches; qualified immunity
—BRUTALITY AND HARASSMENT OF BLACK PEOPLE: Damalas Bouldin beating case resulting in prison time for police chief and national attention to racist abuses by police, 106–7; context of, and lack of freely given consent to searches, 5, 6–7, 8,

212–15; COVID-19 lockdown and, 7; national attention brought to, 106–7
—KILLINGS OF UNARMED BLACK PEOPLE: as context of Clarence Jamison's suit for unconstitutional stop and search, 5, 6–7, 8; Reeves's recitation of recent history of and call for end to qualified immunity (2020 *Jamison* opinion), 7–9; shooting of fourteen students at Jackson State (1970), 20–21, 34
police searches: context of police violence against Black and Brown people and lack of freely given consent to, 5, 6–7, 8, 212–15; Fourth Amendment requirement for voluntary consent as dependent on the "totality of the circumstances," 213, 214–15; the Fourth Amendment right against unreasonable search and seizure as indispensable freedom, 158–59; inability of accused to understand English and could not have consented to the search (*Lopez*, 2011), 156–59; judicial denial of race as determining factor, 215; Supreme Court finding as "common sense" that a child might agree to answer a cop's questions when an adult would feel free to decline (2011), 215. *See also* Easley, Ollisha, and race as factor in searches (*U.S. v. Easley* [D.N.M. 2018]); Jamison, Clarence, lawsuit for damages due to police stop and search (*Jamison v. McClendon* [S.D. Miss. Aug. 2020])
politics, district court judges ordered to stay out of issues involving, 193
Pollack, Milton (judge), 54, 55
Pooler, Rosemary (judge), 203, 205
Populists, 24
Pori, Brian (public defender): background of, and compassion as public defender, 213, 217, 219; and the Easley case (2018), 212–13; and the Marc Dutch case (2016), 216–17, 218–23, 224
poverty: as correlating factor for higher rates of plaintiff's victories and size of awards, 100; emerging as national issue, 49; in Mississippi, 17, 100, 101, 227; of Native Americans, resulting from allotment scheme privatizing Indian lands, 133
Powell, Lewis (justice): appointment of, 34, 56, 57; as lawyer, memo to US Chamber of Commerce as business cri de coeur, 55–57, 86, 94; limits on lawsuits, 57–58
Powe, Lucas, 125
pretrial diversion, 210
Prigg v. Pennsylvania (1842), 23
prison overcrowding and abusive conditions: fixed or mandatory sentencing guidelines as resulting in, 74–75; Mississippi's Parchman Farm, 156; New Mexico Penitentiary riot due to (1980), 74–75; Rockefeller's draconian 1970s drug laws and, 75–76. *See also* incarceration in federal facilities
Pritchett, Jocelyn, 166. *See also* same-sex marriage—lawsuit to strike down Mississippi ban (2014)
privacy, right to: granted to engage in intimate practices (*Griswold v. Connecticut*, 1965), 35; intimate practices not applicable to gay couples (1986), 35

Index [315]

Private Securities Litigation Reform Act (1995), 94
product liability lawsuits, Mississippi law constraining, 95–96
product safety laws, upheld in *Carolene Products* (1938), 26
Progressives, 24
prosecutors: absolute immunity of, who knowingly use perjured testimony, 34. *See also* US Attorney's Office
protests and demonstrations: Black Lives Matter movement, 2, 8; of hate-crime murder of James Craig Anderson (2012), 161–62; of United Fruit Company, 40. *See also* Occupy Wall Street movement
Proust, Marcel, 47–48
public accommodations: segregation of restrooms, 48
—BAN ON SEGREGATION OF: buses/public transportation, 22; the Civil Rights Act (1964), 18, 22; destruction of public pools to avoid, 18; and interstate buses, Freedom Riders aiming to compel compliance with, 155, 164; movie theater segregation practices following, 6, 18; restaurant and motel access, 22
Public Citizen, 58
public defenders. *See* New Mexico Law Office of the Public Defender
public pools, desegregation and destruction of, 18
public relations industry: campaign claiming Mississippi counties as "judicial hellholes" (2002), 102–3; campaign to produce animosity toward trial lawyers (1986), 86–88; grassroots lobbying technique hiding true client, 95–96; Mississippi campaign disparaging "greedy" lawyers (1993), 96
Putnam, Robert, 183–84

qualified immunity: of City of Mendenhall in *Bouldin*, despite prison time for police chief, 107; defined, 90; and dismissal of *Jamison* lawsuit, 6, 7–9; as doctrine fabricated by Supreme Court (1967), 6, 8, 31; inapplicable in criminal cases, 106; for Ohio governor who sent the national guardsmen who shot Kent State University students dead, 34; of police officers who arrested Episcopal priests on "prayer pilgrimage," 31, 34; Rakoff refusing to defer to, in the Occupy Wall Street lawsuit, 199–200; Reeves calling on Supreme Court to abolish, 8–9. *See also* immunity from lawsuits
—EXCEPTIONS TO: legal requirement to find a previous case involving almost precisely the same facts, 6, 35; requiring obvious evidence that a "reasonable officer" would have known the behavior was unconstitutional, 6, 34–35
Quinones, Alan (and codefendant Diego Rodriguez) (*U.S. v. Quinones* [S.D.N.Y. 2002]): background of Quinones, 114–15; cocaine and heroin operation of, 115; guilty pleas of eight codefendants of ten, 115, 121; murder of Edwin Santiago, 115–16; Rakoff speaking to the pain of his brother's murder, 121–22, 123; Santiago's mother speaking at Soto

sentencing, 121-22; trial (2004), and guilty verdict, 126-27
—AS DEATH PENALTY CASE: John Ashcroft (Attorney General) demanding, 116; jurors who strongly favored or opposed the death penalty barred from serving, 126-27; Rakoff's belief that precedent should be questioned if it could lead to bad results (common law), 117-18; as rare in federal courts, 116; requests for briefs on constitutionality of the death penalty, 116-17, 121; schedule set for motions, 116; Second Circuit Judge Guido Calabresi expressing admiration for Rakoff's position, 126; sentenced to life in prison without parole, 127; Supreme Court as consistently upholding statutes for, 117, 125; trial judges expected to follow Supreme Court precedent, 117-18, 124, 125-26
—RAKOFF'S RULING THAT THE DEATH PENALTY IS UNCONSTITUTIONAL: the Antiterrorism and Effective Death Penalty Act as sharply narrowing ability of courts to rectify sentences of even wrongfully convicted inmates, 118; cautiousness of Rakoff in seeking feedback about, 120, 121; despite his personal experience demanding capital punishment, 121-24; DNA testing and other means of proving innocence easily and definitively, 117, 120, 124; Fifth Amendment on due process, 120; final decision that execution is tantamount to murder, 124; and *Herrera* decision, the majority of justices then on the Supreme Court suggested putting an innocent person to death is unconstitutional, 118-20, 125, 126; media reaction to, 124, 126; novelty of the ruling, 124; Rakoff's awareness of the risks he was taking, 125-26; reversed by Second Circuit, 124-25

racial desegregation: the Roberts Court striking down desegregation plans (2007), 154-55; "the Four" judges on the Fifth Circuit who took on the task of enforcing, at risk to their lives, 22, 55. See also *Brown v. Board of Education* (1954); Civil Rights Act (1964); public accommodations—ban on segregation of
racial discrimination: emerging as national issue, 49; Mexican Americans experiencing, 70-71, 72, 208; and Native Americans, prejudices of non-Native jurors about, 137, 138; in New Mexico, Mexicans emphasizing their Spanish roots to avoid, 72-73, 129; the Roberts Court in undermining of *Brown* (2007), 154-55. See also civil rights movement; discrimination; racial segregation; racism; voting rights
racial segregation: of public restrooms, 48; "separate but equal" endorsed by Supreme Court, 23-24. See also racial desegregation
racism: arrest of Reeves's father for raising his voice to a white man, 6, 18; Reeves on slavery and lynchings as racist savagery, 174-75; Reeves's experiences of injustice and, in grade- and high-school, 17-18;

racism *(continued)*
  verbal attacks and threats of violence against judges, 255–56. *See also* police—brutality and harassment of Black people; police—killings of unarmed Black people; racial discrimination; racial segregation; racist murders of Black people; slavery; Southern Manifesto; white supremacy
racist murders of Black people: James Byrd Jr., 163; Zimmerman acquittal of Trayvon Martin murder, 2. *See also* Dedmon, Deryl, and hate-crime co-conspirators in murder of James Craig Anderson; police—killings of unarmed Black people
Rakoff, Abraham (father), 46–47, 123
Rakoff, Doris (mother), 47–48, 123
Rakoff, Jan (brother): as brilliant intellect and talent, 48, 122; as gay man, 48, 122; murder of, 122–23; murder of, and Judge Jed Rakoff ruling the death penalty unconstitutional despite his personal feelings about, 121–22, 123–24; as oldest brother, 47
Rakoff, Jed (judge): overview, 12, 62–63, 246–48; appearance and temperament of, 45; appointment of (1995), 109–10; assigned randomly to financial crisis cases, rumors stemming from, 180, 192, 239; in baby judge school, 109, 111–12; as baseball fan, 48, 236; belief that precedent should be questioned if it could lead to bad results (common law), 117–18; on *Chevron* being overturned (2024), 248; in the Courthouse Follies, 62, 114; the democracy of opportunity advanced via constraints on excessive money and power, 13, 38, 45–46, 50, 63, 183–84, 248, 253–54; desire to become a judge, 54, 62; on the difficult issues faced routinely by trial judges, 113; on his role as a judge, 125–26; and juries, appreciation for, 201, 202; and the lesson of controlling a case and the courtroom to ensure the truth comes out, 54, 55; and the lesson of creative logic, 52; and the lesson to go beyond lawyers' arguments to figure out why the person before you broke the law and what punishment they deserved, 52–55; loneliness and, 109, 112; and "MacJed, or All's Well That Ends: The Life and Times of Jed Rakoff," 246–47; and Occupy Wall Street suit against NYC for false arrest (2012), 191–92, 199–200; optimism of, 48–49, 50; public acclaim for rejection of Citigroup settlement, 197–98; and Second Circuit, respect and friendships between, 204–5; and Second Circuit, tensions with, 200, 204, 205; on self-restraint needed by judges, 188, 189; senior judge status, 236; sense of humor, 45, 46, 62; social justice conscience of, 48–49; "This is going to be fun!," 193, 239; on "troublemakers" of the nation, debt owed to, 200. *See also* Bank of America merger with Merrill Lynch (*SEC v. Bank of America* [S.D.N.Y. 2009]); Citigroup alleged to have misled investors in defaulted mortgage-backed CDO (*SEC v. Citigroup* [S.D.N.Y. 2011]);

Quinones, Alan (and codefendant Diego Rodriguez)—Rakoff's ruling that the death penalty is unconstitutional
—IN CHAMBERS: chamber description, 114; coffee habit, 114, 193-94; courtroom description, 193-94, 200; electronic keyboard, 114; robing room, 193; work process of, 114, 180, 196-97
—CLERKS OF: overview, 112-13; as a sort of family at work, 112, 113; collaborative method for Rakoff's opinions, 196-97; at hearings, 193, 196; hours kept by, 113; and the *Newman* case, 235-36; office logistics assistance by, 113; Rakoff having fun with, 113; Rakoff saying to: "I'm just a district court judge," 236; researching cases, 118, 120, 191-92, 199; work process, 114, 180, 196-97
—EDUCATION: Central High School (Philadelphia), 48, 53; clerking for Judge Abraham Freedman, and women's right to equal pay, 50-52; convincing Swarthmore to create a sociology department, 49-50; Harvard Law School, 50; legal aid bureau (Harvard), 50; master's thesis on independence movement of Mahatma Gandhi, 50, 110; Oxford University scholarship, 50; in private corporate law practice, 52; as Swarthmore College student and student leader, 48-50
—FAMILY AND CHILDHOOD EXPERIENCES: overview as white Jewish family in prosperous Philadelphia neighborhood, 12, 46-48; birth of Jed, 47; discriminatory experiences felt by parents Abraham and Doris, 46-47; Jed jeered for using a men's room marked "colored," 48; Jewish sense of social justice and, 48. *See also* Rakoff, Jan (brother)
—MARRIAGE AND FAMILY LIFE OF: daughters of (Jena, Elana, and Keira), 110, 112; support of wife Ann, 112, 125, 244, 246; vacations, 110
—IN PRIVATE PRACTICE: Debevoise & Plimpton, 52; as partner in Mudge, Rose, Guthrie, Alexander & Ferdon, 60
—IN US ATTORNEY'S OFFICE (SOUTHERN DISTRICT OF NEW YORK): overview, 44-45; application and hiring of, 52; "Dear Top Banana ... ," 46; lessons in what a judge could do, 52-55; and passage of the Foreign Corrupt Practices Act (1977), 59-60; and the wire fraud case against United Brands, 44-46, 59-60. *See also* United Brands (once United Fruit Company)—criminal prosecution for Honduran bribe

Rakoff, Todd (brother), 47, 48, 121, 122-23
Ramirez v. Martinez (5th Cir. 2013), 6
Reagan, Ronald: campaign speech giving "wink of approval" to Southern segregationists, 35-36; "fear of crime" and mandatory sentencing, 75-76; as governor of CA, Edwin Meese and, 61; "judicial restraint" as campaign promise, 60; judicial selection process and appointments based on adherence to "originalism," 60-62; Edwin

Reagan, Ronald *(continued)*
Meese and, 61–62, 76–77; and passage of the Armed Career Criminal Act, 218–19; William French Smith as first attorney general for, 60–61; tough-on-crime stance of, 60, 75, 218

Real, Manuel (judge): appointment of, 78; behavior of, and call for impeachment, 78–79; and desegregation of Pasadena school district, 78; and trial of Ricardo Vázquez (Martha's brother), 79–83, 134

Reconstruction, 7, 23, 96, 166

Reeves, Carlton (judge): overview, 12, 251–52; ambition to become a judge, 38, 153; appearance and temperament of, 5, 6, 16, 19, 84, 231, 232–33, 255; appointment of, and swearing-in ceremony (2010), 108, 152–53; approaching Bennie Thompson about a vacancy on the federal court, 108, 153; chambers of, 5, 156; the democracy of opportunity advanced via inclusion of more people across all races and genders, 13–14, 38, 159–60, 228, 251–52, 253; desire to practice in Mississippi, 37, 88, 91; expectations upon him, 155–56, 162–63; on his role as a judge, 171–72, 227–28; on the law as sometimes leading to rulings that are unfair, and that the law should change, 153; "Let's go do justice," 160; on the need for judges to boldly stand up for the judiciary, 252, 256; optimism of, 16, 19–20, 38; pace of proceedings presided over, 168–69; as public hero in the wake of sentencing statement on lynching as racist savagery (2015), 175–76; quoting Lincoln on *Dred Scott* as wrongly assuming historical facts that were falsehoods, 38; on racist threats of violence against judges of color, 255–56. *See also* abortion ban (Mississippi), challenge to (2018); Dedmon, Deryl, and hate-crime co-conspirators in murder of James Craig Anderson (2012); Jamison, Clarence, lawsuit for damages due to police stop and search (2020); Lopez, Jonatan, motion to suppress due to illegal search (2011); same-sex marriage—lawsuit to strike down Mississippi ban (2014) on Sentencing Commission (*See* Sentencing Commission (US)—Judge Carlton Reeves as chair of); as staff attorney for Mississippi Supreme Court, 88; in US Attorney's office, as head of the civil division (1995–2001), 92

—CLERKS OF: in awe of Reeves, 159, 160; first choices, 152–53; researching cases, 157, 167–68; as startled by Dedmon sentencing statement, 173; women among, as influence on his work, 228

—EDUCATION: ACLU summer work during law school, 37; activism for MLK national holiday (1983), 36; activism for Voting Rights Act (1982), 36; in the "A section" (academic training), 19; clerking for Justice Reuben Anderson, 37–38, 88, 91; friendships and popularity with white and Black classmates, 19; integrated classrooms in first grade (photo) through high school, 15–16, 21, 27, 30, 162; interning for

[320] INDEX

Bennie Thompson, 91; Jackson State University, as student and student leader, 20-21, 27, 36, 37, 38; "judges are heroes," 21-22, 27, 30; racist injustice experienced in grade- and high-school, 17-18; summer work for civil rights attorney Julius Chambers, 37, 88; on tennis team, 19. *See also* University of Virginia Law School (UVA), and Carlton Reeves

—FAMILY AND CHILDHOOD EXPERIENCES: overview as Black family in Yazoo City, Mississippi, 6, 15-21; admonished to "know his place," 17; arrest of father for raising his voice against a white man, 6, 18; and awareness that others had not been able to overcome the discrimination and lack of opportunities he'd faced, 6; birth of Carlton, 16; fascination with politics, 20; Germany, family residence during father's military tour, 16; movie theater segregated seating, 6, 18; nicknamed Baba (pronounced "Bay-bay"), 19; precocious appreciation for the law, 19-20; sisters of, 228, 255; and women, Reeves's admiration for the strength of, 228. *See also* Reeves, Wilhelmina (mother)

—MARRIAGE AND FAMILY LIFE: death of wife Lora, 228, 255; and Reeves's understanding of the goodness and burden of being a woman, 228; support by daughter Chanda, 153, 228, 255; support by wife Lora, 153

—AS PARTNER IN PRIVATE PRACTICE (JACKSON, MS): barnstorming tour to combat animosity toward trial lawyers, 84-86, 101-3; case of police violence against Damalas Bouldin, 104-7; formation of Pigott Reeves Johnson & Minor, 101-2; as president of the Magnolia Bar Association, 154; and the state legislature's constraints placed on the right to legal redress, 103-4

—WITH PHELPS DUNBAR IN CORPORATE PRACTICE: and awkwardness of defending municipal governments against certain claims, 90, 106; on the benefits of toiling in, 90-91; and context of increased difficulty in getting a case heard in federal court, 88-89; Justice Reuben Anderson's invitation to join him at, 88; and removal to federal court as favored by corporate defense lawyers, 89-90; on the respect among young partners for Black lawyers, 90-91; senior partners' stories about the "old Mississippi," 150; as unfamiliar and suspect territory for Black lawyers, 88

Reeves, Jesse W. (father), 6, 16, 18-19

Reeves, Lora (wife): death of, 228, 255; illness during Reeve's clerking period, 37, 38, 88; support for Carlton, 153; wedding, 38

Reeves, Wilhelmina (mother): birth and early childhood of Carlton, 16; job as motel housekeeper washing sheets and towels, 18-19, 21-22, 228; and Reeves's admiration of the strength of women, 228; taking her children to watch her cast her ballot, 20; voting rights due to federal judges, 21-22

Rehnquist, William (justice and then chief justice): appointment to Burger Court, 34; clerks for, 194; on executing the innocent as unconstitutional, 119, 120; and Judicial Conference report stressing avoidance of trials, 112; on limiting suits from investors done wrong, 58

Reich, Charles, 56

religion, discrimination based on, exclusion of Jewish people from University of Pennsylvania medical school, 47

Republican Party: affiliation of federal judiciary in New Mexico, and unwillingness to expand Native American jury pool, 139; antipathy to economic limits to protect workers, 24–25; campaign against lawyers meant to weaken the Democratic Party, 93, 103–4; "Contract with America," 94–95

Rice, John Aaron, 162, 172–75. *See also* Dedmon, Deryl, and hate-crime co-conspirators in murder of James Craig Anderson

Rice, Tamir, 7

Rivera, David, forfeiture case (*U.S. v. Rivera* [D.N.M. 2012]): overview of licensed used car business (David's Auto Mart), 206–7, 210; background as Mexican American, naturalized citizen, 207, 209–10; as cash business in sales and financing (reporting all income and paying taxes), 206, 207, 208; charges for "structuring" cash bank deposits, and deal to plead guilty and forfeit cash and cars, 207–8, 209; and fact pattern that cannot justify significant fine (Supreme Court, 1998), 210; forfeiture law and, 207–8; Judge Vázquez assigned for sentencing, 208; Vázquez determining plea deal was "excessive fine" (Eighth Amendment), 209–10; Vázquez's rejection of plea agreement, and resolution dismissing charges and reducing forfeiture, 210

Rives, Richard (judge), 22, 55

R. J. Reynolds Tobacco Company, 96

Roberts, John (chief justice): and *Salman v. United States*, 240, 241, 242–43; striking down school desegregation plans, 154–55; "we do not have Obama judges or Trump judges," 255

Roberts, Owen (justice), 26

Rockefeller, Nelson, drug laws, 75

Roe v. Wade (1973): decision in, 33; *Dobbs* decision overturning, 229, 230, 253; leaked draft opinion overturning, 230; Mississippi as passing its ban to ask the Supreme Court to overturn, 227; the right "to have an abortion before viability" of the fetus, 226. *See also* abortion ban (Mississippi), challenge to (*Jackson Women's Health v. Currier* [S.D. Miss. 2018])

Roosevelt, Franklin D.: democracy of opportunity, 13; economic program stymied by the "Four Horsemen of the Apocalypse" on Supreme Court, 26; floating the idea of packing the court, 26

Roosevelt, Theodore, on "pulverizing" Native American territory, 132

Rose, Gerald, 161

Rosenfeld, David, 181–82

Russell, Reno Roy (Navajo) (*U.S. v. Russell* [S.D.N.M. 2004]): charged for fight with his cousin (Jonathan Manuelito), 128, 137, 146–47; federal charges and severity of mandatory sentencing for, 129, 137; and federal sentencing guidelines made nonbinding in *Booker* decision, 143–44; high school graduation, delay of trial for, 145; jury prejudices against Native Americans as concern for, 137, 138; Alonzo Padilla (public defender), 137, 143–44, 145, 146–47; sentenced to probation, 147–48; Martha Vázquez assigned to case, 129
—JUDGE VÁZQUEZ BRINGS HER COURT TO NAVAJO LAND: audience, 146; authority as chief judge and logistics of, 144; the clerk's office and, 142, 144; family of Russell present, 146, 149; jury deliberation and guilty verdict on two misdemeanors, 147; jury selection in Albuquerque and arrival to Navajo Nation, 145; the marshal's office and security for, 142, 144, 145; Navajo interpreter translating proceedings, 146; Navajo leaders' assessment as successful, 148–49; other federal judges now holding their court on Indian lands, 148; permissions from tribal leaders and US Attorney's office, 141–42; scheduling of trial, 145; self-defense argument, 137, 147; Joe Shirley (president of Navajo Nation) giving support to, 141, 144, 146; Joe Shirley's positive assessment of, 149; trial, 146–47
Russell, Richard, 28
Rustin, Bayard, 164–65, 171

St. Paul Companies (insurance), 100–101
Salman v. United States (2016). *See* insider trading—Salman case (*Salman v. United States* [2016])
same-sex marriage: Burger Court's refusal to acknowledge as issue, 35; challenge to Defense of Marriage Act (2013), 168; children of same-sex couples and the need for, 166, 170; dozens of federal courts ruled bans unconstitutional, 167; legal rights of marriage and need for, 166; the majority of states and the District of Columbia legalized, 167; Supreme Court striking down bans on (2015), 172
—LAWSUIT TO STRIKE DOWN MISSISSIPPI BAN (2014): the ban as violating the Fourteenth Amendment's guarantee of equal treatment and due process, 166–67, 169; denial of marriage license to lead plaintiffs by court clerk, 165; filed in federal court seeking a preliminary injunction, 166; law barring violation of people's constitutional rights by state officials (Section 1983), as basis of claim, 166–67; Judge Reeves assigned the case, 167; Reeves's hearing on request for preliminary injunction, 168–70; Reeves's opinion recounting the history of the ban and the discrimination experienced by LGBTQ people, 170–72; Reeves's research into the issues, 167–68; the state's appeal of Reeves's ruling, 172; state statute and Constitution as banning, 166–67, 170

Index [323]

Sanders, Andrea, 165–66. *See also* same-sex marriage—lawsuit to strike down Mississippi ban (2014)
Sand, Leonard (judge), 121
Sanford and Son (TV), 19–20
Santa Fe Industries, Inc. v. Green (1977), 59
Santa Fe, New Mexico: Chicano rights movement to reclaim land grants, 73; discrimination in, and Mexican Americans using "Spanish" and "Spanish food" as terms for their culture, 72–73; Martha Vázquez discovering and deciding to practice law in, 72
Santiago, Edwin, 115–16, 121–22, 123, 127
Scalia, Antonin (justice), 119
Scheck, Barry, 117
Scherzer, Aaron, 197
Scheuer v. Rhodes (1974), 34–35
school desegregation. See *Brown v. Board of Education* (1954)
Scruggs, Dickie, 85, 96–97, 100
searches. *See* police searches
SEC (US Securities and Exchange Commission): overview, 43; deference of judges to settlement decisions of, 188, 193, 204, 205; injunctions, 43; limits on available options for enforcement, 43–44; policy of allowing corporations a "neither-admit-nor-deny" bargain, 43–44, 180, 182, 184, 190, 192, 195–96; policy of extracting mea culpas (2013), 247–48; referrals for criminal prosecution, 44; United Brands bribe of Honduran foreign minister, settlement of, 43–44
—CASES: *Dirks v. SEC* (1983), 242, 243; *SEC v. Brian H. Stoker* (S.D.N.Y. 2011), 189–90, 192, 200–202; *SEC v. Texas Gulf Sulphur Co.* (2d Cir. 1968), 57. See also Bank of America merger with Merrill Lynch (*SEC v. Bank of America* [S.D.N.Y. 2009]); Citigroup alleged to have misled investors in defaulted mortgage-backed CDO (*SEC v. Citigroup* [S.D.N.Y. 2011]); Citigroup alleged to have misled investors in defaulted mortgage-backed CDO—appeal (*SEC v. Citigroup* [2d Cir. 2014])
Section 1983 (1871 law barring violation of people's constitutional rights by state officials): overview—history of cyclical suppression of, 7–8; 1961 revival by Supreme Court, 8; 1967 suppression via doctrine of "qualified immunity," 8; in same-sex marriage case (Mississippi), 166–67. *See also* qualified immunity
securities laws: intention to cheat ruled as requirement (1976), 58; "material" fraud requirement (1976), 58–59; not applicable to someone persuaded *not* to buy shares (1975), 58; Private Securities Litigation Reform Act (1995), 94; proof of lie or failure to disclose as requirement (no duty to be fair, 1977), 59; Rakoff's legacy in adjudication of, 247–48; "security," narrowing of definition of (c. 1975, 1979), 59. *See also* class action lawsuits—Supreme Court limits on; financial crisis (2008); insider trading
Senate (US), judicial nomination approval process, 29–30

sentencing: overview as difficult part of a judge's job, 172; attendees, 173; defendant statements, 173-74; in-camera (closed to the public) hearings to hash out, 172-73; judge's statement, 174-75; presentencing reports, 172, 173, 208; scripts for, 173-74, 221; sentencing guidelines (advisory), 172; victim impact statements, 121-22, 173. *See also* sentencing guidelines (federal)

Sentencing Commission (US): bipartisan establishment as keeper of the sentencing guidelines (1984), 76, 231; justices who have served on, 231; original method of determining length of sentences based on average length of past US sentences, plus more time, 76; seven members of, as varying according to party affiliation of the president, 76, 231; as unanimously overhauling drug sentencing rules (2007 and 2014), 231-32

—JUDGE CARLTON REEVES AS CHAIR OF: overview, 230-31; appointment of (2022), and length of tenure, 231, 232; changes instituted in sentencing, as controversial and approved along party lines, 232; as the first Black person to hold job, 231; first public hearing of ("you will be heard"), 232-33; respect for, among those in the criminal justice system, 233

sentencing guidelines (federal): acquitted criminal charges may not be used to increase sentence (2024), 232; changed to nonbinding (with review) in the *Booker* decision (2005), 136-37, 143-44; compassionate release changes (2023), 232-33; defined as attempt to make punishments for the same federal crime uniform, 76; discretion of judges denied in, 76-77, 134; "fear of crime" exploited in campaign for, 76, federal sentences longer than state sentences for similar offenses, 134; for felon in possession of a gun, 218; fixing the 100:1 sentencing disparity between crack and powder cocaine offenses (2007), 231; further overhaul of drug sentencing rules (2014), 231-32; little or no history of committing crimes, reduced sentences for (2023), 232; parole not possible in federal system, 129, 134; the political right and left as initially supporting, 76; prosecutor's choice of charges as determining punishments under, in transfer of power from judiciary to executive branch, 77; and severity of punishments for Native Americans, 129, 134. *See also* Armed Career Criminal Act (1984); Sentencing Commission (US)

—JUDGE MARTHA VÁZQUEZ AND: admirers and detractors of her position, 136; the *Booker* decision as vindication of, 144; on the crippling effects of long-term sentences after release, 223-24, 250; on the discretion of judge as removed by, 134; Geneva Gallegos case and refusal to adhere to, 134-35; personal experience of, with her brother Ricardo, 81-82, 134, 224; reversals by the Tenth Circuit, sentencing guidelines—Judge Martha Vázquez and *(continued)* 135, 136, 144, 219-20, 221; reversals expected, taking controversial stands as form of resistance, 210, 214-16. *See also* Dutch, Marc, and vindication of Judge Vázquez's tailoring of sentences to the individual (*U.S. v. Dutch* [D.N.M. 2016])

sentencing guidelines for fixed or mandatory sentences (states): in 49 of 50 states, 75; in New Mexico, 73-74, 75, 77. *See also* sentencing guidelines (federal)

Sentencing Reform Act (1984), 76

separation of powers, 204, 205

sexism, girls discouraged from pursuing science careers, 47

Shahabian, Matt, 191-92

Shapiro, Alexandra, 240-42, 243

Shepard, Matthew, 163

Shiprock, New Mexico. *See* Russell, Reno Roy (Navajo)—Judge Vázquez brings her court to Navajo land

Shirley, Joe Jr. (president of Navajo Nation), working with Judge Martha Vázquez: accompanying Vázquez on her annual visit to federal detention center for girls under 18, 140; making public service ads to increase Native participation in jury pool, 140-41; supporting Vázquez in bringing her court to Navajo land, 141, 144, 146, 149

Shultz v. Wheaton Glass Company (3d Cir. 1970), 51-52

slavery: *Dred Scott* decision disallowing Congress's efforts to abolish in US territories (1857), 23; Fugitive Slave Act (1793), 23; fugitive slave clause of the Constitution, 23; racist viewpoints taught in civics and history, 18; Reeves on, as Mississippi's cruelest savagery, 174; reversal of Edward Prigg (slave catcher) conviction (1842), 23

Smith, Courtney, 49-50

Smith, William French, 60-61, 75

Sobeloff, Simon (judge), 29-30

sociology, Rakoff and Swarthmore College department of, 49-50

Soto, Janet, 115, 121

Sotomayor, Sonia (justice), and *Salman v. United States*, 242, 243

Souter, David (justice), on executing the innocent as unconstitutional, 119, 120

Southern Manifesto (declaration of war on the federal courts): intimidation of federal courts and forced selection of judges who would toe the Southern line as goals of, 29-30; Olin Johnston as author of, 28-29; presentation to the Senate (1956), 27-28; as racist backlash to *Brown*, 10-11, 28-29, 154; signatories, 28; views in, as having won, 153-55

Southland Corp. v. Keating (1984), 98

Spencer, Herbert, 25

Sporkin, Stanley, 43-44, 184

state courts: jurisdiction of, and corporate defense lawyers' preference for federal court, 89-90; tort suits, 95; the vast majority of cases as handled by, 95. *See also* lawsuits, state laws limiting; Mississippi Supreme Court; sentencing guidelines for fixed or mandatory sentences (states)

State Farm Mutual v. Campbell (2003), 97-98
states' rights: *Brown* claimed to undermine, 28; Ronald Reagan campaign speech giving wink of approval to Southern segregationists, 35-36
stay, 199
Stevens, John Paul (justice), on executing the innocent as unconstitutional, 119, 120
Stevens, Lance, 84
Stoker, Brian (*SEC v. Brian H. Stoker* [S.D.N.Y. 2011]), 189-90, 192, 200-202
Stone, Harlan Fiske (justice and then chief justice): footnote 4 and scrutiny of laws involving minority or political rights, 26; on self-restraint as check on exercise of judicial power, 188
Stout, Michael, 136
Sullivan, Jimmy Charles "Jimbo," prison time for beating of Damalas Bouldin, 105-7
Summers, Twana, 152
Supreme Court (US): Chamber of Commerce turn toward litigation, 56-57; courtroom of, 240; death penalty statutes as consistently upheld by, 117, 125; as giving strength to the most regressive and terrifying forces in society, 10, 22-23; issues placed beyond the reach of judges by, 193; minority rights and Justice Harlan Fiske Stone's footnote 4 in *Carolene Products* (1938), 26; "Money Trust" of, 25; Native American tribal traditions of criminal justice recognized as valid by, but canceled by Congress (1885), 132; Rakoff's belief that precedent should be questioned if it could lead to bad results (common law), 117-18; and Reeves's "judges are heroes," 21-22, 27, 30; sentencing guidelines changed to nonbinding (with review) in the *Booker* decision (2005), 136-37, 143-44; "separate but equal" endorsed by, 23-24; structure of the courts and workload, 110-11; "the switch in time that saved nine," 26; trial judges expected to follow precedents without question, 117-18, 124, 125-26. *See also* labor laws; lawsuit limitations—Supreme Court; securities laws; slavery
—CASES: overview list with full citations, 285-87; *Alexander v. Holmes County Board of Education* (1969), 16, 30; *Baker v. Nelson* (1972), 35; *BFI, Inc. v. Kelco Disposal, Inc.* (1989), 97-98; *Bivens v. Six Unknown Named Agents of Federal Bureau of Narcotics* (1971), 33-34; *Blue Chip Stamps v. Manor Drug Stores* (1975), 58; *BMW of North America v. Gore* (1996), 97-98; *Bowers v. Hardwick* (1986), 35; *Briscoe v. LaHue* (1983), 34; *Brown v. Board of Education* (*Brown II*) (1955), 21, 29; *Bush v. Lucas* (1983), 34; *The Cherokee Nation v. the State of Georgia* (1831), 132; *Citizens United v. Federal Election Commission* (2010), 57; *Crow Dog* (1883), 132; *Davis v. United States* (1973), 35; *Dirks v. SEC* (1983), 242, 243; *Dobbs v. Jackson Women's Health Organization* (2022), 229, 230, 253; *Dred Scott*

Supreme Court (US)—cases *(continued)* *v. Sandford* (1857), 23, 38; *Eisen v. Carlisle & Jacquelin* (1974), 58; *Erie Railroad v. Tompkins* (1938), 89; *Ernst & Ernst v. Hochfelder* (1976), 58; *Ex parte KAN-GI-SHUN-CA* (1883), 132; *Flood v. Kuhn* (1972), 57; *Francis v. Henderson* (1976), 35; *Gilmer v. Interstate/Johnson Lane Corp.* (1991), 98–99; *Gregg v. Georgia* (1976), 117; *Griswold v. Connecticut* (1965), 35; *Harper v. Virginia Board of Elections* (1966), 22; *Heart of Atlanta Motel, Inc. v. United States* (1964), 22; *Herrera v. Collins* (1993), 118–20, 125, 126; *Imbler v. Pachtman* (1976), 34; *International Brotherhood of Teamsters v. Daniel* (1979), 59; *J.D.B. v. North Carolina* (2011), 215; *J.I. Case Co. v. Borak* (1964), 57; *Jones v. Mayer* (1968), 22; *Lochner v. New York* (1905), 24–25; *Mobile v. Bolden* (1980), 36; *Moses H. Cone Memorial Hospital v. Mercury Construction Corporation* (1983), 98; *New York Central & Hudson River Railroad Co. v. United States* (1909), 45–46; *Obergefell v. Hodges* (2015), 172; *Pacific Mutual Life Insurance Co. v. Haslip* (1991), 97–98; *Parents Involved in Community Schools v. Seattle School Dist. No. 1* (2007), 154–55; *Pierson v. Ray* (1967), 6, 31; *Plessy v. Ferguson* (1896), 23–24; *Prigg v. Pennsylvania* (1842), 23; *Santa Fe Industries, Inc. v. Green* (1977), 59; *Scheuer v. Rhodes* (1974), 34–35; *Southland Corp. v. Keating* (1984), 98; *State Farm Mutual v. Campbell* (2003), 97–98; *TSC Industries, Inc. v. Northway, Inc.* (1976), 58–59; *United Housing Foundation v. Forman* (1975), 59; *United States v. Bajakajian* (1998), 210; *United States v. Booker* (2005), 136–37, 143–44; *United States v. Bostick* (1991), 213; *United States v. Carolene Products Co.* (1938), 26; *United States v. Kagama* (1886), 133; *United States v. Richardson* (1974), 35; *United States v. Stanley* (1987), 34; *United States v. Windsor* (2013), 168; *Virginia State Board of Pharmacy v. Virginia Citizens Consumer Council, Inc.* (1976), 57; *Wainwright v. Sykes* (1977), 35; *West Coast Hotel Co. v. Parrish* (1937), 26; *Wooden v. United States* (2022), 221–23. See also *Brown v. Board of Education* (1954); *Chevron v. Natural Resources Defense Council* (1984); insider trading—Salman case (*Salman v. United States* [2016]); *Roe v. Wade* (1973)

—JUSTICES: Samuel A. Alito, 230, 243; Louis Brandeis, 25; Stephen Breyer, 231, 242; Stephen Field, 24; Felix Frankfurter, 10; Oliver Wendell Holmes, 25; Charles Evans Hughes (chief justice), 26; Robert H. Jackson, 159; Ketanji Brown Jackson, 231; Elena Kagan, 242; Sandra Day O'Connor, 98, 119–20, 125; Rufus Peckham, 25; Owen Roberts, 26; Antonin Scalia, 119; Sonia Sotomayor, 242, 243; David Souter, 119, 120; John Paul Stevens, 119, 120; Roger Taney (chief justice), 23; Clarence Thomas, 119, 229; Willis Van Devanter, 26. *See also* Burger, Warren (chief justice); Ginsburg, Ruth Bader (justice);

[328] INDEX

Marshall, Thurgood (justice); Rehnquist, William (justice and then chief justice); Roberts, John (chief justice); Stone, Harlan Fiske (justice and then chief justice); Warren, Earl (chief justice)
Sureño 13 case, Judge Martha Vázquez handling, 130-31
Swarthmore College, Rakoff and, 48-50
Sydnor, Eugene B., Jr., 55

Taney, Roger (chief justice), 23
Tarlow, Barry, 78
Taylor, Breonna, 6-7
Thain, John, 177-79, 181-82
Thomas, Clarence (justice), 119, 229
Thomas, Jim, 39, 41
Thompson, Bennie: and Barack Obama, 107-8; Reeves approaching about federal judgeship, 108, 153; Reeves interning for, 91; and Reeves' return to Mississippi, 91
Thurmond, Strom: attacks on judicial nominees, 30; mandatory sentencing law, 76; and views in Southern Manifesto as having won, 153-54
Tijerina, Reies López, 73
Till, Emmett, 174
tobacco companies: backlash against, and investment of corporations in litigation, 56; massive class action suit for public money states spent for health care, launched out of Mississippi, 85, 96-97; Lewis Powell as director of company, 55; and public relations grassroots lobbying in Mississippi, 95-96
trial lawyers and lawsuits, animosity toward: overview, 85-86; George W. Bush speech encouraging, 85; "grassroots lobbying" as technique used to fuel, 95-96; harshest impacts as falling on the poorest and most vulnerable regions of the nation, 86, 101-3, 104; the Justice Department as fueling, 87; large awards by juries used in public relations campaigns to fuel, 85, 88, 93, 99-100; McDonald's coffee injuries (1994) and, 93; public relations campaign blaming lawyers for insurance premium increases (1986), 86-88; public relations campaign claiming Mississippi counties as "judicial hellholes" (2002), 102-3; public relations campaign disparaging "greedy" lawyers (1993), 96; punitive damages limited by Supreme Court, 97-98; as Republican Party strategy to weaken the Democratic Party, 93, 103-4; rising insurance premiums blamed on lawyers and lawsuits, 85-86, 87-88; viewed as impediments to prosperity, 85, 86. *See also* civil justice system, struggle over the purpose of; lawsuit limitations
—IN MISSISSIPPI: Black juries stereotyped in, but poverty shown as the factor increasing plaintiffs' victories and awards, 100; doctor refusing to treat lawyer's son in ER, 101; doctors threatening to leave the state due to malpractice insurance costs, 85, 102; "joinder" rules as increasing, 100; public relations campaigns to fuel (1993, 2002), 86-88, 95-96, 102-3; rising insurance premiums (and lack of

trial lawyers—in Mississippi *(continued)* coverage) blamed on lawyers, with little evidence, 85–86, 100–101; rising insurance premiums, reasons for, 86–101; state laws limiting lawsuits passed due to (2002 and 2004), 103–4; success of trial lawyers as biggest factor in the campaign against, 99–100; trial lawyers as big-money lobby in the state, 97; trial lawyers' barnstorming tour to educate the people (Reeves, 2002), 84–86, 101–3; trial lawyers' position that the right for legal redress of nation's poorest was under attack in, 86, 101–3, 104

—MISSISSIPPI LAWSUITS OF NOTE IN: fen-phen diet drug, 99–100; Ford Motor Company award, 99; shipbuilders, liability for worker exposures to asbestos, 85, 96–97; tobacco companies, class action for recovery of money states spent for health care due to, 85, 96–97

Tribe, Laurence, 124

Trump, Donald: attacks on the judicial system and judges, 252, 255–56; weakening of "Yates Memo" targeting individual wrongdoers rather than just the companies they work for, 247

TSC Industries, Inc. v. Northway, Inc. (1976), 58–59

Tso, Karletta, 128

Tuttle, Elbert (judge), 22

United Brands (once United Fruit Company): aiding the CIA to topple Guatemalan government (1954), 40; antitrust settlement (1958), 40; Eli Black as CEO, and payment of bribe to Honduran officials, 40–43, 44, 45; Eli Black suicide in wake of, 39–40, 41–42, 45; bribe reported to the SEC, 43; New York offices bombed by Weather Underground (1969), 40; as "The Octopus," dominating economies and governments in service of the banana trade, 40, 45; SEC settlement of bribe complaint, 43–44

—CRIMINAL PROSECUTION FOR HONDURAN BRIBE: absence of anti-foreign bribery law as problem, 44, 46; companies may be held liable for the actions of a single employee (1909), 45–46; indictment of and guilty plea, 46, 59; maximum fine the law would allow, 59; SEC referral for prosecution, 44; the Southern District of New York policy of not prosecuting corporations as hurdle for, 45; the US criminal code did not cover foreign bribes, 44; wire fraud (mail fraud) statute expansion and, 44, 46

United Housing Foundation v. Forman (1975), 59

United States v. Bajakajian (1998), 210

United States v. Booker (2005), 136–37, 143–44

United States v. Bostick (1991), 213

United States v. Carolene Products Co. (1938), 26

United States v. Kagama (1886), 133

United States v. Richardson (1974), 35

United States v. Stanley (1987), 34

United States v. Windsor (2013), 168

University of Pennsylvania: law

school denying admission on basis of age, 47; medical school denying admission to Jewish people, 47; Rakoff enlisting sociology professors to teach classes at Swarthmore, 49–50

University of Virginia Law School (UVA), and Carlton Reeves: alumni group lunching in Jackson, 91; Black woman named to the *Virginia Law Review*, criticized as preferential treatment for Black students, 36–37; discussion of race as broken within, 37; grade average, 37; Reeves on UVA as behind Mississippi on issues of race, 36–37; Reeves's speech on the occasion of receiving its highest honor (2019), 255–56; as student, 36–37, 168; summer work with ACLU Mississippi and civil rights practice in NC, 37, 88

US Attorney's Office: sentencing guidelines made nonbinding in *Booker* decision, and reaction to, 143; sentencing guidelines transferring power to determine punishments to, via choice of offenses charged, 77. *See also* Justice Department (US)

—SOUTHERN DISTRICT OF MISSISSIPPI: criminal prosecution and prison time for police-chief Sullivan's beating of Damalas Bouldin, 106–7; Brad Pigott appointment as, 91–92; Carlton Reeves as head of civil division, 92

—SOUTHERN DISTRICT OF NEW YORK: overview, 44–45; Preet Bharara, 234, 235, 237, 243; most prosecutors enter private practice following period in, 60; policy of prosecuting actual people rather than corporations, 45. *See also* financial crisis (2008); Rakoff, Jed (judge)—in US Attorney's office (Southern District of New York); securities laws; United Brands (once United Fruit Company)—criminal prosecution for Honduran bribe

U.S. Bancorp, judge denouncing deferred prosecution agreement, 248

U.S. v. Dutch (10th Cir. 2020), 219–20, 221

U.S. v. Dylan Wade Butler et al. See Dedmon, Deryl, and hate-crime co-conspirators in murder of James Craig Anderson (*U.S. v. Dylan Wade Butler et al.* [S.D. Miss. 2012])

U.S. v. Easley (10th Cir. 2018), 215

U.S. v. Easley (D.N.M. 2018). *See* Easley, Ollisha, and race as factor in searches (*U.S. v. Easley* [D.N.M. 2018])

U.S. v. Fernando Mendez et al. (C.D. Cal. 1990), 67–68, 77–82

U.S. v. Geneva Gallegos (10th Cir. 1997), 135

U.S. v. Jonatan Lopez (S.D. Miss. 2011), 156–59

U.S. v. Newman. *See* insider trading—Newman case (*U.S. v. Newman* [2d Cir. 2014])

U.S. v. Quinones (2d Cir. 2002), 116–17, 124–26

U.S. v. Quinones (S.D.N.Y. 2002). *See* Quinones, Alan (and codefendant Diego Rodriguez) (*U.S. v. Quinones* [S.D.N.Y. 2002])

Index [331]

U.S. v. Rivera (D.N.M. 2012). See
  Rivera, David, forfeiture case (U.S.
  v. Rivera [D.N.M. 2012])
U.S. v. Russell (S.D.N.M. 2004). See
  Russell, Reno Roy (Navajo) (U.S. v.
  Russell [S.D.N.M. 2004])
U.S. v. Salman. See insider trading—
  Salman case (U.S. v. Salman [9th
  Cir. 2015])
U.S. v. Vazquez (9th Cir. 1992), 80,
  82–83
U.S. v. Wooden (6th Cir. 2019), 222

Vance, Cyrus, 246
Van Devanter, Willis (justice), 26
Vázquez, Consuelo Mendez (mother):
  family history of, 69; and son
  Ricardo's involvement in cocaine
  sting, 78, 79, 80–81, 82; wedded to
  Remigio Vázquez, 69. See also
  Vázquez, Martha (judge)—family
  and childhood experiences
Vázquez, Martha (judge): overview,
  12, 248–51; annual visit bringing a
  feast to federal detention center for
  girls under 18, 140; appointment of
  (1993), 83, 129–30; appreciation for
  court of appeals, 135–36; arduous
  travel schedule in rotations to the
  bench in Las Cruces, 130; as chief
  judge with authority over entire
  New Mexico district court (2003),
  138, 144; compassion as value of,
  82, 129, 144, 208; the democracy of
  opportunity advanced via
  broadening of the middle class, 13,
  83, 208, 253; desire to become a
  judge, 82, 83, 134; discrimination
  experienced by, 70–71, 72, 129;
  health toll of death penalty case
  stresses, 131; indelible sense of the
  wrongness of "throwing them away
  like garbage," 75, 79, 223–24,
  249–51; and life tenure on the
  bench, 136; loneliness as judge, 131;
  "read everything" as mantra of,
  214; on Judge Carlton Reeves as her
  hero, 233; supervised release visits
  with ex-cons, 249–51; tailoring the
  punishment to fit the individual, 73,
  144, 223; taking controversial
  stands she knew would be
  reversed, as resistance, 210, 214–16;
  workload of, 130–31. See also Dutch,
  Marc, and vindication of Judge
  Vázquez's tailoring of sentences to
  the individual (U.S. v. Dutch
  [D.N.M. 2016]); Easley, Ollisha,
  and race as factor in searches (U.S.
  v. Easley [D.N.M. 2018]); Native
  Americans on juries, Judge Martha
  Vázquez's work to increase
  numbers of; Rivera, David,
  forfeiture case (U.S. v. Rivera
  [D.N.M. 2012]); Russell, Reno Roy
  (Navajo)—Judge Vázquez brings her
  court to Navajo land; sentencing
  guidelines (federal)—Judge Martha
  Vázquez and
—EDUCATION: in Catholic school,
  69–70, 71; college at University of
  Notre Dame (South Bend, IN),
  71–72; discovering Santa Fe on her
  drives home for college breaks, 72;
  English, subterfuge to learn, 70;
  Notre Dame law school, 72; as
  student leader in high school, 71;
  summer job as associate in Santa Fe
  law firm, 72
—FAMILY AND CHILDHOOD
  EXPERIENCES: overview as
  Mexican American family in East

Santa Barbara, California, 12, 64–65, 68–71; births of Ricardo and Martha, 69; early determination to become an immigration lawyer, 70; Martha as deeply sheltered from popular culture and forbidden from dating, 71; moving to upscale neighborhood near Santa Barbara mission, 71; the siblings joining their parents to work gardening jobs at nights and weekends, 65, 70; summers in her parents' Mexican village of origin (Atotonilquillo), 64, 71; work ethic of her father and other immigrants, 70–71. *See also* Vázquez, Consuelo Mendez (mother); Vázquez, Remigio (father); Vázquez, Ricardo (brother)
—MARRIAGES AND FAMILY LIFE OF: appointment as judge and inquiries about, 130; children, 73, 77, 130; grandchildren of, talk of retiring to spend time with, 251; married during law school, 72; and the need to leave the public defender's office, 77; rigors of her job, as toll on her children and marriages, 130, 251
—AS PARTNER IN PRIVATE PRACTICE (SANTA FE): overview, 77; brother Ricardo's drug case occurring during, 68, 82–83; founder of firm recommending her for judicial appointment, 83
—IN PUBLIC DEFENDER'S OFFICE (SANTA FE): overview, 73, 77; finding wiggle room in state sentencing guidelines, 77; helping to save Modesto Martinez from death penalty murder conviction, 73, 130

Vázquez, Remigio (father): discrimination experienced by, 70–71; faith in the US to treat him fairly, 70–71; falling in love with Consuelo and following her to the US to be married, 69; life in Atotonilquillo (Mexico) as soccer player and university-educated accountant, 68–69, 71; naturalized as US citizen, 69; as undocumented immigrant, 12, 69, 70, 208; working his way up to own a small Spanish-language radio station and a restaurant, 71, 208. *See also* Vázquez, Martha (judge)—family and childhood experiences
Vázquez, Ricardo (brother): belongings stored in Vázquez's office, 224; children of, and need to care for, 65–66, 77, 224; close relationship between Martha ("Chacha") and her brother ("Chacho"), 64–65, 68; death of, 223–24; education of, 65; employment as assistant manager of grocery store, 65; marriage of, and divorce in the wake of severe health problems and unemployment, 65, 66; special qualities of Ricardo that made people love him, 64–65, 78, 82; summers in their parents' Mexican village of origin (Atotonilquillo), 64; working to help his parents and siblings, 65
—INVOLVEMENT IN COCAINE DRUG STING: "admission" of guilt, 67–68, 78; appeal unsuccessful, 82–83; bail denied by Judge Real (and contempt for family), 79; DEA ("Adam Cobb," informant) set-up and arrest of Ricardo, 66–68, 80; DEA agent offer to

Vázquez, Ricardo—involvement in cocaine drug sting *(continued)* Martha to support release on bail, and subsequent denial of, 77, 79; entrapment defense, Judge Real refusing to allow, 80, 83; health problems in prison and lack of decent care, 223–24; hiring Barry Tarlow and getting Mark Heaney as lawyer, 78, 79–80, 82, 83; Martha filing petition for clemency with President Bill Clinton, 83; Martha's testimony for her brother, 79; Martha's visits to prisons to help her brother, 68, 83, 224; pressure on Ricardo to plead guilty, 78; release from prison, 223–24; scraping together the money for a good lawyer, 78; sentencing guidelines and sentence given by Judge Real (35 years), 81–82, 134; trial and verdict, 79–81

Vázquez, Rosanna (sister), 78

Vietnam War, backlash against companies profiting from, 56

violence: and threats of, against federal judges, 22, 55, 142, 254–56. *See also* police; racist murders of Black people

violent crime: dropping rates of (1981), 75–76; fear of crime exploited to maximize sentencing, 76–77

Virginia State Board of Pharmacy v. Virginia Citizens Consumer Council, Inc. (1976), 57

voting rights: Judge W. Harold Cox's racist opinion of, 151; poll taxes banned (1966), 22; rejection of claims that at-large voting discriminatory (1980), 36; Voting Rights Act of 1982 establishing discriminatory results as support for discrimination claim, 36; for women, Mississippi as last state to ratify, 227

Voting Rights Act (1982), 36

Wachtell, Lipton, Rosen & Katz, 185

Wainwright v. Sykes (1977), 35

Wall Street. *See* financial crisis (2008); Occupy Wall Street movement; SEC (US Securities and Exchange Commission); securities laws

war, district court judges ordered to stay out of issues involving, 193

Warren Court: Warren Burger as outspoken critic of, 33; criticized as boosting the rights of criminals, 31; as largely an exception to Supreme Court's support for regressive forces, 22–23; Edwin Meese as despising expansion of individual rights by, 61; qualified immunity as creation of, 6, 8, 31; as Reeves's heroes, 21–22, 27, 30. *See also Brown v. Board of Education* (1954)

Warren, Earl (chief justice): on qualified immunity, 31; retirement of, 33

Watergate hearings (1973), 20

Weather Underground, 40

Webb, Carla, 166. *See also* same-sex marriage—lawsuit to strike down Mississippi ban (2014)

Wells, Theodore, 190

Wertheim, Jerry, 83

Wertheim, Todd, 129

West Coast Hotel Co. v. Parrish (1937), 26

whistleblowers, 97, 102

White, Byron (justice), 119; appointment of, 34

white flight, 17, 48

white supremacists and white supremacy: history of laws passed to overcome, as crushed by, 7–8; homosexuality and racial justice perceived as threats by, 164. *See also* racism; racist murders of Black people

Wigand, Jeffrey, 97

Wilkins, Roy, 152

Windsor, Edith, 168

Wingate, Henry (judge), 162

Wing, John "Rusty": and *SEC v. Citigroup* (2d Cir. 2014), 203–4; and wire fraud criminal charges for United Brands, 44–46

wire fraud, and United Brands bribery of a foreign official, 44, 46

Wisdom, John Minor (judge), 22

women: Mississippi treatment of health and rights of, throughout its history, 225, 227, 229; Reeves's deep admiration for their strength and all that they endured, 228; right to equal pay, 51–52. *See also* abortion ban (Mississippi), challenge to (*Jackson Women's Health v. Currier* [S.D. Miss. 2018])

Wooden, William Dale (*Wooden v. United States* [2022]), 221–23

Yazoo City, Mississippi: geography and topography of, 16–17; integrated classrooms in, 15–16, 21, 27, 30, 162; politics of, Reeves's precocious interest in, 20; population and poverty rate of, 17; segregated public accommodations in, 18; white flight and, 17. *See also* Reeves, Carlton (judge)

Yazoo County Courthouse, Reeves' precocious interest in the law and, 20

Yazzie, Herb, 141–42, 148–49

Young Americans for Freedom, 32

Zimmerman, George, 2

Founded in 1893,
UNIVERSITY OF CALIFORNIA PRESS
publishes bold, progressive books and journals
on topics in the arts, humanities, social sciences,
and natural sciences—with a focus on social
justice issues—that inspire thought and action
among readers worldwide.

The UC PRESS FOUNDATION
raises funds to uphold the press's vital role
as an independent, nonprofit publisher, and
receives philanthropic support from a wide
range of individuals and institutions—and from
committed readers like you. To learn more, visit
ucpress.edu/supportus.